The Cooperative Extension System serves as the conduit through which scientific knowledge generated by the 130 land-grant colleges and universities in the United States is translated and delivered directly to its constituents. Since its inception over 100 years ago, Extension has been integral in developing, delivering, and applying cutting-edge knowledge in agriculture and natural resources, youth development, family and consumer sciences, and community and rural development. Today, more than ever, Extension will need to lead the way in building and maintaining sustainable partnerships across disciplines and with organizations at the local, state, and national levels to tackle complex issues considering diminishing resources. Bringing together leading and emerging scholars, this volume discusses how Extension is addressing issues and opportunities relevant to children, youth, families, and communities across the country both now and in the future. Topics include Extension's role in supporting childcare, social media use, entrepreneurship, rural communities, and underserved audiences.

MARIA ROSARIO T. DE GUZMAN is a Professor and Extension Specialist in Child, Youth, and Family Studies and Chair of Textiles, Merchandising and Fashion Design at the University of Nebraska-Lincoln. Her programs of Extension and research focus on supporting healthy adolescent development and in understanding the intersections of culture, migration, and family life. She has authored over 50 publications, including the book *Parenting from Afar* (2018), which received the Gielen Award from the American Psychological Association for its contribution to psychology as a global discipline.

HOLLY HATTON is an Associate Professor and Extension Specialist in the Child, Youth, and Family Studies Department at the University of Nebraska-Lincoln. Holly's program of Extension focuses on the use of reflective practice, mindfulness, compassion, and social-emotional learning to support caregivers, early childhood educators, young children, and families drawing upon community-based participatory methods. She is committed to addressing issues of systemic inequities and brings these issues to the forefront of her work.

EXTENSION EDUCATION AND THE SOCIAL SCIENCES

Uplifting Children, Youth, Families, and Communities

EDITED BY

MARIA ROSARIO T. DE GUZMAN
University of Nebraska-Lincoln

HOLLY HATTON
University of Nebraska-Lincoln

CAMBRIDGE
UNIVERSITY PRESS

CAMBRIDGE
UNIVERSITY PRESS

Shaftesbury Road, Cambridge CB2 8EA, United Kingdom

One Liberty Plaza, 20th Floor, New York, NY 10006, USA

477 Williamstown Road, Port Melbourne, VIC 3207, Australia

314–321, 3rd Floor, Plot 3, Splendor Forum, Jasola District Centre, New Delhi – 110025, India

103 Penang Road, #05–06/07, Visioncrest Commercial, Singapore 238467

Cambridge University Press is part of Cambridge University Press & Assessment, a department of the University of Cambridge.

We share the University's mission to contribute to society through the pursuit of education, learning and research at the highest international levels of excellence.

www.cambridge.org
Information on this title: www.cambridge.org/9781108833387

DOI: 10.1017/9781108980562

First published 2024

A catalogue record for this publication is available from the British Library

A Cataloging-in-Publication data record for this book is available from the Library of Congress

ISBN 978-1-108-83338-7 Hardback
ISBN 978-1-108-97037-2 Paperback

Contents

Contributors

MARY E. ARNOLD Oregon State University

CONSTANCE C. BEECHER Iowa State University

ANN A. BERRY University of Tennessee Knoxville

TERESA A. BYINGTON University of Nevada, Reno

MARIA ROSARIO T. DE GUZMAN University of Nebraska-Lincoln

KIEU ANH DO University of Maryland Eastern Shore

JOSEPH L. DONALDSON North Carolina State University

JODI DWORKIN University of Minnesota

KERRIE FANNING University of Wisconsin-Madison

THERESA M. FERRARI The Ohio State University

JEAN ANN FISCHER University of Nebraska-Lincoln

JULIE M. FOX The Ohio State University

LISA FRANZEN-CASTLE University of Nebraska-Lincoln

JEMALYN GRIFFIN University of Nebraska-Lincoln

HOLLY HATTON University of Nebraska-Lincoln

OLIVIA KENNEDY University of Nebraska-Lincoln

MARGARET L. KERR University of Wisconsin-Madison

SURIN KIM University of Nebraska-Lincoln

MICHELLE KREHBIEL University of Nebraska-Lincoln

J. KALE MONK University of Missouri

CLAIRE NICHOLAS University of Oklahoma

IRENE PADASAS University of California Agriculture and Natural Resources

YOSHIE SANO Washington State University Vancouver

CHRISTOPHER T. SNEED University of Tennessee Knoxville

YUNQI WANG University of Nebraska-Lincoln

JIWON YOON University of Wisconsin-Madison

VIRGINIE ZOUMENOU University of Maryland Eastern Shore

PART I

Overview of Extension and the Social Sciences

CHAPTER I

Introduction

The Role of Extension Education in Supporting Children, Youth, Families, and Communities

Maria Rosario T. de Guzman and Holly Hatton

In Douglas County, Nebraska, two graduate students and two Extension educators are working with a dozen youth who are putting finishing touches on their posters as part of their mock presidential campaigns. Situated in a middle school in a predominantly Latinx neighborhood, participants are part of Youth Arise – an afterschool program designed to foster civic engagement among youth from underserved communities. Over 3,000 miles west, two nutrition Extension educators are facilitating a youth photovoice project with twenty-five sixth-grade students in Madera County, California. This school is in a highly agricultural community in the Central Valley Region, with a large population of Hispanic/Latinx residents and indigenous groups from Mexico. The project aims to document youth's experiences and challenges with water access and consumption while in school and provides opportunities for youth to learn about the importance of sleep, good nutrition, and regular physical activity for their health.[1] On the Eastern part of the country, educators are engaging in Wellness Enhancing Physical Activity for Young Children (WE PLAY), an online program designed to foster participants' skills in leading active play, promoting physical activity, and implementing inclusive practices with typically developing preschool children and children with autism spectrum disorder. WE PLAY represents a partnership between Penn State Extension's Better Kid Care and Northeastern University and has to date reached approximately 6,000 educators.[2]

The earlier scenarios illustrate the diversity in audiences, the wide range of contexts, and breadth of programming in which contemporary

---

[1] Example is provided by Dr. Irene Padasas, Community Health and Nutrition Advisor, UCCE Tulare, Kings, Madera, & Freson Counties.

[2] Example provided by Dr. Benjamin Bayly, Assistant Professor of Family Studies, Child, and Youth Development; and Academic Lead for Penn State Extension's Better Kid Care.

Extension professionals engage. As the largest publicly funded, nonformal education system in the United States, Cooperative Extension (a.k.a. "Extension," "Agricultural Extension") serves as the conduit through which scientific knowledge generated in and through state agricultural experiment stations (AES) and land-grant universities (LGUs) in the United States is translated and shared directly to its constituents. Since its inception over 100 years ago, Extension has been integral in developing, delivering, co-creating, and applying cutting-edge knowledge in such domains as agriculture and natural resources, youth development, family and consumer sciences, and community and rural development (Gould, Steele, & Woodrum, 2014). Extension has had a long history of transforming science into everyday solutions through educational programs and collaborative partnerships – shaping the ways in which we cultivate and preserve food, how we educate and care for our children, manage our finances, work with communities, and support populations disproportionately affected by structural inequities.

Scholars and policymakers have long acknowledged that helping the broader population understand the Extension system and preparing future Extension professionals is critical to Extension's sustainability and success in carrying out its charge (Arnold & Place, 2010; Wang, 2014). However, despite Extension's magnitude and knowledge among key constituents and stakeholders regarding its contributions to the US economy and society, Extension has been dubbed as the "best kept secret" in academia. In part, this lack of visibility is not only due to limited marketing and branding of programs within communities but also because of a lack of integration of Extension within the broader undergraduate curriculum (Brodeur et al., 2011; DeBord, 2007). Although the lives of most, if not all, people in the United States have been influenced by advances and technologies resulting from Extension, awareness is lacking even among LGU faculty and students about this entity. Uplifting the importance of Extension as an integral partner in addressing real-world problems can be achieved by fostering stronger connections between Extension and the broader LGU system, and between Extension and the public. Additionally, more robust partnerships between Extension and non-Extension units within land-grant institutions are needed to strengthen research and formal teaching in ways that provide ecological grounding and enhance direct relevance of academic pursuits. In short, helping the broader academe and the public understand the contemporary Extension system can facilitate stronger engagement and broader impact across many fields.

1.1 The Current Volume

The goal of this volume is to extend readers' understanding of the Extension system and its importance, with particular focus on its role in the field of the social sciences, and conversely, the role of the social sciences in Extension. The call for papers generated a broad range of articles – each illustrative of the impact-focused work in which Extension is engaged, the variety of contexts in which it is embedded, and the critically important role that research plays as the basis of programming. This volume brings together leading and emerging scholars to discuss how Extension is addressing issues relevant to children, youth, families, and communities across the country today, as well as how Extension fulfills its charge in the foreseeable future.

Part I provides a broad overview of efforts within Extension to support children, youth, families, and communities. In Chapter 2, J. Kale Monk discusses the critical role of research in the Extension enterprise – both as the basis of program development and as a means of ensuring program quality and impact through evaluation. In Chapter 3, Yoshie Sano, Ann A. Berry, and Christopher T. Sneed discuss the role of Extension in supporting families in rural communities and describe the Rural Families Speak project – a cutting-edge network that brings together researchers and Extension professionals who together address the needs of underserved populations. Chapter 4, by Julie M. Fox, undertakes a critical discussion of the unique factors that need to be taken into consideration when addressing well-being among families in urban contexts. Fox highlights both the common competencies needed across Extension programming and unique considerations needed to address urban needs, as well as provides snapshots of successful programming conducted in large urban areas in several regions of the country.

Part II highlights Extension programs that address key needs and issues facing children, youth, families, and communities today. Constance C. Beecher and Teresa A. Byington (Chapter 5) describe Extension efforts to support young children, illustrating how Extension addresses well-being at multiple levels of programming, for instance, by providing programming for children, caregivers, and educators; and by addressing contextual issues that impact children. Chapter 6, by Jodi Dworkin, is a discussion of various efforts within Extension to support youth development, with a specific focus on programs that engage and empower families – thus building capacity for sustained support of youth. Chapter 7, by Theresa M. Ferrari and Mary E. Arnold, is a discussion of 4-H – the largest youth organization in the country. This chapter illustrates how 4-H exemplifies social science in action, with programming informed by research and continued evolution of program models with new information over the years. In Chapter 8, Lisa Franzen-Castle, Michelle Krehbiel, and Jean Ann Fischer describe how Extension takes a multipronged and collaborative approach to addressing critical issues, leveraging key partnerships at multiple levels (e.g., local, federal), and providing much-needed support for constituents. And in Chapter 9, Surin Kim, Maria Rosario T. de Guzman, Claire Nicholas, Yunqi Wang, Irene Padasas, and Olivia Kennedy describe the growing Extension efforts within the field of youth entrepreneurship education. They propose that Extension can draw insights from the rich body of research on entrepreneurship conducted in the social and behavioral sciences to guide the growing efforts in Extension within this field.

Part III addresses contemporary challenges and issues that Extension is facing. In Chapter 10, Kieu Anh Do and Virginie Zoumenou discuss the demographic shifts and potential implications for the continued relevance of Extension. In Chapter 11, Kerrie Fanning, Jiwon Yoon, and Margaret L. Kerr share promising ways for Extension to engage underserved and underrepresented fathers to highlight potential avenues for engaging historically marginalized communities in Extension work and programming. Chapter 12, by Joseph L. Donaldson, tackles an issue that is critical for the sustainability of Extension, that is, the training of future professionals in the field. Donaldson notes that gaps exist in formal preparation for Extension careers but describes avenues for hopeful Extension professionals to gain experience and training to enter a career in this field. Finally, in Chapter 13, Jemalyn Griffin and Holly Hatton discuss the shifting information landscape and its implications for the continued relevance of Extension and highlight an example of how Extension can partner with university entities with expertise in mass communication.

1.2   Themes, Conclusions, and Remaining Questions

Several key themes are evident from the contributions that highlight the value of Extension and provide insights regarding key challenges and future directions:

1.2.1   Extension's Rich History and Continued Relevance Today

Extension has had a rich history of transforming lives and communities across the country but faces the task of reevaluating its continued relevance in today's rapidly shifting information and demographic landscape. Almost every chapter in this volume noted Extension's history of translating intellectual resources and technological innovations for the direct benefit of individuals and communities. Extension was established through a series of landmark legislations including the Morill Act of 1862 that formed the land-grant colleges and universities, the Hatch Act of 1887 that funded the development of state AES, which continue to generate important knowledge and innovations in agriculture and other fields, and the Morrill Act of 1890 that banned the exclusion of Blacks from land-grant institutions and led to the formation of Historically Black Colleges and Universities across the country. Extension itself was formally established by Congress through the Smith–Lever Act of 1914 that appropriated resources to "aid in diffusing among the people of the United States useful and practical information on subjects relating to agriculture, home economics, and rural energy…" and describing Extension work as consisting of "the development of practical applications of research knowledge and giving of instruction and practical demonstrations of existing or improved practices or technologies in agriculture, home economics, and rural energy," as well as subjects relevant to communities and its residents (Smith–Lever Act, 1914). Thus, for over a century, Extension has served as a unique and robust system to collaborate, generate, and disseminate research, as well as to engage in mission-oriented work to support communities in optimizing their current and future circumstances. Extension has harnessed the expertise of countless scholars and professionals in each of the US land-grant colleges and universities housed on university campuses, experimental stations, and in offices reaching each of the nation's over 3,000 counties.

Yet, across Extension's lifetime, significant shifts have occurred that challenge and/or bring to question its continued relevance. Do and Zoumenou (Chapter 10) contrast the demographics of the US population at Extension's inception versus today. They note that population growth, increasing ethnic and racial diversity shifts in traditional family forms (e.g., higher rates of single parenthood, lower rates of marriage, higher rates of divorce), and changes in the population's age stratification may have the most important implications for how and for whom Extension does its work. As the authors note, Extension is at a "critical junction" and needs to explore ways to fulfill its original charge against a context that has shifted dramatically. Fanning and colleagues (Chapter 11) further highlight the continued relevance of Extension by elevating its critically important role of in reaching and working with historically underrepresented communities. Further, they propose and highlight unique ways that Extension can and has engaged underserved communities to ensure that programming and resources are holistic and reflect community wisdom and representation.

Nonetheless, Extension has shown how it can evolve to meet the needs of its constituents amid times of change. Kim and colleagues' (Chapter 9) discussion of entrepreneurship education efforts illustrates how new fields of inquiry and programming develop within Extension in response to emergent issues and new information and innovations from the social sciences. Extension programming within youth entrepreneurship education is relatively new but draws from a substantial body of scholarship on the potential of entrepreneurial efforts to uplift communities and the value of entrepreneurial thinking. Julie M. Fox (Chapter 4) reminds us that Extension was initially designed to bring the intellectual resources of the land-grant system to rural populations. Yet today, the contemporary Extension system has substantial presence within suburban and urban communities. Fox provides examples of programs specifically designed for audiences residing in more densely populated regions, highlighting how Extension has evolved to reach populations that were not its prime focus when it was created more than a century ago.

Describing yet another type of shift, Griffin and Hatton (Chapter 13) address the issue of accelerating change within the information landscape. Advances in informational technology now facilitate access to information – putting into question Extension's role in disseminating information to the broader population in relevant, responsible, and meaningful ways. However, as opposed to making Extension obsolete, the authors propose that Extension now has the potential to increase engagement by involving audiences as cocreators of content rather than as passive recipients.

1.2.2   Extension's Approach to Supporting Children, Youth, Families, and Communities Is Uniquely Collaborative, Interdisciplinary, and Innovative

In recent decades, there has been growing recognition for the value of interdisciplinary approaches in conducting research and in addressing issues facing children, youth, families, and communities (Bronstein, 2003; Moody & Darbellay, 2019). Interdisciplinary collaborations bring together varied but potentially complementary perspectives that can prove synergistic in addressing complex issues (Derry & Schunn, 2005). By its very structure, Extension takes a collaborative (i.e., "cooperative") approach to engagement. As a nationwide nonformal and translational education system, Extension is operated through each of the nation's LGUs in collaboration with government agencies and entities at the federal (i.e., United States Department of Agriculture [USDA]-National Institute for Food and Agriculture [NIFA]), state (i.e., LGUs, AES) and local levels (e.g., county offices, local organizations) (APLU, n.d.; USDA-NIFA, n.d.). Funding structures similarly reflect this collaborative nature, with state Extension efforts typically supported by a combination of government appropriations at federal, state, and county levels in combination with grants and other funding sources (APLU, n.d.).

Several key examples can be drawn from chapters in this volume to further illustrate the collaborative and interdisciplinary approach taken within Extension, and how efforts address the broader ecology of children, youth, and families. Franzen-Castle and colleagues (Chapter 8) describe Extension programs that support food, nutrition, and health issues of families. They provide an in-depth discussion of Supplemental Nutrition Assistance Program (SNAP), SNAP Education, and other exemplars of programming that leverage community partnerships and address well-being of constituents with both individual-level interventions and changes to the broader context through policy change. Dworkin (Chapter 6) also describes an ecological and collaborative approach to programming – describing Extension youth development programs across the country that do not just address individuals' well-being but also engages families and the broader community as partners to support youth.

Perhaps it is due to Extension's collaborative and issue-focused nature that it has been able to engage constituents in agile and responsive ways. Extension has been at the forefront of rapid responses – "extending" scholarship in real time and in situations wherein immediate responses are needed. Several Extension efforts have been deployed across the country during natural and man-made disasters, for example, in 2019, when historic and catastrophic floods hit the central regions of Nebraska – devastating homes, communities, and farmlands. With hundreds of professionals already situated in or serving the state's ninety-three counties, Extension was able to rapidly deploy assistance and bring to bear the university's intellectual resources to address the challenges that resulted from this event. Responses included organizing and deploying volunteers for debris removal and engaging agricultural scientists to share their expertise on how to handle damaged crops and farmlands, business- and entrepreneurship-focused educators to assist business owners in addressing lost sources of livelihoods, and early childhood and youth Extension scholars to develop resources to mitigate the trauma on children and families (Reed, 2022).

The rapid response of Extension was again needed and applied multiple times over just one year later during the COVID pandemic (Narine & Meier, 2020). Across the country, Extension entities supported children, youth, and families by disseminating information regarding health and safety at the time of COVID, distributing resources about vaccines and helping implement clinics, supporting well-being by providing guidance to help navigate social isolation, and by providing much-needed resources through online and hybrid activities for children during one of the greatest disruptions in education and normative life that the United States had collectively faced (USDA, 2021).

With a focus on addressing issues rather than being siloed within specific disciplinary lines, Extension is primed to bring together the necessary teams and experts to provide rapid and innovative responses both in the field and in research. It is not atypical to find child-, youth-, and family-focused Extension programs that engage early childhood educators alongside entomologists, youth development professionals working with agricultural engineers, and family scientists collaborating with finance experts. A common theme across the chapters was the instrumental role of community-based participatory approaches to effectively address issues facing children, youth, families, and communities that can require a different way of engaging and working with those most affected by gaps in resources, information, and programming. With shifts in the demography of its audience, accelerating advances in information technology, paired with diminishing resources, we propose that Extension continues to be well positioned to make significant and transformative impacts in the lives of children, youth, families, and communities for the foreseeable future.

1.2.3   Remaining Challenges and Potential Responses

Notwithstanding Extensions' potential for impact-focused and transformative work, contributions to this volume make evident several challenges and questions that remain:

Diminishing resources and increased demands. Funding for Extension has declined over the years – in both the amount and the proportion of state and federal dollars that support Extension efforts (Coppess et al., 2018; Wang, 2014). At the same time, Extension professionals are today tasked with increased responsibilities, for instance, to participate in the production of scholarship and to meet expectations for high-quality programming despite (and perhaps partly because of) diminishing resources. Monk (Chapter 2) discusses the complex charge of many

Extension professionals to not just disseminate but also engage in research despite sometimes limited training and/or absent explicit job duties that reflect these responsibilities. Whereas earlier Extension positions focused primarily on translating research and dissemination through program development, today's Extension professionals are also tasked with implementing rigorous evaluations and contributing to the broader research enterprise. Engaged scholarship through both basic and applied research is clearly essential in Extension. Nonetheless, the need to contribute to both programming and evaluation, and at times even basic research, can put a significant strain on an already challenged system.

In response to diminishing resources and increased demands, emergent tools may offer some assistance to ease the burden for the already taxed Extension professionals (e.g., see Griffin & Hatton this volume). However, such tools may also herald in even more challenges such that Extension professionals are not just developing resources but also having to navigate means of information distribution, serving as researchers, content creators, and managers of social media accounts, for example.

Griffin and Hatton discuss in their chapter that the availability of technologies makes it possible to reach a broader audience today at unprecedent levels. Technological innovations are changing how Extension is doing its work, on the one hand facilitating program and content development, and on the other hand imposing potential challenges. They propose at least one path toward easing the burden of navigating this changing information landscape, that is, engaging partners that have specific expertise in addressing such issues. Extension already has a history of leveraging multiple partners to tackle complex issues. Taking a similar approach as a means of navigating diminishing resources may prove beneficial, if not necessary.

Hiring and preparing the next generation of Extension professionals. Donaldson (Chapter 12) points to another challenge within Extension, that is, the need to prepare the next generation of professionals to ensure sustainability of the Extension enterprise. Currently, few programs exist that specifically provide professional learning and development for Extension careers. Some universities offer master's level degrees in agricultural extension and/or extension education (e.g., Colorado State University, Virginia Tech University, University of Arkansas), though such training opportunities are rare. Learning experiences specifically for professionals wishing to undertake a career in Extension focused on children, youth, and families are difficult to find. Instead, personnel receive professional development and experiences in specific fields (e.g., nutrition, early childhood education, family science, youth development) and then gain the "extension" aspect of their profession on-the-job. Thus, there is a substantial gap and opportunity to supplement current training for professionals in early childhood, youth development, and family science with Extension experience and education. This instructional gap may in fact pose an opportunity for departments with Extension charges to include coursework that provides information about Extension, internships, and skills to work therein.

Continued relevance and shifts in how Extension conducts its work. In the 100+ years of its existence, the charge of Extension has remained the same – to translate "research into action" and to bring the intellectual resources, innovations, and insights from research stations and universities directly into the hands of our constituents. Funding structures, the informational landscape, and demographics of our audiences, nonetheless, have shifted dramatically. Against this backdrop, Extension must ask such important questions as how it can continue to be relevant in a world where there is greater access to information, where audiences have also become content creators, where the demographics of our audience have diverged tremendously from the original target for which Extension was developed, and where structural barriers continue to contribute to inequities across racial, ethnic, and other sociodemographic lines as was made evident during the COVID pandemic and the summer of 2020 that spotlighted such realities.

As it did during its first 100 years, Extension continues to evolve and is already showing shifts in the ways it is conducting its work to match the contextual, demographic, and technological changes we are seeing today. Contributions to this volume illustrate the collaborative, innovative, and impact-focused work that continues to make important contributions in supporting children, youth, families, and communities across the country. Perhaps today more than ever, Extension will need to lead the way in building and maintaining sustainable partnerships across disciplines and with organizations at the local, state, and national levels to tackle complex issues considering diminishing resources. Extension will also need to effectively show its impact and return on investment to illustrate its value to federal, state, and local stakeholders (Wang, 2014). Finally, it is critical for Extension to remain agile, to continue focusing on impact that may, in the future, necessitate new methods of engagement, new partners, and new ways of understanding solutions to address issues and in delivering information. Extension has successfully delivered resources to communities since its establishment and has cocreated solutions to wicked problems for decades. Contributions to this volume indicate a promising start to the next century of delivering and cocreating impactful programming to support the well-being of children, youth, families, and communities.

References

APLU. (n.d.). *Cooperative Extension Section (CES)*. Retrieved on July 18, 2023 from www.aplu.org/members/commissions/food-environment-and-renewable-resources/board-on-agriculture-assembly/cooperative-extension-section/

Arnold, S., & Place, N. (2010). What influences agents to pursue a career in Extension? *The Journal of Extension*, 48(1), Article 9. https://tigerprints.clemson.edu/joe/vol48/iss1/9

Brodeur, C. W., Higgins, C., Galindo-Gonzalez, S., Craig, D. D., & Haile, T. (2011). Designing a competency-based new county extension personnel training program: A novel approach. *The Journal of Extension*, 49(3), Article 2. https://tigerprints.clemson.edu/joe/vol49/iss3/2

Bronstein, L. R. (2003). A model for interdisciplinary collaboration. *Social Work*, 48(3), 297–306. https://doi.org/10.1093/sw/48.3.297

Coppess, J., Paulson, N., Schnitkey, G., & Zulauf, C. (2018). Cooperative Extension challenges: Funding and remaining relevant. *AgFax*. 2018 August. Retrieved on November 22, 2023 from www.agfax.com/2018/08/24/cooperative-extension-challenges-funding-and-remaining-relevant/

DeBord, K. (2007). How integrated extension programming helps market Cooperative Extension: The North Carolina recommendation. *The Journal of Extension*, 45(5), Article 2.

Derry, S. J., & Schunn, C. D (2005). Interdisciplinarity: A beautiful but dangerous beast. In S. J. Derry, C. D. Schunn, & M. A. Gernsbacher (Eds.), *Interdisciplinary collaboration: An emerging cognitive science* (pp. xii–xx). Taylor and Francis.

Gould, F. I., Steele, D., & Woodrum, W. J. (2014). Cooperative Extension: A century of innovation. *The Journal of Extension*, 52(1), Article 3. https://tigerprints.clemson.edu/joe/vol52/iss1/3

Moody, Z., & Darbellay, F. (2019). Studying childhood, children, and their rights: The challenge of interdisciplinarity. *Childhood*, 26(1), 8–21. https://doi.org/10.1177/0907568218798016

Narine, L., & Meier, C. (2020). Responding in a time of crisis: Assessing extension efforts during COVID-19. *Advancements in Agricultural Development*, 1(2), 12–23. https://doi.org/10.37433/aad.v1i2.35

Reed, L. (2022). Nebraska U continues to assist with 2019 flooding recovery. *Nebraska Today*. 2022 March. Retrieved on November 23, 2023 from https://news.unl.edu/newsrooms/today/article/nebraska-u-continues-to-assist-with-2019-flooding-recovery/

Smith–Lever Act. (1914). www.govinfo.gov/content/pkg/COMPS-10296/pdf/COMPS-10296.pdf

USDA-NIFA. (2021). *USDA-NIFA, CDC and Cooperative Extension team up for vaccine education in rural America.* Retrieved from www.nifa.usda.gov/about-nifa/press-releases/usda-nifa-cdc-cooperative-extension-team-vaccine-education-rural-america

USDA-NIFA. (n.d.). *Cooperative Extension System.* Retrieved July 18, 2023 from www.nifa.usda.gov/about-nifa/how-we-work/extension/cooperative-extension-system

Wang, S. L. (2014). Cooperative Extension System: Trends and economic impacts on U.S. agriculture. Choices: The Magazine of Food, Farm, and Resource Issues. *Agricultural and Applied Economics Association,* 29(1), 1–8.

CHAPTER 2

Engaged Scholarship
Navigating the Role of Research in Extension
Using a Relationship Education Case Example

J. Kale Monk

The overarching purpose of Extension is to facilitate the application of science to the broader public (Monk, Benson, & Bordere, 2019; Spoth et al., 2020). As Extension professionals, we are tasked to act as an "extension" of our land-grant universities to increase access to education, solve real-world problems, and improve people's lives (Franz, 2014; Patton, 2008). Hamilton and colleagues (2013) argue that "the Extension system exists to disseminate the findings of research beyond the academic community to practitioners, policy makers, and the general public" (p. 1). To accomplish the important goal of community betterment through dissemination, the information we provide the public must be accurate and trustworthy, based on rigorous science (Braverman & Arnold, 2008). This empirical standard is vital in order to "do no harm" by avoiding recommendations or providing guidelines that could be maladaptive. Accomplishing this feat increases the likelihood that our programs will be relevant and beneficial to the communities we serve (Hill & Parker, 2005).

Complicating the task of disseminating research to the broader public is the precipitous decline in the allocation of financial and instrumental resources for Extension (and many universities as a whole) over the last several decades (see Page & Kern, 2018). Consequently, Extension professionals are under heightened pressures from university administrators, funding agencies, and federal, state, and local governments to justify support and demonstrate the public value of Extension (Fetsch et al., 2012; Franz, Arnold, & Baughman, 2014; Taylor-Powell & Boyd, 2008). A few of these pressures include a push to utilize evidence-based programs (Sellers et al., 2017) and demonstrate the impact of programming through rigorous evaluation (Lamm et al., 2013). Both of these expected tasks require the understanding of existing research to inform our work and the ability to conduct research to properly ensure our efforts are accomplishing our goals.

Extension professionals recognize the challenges they face and are interested and willing to take on the charge to enhance research and evaluation efforts, even if not all within the organization (a) feel prepared (e.g., Lamm et al., 2013; Sellers et al., 2017) or (b) feel their organization as a whole has the capacity (Arnold, 2006). Nevertheless, Extension is well positioned to take on these challenges as the active mechanism to fulfill the land-grant mission to disseminate scientific knowledge to the public (Monk, Benson, & Bordere, 2019), especially given research is an important component of the programming process (e.g., research and theory inform the program content and implementation approach, and comprehensive evaluation leads to necessary programmatic improvements; Duttweiler, 2008; Taylor-Powell & Boyd, 2008). Therefore, Extension professionals are well positioned to support universities by demonstrating the value and real-world applicability of research, thereby addressing the crisis of relevance for academia as a whole (see Bell & Lewis, 2023).

In this chapter, I demonstrate the complementarity of Extension practice and the process of research and evaluation by outlining the relevance of Extension as a research-informed, evidence-based, culturally relevant, interdisciplinary, and public scholarship enterprise. To further illustrate each of these qualities of Extension, I will describe the development of a relationship science dissemination program, Relevate. Although still a work in progress, the development of this program underscores the scholar–practitioner, collaborative, innovative, and engaged work that is exemplified by Cooperative Extension as a source of credible prevention education (see Mincemoyer et al., 2008).

Introduction to the case example. Relevate is a team of researchers and practitioners that we established under the leadership of Dr. Amber Vennum to make relationship science available and accessible to the public (Monk, Vennum, & Kanter, 2019). The main avenue through which we intend to disseminate information is via a mobile or website application (app) called *MyRelevate* that we are currently developing. This platform will provide research-based insights in a convenient and adaptable, self-contained program. Throughout this chapter, I will describe Relevate as a project development intuitive to demonstrate the various research attributes of Extension, which illustrates the reciprocal and iterative role research plays in Extension.

2.1   Extension as Research-Informed Application

Critical to the Extension mission is identifying social problems in communities that might be solved through educational programming (Yang et al., 2009). There is not one linear path toward research-informed practice with regard to program development in Extension. Nonetheless, an important first task for an Extension professional is to determine the needs of a particular community. A *needs assessment* can be used as a method to identify the unique issues facing a particular audience, what – if anything – has already been attempted to remedy particular problems, what community strengths or resources are present, and what issues still remain (Garst & McCawley, 2015). As a result, a needs assessment can help professionals learn about relevant partners'[1] concerns and understand how they might respond to these issues (Garst & McCawley, 2015). It is also worth noting that the process of needs assessment and program development does not have to start with the Extension professionals because community members may serve as the initiators and/or key partners in identifying issues of concern and potential solutions in their communities.

Once a problem or need is determined, a natural next step is to see if there is an evidence-based (or at least research-informed) program already in existence; after all, developing a program is a costly and time-intensive process, so it is often best not to "reinvent the wheel" (Fetsch et al., 2012). However, a program for a particular need may not be in existence or a closely aligned program may require significant adaptation to make it relevant for a specific community. This potential limitation in existing programs is not an uncommon concern given the need for Extension to be responsive to the unique needs and experiences within diverse local communities, which reflects the contextual nature of Extension work (Applebee, 2000). Because of the demand for emergent responsivity to local needs (Olson et al., 2015), there may be a necessity to develop a program "in house." Many of these Extension programs developed by professionals themselves are perceived to be equally as effective as evidence-based programs developed by individuals or organizations outside their systems (Hamilton et al., 2013; Hill & Parker, 2005; Perkins et al., 2014). Using a *logic model* can be a useful first step in program planning and evaluation because it can help identify (a) what efforts, personnel, and resources will go into a given program (inputs), (b) what program facilitators plan to do and what populations they plan to target (outputs), and (c) the short-, medium-, and long-term goals (outcomes/impact) (Arnold, 2006; Taylor-Powell & Boyd, 2008). Focusing on the necessary components of the program and explicitly stating the end goal may increase the likelihood that a program will be effective in having the desired impact.

---

[1] I use "community partners," "practitioners," and similar terms to suggest individuals involved in or affected by an action, while avoiding the usage of "stakeholder" as it can conjure colonial and patronizing connotations (Reed & Rudman, 2023; Sharfstein, 2016).

Although a need may be new, no program should truly be "started from scratch" because program development should be theory- and research-driven (see Fetsch et al., 2012, for guidelines). For example, a sound 4-H youth program might be based on positive youth development principles and a parent education program might be based on attachment theory, both of which represent large bodies of empirical research that provide guidance to support optimal child development.

In order to find empirical scholarship to inform the content and implementation of a program, Extension professionals may look to scholarly databases and publication repositories like Google Scholar, PsychInfo, or their university library. Literature searches should focus on peer-reviewed sources of evidence. Credible, peer-reviewed journals may include, for example, *Family Relations, Family Process*, and the *Journal of Marriage and Family* for family life education specialists or the *Journal of Research on Adolescents* and the *Journal of Youth and Adolescence* for 4-H youth development specialists. The *Journal of Extension* may be a good starting point, especially for identifying commonly used and evaluated programs (see Duttweiler, 2008). Extension professionals should scrutinize the design of each study to make sure any claims made in the article match what was actually assessed, how the results were derived, and to whom the findings actually generalize based on the participant sample.

Cutting-edge information may also be disseminated through professional organizations and at academic conferences (e.g., National Council on Family Relations, Society for Research on Adolescence, National Health Outreach Conference, Society for Prevention Research, and American Association for Marriage & Family Therapy). The eXtension (impact.extension.org) and Land Grant Impacts (landgrantimpact.org) websites are also useful resources in finding relevant insights. Similarly, an Extension-affiliated center, consortium, or working group that provides webinars, reports, and other resources may also be useful, such as the National Extension Relationship & Marriage Education Network (NERMEN), the North Central Regional Center of Rural Development (NCRCRD), or the North Central Region Aging Network (NCRAN).

The research informing Relevate. Intimate relationships exert a robust influence on the mental and physical well-being of individual partners (see Holt-Lundstad et al., 2017; Kiecolt-Glaser & Wilson, 2017), as well as other people around the couple (e.g., children; Amato, 2010). Poor quality relationships can also impact local communities at large, for example, through economic impacts in cases of divorce or the cost of addressing resulting challenges to mental health or worker productivity losses (e.g., Shamblen et al., 2018). Therefore, the federal government instituted policy initiatives promoting healthy marriage and relationship education to help partners develop appropriate expectations and attitudes about relationships and supply participants with the skills to bring those expectations to fruition (Fincham et al., 2011). There are many empirically supported educational initiatives that began in Extension, for instance, the relationship education programs developed by renowned scholars like Francesca Adler-Baeder and her team (e.g., Adler-Baeder et al., 2004). These programs are based on decades of research in what makes relationships flourish and what qualities or behaviors need to be avoided to prevent relational distress and dissolution (e.g., Gottman & Gottman, 2017). To reach broad audiences with these and other resources, scholars recommend developing low cost and easily accessible delivery methods, such as Internet-based, self-guided programs (e.g., Hawkins & Ooms, 2010).

Unlike other resources, access to mobile phones is high across all residential areas and racial groups, making interventions through mobile health (mHealth) a burgeoning avenue for reducing health disparities (e.g., Arya et al., 2014) with over 81 percent of all Americans owning smartphones (PEW Research Center, 2019). Additionally, according to a popular press report of digital activity, on average, people in the United States spend approximately six and a half hours online a day (We are Social, 2019). Young adults lead the way in using smartphones to look for relationship advice and health information online (Fox & Duggan, 2012, 2013; see also Percheski & Hargittai, 2011). Consequently, interest in mHealth, telehealth, and other online health interventions has risen sharply in recent decades (e.g., Hong et al., 2020; Tozzi et al., 2015), creating a critical opportunity for Extension programming to expand our reach. Noticing the need for individuals to be able to access quality relationship science remotely, my colleague Amber Vennum approached me with her idea to develop Relevate to fill this gap (Monk, Vennum, & Kanter, 2019). Over the last several years, our team has conducted several focus groups and collected other forms of data to assess what types of information young adults desire to learn and what features of a mobile app they would find most beneficial.

2.2 Extension as Evidence-Based Programming and Practice: The Role of Evaluation and Research

Although certainly not characteristic of Extension as a whole, some Extension professionals may struggle with the differences between evidence-based programs (EBPs) and a program that is research-based (e.g., Sellers et al., 2017), which can stem from a lack of conceptual clarity. Evidence-based programs are those that have been rigorously examined for effectiveness and generally (a) have been evaluated with randomized controlled trials, (b) have shown evidence for positive outcomes over time, (c) are well documented so that they are more easily disseminated with identifiable curricula and practices, (d) have gone through rigorous peer review, and (e) are endorsed by government agencies and well-respected research organizations (Small et al., 2009). In recent years, EBPs and evidence-based practices have gained momentum in Extension (Dunifon et al., 2004) and many EBPs are already in existence (see Fetsch et al., 2012, for examples). In contrast to the strict definition for EBPs, evidence-based practices "are commonly defined as the integration of the best available research evidence with clinical expertise and client values" and may not necessarily be part of a larger program (Small et al., 2009, p. 1).

The increased demand for EBPs is driven by many forces. Among the most central pressures is the external demand for accountability and documented impact through the Government Performance and Results Act (GPRA) of 1993 (Taylor-Powell & Boyd, 2008). Government officials and private taxpayers want evidence that funds, like those provided to Extension, are producing adequate results in terms of return on investment. However, there are also internal demands because Extension professionals are intrinsically motivated to do the most good and improve their programs (Taylor-Powell & Boyd, 2008).

Whether one is aiming to utilize evidence-based practices or develop EBPs, rigorous evaluation is critical (Taylor-Powell & Boyd, 2008) and adds to the evidence that engagement work is rigorous and systematic (Warren et al., 2018). Research is an important component of the programming process because research and theory should inform program content and implementation, and empirically evaluating outcomes is essential in assessing impact and guiding improvements (Duttweiler, 2008). Accordingly, the success of Extension is intertwined with evaluation. The essential elements of *evaluation* directly align and are compatible with day-to-day Extension work. Patton (2008) illustrates this overlap by stating "Extension educators work to get people to use information – and so do evaluators. Extension educators spend a lot of time considering how to overcome resistance to change. So do evaluators. Extension educators worry about communicating knowledge in a form people can understand and use. So do evaluators" (p. 103). Both Extension and evaluation are concerned with determining who needs information and from whom, what types of resources are needed, and the most effective manner of delivering content (see Patton, 2008).

To develop a useful evaluation, King and Cooksy (2008) recommend considering five questions: Who cares? (i.e., Who are the relevant partner groups?) Who came? (i.e., Who were the participants?) What was implemented? (e.g., What is the description of the program or intervention?) What changed and what difference did it make? (e.g., How effective was the program? What from the program was adopted by participants?) How much did the program cost (or earn)? (e.g., What were the resources invested into the delivery of the program)? The responses to the questions can help determine if the program is worth continuing in the future.

The most complicated of these questions is determining what changed and what difference the program made in participants. To measure change and determine impact, it is important that Extension professionals use brief, valid measures that are aligned with program objectives. These measures should also focus on behavioral or attitude changes and not just a participant's satisfaction with the program (or if they would recommend the program to a friend) (see Fetsch et al., 2012). Measures can be identified through the same means as locating empirical research and theory to develop program content (see Fetsch et al., 2012, for other suggested outlets). Indeed, empirical studies and published program evaluations should contain detailed descriptions of the measures used, including information about validity and reliability (or authors point to prior studies that already established these metrics). If an Extension professional is adapting an existing measure, or creating their own, Fetsch and colleagues (2012) recommend consulting with a specialist who has relevant expertise in this area, if psychometric assessment is not in the professional's area of expertise.

Relationship education as evidence-based and the evaluation plan for Relevate. Although Relevate is primarily focused on translating and communicating relationship science to individuals broadly and not focused on a particular relationship education curriculum specifically, the existing evidence base around relationship education (e.g., Hawkins et al., 2008) and critiques of these programs (e.g., Johnson, 2012; Johnson & Bradbury, 2015) served as a starting point to motivate us to develop the program. One of the most highly regarded relationship education programs that served as inspiration for the Relevate team to work in this area is the Prevention and Relationship Enhancement Program (PREP; Stanley et al., 2001). Through PREP, couples learn how to nurture commitment and an intimate bond, in addition to being taught communication, problem-solving, and conflict management skills. The effectiveness of this program in improving relationship outcomes (e.g., improving communication behaviors, reducing risk of divorce) has been demonstrated through several randomized controlled trials (e.g., Stanley et al., 2010, 2014).

After we complete the development of our program, we plan to properly evaluate MyRelevate using established recommendations from the mHealth and prevention science literature (e.g., Martin et al., 2015). This will include providing a randomized intervention group access to the MyRelevate app and administering assessments of relationship quality, interpersonal behaviors, and personal well-being over time. One evaluation strategy we plan to implement is an ecological momentary assessment (EMA), a procedure that involves intensive repeated measurements over a short period of time to capture real-time interactive processes (Bolger et al., 2003). Participants will be prompted to respond daily to a brief assessment through mobile phone notifications.

We intend to recruit a randomized control group that will similarly receive notifications with the same assessments, without receiving access to the MyRelevate program itself (but another resource instead). This design will allow us to assess personal and relational changes over time and compare these changes between those who did and those who did not have access to the app. Additionally, participants in the intervention group will be asked questions pertaining to their level of satisfaction with the program. Although we do want to investigate actual change (action) and not just satisfaction (or intentions), it is still critical to determine if individuals *like* and would *use* the program. Qualitative evaluations of users' experiences would also be incredibly valuable in addition to the quantitative assessments (Patton, 2015).

2.3   Extension as Culturally Relevant Partnerships

There is a growing diversity in the United States that is well documented (e.g., Lichter, 2012). Most of the focus on this diversification is on large cities that have "majority-minority" populations, but there is increasing diversity in rural areas as well (Lichter, 2012). Nevertheless, there is an added push for Extension to increase focus on urban areas, beyond the rural roots of the system (Borich, 2001; Fehlis, 1992; Fox, 2017), which makes the diversity in rural and urban areas all the more relevant. Indeed, these factors ensure that most Extension professionals will encounter individuals in their work who are different for them in a variety of ways (e.g., gender identity, sexual orientation, ability, religion, socioeconomic status/class, language use, race, and ethnicity; see Schauber & Castania, 2001). With the need to deliver programs that are beneficial and not harmful to communities, it is important that Extension professionals demonstrate cultural competence.

That is, the content and implementation of programs need to be *culturally competent* in order to be relevant and beneficial to the communities we serve, particularly populations that are historically underserved, marginalized, and disenfranchised. Involving community members throughout the development and implementation process is an advantageous method to help ensure cultural relevance. *Community-based participatory research* (CBPR) is an approach that supports "collaborative, equitable partnerships in all phases of the research" and promotes "co-learning and capacity building among partners" to "disseminate findings and knowledge gained to all partners" (Israel et al., 2003, pp. 56–58). Based on this belief that programming is strengthened when community insight is included, there is a clear parallel between CBPR and Extension work (Gagnon, Franz et al., 2015). Indeed, Extension also embraces the importance of relinquishing an expert role, and colearning and cocreating products with communities (Franz, 2014; Monk et al., 2022). This approach is incredibly vital in determining cultural appropriateness and developing reciprocal partnerships because CBPR empowers community members to determine activities, cocreate content, and engage throughout the process (Israel et al., 2003). If campus-based researchers or Extension professionals go to a community assuming they are experts and deliver content that was developed for and normed on completely different populations, they may actually be doing harm in addition to potentially not promoting interest or buy-in from the local community (e.g., Stephenson, 2003). Therefore, CBPR can also encourage trust in Extension among community members (see Shelton, 2008), while also working toward health equity and decolonizing the health and well-being of underserved populations at large.

Similarly, despite the noted benefits and importance of EBPs, there are several considerations that are relevant to cultural diversity. For example, it takes significant time to build up evidence of longitudinal effectiveness with Fetsch and colleagues (2012) noting that it could take fifteen to twenty years before a program is ready for distribution. While waiting for programs to be developed and evaluated to ensure they are not harmful, unique needs for particular communities may have changed, especially as demographics evolve. Similarly, EBPs are tightly controlled, often requiring consistency (fidelity) in implementation to ensure replicability of results (DiClemente et al., 2009). This is problematic if responsive adaptation is needed with regard to emerging issues in diverse communities with unique local considerations (e.g., not all participants are responsive to the same types of information or delivery). Based on these factors, adaptation may be necessary to make it relevant or applicable to different populations, while continuing to engage in evaluation practices like consulting with community members about content and delivery to reduce the potential of harm. Scholars and professionals should also note the long colonizing, minoritizing, and gendered history in academia, which further contributes to barriers in doing this engagement work, especially for minoritized researchers and engagement professionals (see Bell & Lewis, 2023).

Like programming itself, evaluation questions also need to be culturally appropriate and comprehensible (Fetsch et al., 2012). In advanced statistical models, measurement invariance tests can be used to approximate if a measure holds a similar meaning across groups (Kim et al., 2017). Member checks are another important tool and include having community members read through assessments and provide feedback about comprehension and appropriateness (see Fetsch et al., 2012). When I was interning as a couple and family therapist, for example, I had a colleague from another country look at a widely used measure of depression that included an item asking how often participants "feel blue." My colleague looked at me perplexed before laughing and saying, "Are you really going to ask people if they feel like they are the color blue?" This idiom did not translate or maintain its meaning and was therefore taken literally, which would be incredibly problematic if I implemented it with clients or participants from cultural backgrounds that did not share this saying. To increase the cultural competence of engagement programming, scholars and professions need to engage in the democratization of knowledge, which requires *reflexivity* (i.e., self-awareness and the critical examination of biases and assumptions in the work), *humility* (i.e., noting that expertise may be questionable or overgeneralized), and the respectful *recognition* that communities hold a great deal of knowledge themselves (see Bell & Lewis, 2023).

Cultural relevance as an impetus for Relevate. One of the major advantages of a mobile or web app is that information, resources, and referrals can be tailored for particular audiences based on background and preferences. This is critical given the fact that many established educational programs were developed for and normed on White, highly-educated, middle-class, heterosexual samples (see Johnson, 2012; c.f., Adler-Baeder et al., 2007; Adler-Baeder & Hawkins, 2010; see also Iverson, 2008). For example, if you are providing an in-person relationship education class to twenty couples, you would likely spend the limited time talking about concepts and strategies that are expected to benefit the majority of attendees (e.g., what works in relationships, generally). However, there are likely couples in the audience that are not receiving critical information that they need; information that is most relevant to their unique circumstances, in addition to the fact that not all information will resonate with all individuals in the same way.

Out of the twenty couples in your class, imagine there is a same-gender couple and an interracial couple in attendance. Professionals may worry that if they tailor the content and adapt to pivot information to be particularly beneficial to these two couples, they may "lose" the other eighteen couples. Although this is a faulty assumption and relevant content should also be provided to these couples within in-person programming, this is precisely when an adaptive app can be especially advantageous. If one partner indicates that they were racialized as White and their partner as Black, for example, the program could provide cutting-edge research focused on important conversations interracial couples report as critical, like how to support a partner best who has experiences that the other partner may not fully understand (e.g., discrimination; see Brooks et al., 2018). If romantic partners report they share the same-gender, they may benefit from information about relationship maintenance behaviors like (a) equity and openness that are demonstrated to be effective buffers against minority stressors for lesbian and gay couples (see Ogolsky et al., 2017) or (b) dyadic coping, which can be particularly advantageous during times of sociopolitical uncertainty (e.g., during times of heightened media coverage about anti-LGBTQ rhetoric) for these couples (Monk & Ogolsky, 2019). Young adults in particular, prefer to have personalized service experiences and the diverse demographic background of individuals means a "one-size-fits-all" content approach will be limited in effectiveness (see Vennum et al., 2017). Not only could mobile relationship education reduce barriers to accessing mental health and relationship resources, but an interactive app could also recommend specific information, self-assessments, and skill-building exercises tailored to cultural considerations, personal preferences, context, and individual goals.

2.4 Extension as Interdisciplinary Teamwork

Meeting community needs often requires a multifaceted array of skills and knowledge given issues are often complex and transcend the expertise of any single discipline. Accordingly, Extension provides programming across many areas that intersect in people's lives, including agriculture and natural resources, family life education and consumer sciences, community and economic development, 4-H Youth Development (Franz & Townson, 2008), and behavioral health education (Spoth et al., 2020). To address multifaceted issues holistically, team science is advantageous in a similar vein of collaborative teams in physical and mental healthcare settings (Sevin et al., 2009). Thus, to meet the myriad challenges facing Extension and higher education more generally, research and programming are being conducted and developed by interdisciplinary, multidisciplinary, and transdisciplinary teams (Adams et al., 2012). For example, in the University of Missouri Extension, we offer programming for estate planning, which involves educating participants about financial concerns. However, Extension financial specialists noticed a lot of communication and relationship concerns that can exist among families as they navigate wills and the estate planning process. Both family and finance specialists came together to teach the curricula to complement the disparate expertise areas. Funders are also recognizing the importance of getting out of disciplinary silos and collaborating across and between specialties, resulting in more funding opportunities for interdisciplinary work (Bruns & Franz, 2015).

Similarly, collaborations between researchers and educators or practitioners are also incredibly advantageous and mutually beneficial given the complementarity of their roles (Monk et al., 2021). As educators embedded in the community, Extension professionals in the field have robust knowledge of the needs, attitudes, and preferences of the local public, making them essential resources and key informants for campus-based researchers. This expertise makes Extension professionals in the field an ideal collaborative partner for campus-based researchers who may not have the time, resources, training, or skillset to disseminate research directly to the general public in a systematic way to promote broader impacts. On the other hand, campus-based researchers have advanced training in research design, measurement, and statistical analyses, and are often expected to conduct empirical studies for a significant percentage of their appointment at research-intensive institutions. Although a scholar may have expertise in both research and Extension/engagement, this research knowledge can be a valuable resource for Extension professionals who may not have (a) the training in advanced research design and statistical analyses or (b) the time and resources to plan out a rigorous empirical study to test program objectives even if they have research training (see Monk, Benson, & Bordere, 2019; Monk et al., 2021).

Interdisciplinary collaboration in the development of Relevate. I am a relationship scientist and a couple and family therapist by training, not a software engineer. Developing a mobile or web app is not within my area of expertise. To create the adaptive, mobile relationship science application, my colleagues and I teamed up with software engineers and e-learning education designers, as well as other relationship researchers, therapists, and Extension professionals. Each member of the team brings unique skills and perspectives that lead to more comprehensive ideas.

2.5   Extension as Public Scholarship Endeavors

The proper communication of results is an important feature of the scientific process (see Monk et al., 2021). For example, application of research in the field creates new knowledge (Yapa, 2006). The research-practice link is bidirectional: research should inform our practice (e.g., providing content based on empirical findings, providing points of improvement based on program evaluation), but also practice informs our research in terms of new research questions and future directions (e.g., Franz et al., 2015).

However, some researchers may see a publication and a conference presentation to other scholars in their discipline as enough to fulfill the need for dissemination. Because of a "publish or perish" culture that exists within academia, scholars may feel increasing pressure to cease additional science communication efforts to start the next publication (see Monk et al., 2021). Scholars may also be reluctant to participate in community engagement due to concerns about (a) how to "count" these efforts or (b) whether their institutions will value these efforts in promotion and tenure decisions (Colbeck & Wharton-Michael, 2006; Grzanka & Cole, 2021).

Insights residing only among privileged academicians in the "ivory tower" create knowledge silos and a social justice issue because the groups that we intend to benefit from our findings often cannot access this information (Monk et al., 2021). For example, many journals require individuals or institutions to pay a fee for temporary access to information. Even if the general public gains access to this information, it is often ladened with scientific jargon that requires specialized training to decipher (see Monk et al., 2021). Proper dissemination is vital because credible information can counteract problematic misconceptions and provide various insights that lead to positive change. After all, if a researcher learns how to better people's lives, keeping that discovery from the public is unethical and counter to standards of beneficence and nonmaleficence in research (see Curtis et al., 2017).

In response to this civic responsibility and social justice imperative for science communication (Beaulieu et al., 2018), there is increasing support and popularity for public scholarship (Bell & Lewis, 2023; Besley et al., 2020; Monk et al., 2021). Monk and colleagues (2021) define *public scholarship* broadly as intentional efforts "to create change through the translation and communication of scholarship to persons outside the research setting" (p. 1613) and can encompass related concepts like the engaged scholarship and translational science. If this definition sounds familiar, it is because it greatly overlaps with the defining feature of Extension to disseminate to the public, which introduced this chapter. Indeed, Cooperative Extension was created as the first formal university–community engagement initiative (Franz, 2014; Franz & Townsend, 2008). Many institutions have begun an internal shift toward increasing engagement work because it has the "capacity to increase trust, transparency, and accountability, which together may positively influence the legitimacy and impact of academic knowledge" (Bell & Lewis, 2023, p. 305). Extension can embrace and take advantage of the engaged/public scholarship movement rather than see it as a competitor (Gagnon, Garst, & Franz, 2015). That is to say, the growing popularity of public scholarship can be leveraged to underscore Extension as an entity that was created for this purpose and has been engaging in these translational efforts since its inception over 100 years ago (see Franz, 2014). With Extension often being considered a "best kept secret" in the academe (McDowell, 2004), there exists a vital opportunity to step out of the shadows and into the spotlight by demonstrating our relevance because it is "our time to shine."

Leveraging public scholarship to create Relevate content. To provide research-based relationship information to participants through an EBP, we needed credible relationship science content to share. Much of this content is not readily available online. In fact, a simple Google search of relationship concepts like "love" or "conflict" will largely yield blogs and webpages developed by individuals without relationship science training, speaking mostly from personal experiences. Thus, much of the advice we found online was anecdotal and often problematic. In order to counteract this maladaptive information, we naturally turned to peer-reviewed journals that publish relationship science. However, we could not simply upload these articles into a mobile or web app and expect the general public to read and understand their contents. We needed the authors of these articles to translate their science to the general public because we did not have the capacity to generate all the content on our own. This led us to promote public scholarship as a worthy and valuable endeavor for scholars who want to have a direct impact beyond publishing their results in an academic journal, while also increasing the visibility of their work. We continually partner with other scholars and practitioners to help them create accessible resources derived from credible science and offer these trainings through a variety of outlets (e.g., Monk et al., 2020).

2.6   Recommendations and Conclusion

Extension is part and parcel with the research, evaluation, and dissemination process. Not only can Extension professionals be critical assets for researchers without Extension appointments as key informants and gatekeepers to a wide variety of populations and need-fulfilling programs, but research is also integral to establishing and continuing quality Extension work. It is for this reason that I offer the following recommendations to Extension professionals and administrators.

Enhance professional development related to research and cultural competence. For Extension to meet the demands of being research-informed and evidence-based, training may be required to augment knowledge and skills regarding research design and evaluation (see Sellers et al., 2017). Given the fact that the development of EBPs requires randomized controlled trials and valid evaluation measures, for example, up-to-date training is needed if this level of testing is expected (see Sellers et al., 2017). Many campus Extension professors have advanced training in research and could provide professional development opportunities for state- and county-level Extension educators who may be seeking this expertise. Trainings could include resources for identifying empirical studies and valid measures and recommendations for research design, evaluation and measure development, statistical analyses, as well as providing state-of-the-science updates on recent findings in an area (see Futris et al., 2004, for example). Partnering with similar scholars and practitioners may also be beneficial to share best practices (e.g., family life educators; see Myers-Walls et al., 2011).

Training in the area of anti-racism, anti-oppression, cultural awareness, and competence is also essential, especially for Extension professionals who may be engaging with audiences from cultural backgrounds that differ from their own (see Abrams & Moio, 2009). These types of trainings might focus on the ability for providers (e.g., educators) to serve individuals with diverse values, beliefs, and behaviors that may require tailoring delivery to meet unique social, cultural, and linguistic needs (American Hospital Association, 2013). Garst and colleagues

(2014) offer recommendations for improving professional development practices, which include introducing and demonstrating new practices and skills, providing opportunities to practice and receive feedback on these new skills, and providing continuous support and follow-up training. Although many Extension professionals are already doing this work, coaching Extension professionals to be able to understand and articulate the public value of engagement is also critical to establishing Extension's credibility across numerous partners (Franz, 2015).

Create opportunities for interdisciplinary partnerships. Given the importance of working within interdisciplinary teams to solve multifaceted problems (see Arnold, 2006), Extension professionals need to be continually connected with practitioners and scholars in other areas to capitalize on existing expertise in various fields that could be of value to Extension. At the same time, it is exceptionally advantageous for non-Extension researchers to connect with Extension given its vast network, connection to audiences "on the ground," and opportunities to develop and implement applied and engaged scholarship in various domains. Administrators, funders, and other key partners can help facilitate such collaborations by incentivizing teamwork and cross-disciplinary collaborations, as well as providing opportunities for collaborations to occur.

Databases or working groups may also be useful for connecting individuals across disciplines and those with complementary roles (e.g., producers of research and distributors of education). For example, at the University of Missouri, the Connector is a joint initiative through the Office of Research and Economic Development and the Office of Extension and Engagement with funding from the National Science Foundation. The core mission of this initiative is to connect "the people, resources, tools and ideas of [University of Missouri] System research and creative activities for the purposes of research development, communication, engagement and professional development to benefit the people of Missouri, the nation, and the world" (The Connector, 2020, para 1). The Connector achieves their mission by providing engagement resources and facilitating meaningful partnerships with faculty, students, staff, and practitioners at the institution and surrounding communities. This program provides professional development opportunities, proposal consulting, and a database of researchers and practitioners and their specific engaged scholarship interests.

Promote engagement. The promotion of public scholarship may be another mechanism through which Extension professionals can encourage connections with researchers to enhance broader impacts and describe the public value of their efforts. By advocating about the importance of public scholarship in bridging gaps between public opinion and scientific consensus (see Monk et al., 2021) and how this work can also demonstrate the relevance and importance of universities (Bell & Lewis, 2023), scholars and other professionals can shift various cultures and form a more united front for the public good. Extension professionals and administrators, for example, could host engagement events and utilize the established Promoting and Engaging in Public Scholarship (P.E.P.S.) program that is aimed at increasing interest in broader impact activities and making connection with others interested in engagement (Monk, Benson, & Bordere, 2019; see also Bell & Lewis, 2023; Monk et al., 2021, for more suggestions).

Focus on new funding streams. Extension professionals need proper resources to continue delivering programs and meet expectations for demonstrating impact through quality evaluation. Given the shrinking support from typical funding outlets for Extension including federal, state, and local governments (see Page & Kern, 2018), Extension professionals are more reliant on entrepreneurial revenue streams, fees, and grants. Each of these endeavors will require specialized professional development training because of the novelty associated with innovative funding avenues. Opportunities like crowdfunding (see Monk, Vennum, et al., 2019) and targeting new grant funding sources in the area of behavioral health (see Spoth et al., 2020) are just a few examples of potential funding streams that Extension professionals can pursue to support engaged scholarship.

Integrate technology. The landscape of education is changing as we continue in a digital age (Selwyn et al., 2006). A strength of Extension is the ability to adapt to changing needs and changing contexts. Extension is incredibly responsive. For example, Extension professionals discussed needs and considered helpful programs in response to natural disasters, farm stress and crises (e.g., Molgaard, 1997; Williams, 1996), the 9/11 terror attacks (see Kaplan et al., 2003), school shootings (Go & Murdock, 2003), and the COVID-19 pandemic (e.g., Arnold & Rennekamp, 2020; Bamka et al., 2020). During the pandemic, for example, many Extension professionals shifted to providing asynchronous online and synchronous virtual programming (e.g., Arnold & Rennekamp, 2020). Not only was this important to comply with health and safety standards, but it opened the opportunity to reach audiences that may not be able to attend in-person programs in a typical year. Although there were certainly Extension programs offered online prior to the pandemic (e.g., Kim et al., 2015;

Monk, in press), the shift to remote work forced many professionals to learn new education technologies and digital communication strategies. Even as life begins to return to a "new normal," the reality of diminished resources and reduced budgets restricts the ability of Extension professionals to travel across counties to deliver programs to only a few attendees in certain geographical areas.

The existing demand for e-learning (see Diem et al., 2011) and the movement to finding health information and relationship advice online (Fox & Duggan, 2012, 2013; see also Percheski & Hargittai, 2011) illustrate that many individuals are gravitating toward online educational opportunities. Extension is well equipped to meet that growing demand. As the case example of Relevate demonstrates, adopting technology may require additional training and working with colleagues across disciplines (e.g., software engineers, online learning experts) to adequately navigate virtual programming. Technology can also be integrated to facilitate professional development through virtual conferencing (Franz, Brekke, et al., 2014). As we move into more technological spaces, Extension professionals need to continue evaluating these efforts in meaningful and rigorous ways.

In its over 100 years of existence, Extension has been at the forefront of community engaged, translational and transformative scholarship. Changes in the landscape of Extension with regard to funding, increased demands around scholarship and evaluation, the need for interdisciplinary work and shifts in the technological context pose challenges as outlined in this chapter. However, such shifts and challenges can also represent new opportunities to be responsive and innovative. Extension is well positioned to continue carrying out its charge of bringing research to the community and conducting impactful, innovative, and engaged scholarship.

References

Abrams, L. S., & Moio, J. A. (2009). Critical race theory and the cultural competence dilemma in social work education. *Journal of Social Work Education*, 45(2), 245–261. https://doi.org/10.5175/JSWE.2009.200700109

Adams, B. L., Cain, H. R., Giraud, V., & Stedman, N. L. (2012). Leadership, motivation, and teamwork behaviors of principal investigator's in interdisciplinary teams: A Synthesis of research. *Journal of Leadership Education*, 11(2). https://doi.org/10.12806/V11/I2/TF2

Adler-Baeder, F., & Hawkins, A. J. (2010). Relationship and marriage education for diverse, lower-income couples. *Journal of Couple & Relationship Therapy*, 9(2), 93–94. https://doi.org/10.1080/15332691003694869

Adler-Baeder, F., Higginbotham, B., & Lamke, L. (2004). Putting empirical knowledge to work: Linking research and programming on marital quality. *Family Relations*, 53(5), 537–546. https://doi.org/10.1111/j.0197-6664.2004.00063.x

Adler-Baeder, F., Kerpelman, J. L., Schramm, D. G., Higginbotham, B., & Paulk, A. (2007). The impact of relationship education on adolescents of diverse backgrounds. *Family Relations*, 56(3), 291–303. https://doi.org/10.1111/j.1741-3729.2007.00460.x

Amato, P. R. (2010). Research on divorce: Continuing trends and new developments. *Journal of Marriage and Family*, 72(3), 650–666. https://doi.org/10.1111/j.1741-3737.2010.00723.x

American Hospital Association. (2013). Becoming a culturally competent health care organization. aha.org. www.aha.org/ahahret-guides/2013-06-18-becoming-culturally-competent-health-care-organization

Applebee, G. (2000). Cooperative Extension. In A. Wilson & E. Hayes (Eds.), *Handbook of adult and continuing education* (pp. 408–422). Jossey-Bass.

Arnold, M. E. (2006). Developing evaluation capacity in extension 4-H field faculty: A framework for success. *American Journal of Evaluation*, 27(2), 257–269. https://doi.org/10.1177/10982140062879

Arnold, M. E., & Rennekamp, R. A. (2020). A time like no other: 4-H youth development and COVID-19. *Journal of Extension*, 58(3), v58-3comm1.

Arya, M., Kumar, D., Patel, S., Street Jr, R. L., Giordano, T. P., & Viswanath, K. (2014). Mitigating HIV health disparities: the promise of mobile health for a patient-initiated solution. *American Journal of Public Health*, 104(12), 2251–2255. https://doi.org/10.2105/AJPH.2014.302120

Bamka, W., Komar, S., Melendez, M., & Infante-Casella, M. (2020). "Ask the Ag Agent" weekly webinar series: Agriculture-focused response to the COVID-19 pandemic. *Journal of Extension*, 58(4), v58-4tt2.

Beaulieu, M., Breton, M., & Brousselle, A. (2018). Conceptualizing 20 years of engaged scholarship: A scoping review. *PloS One*, 13(2), e0193201. https://doi.org/10.1371/journal.pone.0193201

Bell, M., & Lewis Jr, N. (2023). Universities claim to value community-engaged scholarship: So why do they discourage it? *Public Understanding of Science*, 32(3), 304–321. https://doi.org/10.1177/09636625221118779

Besley, J. C., Newman, T. P., Dudo, A., & Tiffany, L. A. (2020). Exploring scholars' public engagement goals in Canada and the United States. *Public Understanding of Science*, 29(8), 855–867. https://doi.org/10.1177/0963662520950671

Bolger, N., Davis, A., & Rafaeli, E. (2003). Diary methods: Capturing life as it is lived. *Annual Review of Psychology*, 54(1), 579–616. https://doi.org/10.1146/annurev.psych.54.101601.145030

Borich, T. O. (2001). The Department of Housing and Urban Development and Cooperative Extension: A case for urban collaboration. *Journal of Extension*, 39(6), 6FEA2.

Braverman, M. T., & Arnold, M. E. (2008). An evaluator's balancing act: Making decisions about methodological rigor. In M. T. Braverman, M. Engle, M. E. Arnold, & R. A. Rennekamp (Eds.), *Program evaluation in a complex organizational system: Lessons from Cooperative Extension* (pp. 71–86). New Directions for Evaluation, 120. Jossey-Bass.

Brooks, J. E., Ogolsky, B. G., & Monk, J. K. (2018). Commitment in interracial relationships: Dyadic and longitudinal tests of the investment model. *Journal of Family Issues*, 39(9), 2685–2708. https://doi.org/10.1177/0192513X18758343

Bruns, K., & Franz, N. K. (2015). Cooperative Extension program development and the community-university engagement movement: Perspectives from two lifelong Extension professionals. *Journal of Human Sciences and Extension*, 3(2), 156–169.

Colbeck, C. L., & Wharton-Michael, P. (2006). Individual and organizational influences on faculty members engagement in public scholarship. *New Directions for Teaching and Learning*, 105, 17–26. https://doi.org/10.1002/tl.220

Curtis, K., Fry, M., Shaban, R. Z., & Considine, J. (2017). Translating research findings to clinical nursing practice. *Journal of Clinical Nursing*, 26(5–6), 862–872. https://doi.org/10.1111/jocn.13586

DiClemente, R. J., Crosby, R. A., & Kegler, M. C. (Eds.). (2009). *Emerging theories in health promotion practice and research*. Jossey-Bass.

Diem, K. G., Hino, J., Martin, D., & Meisenbach, T. (2011). Is extension ready to adopt technology for delivering programs and reaching new audiences? *Journal of Extension*, 49(6), v49–6a1.

Dunifon, R., Duttweiler, M., Pillemer, K., Tobias, D., & Trochim, W. M. (2004). Evidence-based extension. *Journal of Extension*, 42(2), 2FEA2.

Duttweiler, M. W. (2008). The value of evaluation in Cooperative Extension. In M. T. Braverman, M. Engle, M. E. Arnold, & R. A. Rennekamp (Eds.), *Program evaluation in a complex organizational system: Lessons from Cooperative Extension* (pp. 87–100). New Directions for Evaluation, 120. Jossey-Bass.

Fehlis, C. P. (1992). Urban extension programs. *Journal of Extension*, 30(2), 2FEA3.

Fetsch, R. J., MacPhee, D., & Boyer, L. K. (2012). Evidence-based programming: What is a process an extension agent can use to evaluate a program's effectiveness. *Journal of Extension*, 50(5), 5FEA2.

Fincham, F. D., Stanley, S. M., & Rhoades, G. (2011). Relationship education in emerging adulthood: Problems and prospects. In F. D. Fincham & M. Cui (Eds.), *Romantic relationships in emerging adulthood* (pp. 293–316). Cambridge University Press.

Fox, J. (2017). What is unique about Extension personnel in the city? *Journal of Human Sciences and Extension*, 5(2), 22–36.

Fox, S., & Duggan, M. (2012). *Mobile health 2012*. Washington, DC: Pew Research Center. Retrieved from www.pewinternet.org/2012/11/08/mobile-health-2012/

Fox, S., & Duggan, M. (2013). *Tracking for health. Pew research Center's internet & American life project*. Retrieved from www.pewinternet.org/2013/01/28/tracking-for-health/

Franz, N. K. (2014). Measuring and articulating the value of community engagement: Lessons learned from 100 years of Cooperative Extension work. *Journal of Higher Education Outreach and Engagement*, 18(2), 5–16.

Franz, N. K. (2015). Programming for the public good: Ensuring public value through the Cooperative Extension program development model. *Journal of Human Sciences and Extension*, 3(2), 13–25.

Franz, N. K., Arnold, M., & Baughman, S. (2014). The role of evaluation in determining the public value of Extension. *Journal of Extension*, 52(4), 4COM3.

Franz, N. K., Brekke, R., Coates, D. M., Kress, C., & Hlas, J. M. (2014). The virtual Extension annual conference: Addressing contemporary professional development needs. *Journal of Extension*, 52(1), 1TOT1.

Franz, N. K., Garst, B. A., & Gagnon, R. J. (2015). The Cooperative Extension program development model: Adapting to a changing context. *Journal of Human Sciences and Extension*, 3(2), 3–12.

Franz, N., & Townson, L. (2008). The nature of complex organizations: The case for Cooperative Extension. In M. T. Braverman, M. Engle, M. E. Arnold, & R. A. Rennekamp (Eds.), *Program evaluation in a complex organizational system: Lessons from Cooperative Extension* (pp. 5–14). New Directions for Evaluation, 120. Jossey-Bass.

Futris, T. G., Adler-Baeder, F., & Dean, K. J. (2004). Using technology to link researchers and educators: Evaluation of electronic conferencing. *Journal of Extension*, 42(1), 1RIB1.

Gagnon, R. J., Franz, N. K., Garst, B. A., & Bumpus, M. F. (2015). Factors impacting program delivery: The importance of implementation research in Extension. *Journal of Human Sciences and Extension*, 3(2), 68–82.

Gagnon, R. J., Garst, B. A., & Franz, N. K. (2015). Looking ahead: Envisioning the future of the Extension program development model. *Journal of Human Sciences and Extension*, 3(2), 170–176.

Garst, B. A., Baughman, S., & Franz, N. K. (2014). Benchmarking professional development practices across youth-serving organizations: Implications for Extension. *Journal of Extension*, 52(5), 5FEA2.

Garst, B. A., & McCawley, P. F. (2015). Solving problems, ensuring relevance, and facilitating change: The evolution of needs assessment within Cooperative Extension. *Journal of Human Sciences and Extension*, 3(2), 26–46.

Go, C., & Murdock, S. (2003). To bully-proof or not to bully-proof: That is the question. *Journal of Extension*, 41(2), 2RIB1.

Gottman, J., & Gottman, J. (2017). The natural principles of love. *Journal of Family Theory & Review*, 9(1), 7–26. https://doi.org/10.1111/jftr.12182

Grzanka, P. R., & Cole, E. R. (2021). An argument for bad psychology: Disciplinary disruption, public engagement, and social transformation. *American Psychologist*, 76(8), 1334. https://doi.org/10.1037/amp0000853

Hamilton, S. F., Chen, E. K., Pillemer, K., & Meador, R. H. (2013). Research use by Cooperative Extension educators in New York state. *Journal of Extension*, 51(3), 3FEA2.

Hawkins, A. J., Blanchard, V. L., Baldwin, S. A., & Fawcett, E. B. (2008). Does marriage and relationship education work? A meta-analytic study. *Journal of Consulting and Clinical Psychology*, 76(5), 723–734. https://doi.org/10.1037/a0012584

Hawkins, A. J., & Ooms, T. (2010). *What works in marriage and relationship education? A review of lessons learned with a focus on low-income couples.* National Healthy Marriage Resource Center.

Hill, L. G., & Parker, L. A. (2005). Extension as a delivery system for prevention programming: Capacity, barriers, and opportunities. *Journal of Extension*, 43(1), 1FEA1.

Holt-Lunstad, J., Robles, T. F., & Sbarra, D. A. (2017). Advancing social connection as a public health priority in the United States. *American Psychologist*, 72(6), 517. https://doi.org/10.1037/amp0000103

Hong, Y. R., Lawrence, J., Williams Jr, D., & Mainous Iii, A. (2020). Population-level interest and telehealth capacity of US hospitals in response to COVID-19: Cross-sectional analysis of Google search and national hospital survey data. *JMIR Public Health and Surveillance*, 6(2), e18961. https://doi.org/10.2196/18961

Israel, B. A., Schulz, A. J., Parker, E. A., Becker, A. B., Allen, A. A., & Guzman, J. R. (2003). Critical issues in developing and following community-based participatory research principles. In M. Minkler & N. Wallerstein (Eds.), *Community-based participatory research for health* (pp. 53–76). Jossey-Bass.

Iverson, S. V. (2008). Now is the time for change: Reframing diversity planning at Land-Grant Universities. *Journal of Extension*, 46(1), 1FEA3.

Johnson, M. D. (2012). Healthy marriage initiatives: On the need for empiricism in policy implementation. *American Psychologist*, 67(4), 296–308. https://doi.org/10.1037/a0027743

Johnson, M. D., & Bradbury, T. N. (2015). Contributions of social learning theory to the promotion of healthy relationships: Asset or liability? *Journal of Family Theory & Review*, 7(1), 13–27. https://doi.org/10.1111/jftr.12057

Kaplan, M., Liu, S. T., & Radhakrishna, R. (2003). Intergenerational programming in Extension: Needs assessment as planning tool. *Journal of Extension*, 41(4), 4FEA5.

Kiecolt-Glaser, J. K., & Wilson, S. J. (2017). Lovesick: How couples' relationships influence health. *Annual Review of Clinical Psychology*, 13, 421–443. https://doi.org/10.1146/annurev-clinpsy-032816-045111

Kim, E. S., Cao, C., Wang, Y., & Nguyen, D. T. (2017). Measurement invariance testing with many groups: A comparison of five approaches. *Structural Equation Modeling: A Multidisciplinary Journal*, 24(4), 524–544. https://doi.org/10.1080/10705511.2017.1304822

Kim, Y. B., Bowers, J. R., Martin, S., Ebata, A., Lindsey, S. C., Nelson, P. T., & Ontai, L. (2015). Process monitoring evaluation of an online program for parents. *Journal of Extension*, 53(2), 2RIB2.

King, N. J., & Coosky, L. J. (2008). Evaluating multilevel programs. In M. T. Braverman, M. Engle, M. E. Arnold, & R. A. Rennekamp (Eds.), *Program evaluation in a complex organizational system: Lessons from Cooperative Extension* (pp. 27–39). New Directions for Evaluation, 120. Jossey-Bass.

Lamm, A. J., Israel, G. D., & Diehl, D. (2013). A national perspective on the current evaluation activities in Extension. *Journal of Extension*, 51(1), 1FEA1.

Lichter, D. T. (2012). Immigration and the new racial diversity in rural America. *Rural Sociology*, 77(1), 3–35. https://doi.org/10.1111/j.1549-0831.2012.00070.x

Martin, S. S., Feldman, D. I., Blumenthal, R. S., Jones, S. R., Post, W. S., McKibben, R. A., … Blaha, M. J. (2015). mActive: A randomized clinical trial of an automated mHealth intervention for physical activity promotion. *Journal of the American Heart Association*, 4(11), e002239. https://doi.org/10.1161/JAHA.115.002239

McDowell, G. (2004). Is Extension an idea whose time has come – And gone. *Journal of Extension*, 42(6), 6COM1.

Mincemoyer, C., Perkins, D., Ang, P. M. M., Greenberg, M. T., Spoth, R. L., Redmond, C., & Feinberg, M. (2008). Improving the reputation of cooperative extension as a source of prevention education for youth and families: The effects of the PROSPER model. *Journal of Extension*, 46(1), 1FEA6.

Molgaard, V. K. (1997). The extension service as key mechanism for research and services delivery for prevention of mental health disorders in rural areas. *American Journal of Community Psychology*, 25(4), 515–544. https://doi.org/10.1023/A:1024611706598

Monk, J. K. (in press). Changing dynamics after divorce: Evaluation of a co-parent education program. *Journal of Extension*.

Monk, J. K., Benson, J. J., & Bordere, T. C. (2019). Public scholarship: A tool for strengthening relationships across Extension, campus, and community. *Journal of Extension*, 57(3), 3TOT1.

Monk, J. K., Benson, J. J., Bordere, T. C. & Vennum, A. V. (2020). *Creating change through public scholarship*. Webinars available through the National Council on Family Relations at www.ncfr.org/events/creating-change-through-public-scholarship-part-1-2

Monk, J. K., Bordere, T. C., & Benson, J. J. (2021). Emerging Ideas. Advancing Family Science through public scholarship: Fostering community relationships and engaging in broader impacts. *Family Relations*, 70(5), 1612–1625. https://doi.org/10.1111/fare.12545

Monk, J. K., & Ogolsky, B. G. (2019). Contextual relational uncertainty model: Understanding ambiguity in a changing sociopolitical context of marriage. *Journal of Family Theory & Review*, 11(2), 243–261. https://doi.org/10.1111/jftr.12325

Monk, J. K., Ruhlmann, L., Nelson Goff, B. S., Ogan, M., & Miller, M. B. (2022). Translating Discovery Science. Fostering relationships: Service provider perspectives on community building among veteran families. *Family Relations*, 72, 1351–1367. https://doi.org/10.1111/fare.12724

Monk, J. K., Vennum, A. V., & Kanter, J. B. (2019). How to use crowdfunding in Extension: A relationship education example. *Journal of Extension*, 57(4), 4TOT3.

Myers-Walls, J. A., Ballard, S. M., Darling, C. A., & Myers-Bowman, K. S. (2011). Reconceptualizing the domain and boundaries of family life education. *Family Relations*, 60(4), 357–372. https://doi.org/10.1111/j.1741-3729.2011.00659.x

Ogolsky, B. G., Monk, J. K., Rice, T. M., Theisen, J. C., & Maniotes, C. R. (2017). Relationship maintenance: A review of research on romantic relationships. *Journal of Family Theory & Review*, 9(3), 275–306. https://doi.org/10.1111/jftr.12205

Olson, J. R., Welsh, J. A., & Perkins, D. F. (2015). Evidence-based programming within Cooperative Extension: How can we maintain program fidelity while adapting to meet local needs? *Journal of Extension*, 53(3), 3FEA3.

Page, C. S., & Kern, M. A. (2018). Creating and implementing diverse development strategies to support Extension centers and programs. *Journal of Extension*, 56(1), Article 1FEA4.

Patton, M. Q. (2008). Sup wit eval ext? In M. T. Braverman, M. Engle, M. E. Arnold, & R. A. Rennekamp (Eds.), *Program evaluation in a complex organizational system: Lessons from Cooperative Extension* (pp. 101–116). New Directions for Evaluation, 120. Jossey-Bass.

Patton, M. Q. (2015). *Qualitative research & evaluation methods: Integrating theory and practice*. Sage Publications.

Percheski, C., & Hargittai, E. (2011). Health information-seeking in the digital age. *Journal of American College Health*, 59(5), 379–386. https://doi.org/10.1080/07448481.2010.513406

Perkins, D. F., Chilenski, S. M., Olson, J. R., Mincemoyer, C. C., & Spoth, R. (2014). Knowledge, attitudes, and commitment concerning evidence-based prevention programs: Differences between family and consumer sciences and 4-H youth development educators. *Journal of Extension*, 52(3), 3FEA6.

PEW Research Center. (2019). *Mobile fact sheet*. www.pewinternet.org/fact-sheet/mobile/

Reed, M. S., & Rudman, H. (2023). Re-thinking research impact: Voice, context and power at the interface of science, policy and practice. *Sustainability Science*, 18(2), 967–981.

Schauber, A. C., & Castania, K. (2001). Facing issues of diversity: Rebirthing the Extension Service. *Journal of Extension*, 39(6), 6COM2.

Sellers, D. M., Schainker, L. M., Lockhart, P. A., & Yeh, H. C. (2017). Establishing a common language: The meaning of research based and evidence-based programming (in the Human Sciences). *Journal of Extension*, 55(6), 6FEA2.

Selwyn, N., Gorard, S., & Furlong, J. (2006). *Adult learning in the digital age: Information technology and the learning society*. Routledge.

Sevin, C., Moore, G., Shepherd, J., Jacobs, T., & Hupke, C. (2009). Transforming care teams to provide the best possible patient-centered, collaborative care. *The Journal of Ambulatory Care Management*, 32(1), 24–31. https://doi.org/10.1097/01.JAC.0000343121.07844.e0

Shamblen, S. R., Gluck, A., Wubbenhorst, W., & Collins, D. A. (2018). The economic benefits of marriage and family strengthening programs. *Journal of Family and Economic Issues*, 39(3), 386–404. https://doi.org/10.1007/s10834-018-9565-8

Sharfstein, J. M. (2016). Banishing "stakeholders." *The Milbank Quarterly*, 94(3), 476.

Shelton, D. (2008). Establishing the public's trust through community-based participatory research: A case example to improve health care for a rural Hispanic community. *Annual Review of Nursing Research*, 26(1), 237–259.

Small, S. A., Cooney, S. M., & O'connor, C. (2009). Evidence-informed program improvement: Using principles of effectiveness to enhance the quality and impact of family-based prevention programs. *Family Relations*, 58(1), 1–13. https://doi.org/10.1111/j.1741-3729.2008.00530.x

Spoth, R., Franz, N., & Brennan, A. (2020, July). Strengthening the power of evidence-based prevention in Cooperative Extension: A capacity-building framework for translation science-driven behavioral health. *Child & Youth Care Forum.* https://doi.org/10.1007/s10566-020-09559-0

Stanley, S. M., Allen, E. S., Markman, H. J., Rhoades, G. K., & Prentice, D. L. (2010). Decreasing divorce in US Army couples: Results from a randomized controlled trial using PREP for Strong Bonds. *Journal of Couple & Relationship Therapy,* 9(2), 149–160. https://doi.org/10.1080/15332691003694901

Stanley, S. M., Markman, H. J., Prado, L. M., Olmos Gallo, P. A., Tonelli, L., St. Peters, M., ... Whitton, S. W. (2001). Community-based premarital prevention: Clergy and lay leaders on the front lines. *Family Relations,* 50, 67–76. https://doi.org/10.1111/j.1741-3729.2001.00067.x

Stanley, S. M., Rhoades, G. K., Loew, B. A., Allen, E. S., Carter, S., Osborne, L. J., ... Markman, H. J. (2014). A randomized controlled trial of relationship education in the US Army: 2-year outcomes. *Family Relations,* 63(4), 482–495. https://doi.org/10.1111/fare.12083

Stephenson, G. (2003). The somewhat flawed theoretical foundation of the extension service. *Journal of Extension,* 41(4), 4FEA1.

Taylor-Powell, E., & Boyd, H. H. (2008). Evaluation capacity building in complex organizations. In M. T. Braverman, M. Engle, M. E. Arnold, & R. A. Rennekamp (Eds.), *Program evaluation in a complex organizational system: Lessons from Cooperative Extension* (pp. 55–69). New Directions for Evaluation, 120. Jossey-Bass.

The Connector. (2020). Retrieved from https://theconnector.missouri.edu/who-we-are/

Tozzi, A. E., Carloni, E., Gesualdo, F., Russo, L., & Raponi, M. (2015). Attitude of families of patients with genetic diseases to use m-health technologies. *Telemedicine and e-Health,* 21(2), 86–89. https://doi.org/10.1089/tmj.2014.0080

Vennum, A., Monk, J. K., Pasley, B. K., & Fincham, F. D. (2017). Emerging adult relationship transitions as opportune times for tailored interventions. *Emerging Adulthood,* 5, 293–305. https://doi.org/10.1177/2167696817705020

Warren, M. R., Calderón, J., Kupscznk, L. A., Squires, G., & Su, C. (2018). Is collaborative, community-engaged scholarship more rigorous than traditional scholarship? On advocacy, bias, and social science research. *Urban Education,* 53(4), 445–472. https://doi.org/10.1177/0042085918763511

We are Social. (2019). https://wearesocial.com/us/digital-2019-us

Williams, R. T. (1996). The on-going farm crisis: Extension leadership in rural communities. *Journal of Extension,* 34(1), 1FEA3.

Yang, R. K., Fetsch, R. J., McBride, T. M., & Benavente, J. C. (2009). Assessing public opinion directly to keep current with changing community needs. *Journal of Extension,* 47(3), 3FEA6.

Yapa, L. (2006). Public scholarship in the postmodern university. *New Directions for Teaching and Learning,* 105, 73–83. https://doi.org/10.1002/tl.226

CHAPTER 3

Extension's Role in Promoting Resilience among Rural Families with Low Incomes

Yoshie Sano, Ann A. Berry, and Christopher T. Sneed

Rural: The very word evokes a host of images that include pastoral fields and community gatherings, bringing to mind strong family bonds and positive and idealistic imagery of a day and time gone by. Indeed, research suggests various strengths and assets of rural communities at multiple levels including individual (e.g., strong individual relationships and connections), organizational assets (e.g., faith-based organizations), community (e.g., natural resources), and cultural assets/historical context (e.g., self-reliance and independence) (Meit, 2018). Nonetheless, although rural communities demonstrate strong resilience by many measures, they also face unique challenges including population decline, lower labor participation rates, and demographic shifts that threaten community vitality. Leveraging the strengths and assets of rural communities, Extension plays a vital role in serving the needs of families and communities in rural America.

According to the Economic Research Service (2017), only 14 percent of the United States population resides in rural communities, which in contrast covers 72 percent of the nation's land area. There has been general population loss in rural areas over the last few decades, except for a brief reversal in 2016, during which time there was modest population growth. Racial and ethnic diversity is also increasing in rural America. Hispanics[1] were the fastest-growing segment of the rural population in 2017, making up 9 percent of the rural population. Whites made up 80 percent of the population in 2017, while Blacks[2] accounted for 8 percent (Cromartie & Vilorio, 2019). Since 2013, national population trends indicate that rural areas have experienced declining unemployment, rising incomes, and declining poverty. However, not all rural communities have experienced

---

[1] Based on the US Census Bureau, Population Estimates Program, Hispanics may be of any race.
[2] Based on the US Census Bureau, Population Estimates Program, Blacks include person self-reporting only one race as Black or African American.

these positive outcomes. Economic development is challenging in rural communities located in less populated, less scenic, and more remote areas where there is lower population growth.

Several economic challenges face rural locales specifically, for instance, lower labor participation rates in rural (57.6 percent) compared to urban areas (63.7 percent). Factors that may contribute to this difference are in part a result of unique demographic characteristics of rural populations. Rural populations are generally older, with the age at 48.9 years compared to 46.1 years in urban areas; 17.5 percent of the rural population is older than sixty-five years compared to 13.8 percent in urban areas. Education levels also tend to be lower. Education among adults in rural communities sits at the median level of high school, compared to some college in urban areas. The share of rural residents with a disability is 16.5 percent compared to 10.9 percent of urban residents (Cromartie & Vilorio, 2019).

Given the challenges and rapid changes facing rural communities, Extension is even more relevant to serving the needs of families and communities residing therein. Some examples of how Extension is responding to the changing demographics across the country include hiring staff who racially/ethnically represent the diverse audiences being served by Extension, producing culturally sensitive materials and translating materials, and disseminating information through social media in native languages. Audience-specific initiatives such as Latinx 4-H programs, Latinx diabetes education initiatives, and programs for minority farmers are being designed and implemented by Extension entities across the country. Extension has a long history of work in rural communities with the goal of helping farmers, ranchers, families, and communities thrive and prosper. Thanks to its geographic footprint, including state-, region-, and county-based offices across the nation, Extension is well positioned to continue to bring research-based information to and cocreate programming with rural communities and families.

This chapter provides an overview of Extension's work in rural communities. It focuses on how Extension educators, paraprofessionals, and volunteers have promoted the well-being and resilience of individuals, families, and communities through work across four areas: food insecurity, economic security, health, and family well-being. This chapter does not seek to provide a comprehensive review of Extension's engagement in each of these areas but instead highlights examples of Extension's work in each domain. To illustrate specific examples, each subject area begins with an overview of research findings from the *Rural Families Speak* (RFS) projects, a longitudinal multistate research endeavor that began in 1998. Following these overviews of relevant RFS research, examples of educational programming and community interventions implemented by Extension as well as suggestions for future Extension roles are shared.

3.1   Overview of Rural Families Speak Projects

A significant body of knowledge about the lives of rural families with limited resources has been produced over the last twenty years through a series of multistate collaborative research projects titled *Rural Families Speak* (RFS, 1998–2008), *Rural Families Speak about Health* (RFSH, 2008–2019), and *Rural Families Speak about Resilience* (RFSR, 2019–present). These projects employ multiple research approaches that engage quantitative, qualitative, and mixed-methods; and utilize a variety of sampling methods for collecting data such as purposive sampling, respondent-driven sampling, and mixed purposive sampling (Mammen & Sano, 2012). This diversity in approaches ensured broad reach and enriched our understanding of different aspects and extent of knowledge regarding rural families and communities. Figure 3.1 illustrates the timeline of the development and implementation of the RFS projects and relevant contextual information. These three initiatives, referred to collectively as "RFS projects," were designed to create a strong alliance between research and Extension with the goal of understanding and improving the lives of family in rural communities.

The original research project, *Rural Families Speak* (RFS),[3] was designed as an attempt to respond to a major welfare reform legislation, namely the Personal Responsibility and Work Opportunity Reconciliation Act (PRWORA) of 1996. A multistate alliance of research and Extension faculty, including family scientists, family economists, nutritional scientists, psychologists, and sociologists, proposed studying the impact of the PRWORA on rural families with limited resources. The findings of RFS identified multiple risks and protective factors for family well-being. Utilizing their social support networks, life skills, and knowledge of community resources, many RFS families demonstrated resilience in a context of rural poverty. However, they also faced many health issues, including physical and mental health problems, lack of access to health care services

---

[3] Cooperating states are California, Hawaii, Illinois, Indiana, Iowa, Kentucky, Louisiana, Maryland, Massachusetts, Michigan, Minnesota, Nebraska, New Hampshire, New York, North Carolina, Ohio, Oregon, South Dakota, Tennessee, Texas, Washington, and Wyoming with later participation from Arizona, Florida, Kansas, Mississippi, and Oregon.

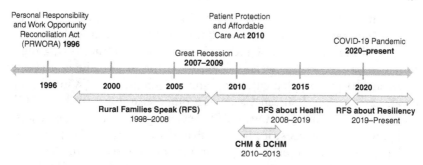

Figure 3.1   Timeline of the Rural Families Speak Project.

and providers, and inadequate health insurance coverage. These findings prompted many members of the RFS group, along with others, to launch a second study, NC1171, Interactions of Individual, Family, Community, and Policy Contexts on the Mental and Physical Health of Diverse Rural Low-Income Families (referred to as RFSH) (2008–2019).[4] Coincidently, this was also a time when the United States was undergoing the Great Recession (2007–2009) and enactment of a comprehensive health care reform law, Patient Protection and Affordable Care Act (ACA) (2010). The overall goal of RFSH was, therefore, to identify factors leading to positive physical and mental health among rural families with low incomes in the context of economic adversity.

The findings of RFSH also gave rise to two one-year studies:[5] (a) "Core Health Messages: A Strategy to Improve the Health and Well-Being of Rural, Low-Income Families" (CHM),[6] and (b) "Dissemination of Core Health Messages: Using Community-Based Participatory Research to Strengthen the Health of Rural, Low-Income Families" (DCHM).[7]

---

[4] Cooperating states are California, Hawaii, Illinois, Indiana, Iowa, Kentucky, Louisiana, Maryland, Massachusetts, Michigan, Minnesota, Nebraska, New Hampshire, New York, North Carolina, Ohio, Oregon, South Dakota, Tennessee, Texas, Washington, and Wyoming with later participation from Arizona, Florida, Kansas, Mississippi, and Oregon.

[5] CHM (Grant 2010-46100-2179) and DCHM (Grant 2011-46100-3113) were both supported by the Rural Health and Safety Education Competitive Program of the USDA Cooperative State Research, Education and Extension Service, National Institute of Food and Agriculture.

[6] Cooperating states are California, Hawaii, Illinois, Indiana, Iowa, Kentucky, Louisiana, Maryland, Massachusetts, Michigan, Minnesota, Nebraska, New Hampshire, New York, North Carolina, Ohio, Oregon, South Dakota, Tennessee, Texas, Washington, and Wyoming.

[7] Cooperating states are California, Illinois, Indiana, Iowa, Kentucky, Louisiana, Maryland, Massachusetts, Michigan, Minnesota, Nebraska, New Hampshire, New York, North Carolina, Ohio, Oregon, South Dakota, Tennessee, Texas, Washington, and Wyoming along with Arizona, Florida, Kansas, Mississippi, and Oregon.

A community-based participatory research (CBPR) approach is built on the equitable engagement of both researchers and stakeholders (i.e., rural mothers with low incomes) where both partners bring their own strengths in the process of identifying the issue to be addressed, research design, implementation, and dissemination (Winterbauer et al., 2016) (See Franzen-Castle for other examples of the CBPR approach, this volume). Thus, CBPR benefits participants, researchers, and practitioners because it produces shared knowledge and experiences which result in more effective prevention and intervention. Working *with* – not *for* – rural mothers with low incomes, the goals of CHM and DCHM were to improve health outcomes of rural families with low incomes through the creation of learner-driven Core Health Messages, and to determine effectiveness of various methods of disseminating these messages by involving a subsample of RFSH mothers as well as community stakeholders.

Currently, the focus of RFS has been expanded to explore dynamic resilience processes of rural families and their communities. Resilience is generally defined as "the capacity of a system to adapt successfully to significant challenges that threaten the function, viability, or development of that system" (Masten, 2018, p. 12). In other words, resilient individuals, families, and communities can survive, and potentially thrive, through adversity. Our third study, RFSR, 2019–present,[8] coincided with the time of the COVID-19 global pandemic. The multistate research team collected data about risks and resilience factors in a time of adversity at individual, family, and community levels.

Collectively, the RFS projects have identified the diverse needs, challenges, and resilience of families with low incomes in the rural context. Extension specialists associated with the RFS projects have incorporated the findings of the twenty-year study into the implementation of various programs. At the same time, they also gained valuable knowledge and perspectives from rural families with low incomes. This collaborative relationship between researchers and rural families collectively addresses a broad spectrum of issues that impact rural communities. In Section 3.2, we briefly highlight some critical findings of the RFS projects related to Extension work in the areas of food insecurity, economic security, health, and family well-being.

---

[8] Cooperating states are Arizona, California, Florida, Hawaii, Indiana, Iowa, Kansas, Kentucky, Michigan, Mississippi, Montana, Nevada, North Carolina, Oklahoma, Oregon, Tennessee, and Washington.

3.2 Current Issues Addressed by Extension in Rural Communities

3.2.1 Food Insecurity and Nutrition

3.2.1.1 Findings of RFS Projects: Barriers and Opportunities for Extension Engagement

Findings of the RFS projects demonstrated that the causes and consequences of food insecurity are complex and are embedded in contextual factors faced by rural families. Rural mothers reported their efforts to provide healthful food to their children (Sano et al., 2019). However, financial struggles and lack of access to quality food in rural locales hampered their ability to create optimal food environments for their families (Bao & Greder, 2015). For mothers, knowledge, skills, and strategies to stretch food, as well as informal and formal support were especially critical as protective factors against food insecurity (Sano et al., 2018). The RFS findings revealed that food-insecure families relied on various informal supports, including community-based (e.g., food pantries, churches) and individual (e.g., family, friends) sources (Swanson et al., 2008). Social support was particularly important for Latinx immigrant families primarily because of the many obstacles they faced when trying to access public assistance, as well as the need to negotiate their new food environments to maintain cultural food practices (Greder et al., 2008; 2012).

Rural Families Speak mothers' participation rates in public assistance programs were high – Supplemental Nutrition Assistance Program (SNAP) (54–70 percent); Special Supplemental Nutrition Program for Women, Infants, and Children (WIC) (53–84 percent); and National School Lunch Program (NSLP) (66–86 percent) – depending on the project (Anderson & Swanson, 2002; Mammen & Sano, 2013). Participation in these programs was associated with decreased difficulties in purchasing food (Grutzmacher & Braun, 2004), higher levels of healthful eating and physical activity routines (Downey & Greder, 2014), and lower maternal depression among Latinx immigrant mothers (Browder et al., 2013). Families' use of these formal supports was, however, influenced by their awareness, past experiences, and cultural norms regarding such assistance (Sano et al., 2011).

Findings highlight the fact that food insecurity is not simply a result of having low income but instead is rooted in a host of factors, including deficiencies in economic, social, and community resources, as well as gaps in knowledge and skills. Together, the findings indicated the importance of building multidisciplinary, multilevel programs (i.e., individual, family, and community) and policies to reduce food insecurity. With a long history of providing such programming, Extension was well positioned to address those needs. Programming and interventions such as community gardens, food pantries, food retail work, and partnerships with farmers' markets are but a few examples of the power of multidisciplinary, multilevel programming in which Extension was already engaged throughout the nation.

3.2.1.2   The Role of Extension in Addressing Food Insecurity: EFNEP and SNAP-Ed

Extension has and continues to provide education related to food and nutrition through direct and indirect education, community interventions, and by implementing policy, systems, and environmental changes. These programs cover, among other topics, how to safely secure, store, preserve, and prepare foods. Sizeable financial support for Extension's work in nutrition education comes from two federal programs: the Expanded Food and Nutrition Education Program (EFNEP) and the Supplemental Nutrition Assistance Program Education (SNAP-Ed). While EFNEP and SNAP-Ed are complementary, both programs are unique in terms of their focus, target audience, delivery, impact, and outcomes. Most, but not all Extension agencies conduct EFNEP and SNAP-Ed programming to reach rural families where they live, work, worship, and play (National Institute of Food and Agriculture, 2017). Chapter 7 (this volume) provides additional information regarding EFNEP and SNAP-Ed programming.

Expanded Food and Nutrition Education Program. Established in 1969 as part of President Johnson's War on Poverty, EFNEP is part of the National Institute for Food and Agriculture. As the nation's first nutrition education program, EFNEP uses a peer-to-peer, intensive, and direct approach to deliver hands-on nutrition education to adults who are caregivers of young children as well as school-age youth at risk of food insecurity. Education addressing EFNEP's core areas of diet quality and physical activity, food resource management, food safety, and food security is delivered by Extension professionals, paraprofessionals, and volunteers (National Institute of Food and Agriculture, 2021a).

Currently, EFNEP education is conducted through seventy-six land-grant universities. EFNEP programming is delivered in all fifty states, US territories, and the District of Columbia, and each year it reaches approximately 200,000 adults and 450,000 youth living with low incomes (National Institute of Food and Agriculture, 2021b). In federal year 2019,

EFNEP reached a total of 88,456 families. Of the 88,456 families, 1,250 (1 percent) lived on farms, 13,234 (15 percent) lived in towns with a population under 10,000 and rural nonfarm areas, and 22,220 (25 percent) lived in towns and cities with populations of 10,000 to 50,000. Smaller target audiences, geographic distance, and staffing present challenges for EFNEP programming in rural areas. Increased technology usage and availability in rural communities present unique opportunities for reimagining the delivery of EFNEP programming. Although EFNEP's reach in rural communities is not as deep as its reach in urban areas, EFNEP has demonstrated positive impacts for participants in both settings. EFNEP has a consistently high positive return on investment with over 90 percent of EFNEP adult participants reporting improved nutrition behaviors following program participation (National Institute of Food and Agriculture, 2021a).

Supplemental Nutrition Assistance Program Education. Started as part of the Food and Nutrition Service to promote healthful diets through partnerships with states, the SNAP-Ed (formerly known as Food Stamp Nutrition Education) seeks to reduce nutrition-related health risks through nutrition education, community engagement, and multilevel interventions. SNAP-Ed supports nutrition education and obesity-prevention projects for persons eligible for the SNAP. SNAP-Ed's effectiveness is rooted in its community orientation. Land-grant universities, community partners, and other organizations work within communities to deliver direct nutrition education, policy, systems, and environmental change interventions, and multilevel, complementary approaches to promote healthy eating and obesity prevention. The strategies implemented through SNAP-Ed are designed to assist families of limited resources in making healthy food choices and physically active lifestyles consistent with the Dietary Guidelines for Americans (Food and Nutrition Service, 2020).

Within Extension, SNAP-Ed programs and interventions are implemented in rural, suburban, and urban communities. While the implementation of SNAP-Ed activities in any community has its pathways and challenges, research has identified unique barriers and pathways for the delivery of SNAP-Ed in rural communities. Lack of food access and physical activity opportunities, funding restrictions, transportation barriers, participant recruitment/retention challenges, and SNAP-Ed staff not being part of the community have all been identified as challenges (Haynes-Maslow et al., 2019). However, Extension and other SNAP-Ed implementing agencies in rural communities continuously navigate these challenges, thus allowing them to reach families of limited resources residing in rural

communities with nutrition education and environmental support interventions. Through direct education, community gardens, corner-store
interventions, faith-based programs, physical activity assessments, and
more, SNAP-Ed is impacting rural families of limited resources by promoting healthy food choices and physically active lifestyles. SNAP-Ed
Connection (https://snaped.fns.usda.gov/success-stories) presents numerous success stories demonstrating the impact of SNAP-Ed, including the
benefits created in rural areas. Even when SNAP-Ed staff are not living in
the rural communities they serve, they can still make a positive impact on
participants through the establishment of strong partnerships and development of strategic relationships with community leaders (Haynes-Maslow
et al., 2019).

3.2.2   Economic Security

3.2.2.1   Findings of RFS Projects: Identifying the Barriers and Opportunities for Extension to Engage

The RFS projects were uniquely positioned to capture the economic functioning of rural families with limited resources immediately after welfare
reform, as well as before and after the Great Recession. Among numerous
works the RFS projects produced, the stories told by mothers, in particular, gave deep insights as to the challenges they faced daily to provide for
their families and provided context regarding the communities in which
they lived. Findings clustered around two themes: (1) economic well-being
with emphasis on the importance of family and social supports and public assistance programs; and (2) rural employment and use of the Earned
Income Tax Credit.

Economic self-sufficiency was a struggle for many of the RFS families.
Even when employed, the household incomes were not adequate, with
many families not earning enough to keep them out of poverty (Bauer et
al., 2002; 2003). To meet their financial needs, rural families often relied on
family and social supports to extend their resources (Simmons et al., 2007).
Public assistance programs also contributed to the economic functioning
of families. Commonly utilized resources were Temporary Assistance for
Needy Families, SNAP, Medicaid, and other food assistance programs.
However, even with supplemental support, many families' earned income
was not enough for self-sufficiency (Barun et al., 2002).

Employment options, particularly jobs paying a living wage, in rural
areas are scarce. For rural residents, especially those with limited resources
and skills, securing and maintaining employment can be difficult. Findings

from the RFS studies revealed the mothers' labor force participation began at an early age with many mothers working one to three jobs (Bauer & Braun, 2002). Types of employment held by the mothers included waitressing at family-owned restaurants and serving as nurses' aides and real estate agents (Berry et al., 2008). These types of jobs offered flexibility to allow for parenting responsibilities, but often did not provide sufficient income. Respondents noted job volatility as an issue, though participants whose employers offered flexibility also tended to maintain stable employment over time (Berry et al., 2008). Mothers mentioned that their communities lacked healthcare and community and family support services, both of which can impact labor force participation (Bauer et al., 2003).

The Earned Income Tax Credit (EITC) is a federal tax credit for low-income wage earners. It can serve to assist the income security of families. However, many qualifying families do not take advantage of this benefit. *Rural Families Speak* researchers found that more than one third of the RFS participants who qualified for the credit did not claim it (Gudmunson et al., 2010). Mothers who did claim this credit used the EITC refund to pay bills, acquire/maintain transportation, purchase necessities, and build savings (Mammen & Lawrence, 2006). The EITC can have significant benefits in the economic situations of rural families with limited resources.

3.2.2.2 *The Role of Extension in Economic Security*

Findings from the RFS projects highlight areas of opportunity for Extension programming that can help rural residents obtain sustainable employment and improve their economic security. Extension provides educational programs in budgeting, credit and debt management, workforce development, and other areas for families with limited resources. Many state Extensions offer programs similar to the University of Tennessee Extension's "Who Gets Paid First When You Can't Pay Everybody," which teaches participants how to triage debt. Although these programs can be helpful, agents must be creative in marketing their programs, many times taking the programs to where the audiences are by partnering with other agencies serving the same audience. Schools, senior centers, and banks are a few of the establishments through which educators deliver educational programs. Along with educational programming, many county educators serve as the glue connecting individuals and families with community resources, social supports, and education about public assistance programs. The educators also serve as facilitators, bringing community leaders, such as employers, government officials, and community service agencies together to address issues. Extension agents in rural areas work with other community leaders to identify county and community needs and to build upon each other's strengths to meet those needs.

Preparing rural residents for better jobs is performed by Extension in some states. Skill Up Tennessee is UT Extension's SNAP Employment and Training program. Supplemental Nutrition Assistance Program Employment & Training (SNAP E&T) is a partnership between the United States Department of Agriculture and the states to provide training and employment services to eligible SNAP participants. The purpose of the program is to assist eligible SNAP participants in gaining skills, training, work, and other experience that will increase their ability to obtain regular employment. The ultimate goal is self-sufficiency. In Tennessee, the program is administered by the Tennessee Department of Labor and Workforce Development through a partnership with the Tennessee Department of Human Services. UT Extension provides Skill Up Tennessee as a SNAP E&T partner. Since its inception, the Skill Up Tennessee program has shown success in using the Extension model to deliver SNAP E&T services. Extension in other states should consider providing SNAP E&T programming to assist in addressing the employment needs in their own rural communities. *Rural Families Speak* found that many of the study participants did not take advantage of the EITC because they were not aware of its existence. Extension is well positioned to address this need by developing educational programs and outreach campaigns for constituents to spread awareness of the EITC and its benefits among qualified families.

The economic needs of rural families and communities are great. Extension can play a role as an educator, facilitator, and connector to improve family economic well-being. As Extension continues to address the economic security of rural families, Extension professionals must pay attention to the changing demographics of the rural landscape. For example, with the growing Latinx population, cultural sensitivity concerning finances need to be considered when developing and delivering programs.

3.2.3   Health

3.2.3.1   Findings of RFS Projects: Identifying the Barriers and Opportunities for Extension to Engage

Findings of the RFS projects consistently revealed that families face physical and mental health challenges, as well as limited access to healthcare (Dyk et al., 2018). The many stressors associated with poverty and living in rural locations contribute to greater vulnerability to health outcomes such as low ratings of health status, low physical activity, high BMI, and obesity (Dyk et al., 2018). More than one third of the RFS sample reported engaging in two or more risky behaviors that decreased their overall well-being such as tobacco use (Noonan et al., 2016). Further, the bi-directionality of physical health with education and economic self-sufficiency was highlighted (Bauer & Dolan, 2011). For example, the mothers' health problems can limit their ability to secure and retain work or acquire an education. Such problems can also create economic hardship imposed by out-of-pocket healthcare expenditures when adults are uninsured or underinsured (Corson, 2001). Similarly, the health status of children impacts the ability of mothers to obtain and maintain a job (Sano & Richards, 2011).

Numerous RFS studies examined the association between rural poverty and mental health, in particular mothers' depressive symptoms. In our samples, depressive symptoms were associated closely with physical health issues. Mothers reporting more depressive symptoms also reported more doctor visits (Simmons et al., 2007), and those who screened positively for depression were more likely to report health issues (Braun & Rudd, 2003). Physical health issues among mothers were more likely even when the depressed person was another household member, such as a spouse or child (Guyer, 2003). Obesity prevention behaviors such as exercise and good nutrition were significantly less likely when high degrees of depressive symptoms were present (Burney et al., 2015). Extension programming focused on emotional well-being, chronic disease management, and healthy eating are implemented as part of Family and Consumer Sciences (FCS) Extension programming. These programs and others seek to provide participants with information and resources that can empower them to make improvements across all health domains.

Access to healthcare is critical in providing physical, mental, and financial protection to families from expected and unexpected health conditions (Byrne & Greder, 2014). A significant number of the RFS participants, however, reported that they or their adult family members were uninsured or underinsured. Public assistance (i.e., Medicaid, State Children's Health Insurance Program) appeared to be an important safety net for the RFS mothers and particularly children, as health insurance coverage was undoubtedly associated with access to and use of healthcare services. Rural context presents unique challenges in access to health services due to geographic distance to healthcare facilities, limited availability of community health services and specialists, and lack of access to reliable transportation. All of these challenges discouraged families from seeing health professionals, affecting their health to the point that many reported having to seek emergency medical care (Greder & Sano, 2011). Seeking help for mental health issues appeared to be even more challenging due to a stigma in small rural communities (Sano et al., 2011). An emphasis on self-reliance, culturally negative beliefs about certain mental health problems, and lack of knowledge and education about mental health issues are just a few examples of obstacles to a person's ability to accept mental health care.

3.2.3.2   *The Role of Extension in Health*

Extension educators are uniquely positioned to not only serve as health educators but also as facilitators of system-level changes. Indeed, Extension has brought and continues to bring a wide array of assets to rural America, positioning itself as an ideal leader in health and wellness. Numerous examples of health programming can be found in the Extension literature. National, regional, state, and local educational efforts have sought to improve the health of rural Americans through education, experiential learning, and community engagement. Evidence-based health education programming has empowered program participants to better manage their chronic health conditions. Extension educators and community leaders have coalesced to address the opioid crisis gripping rural America. Family and Consumer Sciences educators have partnered with Extension educators and leaders in agriculture to build the resilience of farm families, supporting them as they navigate the stressors of farm and family life. Additionally, research-based community programming has helped improve the health literacy of those attending.

Extension's work in health and wellness is not limited to direct education. Instead, recent momentum for broader systems-level engagement has helped Extension start and expand work to address health needs through policy, systems, and environmental changes (Sneed et al., 2020). With support from programs such as SNAP-Ed and projects supported by the Centers for Disease Control and Prevention (CDC) and Robert Wood Johnson Foundation, Extension educators have incorporated Policy, System and Environmental (PSE) approaches as part of the traditional Extension model of direct education (Washburn et al., 2021). Through PSE approaches, Extension educators have encouraged active routes to community destinations by enhancing built environments, increasing access to fresh produce through community gardens, and reimagining early-learning environments through PSE changes.

While the health needs facing rural America are great, they present rich opportunities for Extension to demonstrate the power of its research-based, localized programming. This power, combined with Extension's ability to coalesce communities around critical issues, position Extension as a leader in advancing health and wellness across rural America.

3.2.4   *Family Well-Being*

3.2.4.1   *Findings of RFS Projects: Identifying the Barriers and Opportunities for Extension to Engage*

Family well-being is a multifaceted construct that includes family health, self-sufficiency, and resiliency. It is, however, vulnerable to various social constraints including poverty. Findings from the RFS projects documented various factors that promote and/or hinder family well-being, most significantly, in the areas of work–family balance, childcare, and parenting.

To maintain economic well-being of the family, rural mothers with low incomes often work outside their homes, typically engaging in jobs characterized by low wages, minimal flexibility, and nonstandard hours (Berry et al., 2008). Many mothers, particularly those caring for young children, struggled to meet both family demands (e.g., unreliable childcare, children's emergencies) and job demands (e.g., irregular work hours). While the mothers listed time constraints, tiredness, and stress as the obstacles to attaining work–family balance, the main barrier to work–family balance for them appeared to be lack of access to affordable childcare (Katras et al., 2004).

To alleviate work–family conflicts, rural mothers often developed informal support networks consisting of family, friends, and neighbors. Katras and colleagues (2004) described this kind of network as a "private safety net" essential to meeting obligations of work and family. Although most mothers expressed confidence in the availability of family members to care for children when necessary, these family members often had other obligations and/or their own health issues, and flexibility of available informal caregivers varied considerably.

Evidence suggests that while social support from family members was critical to the survival of the RFS families, it also came with costs. It was not uncommon that some mothers noted troublesome aspects of grandparent caregivers including blurred boundaries in their roles and different parenting philosophies. The substantial parental role of grandmothers was particularly evident in multigenerational households. In studying one-parent versus two-parent households with at least one grandparent, Barnett et al. (2016) found that the quality of communication and co-parenting coalition appear to be higher in one-parent families than in two-parent families, suggesting that unhealthy coalitions are more likely when parenting is shared among three adults.

Being a "good mother" was the most salient role for a majority of the RFS mothers (Sano et al., 2012). The mothers' sense of parenting efficacy appeared to be a central factor in making decisions about and maintaining their romantic relationships, as well as in allowing nonresident fathers to see their children. Mothers consistently indicated that the well-being of their children was their top priority, with many of their behaviors aimed at facilitating child well-being even when they came at costs to their own economic progress and romantic relationships. Mothers' decisions to stay, enter, or leave relationships were driven largely by contextual constraints such as partners' income, employment, and financial contributions, rather than by notions of romantic love alone. Above all, mothers considered the well-being of children and the availability of support from other family members when making partnership decisions. This appeared to be a part of the strategies to create stability for themselves and their children. Overall, the findings point to the importance of programs and policies that recognize and strengthen multigenerational and extended family networks, as well as mothers' sense of parenting efficacy as critical elements for family well-being.

3.2.4.2 *The Role of Extension in Family Well-Being*

Extension is well positioned to address the family well-being issues that were revealed by the RFS studies. Extension family programming focuses on building healthy relationships, cultivating emotional wellness, supporting child and youth development, and providing support during family transitions. Extension educators in rural communities are generally viewed as sources of unbiased information which can facilitate the education of clientele as well as connections to like-missioned community partners serving families. As revealed through RFS research, the well-being of their children was the primary concern of rural mothers. Extension professionals should capitalize on mothers' desires to improve the lives of children when developing, as well as delivering educational programs. (See also Chapter 11 for a discussion of the role of Extension in engaging fathers.) Because many mothers juggle multiple jobs and may have childcare issues, delivery methods that will accommodate these factors should be considered. Additionally, recognizing the importance of informal support, the presence of work–family conflict, and the increase in multigenerational households, Yancura et al. (2020) offered specific program suggestions for Extension personnel working with rural families. Those recommendations include providing programs on best parenting practices; fostering relationships with all household members, including grandparents and partners; using technology to engage clientele in educational programs; and implementing programs focused on communication skills. Extension programs are also needed in the areas of childcare, parenting, time management, grandparent/parent conflict, caregiving, and healthy relationships, all taking into consideration the unique needs of rural families with low incomes. In rural communities with increasing Latinx populations, cultural sensitivity and translation of program materials are critically important.

3.3   Future Directions

The purpose of this chapter was to provide an overview of four domains of Extension work in rural communities: food insecurity, economic security, health, and family well-being. Findings from studies conducted by the RFS projects were used to introduce and frame each domain. Although this chapter did not seek to provide a complete overview of all Extension's efforts in the areas of food insecurity, economic security, health, and family well-being, we were able to illustrate the translational linkage between research and Extension work, highlighting the importance of integrating research and practice.

One example of such efforts made by RFS projects is a creation of *Core Health Messages* (for details, see Mammen et al., 2019). The data from the CHM project revealed that simply distributing health information in generic forms does not resonate well with audiences. For a family to make better decisions and take appropriate actions, health information needs to be timely, culturally relevant, based on principles of health literacy, and disseminated in a culturally acceptable manner (Tabatabaei-Moghaddam et al., 2014). According to Tabatabaei-Moghaddam et al., the mothers preferred health messages that: (a) have a clear connection between recommendations presented in the message and future economic consequences of inaction, with sufficient explanation; (b) mention problem-specific economic struggles and inaccessibility of resources; and (c) include community barriers and availability of professional resources in the community. Based on findings gleaned from this research, a set of core health messages was developed. The messages translated evidence-based information into concrete outputs that could then be disseminated to the general public by Extension agents, specialists, and faculty.

3.3.1 Food Insecurity and Nutrition

Impacted by a variety of familial, economic, social, and communal factors, food insecurity and challenges in making healthy food choices continue to plague rural families with lower resources. A variety of individual and family strategies have been employed by rural households to alleviate food insecurity and manage food resources (Sano et al., 2018). Additionally, our findings consistently demonstrated that food-related programs and education are highly effective. By translating research findings into accessible education that meets the needs of their communities, Extension FCS professionals work to address the nutritional needs of rural families with low resources.

While Extension has offered a variety of nutrition and consumer education programs, its work on larger systems and environmental levels has only begun. The areas of food insecurity and nutrition offer Extension educators the opportunity to transform the places where rural families live, work, worship, and play; evolving them into environments that support healthy food choices, behaviors, and active lifestyles. Most recently, funding sources such as SNAP-Ed, CDC High Obesity Program, and the Robert Wood Johnson Foundation have provided the impetus for Extension's work in this area. In the future, it will be up to the Extension organization to adopt community-building practices and make them a common part of the Extension lexicon and culture. Additionally, the stigma around accessing supports such as SNAP, WIC, government-supported commodities, and emergency food resources must be reduced, and the participation of families must be increased. Extension professionals can and should assist in making this happen.

3.3.2 Economic Security

Rural families with lower resources face multiple challenges in their quest for financial security. Even when employed, members of rural, low-income households have to utilize a variety of strategies to maximize financial well-being, including seeking public assistance, developing social support networks, and managing resources. Yet, despite the utilization of these strategies, rural Americans continue to face higher poverty rates than their urban counterparts (Mammen et al., 2018).

With a deep understanding of rural America, Extension has been a seminal resource for research-based, unbiased financial education and information. As Extension professionals continue to build upon their work in advancing the financial capacity of rural households, it is critical that Extension professionals approach their work in this area using a capacity-based lens. In other words, Extension professionals should look at the resources, knowledge, and skills rural households already have and seek to build upon those resources. This approach contrasts with those in which the deficiencies and shortcomings of rural households are lifted up while the inherent strengths of the household unit are diminished. Additionally, as part of their outreach efforts, Extension professionals should serve as a bridge connecting rural households to support services and resource providers in their communities. These sources of help can be instrumental in aiding rural households who face economic hardships while at the same time offering opportunities for resource management education. Finally, Extension professionals should feel empowered to have a voice and place at the table when it comes to economic decision-making that impacts households in their communities. Serving on local economic development boards, developing strong partnerships with local chambers of commerce, and developing recognition among elected officials as an authority in family financial management lend credibility to the work of Extension in this subject area while also advancing the Extension professional as an agent of change in the community.

3.3.3 Health

The numerous stressors of living in poor, rural communities contribute to great vulnerability among rural families. The health vulnerability of rural households is further exacerbated by challenges in health care access, unemployment, lifestyle factors, and transportation. Lower rates of physical activity and increased prevalence of smoking and food insecurity, combined with high rates of uninsurance, worsen health disparities that impact rural America today (Routh et al., 2020).

Extension has been a leader in the delivery of health programming embedded in the rural context (Routh et al., 2020). As Extension looks to the future and specifically the future of health outreach, it is imperative that emerging educational programs and interventions be situated in the context of the socio-ecological model. Using the socio-ecological perspective as the foundation of future health programming, Extension educators will be able to harness the capacity of their role as agents of change while leveraging the power of multigenerational engagement and technology. Extension educators should see themselves as more than just purveyors of research-based information but as agents of change – change that can be facilitated only when Extension uses its deep community connections to coalesce a variety of key players and community leaders to address rural health challenges. This perspective of Extension professionals as agents of change for health disparities can be further accentuated by Extension educational programming that embraces technology and approaches education through a whole-family approach.

As Extension's work in health programming continues to grow, it is important that the educational materials, health messages, and delivery methods are congruent with the needs of the audiences being served. Simply implementing a health education program within rural communities without considering the nuances and sociodemographic differences inherent in rural America is shortsighted at best and ineffective at worst. Health programming that recognizes the intersectionality of rural Americans and is tailored to the specific needs of rural racial and ethnic minorities, the growing Latinx population, participants with limited literacy skills, persons for which English is a second language, individuals identifying as LGBTQ+, and others in need will be a continual necessity as the landscape of rural America continues to evolve.

3.3.4   *Family Well-Being*

Rural families, like all families, need help navigating challenges that threaten family well-being. Poverty, limited social services, issues of work–life balance, and limited formal childcare supports adversely impact the well-being of rural families, particularly rural mothers (Ontai et al., 2018). Strong social networks and deep extended family support have proven instrumental in helping rural families mitigate these challenges, meet household needs, and overcome financial constraints.

The unique landscape of family life in rural America holds implications for Extension programming while also offering ample opportunities for future involvement in advancing family well-being. The importance of extended family and the larger community to the well-being of rural families must be recognized and incorporated into Extension programming. A holistic family systems approach should help frame Extension's educational responses and outreach to rural communities (Ontai et al., 2018). Additionally, given the centrality of children to rural families – especially rural mothers – Extension programming should be framed in the context of child well-being. In other words, Extension professionals should clearly articulate how their programming efforts benefit not only the direct recipient but also children under that recipient's care. As demographics of rural populations change, Extension must also take proactive steps to meet the needs of growing minority/marginalized populations including people of color, immigrants, LGBTQ+ individuals, people with disabilities, and so on. In particular, addressing the needs of expanding Latinx population is essential in rural communities (Greder et al., 2020). However, simply extending an invitation to participate in Extension programming or making blanket nondiscrimination statements is not enough. Instead, Extension must make intentional, proactive efforts to create culturally sensitive and appropriate content while hiring a workforce that mirrors emerging rural populations. Finally, as academia continues to advance its understanding of rural family well-being, Extension professionals must sharpen their education and advocacy skills to help decision-makers and other family life professionals better understand the unique needs of rural households in order to establish more equitable social systems for diverse rural residents. Such a role will require Extension professionals to pivot from a direct-education model in which the lay public is the target of education to a model that seeks to inform the policies and practices of decision-makers and professionals while simultaneously educating families and the community.

3.4   Conclusion

Extension has been a bedrock of rural America for over 100 years. From its early roots in agrarian work to today, Extension has met challenges facing rural communities, families, and individuals with research-based information embedded in a grass-roots context. As we look ahead to the next 100 years of Extension, we can see a future ripe with possibilities – possibilities for not only continuing Extension's legacy in rural communities but also advancing that legacy through new partnerships, novel approaches, and emergent programming designed to enhance family well-being and promote resilience. The challenge for Extension professionals will be to strike a balance between embracing our rich past and pivoting to move toward the work of new realms and new opportunities. Indeed, the people and communities of rural America deserve (and expect) nothing less.

References

Anderson, K., & Swanson, J. (2002). *Rural families: Welfare reform and food stamps.* Policy Brief. Retrieved from www.cehd.umn.edu/FSoS/projects/ruralspeak/pdf/rural-families-brief2.pdf

Bao, J., & Greder, K. (2015). *Effects of food insecurity and expectation of family involvement on rural Latina immigrant mothers' mental health.* Poster presentation at Iowa State University. Retrieved from https://iastate.box.com/s/ouwq9y7hcz9j2vjl7053jp3nz350ai4b

Barnett, M. A., Yancura, L., Wilmoth, J. D., & Sano, Y. (2016). Well-being among rural grandfamilies in two multigenerational household structures. *GrandFamilies: The Contemporary Journal of Research, Practice and Policy*, 3. Retrieved from http://scholarworks.wmich.edu/grandfamilies/vol3/iss1/4

Bauer, J. W., & Braun, B. (2002). *Rural families and welfare issues*. Rural Families Speak Research Project.

Bauer, J. W., Braun, B., & Dyk, P. H. (2003). Health and the economic well-being of rural families. *A public policy fact sheet*. National Council on Family Relations.

Bauer, J. W., & Dolan, E. M. (2011). Rural families and work overview. In J. W. Bauer & E. M. Dolan (Eds.), *In rural families and work* (pp. 1–15). Springer.

Berry, A. A., Katras, M. J., Sano, Y., Lee, J., & Bauer, J. W. (2008). Job volatility of rural, low-income mothers: A mixed-methods approach. *Journal of Family and Economic Issues*, 29(1), 5–22. https://doi.org/10.1007/s10834-007-9096-1

Braun, B., & Rudd, M. (2003). *About mental health: Maryland rural families speak*. Issue Brief. Retrieved from https://sph.umd.edu/sites/default/files/files/MentalHealthResearchBrief.pdf

Browder, D., Greder, K., & Jasper Crase, S. (2013). *Individual and family factors related to depression among rural Latina immigrant mothers*. Julian Samora Research Institute, Michigan State University.

Burney, J., Routh, B., Greder, K., & Greer, B. (2015). *Associations between maternal depression and family nutrition and physical activity behaviors*. Rural Families Speak about Health. Retrieved from https://iastate.box.com/s/e39g12cdgdq3rjzf4pusuea7ncujnvsx

Byrne, M., & Greder, K. (2014). *Health insurance access and participation among Latinos in Iowa*. Policy Brief. Iowa State University.

Corson, C. M. (2001). *Health, well-being, and financial self-sufficiency of low-income families in the context of welfare reform*. [Unpublished master's thesis]. Oregon State University.

Cromartie, J., & Vilorio, D. (2019). *Rural population trends*. U.S. Department of Agriculture. Retrieved from www.ers.usda.gov/amber-waves/2019/february/rural-population-trends/

Downey, J., & Greder, K. (2014). Depressive symptomology among rural low-income Latina and non-Latina white mothers. In S. L. Blair and J. H. McCormick (Eds.), *Family and health: Evolving needs, responsibilities, and experiences* (pp. 247–269). Emerald Group.

Dyk, P. D., Radunovich, H., & Sano, Y. (2018). Health challenges faced by rural, low-income families: Insights into health disparities. *Family Science Review*, 22(1), 54–69. https://doi.org/10.26536/FSR.2018.22.02.04

Economic Research Service. (2017). *Rural America at a glance, 2017 edition*. United States Department of Agriculture. Retrieved from www.ers.usda.gov/webdocs/publications/85740/eib-182.pdf?v=9533.8

Food and Nutrition Service. United States Department of Agriculture. (2020). *FY 2021 Supplemental Nutrition Assistance Program Guidance*. https://snaped.fns.usda.gov/program-administration/guidance-and-templates

Greder, K., Cancel-Tirado, D. I., Rough, B., & Bao, J. (2020). Engaging with rural Latinx families. *The Forum for Family and Consumer Issues*, 23(1). www .theforumjournal.org/2021/03/01/engaging-with-rural-latinx-families/

Greder, K., Cook, C., Garasky, S., & Ortiz, L. (2008). *Latino immigrants in Iowa and the United States: Food and housing insecurity.* Policy Brief. Iowa State University.

Greder, K., & Sano, Y. (2011). Health-seeking behavior in families. In M. J. Craft-Rosenberg & S. R. Pehler (Eds.), *Encyclopedia of family health.* S. R. Sage.

Greder, K., Slowing, F. R., & Doudna, K. (2012). Latina immigrant mothers: Negotiating new food environments to preserve cultural food practices and healthy child eating. *Family and Consumer Sciences Research Journal*, 41(2), 145–160. https://doi.org/10.1111/fcsr.12004

Grutzmacher, S., & Braun, B. (2004). *Food resource management: Key to food security outcomes among rural, low-income families.* Research brief. Family Policy Impact Seminar. University of Maryland.

Gudmunson, C. G., Son, S., Lee, J., & Bauer, J. W. (2010). EITC participation and association with financial distress among rural low-income families. *Family Relations*, 59(4), 369–382. https://doi.org/10.2307/40864558

Guyer, A. (2003). *Depression risk: An examination of rural low-income mothers.* [Unpublished master's thesis]. Oregon State University.

Haynes-Maslow, L., Osborne, I., & Pitts, S. J. (2019). Examining barriers and facilitators to delivering SNAP-Ed direct nutrition education in rural communities. *American Journal of Health Promotion*, 33(5), 736–744. https://doi .org/10.1177/0890117118821845

Katras, M. J., Zuiker, V. S., & Bauer, J. W. (2004). Private safety net: Childcare resources from the perspective of rural low-income families. *Family Relations*, 53, 201–209. https://10.1111/j.0022-2445.2004.00010.x

Mammen, S., Berry, A. A., Bird, C., & Chandler, K. D. (2018). Rural low-income families' quest for economic security: It takes more than a paycheck. *Family Sciences Review*, 22(1), 9–25. https://doi.org/10.26536/FSR.2018.22.01.01

Mammen, S., & Lawrence, F. (2006). *Use of the earned income tax credit by rural working families.* Proceedings of the 33rd Conference of the Eastern Family Economics Resource Management Association, 29–37.

Mammen, S., & Sano, Y. (2012). Gaining access to economically marginalized rural populations: Lessons learned from non-probability sampling. *Rural Sociology*, 77(3), 462–482. https://doi.org/10.1111/j.1549-0831.2012.00083.x

Mammen, S., & Sano, Y. (2013). Basebook Report. Rural Families Speak about Health (RFSH) (2008–2014). Technical report prepared for the Rural Families Speak about Health project team.

Mammen, S., Sano, Y., Braun, B., & Maring, E. F. (2019). Shaping core health messages: Rural, low-income mothers speak through participatory action research. *Health Communication*, 32(10), 1141–1149. https://10.1080/10410236 .2018.1465792

Masten, A. S. (2018). Resilience theory and research on children and families: Past, present, and promise. *Journal of Family Theory & Review*, 10, 12–31. https://doi .org/10.1111/jftr.12255

Meit, M. (2018). *Exploring strategies to improve health and equity in rural communities*. The Walsh Center for Rural Health Analysis. NORC at the University of Chicago.

National Institute of Food and Agriculture. (2017). *Nutrition education: A path forward for EFNEP*. United States Department of Agriculture. https://nifa .usda.gov/sites/default/files/resource/EFNEP-point-of-departure-03.13.2017-FINAL.pdf

National Institute of Food and Agriculture. (2021a). *2020 impacts: The Expanded Food and Nutrition Education Program (EFNEP)*. United States Department of Agriculture. Retrieved from https://nifa.usda.gov/sites/default/files/ resource/2020%20EFNEP%20National%20Data%20Reports.pdf

National Institute of Food and Agriculture. (2021b). *About EFNEP*. United States Department of Agriculture. Retrieved from https://nifa.usda.gov/program/ about-efnep

Noonan, D., Dardas, L., Bice-Wigington, T., Huddleston-Casas, C. A., Sloan, R., Benjamin, R., Choi, S. & Simmons, L. A. (2016). Understanding multiple behavioral risk factors for cancer in rural women. *Public Health Nursing*, 33(6), 519–528. https://doi.org/10.1111/phn.12282

Ontai, L. L., Barnett, M. A., Smith, S., Wilmoth, J. D., & Yancura, L. (2018). Understanding family well-being in the context of rural poverty: Lessons from the Rural Families Speak Project. *Family Science Review*, 22(1), 39–53. https:// doi.org/10.26536/FSR.2018.22.01.03

Routh, B., Burney, J., Greder, K., Katras, M. J., & Johnson, K. (2020). Rural health disparities: Connecting research and practice. *The Forum for Family and Consumer Issues*, 23(1). www.theforumjournal.org/2021/03/01/ rural-health-disparities-connecting-research-and-practice/

Sano, Y., Garasky, S., Greder, K. A., Cook, C. C., & Browder, D. E. (2011). Understanding food insecurity among Latino immigrant families in rural America. *Journal of Family and Economic Issues*, 32(1), 111–123. https://doi.org/10.1007/ s10834-010-9219-y

Sano, Y., Mammen, S., & Oliver, B. (2018). Food insecurity among rural, low-income families. *Family Science Review*, 22(1), 26–38. https://doi.org/10.26536/ FSR.2018.22.02.02

Sano, Y., Manoogian, M. M., & Ontai, L. L. (2012). "The Kids Still Come First": Creating family stability during partnership instability in rural, low-income families. *Journal of Family Issues*, 33, 942–965. https://doi.org/10.1177/0192513 X11430820

Sano, Y., Richards, L. N., & Lee, J. (2011). Invisible barriers to employment: Mental and behavioral health problems that hinder self-sufficiency. In J. W. Bauer & E. M. Dolan (Eds.), *Rural mothers and work: Contexts and problems* (pp. 77–98). Springer.

Sano, Y., Routh, B., & Lanigan, J. (2019). Food parenting practices in rural poverty context. *Appetite*, 135(1), 115–122. https://doi.org/10.1016/j.appet.2018.11.024

Simmons, L. A., Huddleston-Casas, C., & Berry, A. A. (2007). Low-income rural women and depression: Factors associated with self-reporting. *American Journal of Health Behavior*, 31(6), 657–666. https://doi.org/10.5993/AJHB.31.6.10

Sneed, C. T., Franck, K. L., Norman, H., Washburn, L., Kennedy, L., Jarvandi, S., & Mullins, J. (2020). Two states, one mission: Building PSE capacity of county Extension educators. *Journal of Extension*, 58(4). https://joe.org/joe/2020august/iw1.php

Swanson, J. A., Olson, C. M., Miller, E. O., & Lawrence, F. C. (2008). Rural mothers' use of formal programs and informal social supports to meet family food needs: A mixed methods study. *Journal of Family and Economic Issues*, 29(4), 674–690. https://doi.org/10.1007/s10834-008-9127-6

Tabatabaei-Moghaddam, H., Sano, Y., & Mammen, S. (2014). A case study in creating oral health messages for rural low-income families: A comparison to the Cultural Appropriateness (CA) framework. *Health Promotion and Practice*, 15(5), 646–653. https://doi.org/10.1177/1524839914533567

Washburn, L. T., Norman, H., Franck, K. L., Kennedy, L. E., & Sneed, C. T. (2021). Integrating PSE work into FCS Extension programming: Lessons learned from a multi-state training. *Journal of Human Sciences and Extension*, 9(1). www.jhseonline.com/article/view/1031

Winterbauer, N. L., Bekemeier, B., VanRaemdonck, L., & Hoover, A. G. (2016). Applying community-based participatory research partnership principles to public health practice-based research networks. *SAGE Open*, 6(4). https://doi.org/10.1177/2158244016679211Top of FormBottom of Form

Yancura, L. A., Piper, J. L., Wallace, H. S., & Berry, A. A. (2020). How does research inform work with multigenerational and skipped-generation households in rural America?. *The Forum for Family and Consumer Issues*, 23(1), 1–15.

CHAPTER 4

Extension Programming to Enhance Urban Well-Being

Julie M. Fox

Access to meaningful education empowers people to foster both individual and community well-being (Fields, 2017; Suarez-Balcazar, 2020). Extension's commitment to improving the quality of life of its constituents through nonformal education is constant across the rural–urban continuum. Throughout Extension's history, teams of faculty, staff, students, and volunteers have pursued relevance – a quest that reflects both respect for tradition and as a desire for innovation (Gagnon et al., 2015). Over time, as people moved from rural areas into more suburban and urban communities, Extension has offered more diverse programming (Franz & Townson, 2008).

Although urban, suburban, and rural communities share common issues such as food access, water quality, and health equity, addressing issues of well-being in urban areas requires entrepreneurial approaches that recognize the unique urban context. Understanding context increases awareness of situational factors and informs decision-making (Bamberger, 2008). The complex dynamics in metropolitan areas influence community-engaged research and education relevant to social scientists, including university Extension professionals.

This chapter begins with a brief discussion focused on the urban context and strategies Extension employs in metropolitan areas. Much of the chapter draws upon the National Urban Extension Framework to feature urban Extension engagement to foster well-being in diverse settings across the country. The chapter also discusses and describes the work of the National Urban Extension Leaders (NUEL), an entity developed to mobilize a system-level support and a collaborative network focused on better linking the LGU Extension mission with urban community priorities.

The chapter then concludes with insights and recommendations based on a synthesis of common threads and themes in the scholarly and applied literature, with unique considerations for Extension in urban communities.

4.1 Urban Context

Our affection for cities continues to grow, with forecasts predicting that three out of every four humans globally will live in an urban setting by 2050 (Gleeson, 2014). Urbanization has important implications for health and well-being (Galea & Vlahov, 2015; World Health Organization, 2014) including the challenge of building sustainable and healthy cities (Larson et al., 2016). Many researchers and practitioners across multiple disciplines are exploring quality of life measures and the social and environmental determinants of human well-being in urban areas (Larson et al., 2016; Maggino, 2016). A fresh future is taking shape, with urban areas around the world becoming not just the dominant form of habitat, but also the engine of human development, with people living, working, playing, learning, and serving in urban communities (UN Habitat, 2013). Complex, rapidly unfolding urban developments require new insight from diverse perspectives to inform future development of densely populated communities.

To define Extension's work in densely populated areas, terms like urban, metro, and city have been used almost synonymous but may denote different meanings. "City" is one term used by the Census Bureau to refer to a concentration of population within a given area. In contrast, the Census Bureau's urban–rural classification recognizes urban land use in geographical areas. Metropolitan Statistical Areas, from the United States Office of Management and Budget, are geographic areas used by many federal statistical agencies to denote a locale with high population concentration and economic ties to surrounding areas. Thus, such terms do not just refer soley to population and geography. For example, the US Department of Agriculture's Economic Research Service uses urban influence codes and assesses economic and social diversity of nonmetro America through classifications such as rural–urban continuum codes. Other related terms, such as suburban and peri-urban, are used by the US Department of Housing and Urban Development's (HUD's) Office of Policy Development and Research, the National Center for Education Statistics, and professionals engaged in regional planning. Urbanized areas, as delineated by the Census Bureau, continue to be refined. Regardless of the term and definitions, Extension personnel continue to explore best practices to apply as a catalyst for co-discovery and community change that reflect the similarities and the nuances of metropolitan areas.

While urban and rural areas share common issues, addressing these concerns in urban areas requires approaches that recognize *scale, diversity, complexity*, and the *urban–rural* interface. Each of these factors is discussed in more detail with exemplar case studies provided later in the chapter for illustration. Simply adapting approaches used in rural areas, from rural perspectives, is not sufficient to address those same issues within urban communities (Haynes et al., 2021). Traditional Extension engagement, programming, evaluation, applied research, and operations might not be as effective with urban audiences (Hains et al., 2021; Ruemenapp, 2018; Warner et al., 2017). For example, community assessments with county-level data don't acknowledge or address the distinct needs and assets in neighborhoods throughout the county (Krohn et al., 2022). Youth engagement that culminates in participation at a county fair or residential camp may not be culturally or practically relevant for those in urban regions. Furthermore, many educators and agents engage with their urban communities in ways that are not evaluated as teaching, challenging typical performance reviews. University Human Resources is not geared toward the attraction and hiring of short-term project staff and volunteers who may be needed in urban programming. These examples of unique needs within urban areas show how the local context impacts Extension's relevance, capacity, and program impacts in metropolitan areas. Identifying and agreeing on what makes metropolitan areas unique can have important implications for Extension (Lyon & Driskell, 2011; Wirth, 1938).

4.1.1 Scale

The population size and density in urban areas creates opportunities and challenges for Extension to have a strong presence, engagement, and impact with a large group of people. The ratio of Extension personnel to community members and partners is much higher in urban counties compared with other counties. In the article *Extension in the City: Meeting the Challenges of Scale*, Tiffany (2017) illustrated how the population in the United States increased steadily since before the inception of Extension. Recognizing shifts in population provides Extension with the opportunity to address scale in urban communities (Figure 4.1).

4.1.2 Diversity

A high degree of ethnic and racial diversity enriches and challenges metropolitan communities (Farrell & Lee, 2011; Graham et al., 2014; Meissner & Vertovec, 2015). Large cities are rich in diversity, broadly illustrated through the presence of differences that may include race, gender, religion,

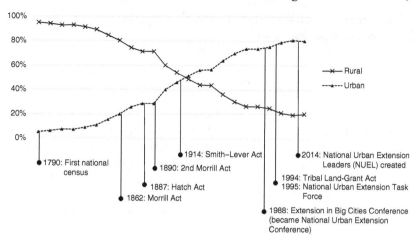

Figure 4.1   Timeline of Extension historical events in relation to urbanization of the US population.

sexual orientation, ethnicity, nationality, socioeconomic status, language, (dis)ability, age, religious commitment, or political perspective.

According to Nicole DuPuis, Manager for *Urban Innovation in the Center for City Solutions* at the National League of Cities, 98 percent of growth in the hundred largest cities since 2000 was accounted for by growth in minority populations (DuPuis, 2019). It is essential for Extension to employ and value diverse personnel, inclusively engage multilingual stakeholders in programming and partnerships, and integrate authentic images and culturally responsive practices that reflect the diversity in Extension's audiences and environments. Ideally, Extension creates a sense of belonging with diverse clientele, personnel, and partners.

4.1.3   Complexity

Extension navigates a challenging environment through both collaboration and competition. Metropolitan areas have multiple jurisdictions and school districts, thousands of public, nonprofit, and private organizations; and complex multifaceted issues. Addressing comprehensive issues with diverse community partners creates layers of complexity that urban Extension professionals manage. As part of land-grant universities (LGUs), the complexities of large educational institutions, combined with urban context present opportunities and challenges for national, state, and local Extension professionals.

4.1.4   Urban–Rural Interface

Rural, suburban, and urban communities are interdependent. Various indicators demonstrate a dynamic flow of people and other resources throughout all geographic areas along the urban and rural continuum. Extension recognizes that many people live in one county, work in another, and enjoy recreation and tourism in other locales. Although there may be some similarities to Extension in nonurban areas, awareness of the urban distinction provides Extension with opportunities to conduct programming intentionally. The purpose is not to minimize the value of Extension's good work and impact in rural and suburban communities, but instead to increase Extension's impact in urban areas through improved knowledge of the urban context and a framework for strategic approaches. Extension is uniquely positioned to help build stronger awareness, connection, and relationships between people in urban, suburban, and rural communities – addressing what is unique in each and what is shared across all perspectives. When Extension draws upon these tenets, there is an opportunity for addressing well-being in urban communities more effectively.

4.2   Well-Being in Urban Communities

Improving well-being and quality of life are at the heart of all Extension programming. However, the underlying frameworks guiding efforts and definitions of terms have not always been transparent. For several decades, researchers all over the world have worked on defining multidimensional concepts to measure and monitor well-being (Maggino, 2016; Prilleltensky et al., 2015). Conceptualizing and clarifying well-being allows for relevant and aspects of life in which people can thrive. One useful framework is the five interrelated elements of well-being proposed by Rath et al. (2010) that encompass physical, social, career, financial, and community components. The following examples illustrate how Extension's engagement with urban communities can address the elements of well-being.

- **Physical Well-Being**. Refers to good health and having enough energy to accomplish necessary tasks daily. *Examples*: Extension's commitment to physical well-being is evident through education, as well as policy, system, and environmental initiatives. For example, the Urban EFNEP (Expanded Food and Nutrition Education Program) in Alabama engages limited-resource Hispanic mothers with children under five, teaching them how to prepare healthy foods on limited budgets and encouraging daily physical activity. Classes are offered in English and Spanish by paraprofessionals from the community in convenient locations, often through a *Nutrition Education on the Move* bus with a fully functional mini-kitchen. EFNEP is a Federal Extension community outreach program that operates through LGUs to support participants' efforts toward self-sufficiency, nutritional health, and well-being. The Healthful Homes for Urban Youths and Families curriculum created by the University of Connecticut's Department of Extension recognizes that thirty-five million US metropolitan homes had one or more health and safety hazards that could be reduced or eliminated to improve health outcomes (National Center for Healthy Housing [NCHH], 2013). The award-winning Tools for Healthy Living program incorporates relevant National Health Education Standards (Centers for Disease Control and Prevention, 2015), the general principles of healthful homes (NCHH, 2011), and education to help develop the skills to advocate for themselves and to become agents for positive change in their homes, schools, and communities.

- **Social Well-Being**. Refers to having strong relationships and love in your life. *Example*: Inclusive engagement has been fundamental throughout Extension's history. With increasing diversity, Extension creates spaces and programs for people in all communities to engage in learning and deliberative dialogue. One example is addressing needs of youth who identify as lesbian, gay, bisexual, transgender, or queer/questioning (LGBTQ+), as illustrated by Soule (2017) and Gonzalez et al. (2020). With a focus on access, equity, belonging, and nondiscrimination, the National 4-H Council and Cooperative Extension affirmed the inclusion of youth of all genders and sexual orientations in the 4-H Youth Development Program. The scholarly literature on the social marginalization of LGBTQ+ populations is expanding (Gonzalez et al., 2020). However, evidence of Extension engagement with LGBTQ+ clientele across the lifespan remains limited across rural, suburban, and urban settings. Extension has the opportunity to illustrate diverse, rather than heteronormative engagement, demonstrate that Extension is an LGBTQ+ ally, explore partnerships with organizations such as the National Resource Center on LGBT Aging, and cultivate a welcoming space for all (Howard et al., 2021; Smith et al., 2021). For those exploring or embracing an identity that does not mirror dominant social norms, an increased sense of belonging and support contributes to positive well-being (Kosciw et al., 2020).

- **Career Well-Being or Purpose**. Refers to how you occupy your time and appreciating what you do each day. *Example*: Extension fosters entrepreneurship and workforce development in many areas, from youth STEM and food system careers to adults working or volunteering in urban agriculture. Certificate programs, best practice studies, business networking opportunities, and policy support are a few examples relevant to urban settings. In various parts of the country, Extension promotes workplace wellness through publications (e.g., see Kinsey, 2019), education (e.g., see University of Nevada-Reno, n.d.), and awards programs (e.g., University of Missouri, n.d.).

- **Financial Well-Being**. Refers to being able to effectively manage your economic life to reduce stress and increase security. *Examples*: The University of Maryland Extension's Master Money Mentor (University of Maryland, n.d.) volunteers assist local individuals and families in acquiring valuable financial management knowledge and skills to build their financial capacity and stability. They also provide group financial education classes and participate in community outreach events. The Ohio State University Extension offers HUD approved home buyer education and financial literacy training and counseling to prospective home buyers in Franklin County (Ohio State Univeristy, n.d.). In an OSU Community Connectors feature article (April 2021), an OSU Extension community engagement director embedded in the urban university district summarized, "To remain true to our mission, we help families accumulate assets, build wealth, and become financially stable. Homeownership is something that will have long-lasting implications on the community, the residents, their children, and generations to come" (Ohio State University, 2021).

- **Community Well-Being**. Refers to engagement and involvement in the area where you live. *Examples*: Prioritizing community needs helps ensure Extension programs are relevant and designed for specific audiences. In Utah, affordable housing, affordable medical clinics, well-paying jobs, quality public schools, and affordable Internet were the top five needs in urban areas (Narine et al., 2021). In Wisconsin, Urban Nature Master Naturalist training engages volunteers in connecting with their natural ecosystem. In the article "4-H and Its Relevance in the Era of #Moments in Urban Communities," Webster (2016) emphasize the need for positive outlets for young people to engage as agents of change in their communities. With the support of the Robert Wood Johnson Foundation, the National 4-H Council and Cooperative Extension are empowering communities to come together to help their residents become healthier at every stage of life. Youth work alongside community members, local public health organizations, businesses, government entities, and nonprofit agencies to address top public health priorities, such as individual and community well-being. At Penn State Extension, the Well Connected Communities program foster coalition building and youth leadership that brought together rural–urban partnerships and a vital connection between regional farms and urban food systems (Byrnes, 2023).

Naturally, some programs align with multiple well-being elements as Extension typically addresses well-being across various domains. For example, the *Wellness and Well-being: What About Me?* program in Iowa increased participants' knowledge and awareness of well-being and intention to implement self-identified lifestyle changes in rural and urban communities (Sellers et al., 2020). Most recently, Extension has an emerging framework for health equity and well-being that applies a community development model and engages Extension personnel from multiple disciplines, which can be a promising model for future programming that involves multiple aspects of well-being.

4.3 Extension Strategy in Urban Communities

A sustainable and integrated approach to Extension's role in urban communities revolves around the interwoven strategic themes of programs, positioning, personnel, and partnerships (NUEL, 2015). Addressing all these aspects ensures an explicit understanding of respectful community-engagement and resources needed to achieve objectives.

4.3.1   *Programs for Relevance and Impacts*

When programming is locally relevant and culturally responsive, outcomes bring private and public value for individuals, families, businesses, and communities (Durlak & DuPre, 2008; Franz, 2015). National Urban Extension Leaders is a group of Extension leaders that focused on scholarship, programming, and advocacy to address the multitude of issues and priorities in the city. Primary program areas in urban communities that are within the focus of NUEL are naturally interdisciplinary. For example, urban agriculture incorporates business and community development, health, food systems, and youth engagement. National Urban Extension Leaders' focus areas include improving our health, enriching youth, feeding the future, strengthening communities, and protecting the environment. Program delivery methods and techniques must vary widely to account for the rich urban tapestry of diversity and commonalities found in metropolitan centers (Fehlis, 1992). For example, urban audiences may have difficulty relating in meaningful ways to examples in teaching materials that were not designed from an urban perspective (Argabright et al., 2012; Borich, 2001; Gould et al., 2014; Krofta & Panshin, 1989; Webster & Ingram, 2007). Extension has diversified its educational programming portfolio in many ways (e.g., 2022 urban-themed issue of the *Journal of Human Sciences and Extension*) to respond to the needs of people living in urban areas (Beaulieu & Cordes, 2014; Christenson & Warner, 1985; Schafer et al., 1992).

4.3.2   *Positioning for Awareness and Accessibility*

Historically, Extension has been perceived as rural, with an agrarian focus that has consequently left many urbanites and urban advocates unaware of Extension's existence (Fox et al., 2017). Several studies have indicated that urban populations traditionally have low awareness of Extension, use of Extension resources, and participation in Extension programs (NUEL, 2015). Urbanites with some knowledge of Extension are often skeptical that Extension has the expertise or commitment to apply its resources toward playing important roles in cities (Christenson & Warner, 1985; Jacob et al., 1991; Warner et al., 1996). The gap in awareness of and support for Extension in cities affects funding streams (Henning et al., 2014; Raison, 2014). In urban communities, Extension sometimes has a relatively small presence relative to the larger population and crowded market. To compete and make the best of Extension accessible in urban communities, Extension must continue to invest in a strategic approach to make its presence known and for communications to distinguish its relevance and unique value. Efforts from Alabama Extension illustrate an example of attempts to increase awareness, with educational materials directly addressing the gap in awareness regarding Extension in urban areas to alert constituents regarding their presence (Alabama Extension, 2021).

4.3.3 Personnel for Capacity and Alignment

Extension personnel are embedded in communities as trusted resources and serve as neutral, trusted facilitators who bring people together to deliberate and deal with local issues (Fox et al., 2017; Kellogg Commission, 1999). The work of NUEL includes supporting urban Extension entities to attract, develop, retain, and structure competent talent for long- and short-term priorities. Personnel include administrative leaders, faculty, staff, students, and volunteer community members. Ideally, personnel reflect the diversity of the community, understand the urban context, collaboratively address complex issues, and are supported from attraction through succession planning.

Extension personnel working in metropolitan areas need the same set of core competencies as Extension professionals in other geographic settings (Fox, 2021). However, because of unique community conditions previously described, these individuals and teams must have additional skills and attributes to effectively address the needs of metropolitan constituents (Fehlis, 1992; Fox et al., 2017; National Extension Urban Task Force, 1996; Webster & Ingram, 2007; Western Extension Directors Association Urban Task Force, 2010). Extension benefits from flexible staffing models that incorporate varied positions, including project-driven hiring that allows for a greater mix of core personnel and additional professionals who have the specific expertise needed to address the broad array of metropolitan issues. Retrofitting traditional strategies and one-size-fits-all approaches are inadequate. The processes of hiring and retaining urban personnel can present challenges in the areas of human resources and professional development. Social scientists interested in engaging with urban communities to address priorities through applied research, education, and Extension bring tremendous capacity to the Extension mission.

4.3.4 Partnerships for Connections and Resources

National Urban Extension Leaders is also focused on partnerships to support Extension collaborations that leverage resources for collective impact. Engaged scholarship through Extension involves linking and leveraging university resources with those in the public and private sectors to enrich knowledge, address and help solve critical societal issues, and contribute to the public good (Stanton, 2012). Urban counties host thousands of organizations, from neighborhood groups to county and city government agencies; not-for-profit and philanthropic foundations; libraries and metroparks; schools and universities; and hospitals, financial institutions, faith-based organizations, media groups, and consulting companies. Extension partnerships often require the management of multiple stakeholder agendas, project timelines, reporting commitments, and other expectations inherent in diversified funding portfolios beyond traditional county, state, and federal fiscal cycles (Krofta & Panshin, 1989). Although many Extension professionals are content experts first and program managers second, in the city, the need for Extension is so vast that many become more engaged in capacity building and management. For urban Extension to thrive, leaders must accept that the most effective way to operate is in partnership with a well-developed group of organizations, where roles are distinct yet missions are aligned and where visibility, credit, and resources are shared (De Ciantis et al., 2015; Jongbloed et al., 2008). To manage multijurisdictional and multidisciplinary networks, different ways of thinking are needed to determine how the resources of the LGU system can be accessed to help address the complex issues that exist in metropolitan areas. Building strong metropolitan advisory councils and relationships with key community decision-makers and other influencers is an effective strategy for Extension to use when navigating a robust set of partnerships that involve varying degrees of connection, coordination, cooperation, and collaboration (Henning et al., 2014; Morrison et al., 2019).

4.4   Urban Extension Program Snapshots

For over a century, Extension has contributed to its mission of working with communities to bring local knowledge and science-based information together to cocreate solutions to support well-being. Extension has increasingly recognized the unique context of engagement in urban communities that need to be addressed to improve social, economic, and environmental conditions (Crossgrove et al., 2005; Gaolach et al., 2017).

One effective way that Extension has sought to understand and expand programming in urban communities is to conduct research with the use of qualitative methods, particularly with cases that are descriptive and present program snapshots. For this chapter, we conducted a study to examine themes and trends in urban programming, and to provide snapshots of programs conducted. We utilized a multiple case study approach, which is a method that can illuminate contextual aspects of the situation by gathering both agreed upon and diverse views (Lauckner et al., 2012; Thomas, 2011). Case studies allow researchers to investigate contemporary complex phenomenon within real-life contexts (Creswell, 2013; Yin, 2011) and are often used in organizational (Hartley, 1994) and social science research (Yin, 2003). The cases selected for this chapter highlight programs in the urban context, and strategies used therein to address the elements of well-being noted earlier (NUEL, 2015; Rath et al., 2010). Program snapshots and/or case studies in urban Extension allow for readers to better understand: (a) the real-life context of urban Extension in communities across the country; (b) urban Extension strategies, programs, and impacts as illustrated in alignment with the NUEL framework (De Ciantis et al., 2015); (c) meaningful connection between urban Extension and the urban perspective in social science; and (d) opportunities to further advance how Extension addresses the urban context in ways that result in Extension being relevant locally, responsive statewide, and recognized nationally.

We culled the literature and various resources to identify Extension programs that exemplify quality efforts in urban settings, selecting programs that occurred in urban cities, and wherein contributors have a connection to a national urban Extension network. We included different geographic regions and a range of programmatic foci to illustrate the breadth of coverage and variety in approaches in Extension. Program cases were identified using a search of national searchable sources including websites of the Extension Foundation, Joint Council of Extension Professionals, Western Center for Metropolitan Extension and Research, NUEL, as well as the *Journal of Extension*, and two special issues of the *Journal of Human Sciences and Extension* that focused on urban programming (2017, 2022).

After identifying examples of urban programming through the sources noted above, we engaged contributors to explore and describe how the programs are relevant locally, responsive statewide, and/or recognized nationally; represent each region as designated by the Extension Committee on Organization and Policy; and demonstrate contributor connections with national urban Extension initiatives. Case contributors conducted interviews of key stakeholders with connections to the identified programs (Hancock & Algozzine, 2017), recorded observations (Furlong & Lawn, 2010; Mays & Pope, 1995; Morgan et al., 2017), and reviewed program documents (Bretschneider et al., 2017).

The researchers' approach was interpretive and analytical, rather than solely descriptive (Merriam, 1988; Stake, 1995). This approach was selected to illuminate contextual aspects of the situation to gather both agreed upon and diverse views (Lauckner et al., 2012). Data were analyzed using the constant comparative method (Merriam & Tisdell, 2016) of analysis, assigning and organizing codes into meaningful concepts. To address dependability, confirmability, and credibility, an audit trail included coded case notes from multiple reviewers and multiple sources (Lincoln & Guba, 1985). Comparative research has become an established research strategy in urban studies for deducting conclusions based upon the understanding of commonalities and differences across places (Krehl & Weck, 2020). The approach was to contextualize not generalize insights into the urban perspective (Tasan-Kok et al., 2013). The following five urban Extension program snapshots summarize cases from contributors across the country.

4.4.1   Urban Extension Program Snapshot 1: Rutgers 4-H STEM Ambassador Program

Despite modest gains in the last twenty-five years, racial and ethnic minority workers continue to be underrepresented in the STEM workforce (Chiappinelli et al., 2016). To address career well-being, the Rutgers 4-H STEM Ambassador Program (Rutgers, n.d.) engages urban youth from groups underrepresented in Science, Technology, Engineering, and Math (STEM). The program has three primary focus areas, namely, (a) STEM exposure, skill development, and identity, (b) college readiness and access, and (c) leadership and contribution. Youth ambassadors are selected by their local 4-H staff to participate in a week on campus, where they engage in discussions, workshops, research projects, and engineering challenges alongside faculty, staff, and graduate students. This collaboration of seven counties serves high school youth from urban communities between Philadelphia and New York City, including young women, African Americans, and Latinos. These communities are racially and ethnically diverse and represent some of the most densely populated urban areas in the country.

Each year, a new cohort of forty-five to sixty-five 8th to 9th graders are selected to receive full scholarships to participate in the multiyear precollege program. More than 500 teenagers have become ambassadors. Many participants are of the first generation in their family to pursue a college education. The program begins with online learning modules for participants to complete prior to a week of campus experiences. After their initial week on campus, the ambassadors continue to receive pre-college support and guidance during their four years of high school. Program staff provide additional opportunities for career and college exploration and assist the ambassadors with the college application process. Ambassadors have participated in various programs including the National 4-H STEM Challenge, the CYFAR-funded Science Pathways program, and service with younger youth, as they facilitate science and engineering projects through afterschool, weekend, and summer programs in their home communities.

A diverse group of 4-H faculty and staff have been collaborating for several years to redefine how 4-H can serve expanded and diverse audiences through a variety of STEM initiatives, while still providing the essential elements of the 4-H experience. Rutgers professors, post docs, graduate students, and undergraduates from numerous schools within the university support the program by contributing their time to lead full-day research projects, inviting Ambassadors into their labs and classrooms, participating in roundtable discussions about their journey in STEM, and mentoring the youth. Internal partners extend across campus and include schools, departments, centers, the office of communications and marketing, the office of urban Extension and engagement, and Rutgers iTV Studio for the online learning modules. Partnerships with urban schools and other youth-serving organizations have been key to building awareness of Extension programs and increasing access to programs by those underrepresented. An internal Rutgers Cooperative Extension Community Enhancement grant provided initial funding. Some of the most important outcomes of STEM pathway programs are engagement of educators, mentors, peer networks, and corporate, public, and philanthropic partners (Contreras, 2011; Stanton-Salazar and Spina, 2005; Wickliffe et al., 2020). In metropolitan areas, these resources are near urban youth, but not always easily accessible.

The program team conducted pre- and postsurveys, focus groups, and a longitudinal study, documenting program impacts through a variety of journal articles (McDonnell et al., 2019), conference presentations, and other publications, such as the *4-H Science in Urban Communities Promising Practices Guide*. A majority of ambassadors (80 percent) reported that their experience with the program was positive and helped shape their goals, widening their perspective in terms of possible STEM careers and areas of scientific study and research. Most importantly, most ambassadors said that their interaction with scientists, interaction with fellow participants, and opportunities to share their projects resulted in increased confidence in themselves, improved interpersonal skills, and strengthened interest in science and engineering. In 2015, the program received the National Excellence in Urban Programing Award from the National Association of Extension 4-H Agents. In 2020, the program team was awarded the Rutgers School of Environmental and Biological Sciences/New Jersey Agricultural Experiment Station Team Excellence Award. (Case contributors: Chad Ripberger, with Janice McDonnell, Marycarmen Kunicki, Marissa Staffen, and James Nichnadowicz from 4-H Youth Development, Rutgers Cooperative Extension.)

4.4.2   *Urban Extension Program Snapshot 2: Produce Perks in Cleveland, OH*

The Cleveland-Cuyahoga Food Policy Coalition (FPC), co-led by the local Ohio State University (OSU) Extension initiated the Produce Perks, Supplemental Nutrition Assistance Program (SNAP) incentive program which offers a dollar-for-dollar match on the purchase of fresh fruits and vegetables to all SNAP participants. This program was initiated, recognizing the need to improve the health of people living in food insecure communities by increasing access to affordable healthy food (Tiwari & Ambinakudige, 2021). The setting for this program was Cleveland (pop. 380,000), which is the largest city in Cuyahoga County, Ohio (pop. 1.24 million) (US Census Bureau, 2020). In the popular press, Cleveland has been described as "a city of ethnic enclaves divided into east and west by the Cuyahoga River" (Hallal, 2016). Cuyahoga County is complex, with forty-nine cities and towns, thirty-three school districts, twelve colleges and universities, and a substantial health care sector.

Four local foundations solely funded the Produce Perks program in its first eight years. The 2014 Farm Bill solidified the program within the county and eventually in the state of Ohio with the support of Wholesome Wave, a nonprofit organization focused on alleviating food insecurity through partnerships. In 2016, the multisector Ohio Nutrition Incentive Network was formed and identified Produce Perks Midwest as its intermediary. As Produce Perks expanded, additional incentives were added in Cuyahoga County as part of the SNAP for Women and Children (WIC) and Temporary Assistance for Needy Families (TANF) (see Franzen-Castle et al., this volume, for detailed descriptions of these programs).

Produce Perks has continued to grow over the years, including in its impact on the local economy and healthy eating behaviors of constituents and has thus been recognized by the USDA (its main funder), as a model SNAP incentive program. Growing evidence shows that fruit and vegetable incentives improve healthy eating behaviors (John et al., 2021) and have local economic benefits for families, farmers, and the local economy. Interactions among families and farmers also foster a sense of community. The farmers' market managers and Extension staff are positively impacted by implementing Perks. Gatherings of the market managers provide one of the few opportunities for them to network as a group. Urban food security depends on an extensive and complex array of processes occurring at many scales and geographies (Biehl et al., 2018). With a diverse team of twenty Extension professionals and hundreds of volunteers, OSU Extension partners with city, county, state, and national organizations for multidisciplinary food system and other related programs for well-being. Urban communities are rich in resources. In addition to traditional partners, the Extension team navigates more than thirty grants and contracts each year with groups that include NASA, the NFL, and numerous other collaborators. (Case contributor: Nicole Debose, leader of OSU Extension, Cuyahoga County and representative on the NUEL Steering Council. Prior to joining OSU Extension, Nicole worked for Cuyahoga County Health and Human Services.)

4.4.3   Urban Extension Program Snapshot 3: University of Idaho Diabetes Prevention Program

Diabetes affects approximately 30.3 million people nationally (CDC, 2017). Among the fifty most populous US cities, diabetes mortality rates are disproportionately higher for Blacks compared to Whites, with poverty rates accounting for much of the disparity (Rosenstock et al., 2014). In Idaho, direct and indirect financial burden of diabetes on the state's health care system was approximately $1.32 billion in 2012. Addressing these challenges, the University of Idaho (UI) Diabetes Prevention Program (DPP) started in partnership with the Idaho State Department of Health and Welfare (IDHW). Several Extension faculty and staff in urban Idaho participated in the CDC National Diabetes Prevention Program (NDPP) training to become certified DPP Healthy Lifestyle Coaches to serve the large population in the Boise area. Although Idaho is primarily rural, Ada and Canyon counties have a combined population of nearly 700,000 residents.

Collaboration has been key in meeting the needs of urban areas in Idaho. In addition to the IDHW, UI Extension partners with over twenty state agencies, employers, schools, health organizations, and individuals to market, recruit, and offer NDPP, delivering programs onsite, online, and as a hybrid. Programs are hosted at worksites, health clinics, recreation facilities, libraries, and other locations. In the first five years, nine certified lifestyle coaches engaged with eighteen cohorts, providing education for more than 200 participants. In 2019, the UI DPP received full recognition from the Centers for Disease Control and Prevention and is now listed on the national registry. Today, the team is exploring additional initiatives including processing health insurance reimbursement for the program. (Case contributor: Bridget Morrisroe-Aman, Assistant Professor, University of Idaho Extension. She has worked with children, youth, and families in Extension programs for twenty years and serves in the most urban area in Idaho. She leads the UI Extension Diabetes Prevention Program and a Master Food Safety Advisor volunteer program.)

4.4.4   Urban Extension Program Snapshot 4: Fostering Sustainability at the Community Level

Sustainable urban development is essential for protecting the natural environment as well as the well-being of people and society at large (Bai et al., 2012; Kaur & Garg, 2019). To address community well-being in the Tampa Florida metropolitan area, Extension focused on fostering sustainability at the community level. The Tampa Bay Metropolitan Statistical Area (MSA) is ranked 18th among metropolitan areas in the United States and is home to over three million residents. The region is highly urbanized but still retains its agricultural heritage, renowned for cattle, strawberries, and now hops and hemp. The densely populated and heavily visited coastal community faces issues such as land use planning, sea level rise, economic development, and sustainability. Multiple local municipalities and a plethora of partners make it much more complicated to address and navigate multifaceted issues that often cross geographic borders. The region is made up of highly urban areas and rural enclaves, and there are well-established flows of people, goods, capital, information, and natural resources, as well as waste and pollution.

For the past ten years, a regional specialized agent in urban sustainability with the University of Florida/IFAS Extension developed, implemented, and evaluated educational programs and initiatives to promote sustainability. This unique position has allowed Extension to showcase its ability to use research-backed information to develop an innovative response to sustainability. Working across county borders leverages the interdisciplinary expertise of the university and increases visibility of Extension and the land-grant system as a resource. By positioning Extension in partnerships with other urban universities and regional entities, this addresses the distance disconnect between the LGU headquartered in Gainesville and potential clientele in the Tampa Bay region. Fostering sustainability at a community level in a highly urbanized area requires engagement on multiple levels – local governments, residents, advisory members, regional partners, youth (K-12), and college/university students. At the community level, the agent created regional awareness by partnering with highly visible partners for Green Expo events and pioneered the deployment of a seven-week community-oriented sustainability training program, "Sustainable Floridians^{SM}," a multidepartment project facilitated by the Department of Family, Youth, and Community Sciences at the University of Florida. In addition to creating knowledgeable sustainability stewards, this program served as a pipeline of newly developed sustainability volunteers who increased visibility of Extension at sustainability activities and events. This complemented the county's goal of increasing the number of volunteers retained and hours of service contributed. One Sustainable Floridians volunteer commented, "Our class was comprised of people from all ages, backgrounds, interests yet we found common ground in this course." Additional community-oriented programs included biennial symposia on energy, local and regional film series with colleges and universities, energy efficiency educational programs, and workshops on coastal hazard preparedness, climate change, sea level rise, and food systems planning.

To reach diverse audiences, energy efficiency programs for youth and adults were offered in Spanish and translated materials were provided to encourage behavior change. The agent actively recruited interns from local urban university partners and benefitted from interns placed through a competitive matching process by the LGU (University of Florida). Interns contributed to developing social media marketing campaigns, writing blogs, and outreach education at sustainability and environmentally themed events. At the local government level, the agent created a website "Green Pinellas" to showcase the county's efforts toward achieving sustainability and the educational role that Extension provided through classes, factsheets, blogs, and videos. The website development and content were supported in part by the Sustainable County Education Committee, a county partner group convened by Extension to provide input and support

Extension in its role to promote sustainability awareness and education. The agent directed the development of an employee education program consisting of training modules and a green employee pledge to create sustainability awareness among new and existing employees and comanaged the Green Business Partnership Program. Most importantly, the agent engaged in state and national certification programs to brand the local government as a pioneer in sustainable local government operations, a reflection of its commitment to creating a sustainability ethic and culture. In 2018, for example, the county earned a 3-STAR (Sustainability Tools for Assessing and Rating) rating with STAR Communities and is recognized as a Leadership in Energy and Environmental Design (LEED) community among ninety national and international cities and communities. The LEED performance score combines fourteen metrics across five categories: energy, water, waste, transportation, and quality of life (education, equitability, prosperity, health, and/or safety efforts will focus on employee training programs to support the local municipalities to create educated workforces to support regional work of sustainability and resiliency.

As communities update and revise sustainability action plans, an emphasis will be on integrating principles of diversity, equity, and inclusive authentic community engagement processes. The agent will create train-the-trainer programs that contribute to building community capacity which ultimately supports quality of life and increases community vitality. Educational programs will integrate information from the United Nations Sustainable Development Goals, the UN Urban Agenda, the National Sustainability Summit, and the World Community Development Conference. (Case contributor: Ramona Madhosingh-Hector, regional specialized agent in urban sustainability with the University of Florida/IFAS Extension, serving the eleven-county Southwest Extension District, with a primary focus on the urban corridor. In addition to multiple urban Extension leadership roles, she is active with the Epsilon Sigma Phi (ESP) Urban and Culturally Diverse Audiences Affinity Group and she is engaged in a learning exchange cohort with the Kettering Foundation to explore Democratic Practices: Creating Spaces for Deliberative Public Life.)

4.4.5   *Urban Extension Program Snapshot 5: Central Kentucky Job Club*

According to the Urban Institute, work is at the heart of our most important social issues and public policy debates. To advance career well-being, a Family and Consumer Science agent in Fayette County (Lexington) created the Central Kentucky Job Club. Following a community assessment that determined that no other organization offered a free community job search program, Job Club was created in 2012 to provide free resources to those who were facing joblessness – many for the first time. Job Club was designed to improve employability skills needed to compete in today's workplaces. Meetings feature a guest speaker or panel presenting job search topics such as resume writing, interviewing, LinkedIn, salary negotiation, networking, and transferable skills. Meeting times are reserved for networking and sharing job leads.

Research shows that the unemployed face numerous health challenges beyond the loss of income (Reine et al., 2012; Robert Woods Johnson Foundation, 2013). Job Club addresses health challenges by providing a positive environment for motivated job seekers to meet, connect, share, and learn – demonstrating Extension's commitment to improving health and well-being during difficult times. Since its inception, Job Club has reached more than 5,000 job seekers and more than 200 employment recruiters with 186 jobs secured. Postprogram evaluations indicated that 86 percent of past participants reported improved employability skills as a result of Job Club. Beginning in March 2020, Job Club began meeting online, which tripled program attendance. Participant testimonials reinforce the value of the program. As one participant commented, "Losing a job equals losing identity, never mind the practical concerns. Job Club offered concrete suggestions and ideas to move the search for a new position forward. The encouraging environment of Job Club helped me maintain a positive attitude to secure employment."

To communicate Job Club opportunities, Fayette County Extension sends Job Club public service announcements to sixty-eight mass media venues, leveraging university and community resources. In recognition of the program impact within the city of Lexington, the mayor endorsed Job Club for Lexington's urban community and the unemployment office officially recommends attendance. Successful job seekers frequently serve as panelists and share the value of Job Club during their job search. In 2020, the founding Extension agent, Diana Doggett was awarded the Southern Region National Urban Extension Leaders Leadership Award for her work with Job Club. In addition to meeting important local needs, Job Club also addresses two of the NUEL primary focus areas of strengthening communities and improving health.

This case was contributed by Dr. Jeffery Young, Director for Urban Extension, and Diana Doggett, Family and Consumer Sciences Agent,

University of Kentucky Cooperative Extension Service. In addition to supporting county and state Extension professionals working to address the challenges facing urban communities, Dr. Young serves on the NUEL Steering Committee and developed a unique undergraduate course focusing on urban issues and Cooperative Extension engagement.

4.5   Reflection and Conclusion on Extension Programming to Enhance Urban Well-Being

The five program snapshots illustrate Extension engagement for well-being in urban communities and inform emerging practices in program planning, marketing, implementation, evaluation, reporting, and engagement of faculty, staff, students, partners, and community. An entrepreneurial thread flows through the cases, as urban Extension professionals proactively developed relationships and pursued opportunities without regard to resources controlled (Stevenson, 1983). They demonstrated an understanding of their context, making them more aware of situational factors and connections as they made decisions and took actions (Bamberger, 2008). Urban Extension professionals are stakeholder-driven and turn problems into opportunities that create economic and social value. Case contributors represented different geographic areas, diverse perspectives, and similar experiences of linking and leveraging community and university assets.

In diverse and dynamic urban communities, Extension benefits from taking an asset-based approach to engagement, rather than a deficit perspective. Universities in urban society can progressively transform the power relations underpinning the production of urban space and urban knowledge (Addie, 2017). With a historical ebb and flow of support, Extension and university-level leadership play a significant role by consistently supporting urban Extension offices and being responsive to their unique needs in terms of positioning, programming, personnel, and partnerships. Positioning requires intentionally communicating relevance and inclusion that attracts urbanites to Extension resources, experiences, and professionals. Programs reflect local priorities and leverage national Extension networks. Best practices, meaningful data, and stakeholder engagement methods inform program design. Personnel and volunteers reflect diversity, increase capacity, and manage both technical and adaptive challenges. Partnerships span boundaries and endure the contradictions, power relations, and opportunities that are present across highly variegated urban structures. With multiple partners, Extension needs to measure and articulate its public value, with the shared interests in economic, environmental, and social change (Franz, 2015). New urban advocates need to be identified and stronger relationships with urban power brokers and political leadership need to be forged (Ruemenapp, 2018). Society's changing values now require a focus on contributing to economic, environmental, and social condition change rather than simply disseminating information or conducting educational activities (Franz, 2014; King & Boehlje, 2013).

There is significant value in continuing to explore and learn from the similarities, unique contexts, and connections with Extension's community engagement along the urban–rural continuum. Despite differences, complex issues do not stop at geographic boundaries as reflected in interconnected economic, social, and environmental perspectives (Henning et al., 2014). National Extension networks continue to honor rural agendas, while increasingly supporting innovation in recognition of changing demographics. Extension is well positioned to respectfully address urban issues through strategic approaches that address immediate priorities while systematically futuring to *continuously co-align university Extension with the dynamic urban environment*. Census and other data confirm that the number and diversity of people living and working in urban communities continues to increase (Desilver, 2017; Frey, 2021). Extension can help communities move beyond abstract data to better understand the contextual story about people and place and the issues that are impacting local communities.

Full cases are available online https://urban-extension.cfaes.ohio-state.edu/programs/national-program-highlights. The author acknowledges Michelle Gaston, Ohio State University Extension program coordinator, for her project management and editing assistance.

References

Addie, J. P. D. (2017). From the urban university to universities in urban society. *Regional Studies*, 51(7), 1089–1099. https://doi.org/10.1080/00343404.2016.1224334

Alabama Extension. (2021). *More in our cities*. www.aces.edu/blog/topics/products-programs-urban/more-in-our-cities/

Argabright, K., McGuire, J., & King, J. (2012). Extension through a new lens: Creativity and innovation now and for the future. *Journal of Extension*, 50(2). https://archives.joe.org/joe/2012april/comm2.php

Bai, X., Nath, I., Capon, A., Hasan, N., & Jaron, D. (2012). Health and well-being in the changing urban environment: Complex challenges, scientific responses, and the way forward. *Current Opinion in Environmental Sustainability*, 4(4), 465–472. https://doi.org/10.1016/j.cosust.2012.09.009

Bamberger, P. (2008). From the editors beyond contextualization: Using context theories to narrow the micro-macro gap in management research. *Academy of Management Journal*, 51(5), 839–846. https://doi.org/10.5465/amj.2008.34789630

Beaulieu, L. J., & Cordes, S. (2014). Extension community development: Building strong, vibrant communities. *The Journal of Extension*, 52(5), Article 23. https://archives.joe.org/joe/2014october/comm1.php

Biehl, E., Buzogany, S., Baja, K., & Neff, R. A. (2018). Planning for a resilient urban food system: A case study from Baltimore City, Maryland. *Journal of Agriculture, Food Systems, and Community Development*, 8(B), 39–53. https://doi.org/10.5304/jafscd.2018.08B.008

Borich, T. O. (2001). The department of housing and urban development and cooperative extension: A case for urban collaboration. *Journal of Extension*, 39(6). https://archives.joe.org/joe/2001december/a2.php

Bretschneider, P. J., Cirilli, S., Jones, T., Lynch, S., & Wilson, N. A. (2017). Document review as a qualitative research data collection method for teacher research. *SAGE Publications Ltd*. https://doi.org/10.4135/9781473957435

Byrnes, J. (2023). *Well connected communities*. https://extension.psu.edu/well-connected-communities

Centers for Disease Control and Prevention. (2015). *National health education standards*. www.cdc.gov/healthyschools/sher/standards/index.htm

Centers for Disease Control and Prevention. (2017). *About diabetes*. www.cdc.gov/diabetes/basics/diabetes.html

Chiappinelli, K. B., Moss, B. L., Lenz, D. S., Tonge, N. A., Joyce, A., Holt, G. E., … Woolsey, T. A. (2016). Evaluation to improve a high school summer science outreach program. *Journal of Microbiology & Biology Education*, 17(2), 225. https://doi.org/10.1128/jmbe.v17i2.1003

Christenson, J. A., & Warner, P. D. (1985). Extension's future is today. *Journal of Extension*, 23(2). https://archives.joe.org/joe/1985summer/a6.php

Contreras, F. (2011). Strengthening the bridge to higher education for academically promising underrepresented students. *Journal of Advanced Academics*, 22(3), 500–526. https://doi.org/10.1177/1932202X1102200306

Creswell, J. W. (2013). *Qualitative inquiry and research design: Choosing among five approaches*. Sage.

Crossgrove, J., Scheer, S. D., Conklin, N. L., Jones, J. M., & Safrit, R. D. (2005). Organizational values perceived as evident among Ohio State University Extension personnel. *Journal of Extension*, 43(5). https://archives.joe.org/joe/2005october/rb6.php

De Ciantis, D., Fox, J., Gaolach, B., Jacobsen, J., Obropta, C., Proden, P., Ruemenapp, M. A., Squires, J., Vavrina, C., Wagoner, S., Willis, M. J., & Young, J. (2015). *A national framework for urban extension*. https://docs.wixstatic.com/ugd/c34867_668cd0780daf4ea18cb1daddad557c72.pdf

Desilver, D. (2017). 5 ways the U.S. workforce has changed, a decade since the Great Recession began. *Pew Research.* www.pewresearch.org/fact-tank/2017/11/30/5-ways-the-u-s-workforce-has-changed-a-decade-since-the-great-recession-began

DuPuis, N. (2019). America's fastest growing cities are becoming more diverse, but face rising inequity. *CitiesSpeak*, National League of Cities, April 5. www .nlc.org/article/2019/04/05/americas-fastest-growing-cities-are-becoming-more-diverse-but-face-rising-inequity/

Durlak, J. A., & DuPre, E. P. (2008). Implementation matters: A review of research on the influence of implementation on program outcomes and the factors affecting implementation. *American Journal of Community Psychology*, 41(3), 327–350. https://doi.org/10.1007/s10464-008-9165-0

Farrell, C. R., & Lee, B. A. (2011). Racial diversity and change in metropolitan neighborhoods. *Social Science Research*, 40(4), 1108–1123. https://doi .org/10.1016/j.ssresearch.2011.04.003

Fehlis, C. P. (1992). Urban extension programs. *Journal of Extension*, 30(2). https://archives.joe.org/joe/1992summer/a3.php

Fields, N. I. (2017). The contribution of urban 4-H to social capital and the implications for social justice. *Journal of Extension*, 55(6), 52. https://tigerprints .clemson.edu/joe/vol55/iss6/52

Fox, J. (2021). Staffing: Preparing the urban Extension workforce. In M. E. Aitken, J Norman, & B. Gaolach (Eds.), *National urban extension conference: Leading edge dialogue series.* Western Center for Metropolitan Extension and Research. https://s3.wp.wsu.edu/uploads/sites/2164/2021/01/Workforce-LED-1.19.21.pdf

Fox, J. M., Ruemenapp, M. A., Proden, P., & Gaolach, B. (2017). A national framework for urban Extension. *Journal of Extension*, 55(5). https://tigerprints .clemson.edu/joe/vol55/iss5/21

Franz, N. (2014). Measuring and articulating the value of community engagement: Lessons learned from 100 years of Cooperative Extension work. *Journal of Higher Education Outreach and Engagement*, 18(2), 5–18. http://openjournals .libs.uga.edu/index.php/jheoe/article/view/1231/75

Franz, N., & Townson, L. (2008). The nature of complex organizations: The case of Cooperative Extension. In M. T. Braverman, M. Engle, M. E. Arnold, & R. A. Rennekamp (Eds.), *Program evaluation in a complex organizational system: Lessons from Cooperative Extension* (pp. 5–14). New Directions for Evaluation, 120. Jossey-Bass. https://doi.org/10.1002/ev.272

Franz, N. K. (2015). Programming for the public good: Ensuring public value through the Cooperative Extension program development model. *Journal of Human Sciences and Extension*, 3(2), 13. https://lib.dr.iastate.edu/ edu_pubs/13

Frey, W. H. (2021, October 28). 2020 Census: Big cities grew and became more diverse, especially among their youth. *Brookings.* www.brookings.edu/ research/2020-census-big-cities-grew-and-became-more-diverse-especially-among-their-youth/?utm_campaign=Brookings%20Brief&utm_medium=email&utm_content=176605830&utm_source=hs_email

Furlong, J., & Lawn, M. (Eds.). (2010). *Disciplines of education: Their role in the future of education research*. Routledge. https://doi.org/10.4324/9780203844137

Gagnon, R. J., Garst, B. A., & Franz, N. K. (2015). Looking ahead: Envisioning the future of the Extension program development model. *Journal of Human Sciences and Extension*, 3(2), 170. https://lib.dr.iastate.edu/edu_pubs/10

Galea, S., & Vlahov, D. (2015). Urban health: Evidence, challenges, and directions. *Annual Review of Public Health. 2005*, 26, 341–365. https://doi.org/10.1146/annurev.publhealth.26.021304.144708

Gaolach, B., Kern, M., & Sanders, C. (2017). Urban Extension: Aligning with the needs of urban audiences through subject-matter centers. *Journal of Human Sciences and Extension*, 5(2). www.jhseonline.com/article/view/713

Gleeson, B. (2014). *The urban condition*. Routledge.

Gonzalez, M., White, A. J., Vega, L., Howard, J., Kokozos, M., & Soule, K. E. (2020). "Making the Best Better" for Youths: Cultivating LGBTQ+ Inclusion in 4-H. *Journal of Extension*, 58(4), Article 3. https://tigerprints.clemson.edu/joe/vol58/iss4/3

Gould, F. I., Steele, D., & Woodrum, W. (2014). Cooperative extension: A century of innovation. *Journal of Extension*, 52(1). https://archives.joe.org/joe/2014february/comm1.php

Graham, S., Munniksma, A., & Juvonen, J. (2014). Psychosocial benefits of cross ethnic friendships in urban middle schools. *Child Development*, 85(2), 469–483. https://doi.org/10.1111/cdev.12159

Hains, K., Young, J., Reinhard, A., & Hains, B. (2021). Reconsidering Extension: Defining urban Extension in Kentucky. *Journal of Human Sciences and Extension*, 9(2), 191–205.

Hallal, B. (2016, August 17). Cleaving the crooked mirror: What's really behind the East & West side rivalry. *Thrillist*. www.thrillist.com/lifestyle/cleveland/cleveland-ohio-east-west-side-history

Hancock, D. R., & Algozzine, B. (2017). *Doing case study research: A practical guide for beginning researchers*. Teachers College Press.

Hartley, J. F. (1994). Case studies in organizational research. In C. Cassell and G. Symon (Eds.), *Qualitative methods in organizational research: A practical guide* (pp. 208–229). Sage.

Haynes, D., Michaels, A., & Fox, J. (2021). *OSU Extension in urban communities: A case study* [Manuscript submitted for publication]. Department of Extension, The Ohio State University.

Henning, J., Buchholz, D., Steele, D., & Ramaswamy, S. (2014). Milestones and the future for cooperative extension. *Journal of Extension*, 52(6). https://archives.joe.org/joe/2014december/comm1.php

Howard, J., McCoy, T., & Wang, C. (2021). Nationwide perspectives and experiences of gay and bisexual male 4-H alums. *Journal of Human Sciences and Extension*, 9(3), 107–132. www.jhseonline.com/article/view/1152

Jacob, S. G., Willtis, F. K., & Crider, D. M. (1991). *Citizen use of cooperative extension in Pennsylvania: An analysis of statewide survey data*. Pennsylvania State University College of Agriculture.

John, S., Lyerly, R., Wilde, P., Cohen, E. D., Lawson, E., & Nunn, A. (2021). The case for a National SNAP Fruit and Vegetable Incentive Program. *American Journal of Public Health*, 111(1), 27–29. https://doi.org/10.2105/AJPH.2020.305987

Jongbloed, B., Enders, J., & Salerno, C. (2008). Higher education and its communities: Interconnections, interdependencies and a research agenda. *Higher Education*, 56(3), 303–324. https://doi.org/10.1007/s10734-008-9128-2

Kaur, H., & Garg, P. (2019). Urban sustainability assessment tools: A review. *Journal of Cleaner Production*, 210, 146–158. https://doi.org/10.1016/j.jclepro.2018.11.009

Kellogg Commission on the Future of State, Land-Grant Universities, National Association of State Universities, & Land-Grant Colleges. (1999). *Returning to our roots: The engaged institution* (Vol. 3). National Association of State Universities and Land-Grant Colleges, Office of Public Affairs.

King, D. A., & Boehlje, M. D. (2013). A return to the basics: The solution for eXtension. *Journal of Extension*, 51(5), 5. https://archives.joe.org/joe/2013october/comm2.php

Kinsey, J. (2019). *Workplace wellness: Ways to increase your physical activity on the job.* Cooperative Extension Fact Sheet FS1107. Accessed from https://njaes.rutgers.edu/fs1107/

Kosciw, J. G., Clark, C. M., Truong, N. L., & Zongrone, A. D. (2020). *The 2019 national school climate survey: The experiences of lesbian, gay, bisexual, transgender, and queer youth in our nation's schools.* GLSEN. www.glsen.org/sites/default/files/2021-04/NSCS19-FullReport-032421-Web_0.pdf

Krehl, A., & Weck, S. (2020). Doing comparative case study research in urban and regional studies: What can be learnt from practice? *European Planning Studies*, 28(9), 1858–1876. https://doi.org/10.1080/09654313.2019.1699909

Krofta, J., & Panshin, D. (1989). Big-city imperative: Agenda for action. *Journal of Extension*, 27(3). https://archives.joe.org/joe/1989fall/a1.php

Krohn, J., Davis-Manigaulte, J., Fulcher, C., & Tiffany, J. S. (2022). Visualizing Diversity: Spatial Data as a Resource Enabling Extension to Better Engage Communities. Journal of Human Sciences and Extension, 10(2), 4.

Larson, L. R., Jennings, V., & Cloutier, S. A. (2016). Public parks and well-being in urban areas of the United States. *PLOS One*, 11(4), Article e0153211. https://doi.org/10.1371/journal.pone.0153211

Lauckner, H., Paterson, M., & Krupa, T. (2012). *Using constructivist case study methodology to understand community development processes: Proposed methodological questions to guide the research process.* Qualitative Report, 17, Article 25.

Lincoln, Y. S., & Guba, E. G. (1985). *Naturalistic inquiry.* Sage Publications Inc. https://doi.org/10.1016/0147-1767(85)90062-8

Lyon, L., & Driskell, R. (2011). *The community in urban society.* Waveland Press.

Maggino, F. (2016). *Challenges, needs, and risks in defining well-being indicators. A life devoted to quality of life* (pp. 209–233). Springer. https://doi.org/10.1007/978-3-319-20568-7_13

Mays, N., & Pope, C. (1995). Qualitative research: Rigour and qualitative research. *BMJ*, 311(6997), 109–112. https://doi.org/10.1136/bmj.311.6997.109

McDonnell, J., Staffenova, M., Ripberger, C., Shernoff, D., et al. (2019). *Promoting STEM interest and identity through the 4-H STEM Ambassadors Program.* Accessed from www.nsta.org/connected-science-learning/connected-science-learning-january-march-2019/promoting-stem-interest

Meissner, F., & Vertovec, S. (2015). Comparing super-diversity. *Ethnic and Racial Studies,* 38(4), 541–555. https://doi.org/10.1080/01419870.2015.980295

Merriam, S. B. (1988). *Case study research in education: A qualitative approach.* Jossey-Bass.

Merriam, S. B., & Tisdell, E. J. (2016). *Qualitative research: A guide to design and implementation.* John Wiley & Sons.

Morgan, S. J., Pullon, S. R., Macdonald, L. M., McKinlay, E. M., & Gray, B. V. (2017). Case study observational research: A framework for conducting case study research where observation data are the focus. *Qualitative Health Research,* 27(7), 1060–1068. https://doi.org/10.1177/1049732316649160

Morrison, E., Hutcheson, S., Nilsen, E., Fadden, J., & Franklin, N. (2019). *Strategic doing: Ten skills for agile leadership.* John Wiley & Sons.

Narine, L. K., Ali, A. D., & Hill, P. A. (2021). Assessing rural and urban community assets and needs to inform Extension program planning. *Journal of Human Sciences and Extension,* 9(1), 109–122. www.jhseonline.com/article/view/1012

National Center for Healthy Housing. (2011). *Seven principles of healthy homes.* Retrieved from www.nchh.org/WhatWeDo/HealthyHomesPrinciples.aspx

National Center for Healthy Housing. (2013). *State of healthy housing.* Retrieved from www.nchh.org/Policy/2013StateofHealthyHousing.aspx

National Extension Urban Task Force. (1996). *Urban extension: A national agenda.* Extension Committee on Organization and Policy National Extension Urban Task Force.

National Urban Extension Leaders (NUEL). (2015). *A national framework for urban Extension: A report from the National Urban Extension Leaders.* http://media.wix.com/ugd/c34867_668cd0780daf4ea18cb1daddad557c72.pdf

Ohio State University. (2021). *Community connectors: Susan Colbert.* https://engage.osu.edu/community-connectors-susan-colbert

Ohio State University. (n.d.). *Home buyer education.* https://franklin.osu.edu/program-areas/community-development/home-buyer-education

Prilleltensky, I., Dietz, S., Prilleltensky, O., Myers, N. D., Rubenstein, C. L., Jin, Y., & McMahon, A. (2015). Assessing multidimensional well-being: Development and validation of the I COPPE scale. *Journal of Community Psychology,* 43(2), 199–226. https://doi.org/10.1002/jcop.21674

Raison, B. (2014). Doing the work of Extension: Three approaches to identify, amplify, and implement outreach. *Journal of Extension,* 52(2). https://archives.joe.org/joe/2014april/a1.php

Rath, T., Harter, J. K., & Harter, J. (2010). *Well-being: The five essential elements.* Simon and Schuster.

Reine, I, Novo, M, & Hammarström, A. (2012). Unemployment and ill health – A gender analysis: Results from a 14-year follow-up of the northern Swedish

cohort. *Public Health (London)*, 127(3), 214–222. https://doi.org/10.1016/j
.puhe.2012.12.005

Robert Woods Johnson Foundation. (2013). How does employment – Or
unemployment – Affect health? *Health Policy Snapshot.* www.rwjf.org/en/
insights/our-research/2012/12/how-does-employment--or-unemployment--
affect-health-.html

Rosenstock, S., Whitman, S., West, J. F., & Balkin, M. (2014). Racial disparities in diabetes mortality in the 50 most populous US cities. *Journal of Urban
Health*, 91(5), 873–885. https://doi.org/10.1007/s11524-013-9861-4

Ruemenapp, M. A. (2018). *Factors influencing delivery of Cooperative Extension
Service programs to urban audiences.* Michigan State University.

Rutgers. (n.d.). *Join the 4-H STEM ambassadors program.* https://nj4h.rutgers
.edu/join-stem-ambassadors/

Schafer, J. M., Huegel, C. N., & Mazzotti, F. J. (1992). Expanding into the urban
arena. *Journal of Extension*, 30(2). https://archives.joe.org/joe/1992summer/a2.php

Sellers, D. M., Meinertz, N. R., & Schainker, L. M. (2020). The development,
implementation, and evaluation of a pilot program designed to enhance well-
being through self-identified lifestyle changes. *Journal of Human Sciences and
Extension*, 8(2), 223–236. www.jhseonline.com/article/view/1066

Smith, S. D., Rowan, N. L., Arms, T. E., Hohn, K. L., & Galbraith, C. S. (2021).
An interdisciplinary approach to enhancing health knowledge and cultural
awareness with LGBT older adults. *Educational Gerontology*, 47(2), 79–85.
https://doi.org/10.1080/03601277.2021.1876584

Soule, K. E. (2017). Creating inclusive youth programs for LGBTQ+ communities. *Journal of Human Sciences and Extension*, 5(2). www.jhseonline.com/
article/view/712

Stake, R. E. (1995). *The art of case study research.* Sage.

Stanton, T. K. (2012). New times demand new scholarship II: Research universities and civic engagement: Opportunities and challenges. *Journal of Higher
Education Outreach and Engagement*, 16(4), 271–304.

Stanton-Salazar, R. D., & Spina, S. U. (2005). Adolescent peer networks as a
context for social and emotional support. *Youth and Society*, 36(4), 379–417.
https://doi.org/10.1177/0044118X04267814

Stevenson, H. H. (1983). *A perspective on entrepreneurship* (Vol. 13). Harvard
Business School.

Suarez-Balcazar, Y. (2020). Meaningful engagement in research: Community residents as co-creators of knowledge. *American Journal of Community Psychology*,
65(3–4), 261–271. https://doi.org/10.1002/ajcp.12414

Taşan-Kok, T., Stead, D., & Lu, P. (2013). *Conceptual overview of resilience:
History and context. Resilience thinking in urban planning* (pp. 39–51). Springer.
https://doi.org/10.1007/978-94-007-5476-8_3

Thomas, G. (2011). A typology for the case study in social science following a
review of definition, discourse, and structure. *Qualitative Inquiry*, 17(6),
511–521. https://doi.org/10.1177/1077800411409884

Tiffany, J. S. (2017). Extension in the city: Meeting the challenges of scale. *Journal of Human Sciences and Extension*, 5(2). www.jhseonline.com/article/view/708

Tiwari, S., & Ambinakudige, S. (2021). Neighborhood food insecurity index to identify food vulnerability and food deserts in the United States. *Journal of Food Security*, 9(4), 148–159. https://doi.org/10.12691/jfs-9-4-2

UN Habitat. (2013). *State of the world's cities 2012/2013: Prosperity of cities.* Routledge.

University of Maryland. (n.d.). *Master Money Mentors.* https://extension.umd.edu/programs/family-consumer-sciences/financial-wellness/master-money-mentors

University of Missouri. (n.d.). *About worksite wellness.* https://extension.missouri.edu/programs/worksite-wellness/about-worksite-wellness

University of Nevada-Reno. (n.d.). *Results from a workplace health and wellness program.* https://extension.unr.edu/publication.aspx?PubID=2516

US Census Bureau. (2020, September 15). *Income and Poverty in the United States: 2019.* The United States Census Bureau. www.census.gov/library/publications/2020/demo/p60-270.html#:%7E:text=Median%20household%20income%20was%20%2468%2C703,and%20Table%20A%2D1

Warner, L. A., Vavrina, C. S., Campbell, M. L., Elliott, M. L., Northrop, R. J., & Place, N. T. (2017). A strategic plan for introducing, implementing, managing, and monitoring an urban Extension platform. *Journal of Extension*, 55(3). https://tigerprints.clemson.edu/joe/vol55/iss3/22/

Warner, P. D., Christenson, J. A., Dillman, D. A., & Salant, P. (1996). Public perception of Extension. *Journal of Extension*, 34(4). https://archives.joe.org/joe/1996august/a1.php

Webster, N. (2016). 4-H and its relevance in the era of# moments in urban communities. *Journal of Extension*, 54(1), 29. https://tigerprints.clemson.edu/joe/vol54/iss1/29/

Webster, N., & Ingram, P. (2007). Exploring the challenges for Extension educators working in urban communities. *Journal of Extension*, 45(3). https://archives.joe.org/joe/2007june/iw3.php

Weinfield, N. S., Mills, G., et al. (2014). *Hunger in America Report 2014.* Chicago, IL. Feeding America. Accessed from www.feedingamerica.org/sites/default/files/2020-02/hunger-in-america-2014-full-report.pdf

Western Extension Directors Association Urban Task Force. (2010). *Final report of the urban task force.* http://extension.oregonstate.edu/weda/reports-publications

Wickliffe, J., Coates, T., Rodas, J., Pomeroy, M., Carrillo, U., Luaces, M. A., Twillman, N., Ilabaca-Somoza, X., Meyer, M., Williams, L. H., & Ramaswamy, M. (2020). Description of a Twenty-Year Initiative to Bring STEM Career Exploration to Urban Minority Youth in Kansas City, Kansas: Multi-Sector Investment and Program Evolution. *JSO*, 3(2).

Wirth, L. (1938). Urbanism as a way of life. *American Journal of Sociology*, 44(1), 1–24. https://doi.org/10.1086/217913

World Health Organization. (2014). *Urban population growth*. Geneva, Switzerland: Global Health Observatory Database. www.who.int/gho/urban_health/situation_trends/urban_population_growth_text/en

Yin, R. K. (2003). *Case study research: Design and methods* (3rd ed.). Sage.

Yin, R. K. (2011). *Applications of case study research*. Sage.

individual who is the direct biological parent. One vitally important way to support families is for communities to support the provision of high-quality early childhood experiences for *all* children.

5.1 Evidence for Quality of Early Experiences: A Bioecological Framework

Early childhood is a critical period of lifespan development and can be understood using Bronfenbrenner's bioecological framework. The framework recognizes the bidirectional associations among children's early health and development and the contextual experiences that either enhance or impede it over time (Bronfenbrenner, 2005; Swick & Williams, 2006). The framework highlights community systems, which include cultural values, institutional structures, interactions among and between families and other systems; the family system itself, and individuals all interact to influence child and family well-being. The ecological feature of this framework, with its emphasis on proximal processes, suggests that the experiences children have with their primary caregivers during the first few years of life have the potential to create rich opportunities for early skill development, but that children are not passive recipients of influence in the process (Huston & Bentley, 2010). For example, when parents and caregivers talk to and read with young children, pointing to the pictures in the book and naming the objects, the child is learning about concepts, vocabulary, and how to respond to the caregiver. The child's responses encourage the adult to continue the interaction. The increase in language input and positive feedback creates a cascade of neuronal development and faster neural networks in the brain that drive cognitive development (Romeo et al., 2018).

Bronfenbrenner's bioecological framework also draws attention to the environments in which child and caregiver interactions occur. Families' and caregivers' abilities to provide the type of support that promotes optimal child development are often dependent on caregivers' knowledge and education, as well as the norms and expectations within the community where they reside. Factors that exist within the caregivers' most proximal environments, such as having differential access to health care, education, parenting knowledge, and information can impact a child's well-being (Rowe, 2017). Communities vary in accessibility of resources and programming including the amount and visibility of educational resources, availability of books, and occupational opportunities (Neumann et al., 2012).

Adults are more likely to provide the type of environment and experiences needed to support optimal child development when they have more

PART II

Addressing Key Issues in the Well-Being of Children, Youth, and Families

Extension's Role in Supporting
Young Children's Well-Being

Constance C. Beecher and Teresa A. Byingt[...]

The Cooperative Extension System (CES) land-grant mission [...]
the public good through higher education and to more fully [...]
fits for society" (APLU Task Force on the New Engageme[...]
Team, 2016). To fulfill this mission, CES broadly aims to [...]
knowledge, integrate with and expand community partne[...]
advance the translation of research into evidence-based practic[...]
residents of the states. The research that is translated and the fo[...]
gramming have evolved over time, from Extension's initial em[...]
innovative farming practices to today's inclusion of STEM (scie[...]
nology, engineering, and math) in youth-based programming, an[...]
ship in innovation to improve community health (e.g., Gould et a[...]
This chapter focuses on an area of programming that has not alw[...]
at the forefront of Extension efforts but that is gaining increased i[...]
supporting health and well-being in early childhood.

In this chapter, we will discuss the various approaches, theoretic[...]
els, and issues addressed by Extension in early childhood progran[...]
Many of the programs focus on families, which are critically import[...]
supporting young children's optimal development. It is important t[...]
that families can be thought of as units that have many different con[...]
tions. According to Learning for Justice (n.d.), a family is "a group o[...]
ple going through the world together, often adults and the children[...]
care for." Families are diverse and include single-parent, adoptive,[...]
foster families. Lesbian, gay, bisexual, and transgender individuals [...]
be raising one or more children as parents. Children may be living [...]
grandparents, extended family members, or splitting time among differ[...]
family members. Thus, in this chapter, we will use the term "family"[...]
mean a single adult or group of adults caring for a child. We will use t[...]
terms "parent" and "caregiver" to indicate an adult with legal responsib[...]
ity for the child, with the understanding that this may or may not be a[...]

Addressing Key Issues in the Well-Being of Children, Youth, and Families

Extension's Role in Supporting Young Children's Well-Being

Constance C. Beecher and Teresa A. Byington

The Cooperative Extension System (CES) land-grant mission is "to achieve the public good through higher education and to more fully realize benefits for society" (APLU Task Force on the New Engagement Planning Team, 2016). To fulfill this mission, CES broadly aims to democratize knowledge, integrate with and expand community partnerships, and advance the translation of research into evidence-based practice to benefit residents of the states. The research that is translated and the focus of programming have evolved over time, from Extension's initial emphasis on innovative farming practices to today's inclusion of STEM (science, technology, engineering, and math) in youth-based programming, and leadership in innovation to improve community health (e.g., Gould et al., 2014). This chapter focuses on an area of programming that has not always been at the forefront of Extension efforts but that is gaining increased interest – supporting health and well-being in early childhood.

In this chapter, we will discuss the various approaches, theoretical models, and issues addressed by Extension in early childhood programming. Many of the programs focus on families, which are critically important for supporting young children's optimal development. It is important to note that families can be thought of as units that have many different compositions. According to Learning for Justice (n.d.), a family is "a group of people going through the world together, often adults and the children they care for." Families are diverse and include single-parent, adoptive, and foster families. Lesbian, gay, bisexual, and transgender individuals may be raising one or more children as parents. Children may be living with grandparents, extended family members, or splitting time among different family members. Thus, in this chapter, we will use the term "family" to mean a single adult or group of adults caring for a child. We will use the terms "parent" and "caregiver" to indicate an adult with legal responsibility for the child, with the understanding that this may or may not be an individual who is the direct biological parent. One vitally important way to support families is for communities to support the provision of high-quality early childhood experiences for *all* children.

5.1   Evidence for Quality of Early Experiences: A Bioecological Framework

Early childhood is a critical period of lifespan development and can be understood using Bronfenbrenner's bioecological framework. The framework recognizes the bidirectional associations among children's early health and development and the contextual experiences that either enhance or impede it over time (Bronfenbrenner, 2005; Swick & Williams, 2006). The framework highlights community systems, which include cultural values, institutional structures, interactions among and between families and other systems; the family system itself, and individuals all interact to influence child and family well-being. The ecological feature of this framework, with its emphasis on proximal processes, suggests that the experiences children have with their primary caregivers during the first few years of life have the potential to create rich opportunities for early skill development, but that children are not passive recipients of influence in the process (Huston & Bentley, 2010). For example, when parents and caregivers talk to and read with young children, pointing to the pictures in the book and naming the objects, the child is learning about concepts, vocabulary, and how to respond to the caregiver. The child's responses encourage the adult to continue the interaction. The increase in language input and positive feedback creates a cascade of neuronal development and faster neural networks in the brain that drive cognitive development (Romeo et al., 2018).

Bronfenbrenner's bioecological framework also draws attention to the environments in which child and caregiver interactions occur. Families' and caregivers' abilities to provide the type of support that promotes optimal child development are often dependent on caregivers' knowledge and education, as well as the norms and expectations within the community where they reside. Factors that exist within the caregivers' most proximal environments, such as having differential access to health care, education, parenting knowledge, and information can impact a child's well-being (Rowe, 2017). Communities vary in accessibility of resources and programming including the amount and visibility of educational resources, availability of books, and occupational opportunities (Neumann et al., 2012).

Adults are more likely to provide the type of environment and experiences needed to support optimal child development when they have more knowledge on how children grow and develop (Leung & Suskind, 2020). Children living in communities where there is ready access to learning opportunities and supportive social networks generally have more enriching environments and experiences. Conversely, when adults have less education, higher levels of stress, and less access to resources and support, they are less likely to provide enriching environments that optimize child development (e.g., see DeVoe et al., 2019). Therefore, ecological approaches that foreground individuals' and communities' needs, assets, and circumstances will create the kind of long-term impact necessary to support children's well-being and positive development.

5.2   Child Well-Being

The Research Center for Childhood Well-being defines well-being as the quality of an individuals' life, noting that "it is a dynamic state of living that is enhanced when people are able to fulfill their personal and social goals" (Statham & Chase, 2010, p. 2). In a systematic review of child well-being studies, Pollard and Lee (2003) identified five distinct domains therein, namely:

- Physical well-being: Nutrition, physical activity, personal body care, immunizations, and safety-related behaviors;
- Psychological well-being: Emotions, attachment, coping skills, resilience, and mental health;
- Cognitive well-being: Intellectual, school attendance, and educational experiences;
- Social well-being: Family relationships, quality of life, peer and other relationships; and
- Economic well-being: financial aspects and support for daily living needs (e.g., food security).

Child well-being must also be considered in the context of family well-being, regardless of the family structure. In addition to the five elements identified, family factors such as caregiver education levels, stress levels, and the relationship stability of adults can also impact child well-being (Moeller et al., 2016). Programs that will be described later focus on the broader family.

5.3   The Role of Extension as a System of Support and Influence

The CES has a history of delivering programming designed to positively impact participants' knowledge, attitudes, skills, and behaviors. Extension professionals disseminate information to clientele through both research and various practitioner outlets, as well as direct programming (Burkhart-Kriesel et al., 2019). One strength of Extension is its collaborative approach, particularly in establishing long-term partnerships with community organizations to address issues. Well-established partnerships allow for rapid responses to community needs and sustained efforts. When a crisis or natural disaster occurs, Extension can serve a critically important need by providing evidence-informed programming. For example, the Read for Resilience program at the University of Nebraska provided storybook guides and recommended children's books to support young children's coping and understanding of emotions in the aftermath of the blizzards and floods that rampaged the central regions of the state in 2019. As part of these efforts, Extension professionals also engage in translational research by evaluating their efforts to ensure that programs are relevant to the needs of the community and achieving targeted outcomes (see Monk, this volume).

Figure 5.1 is a depiction of a holistic approach to Extension programming focused on the young child's well-being. This diagram highlights how child well-being can be supported by programs that increase capacity among childcare providers and educators, as well as by efforts that foster family well-being. For example, Extension programs designed to bolster adult relationships, financial stability, and health and nutrition indirectly support a healthy family environment, which in turn supports child development. Figure 5.1 also summarizes the connections among Extension programming for adults, family well-being, parenting, childcare provider/ teacher education, and child well-being.

Indeed, Extension systems in many states take a comprehensive, multidisciplinary approach to addressing complex problems that directly or indirectly impact children's well-being. For example, Colorado State University's multifaceted family enrichment program taught families strategies designed to support healthy relationships, parenting, and financial literacy. Evaluation of this program indicated positive participant outcomes in measures of positive family functioning, parenting alliance, and relationship satisfaction (Tompkins et al., 2014). These findings highlight the effectiveness of delivering education on the full range of parenting that in turn impact the quality of parent–child relationships and family functioning, and ultimately improve child well-being. In Section 5.4, we provide examples of programs targeting well-being in early childhood, recognizing that other types of Extension programming also have positive impacts on this population. We will also identify some themes that cut across programming approaches and propose suggestions for future research and program considerations.

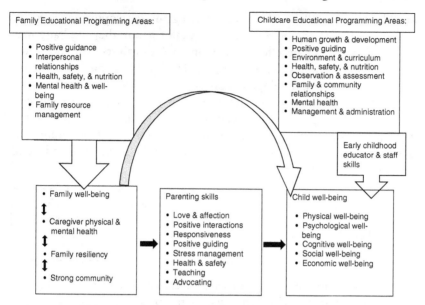

Figure 5.1   Holistic model of the Cooperative Extension System support for child well-being.

5.4   Extension Early Childhood Programming

Within the field of early childhood, Extension provides a variety of programs that directly target young children, families, and early childhood educators. We will give examples that illustrate the responsiveness of Extension personnel to community needs in four main areas: parenting education, early childhood education, health and nutrition education, and emergent and evolving trends in early childhood. The programming in each of these areas focuses on a wide range of topics that include school readiness, childhood obesity, and mindfulness; and which help educators gain knowledge and skills to support children's socio-cognitive, physical, language, and social-emotional development.

5.4.1   Areas of Early Childhood Extension Programming

5.4.1.1   Parenting Education

Parenting young children is an important and challenging responsibility. "Parenting" here includes the multiple roles and identities of adults who are caring for children. Although all parents and caregivers need knowledge and skills in effectively meeting the developmental needs of young children, many do not receive the information they need and may feel ill-equipped to be effective parents and caregivers. Families often struggle with children's challenging behaviors. They may not know how to identify effective and developmentally appropriate ways to enhance young children's growth and development. As a result, some parents need support in establishing realistic expectations of what children can and cannot do. Parenting education can help families and caregivers feel more confident in their skills and abilities to provide positive guidance and build healthy relationships with young children.

> The National Association for Education of the Young Child (2019) defines "developmentally appropriate practice" as methods that promote each child's optimal development and learning through a strengths-based, play-based approach to joyful, engaged learning.

Parenting education programs are diverse and sometimes focus on specific age groups of children, such as the preschool or teenage years. Parenting education programs can also target specific audiences such as divorced parents, grandparents, foster parents, or families that have experienced domestic violence. One common factor among most of Extension's parenting education programs is that they provide access to research-based information, often through educational classes. Teaching positive parenting skills to improve parents' knowledge, coping, and problem-solving skills has been shown to promote positive long-term outcomes for children (Bornstein, 2003). When caregivers develop warm and responsive relationships with young children, they reduce the long-term negative effects of poverty, stress, and trauma that children may experience (Prenatal-to-3 Policy Impact Center, 2021). Additionally, parental knowledge of child development is a contributing factor in the increase of positive interactions between adults and children (Leung & Suskind, 2020). These studies, as well as many others, demonstrate the importance of parenting education in positively influencing child well-being. The following are examples of programs offered within Extension across the United States.

Just in Time Parenting, National Network of Extension Specialists (JITP). JITP is an electronically delivered age-paced parenting newsletter developed by a national network of Extension Specialists from twenty-four land-grant universities. JITP is designed to reach parents at teachable, transitional moments with research-based information about pregnancy, parenting, and child development from prenatal to five years old. Newsletters are designed to provide families with relevant information in a timely manner and are available in English and Spanish. Over 50,000 website users from all fifty states view the JITP website each year with over 13,000 families subscribing to the newsletter. Evaluations of the effectiveness of these parenting newsletters have shown that they increase parents' knowledge of child development, their parenting self-confidence, and their ability to be nurturing and engage in positive parenting behaviors (Kim et al., 2015). (Contact: Anne Clarkson, anne.clarkson@wisc.edu, https://jitp.info)

Building Early Emotional Skills (BEES), Michigan State University Extension. BEES is a series of classes for parents and caregivers of children ages zero to three years. It was designed to help audiences support children's social and emotional development. The curriculum focuses on four main goals: (1) building parental awareness of emotions in self and child; (2) listening and interacting sensitively with the child; (3) identifying and labeling emotions; and (4) intentionally supporting early self-regulation skills. Over the course of eight units, participants learn about temperaments and how these traits can impact behavior. They learn strategies for strengthening their child's social emotional development as well as how to manage stress and conflict within their families. The program is available in multiple format options including in-person, synchronous live webinars, and as an asynchronous cohort-based online course. A recent study of the program including delivery online or face-to-face platforms (N = 264 female caregivers; n = 214 online, n = 50 face-to-face) showed significant increases in knowledge, acceptance of negative emotions, and self-reported emotionally supportive responses to emotions. Additionally, there was a significant decrease in rejection of emotions, emotionally unsupportive responses, and parenting distress. Results suggested no differences in rate of change by program delivery type (Brophy-Herb et al., 2021). (Contact: Kendra Moyes, kmoyses@msu.edu)

Sustainable Community Project to Promote Early Language and Literacy Development in Native Communities, University of Arizona Extension. This comprehensive, community-based, and sustainable program is designed to promote early literacy in two American Indian communities in Arizona: the Nahata Dziil, Wide Ruins, Pine Springs, and Houck Chapters of the Navajo Nation and the communities on the San Carlos Apache Tribal Lands. The program was developed in collaboration with community stakeholders and in partnership with two community advisory boards to ensure that programming addressed community-identified needs and was culturally responsive. Programming targets a wide and inclusive range of caregivers including parents and other guardians; grandparents; extended family and other caring adults; Head Start teachers; pre-K teachers; center- and home-based childcare providers; and family, friend, and neighbor care providers. The program includes both single-session and multi-session programing designed to encourage caregivers to increase their time reading with young children, to improve the quality of their book-reading practices, and to increase the use of non-book-reading activities that promote early literacy. For example, non-book-reading activities (e.g., singing and storytelling) are encouraged because Apache and Navajo families have strong oral storytelling traditions. An aim of the program is to enhance community capacity to sustain high-quality early literacy programming through professional development workshops for early care and education teachers and providers. (Contact: Katherine Speirs, kspeirs@email.arizona.edu)

Gay, 2002 defines culturally responsive practice as using the experiences, strengths, and perspectives of children and their families as a tool to support them more effectively.

Magic Years, Cornell Cooperative Extension. Decades of research shows that children are affected by who their parents are, what their parents know, what their parents believe, what their parents value, what their parents expect of them, and what their parents do (Pew Charitable Trusts, 2009). Based on these findings, the Magic Years lessons are designed to provide Extension educators with tools and resources to explain best practices in child development and parenting to caregivers. The program targets families with children from birth to age four who want to enhance their parenting skills and aims to benefit the whole family. Classes assist participants in developing a deeper understanding of how their self-knowledge, parenting knowledge, and behavior affect their children. Participants have included military families, Head Start families, and families referred through the Department of Social Services Child Protective Services program. Program leaders reported the results of a pre/post survey from participants ($n = 48$). They found significant increases in six out of ten indicators of parenting knowledge and belief. Specifically, participants reported increased confidence in making rules which take their child's needs into consideration, increased time spent reading with their child, increased feelings of support, increased self-efficacy in the skills necessary to be a good caregiver, increases in how often they praise their child, and increased use of explanations for the rules they make (Korjenevitch, Dunifon, & Kopko, 2010). (Contact: Amanda Rae Root, arr27@cornell.edu)

The programs highlighted thus far are examples of Extension education targeted at increasing parents' and caregivers' knowledge of child development, with emphasis on cognitive and social-emotional development. Next, we will look at programming focused on children's health and physical development.

5.4.1.2   Health and Nutrition Education

Extension health and nutrition programming is designed to improve the physical health of community members through healthy food choices and physical activity. One of the most well-known examples of initiatives with broad reach in this area is the Supplemental Nutrition Assistance Program – Education (SNAP-Ed, see Franzen-Castle, this volume). SNAP-Ed targets individuals using or eligible for the Supplemental Nutrition Assistance Program (SNAP) and is designed to help participants increase their knowledge about healthy eating habits, how to make their food dollars stretch further, and strategies for increasing physical activity. In addition to SNAP-Ed, numerous Extension programs are developed and delivered in partnership with community organizations as they collaborate to teach nutrition education classes, employ social marketing campaigns, and work to improve the policies, systems, and environment of their communities. Below are some examples, along with contact information of key leaders.

Little Book and Little Cooks, University of Nevada, Reno Extension. Little Books and Little Cooks (SNAP-Ed funded) is a seven-week parenting education program for preschool-age children (three–five years old) and their parents designed to promote healthy eating, family literacy, parent–child interaction, and children's school-readiness skills. During the program, children and parents come together to learn about healthy eating and nutrition, gain positive parent–child interaction skills, and practice school-readiness skills. Parents and children read children's books about healthy eating and nutrition and have opportunities to cook and eat together. Each weekly session features a new book about healthy eating and a corresponding recipe. Researchers use a pre/post evaluation consisting of parent reports and an observation checklist to assess impact. Results indicate that parents view the program positively, and that there are significant increases in target behaviors including positive parent/child interactions, children and parents trying new foods, and consumption of fruits and vegetables (Kim, 2016). (Contact: YaeBin Kim, kimy@unr.edu)

The Kids Coupon Program – West Virginia University Extension. The Kids Coupon (or Kids Farmers Market) program gives children from low-income households $4 in tokens with which to purchase fresh, local fruits and vegetables from a market that is brought to childcare centers, schools, and community locations. Children and families also participate in nutrition education and food sampling. The program is organized and operated through SNAP-Ed and tokens are funded by private donors. The program has provided over 5,400 children across the state of West Virginia with vouchers. The overall objective of the program is to encourage young children to try new fruits and vegetables by giving them the buying power to make their own choices. Program directors have used parent-report surveys to evaluate impact. Results are promising, with 91 percent of parents reporting that their children ate the produce they purchased and that those children increased their knowledge about fruits and vegetables (McCartney et al., 2019). (Contact: Kristin McCartney, Kristen.McCartney@mail.wvu.edu)

iGrow Readers, South Dakota State University Extension. iGrow Readers is a series of six book-based lessons focused on helping children (pre-K to 3rd grade) understand the benefits of making healthy decisions involving nutrition and physical activity. In groups, children read books that reflect the themes of the program and then participate in nutrition and physical activities that reinforces the concepts covered in the readings. Companion parent newsletters encourage reading and healthy lifestyles at home. The program is designed for limited-resource audiences served through the SNAP-Ed and Expanded Food and Nutrition Education Program (EFNEP) and reaches approximately 4,000 young children each year. An initial evaluation using a pre/post survey with children and a feedback survey collected from teachers found a significant increase in knowledge of nutrition and physical activity for participants (Loes et al., 2015). (Contact: Kimberly Cripps, kimberly.cripps@sdstate.edu)

My TIME to Eat Healthy and Move More, University of Minnesota Extension. My TIME to Eat Healthy and Move More is a home-based program for parents or caregivers (e.g., grandparents, home-based early childhood providers) and their children ages three to five years. This unique program actively engages parents and children in a co-learning process as they experience making healthy food choices and becoming more physically active. By participating in this home-based program, parents and children learn about the importance of varying foods and physical activity for better health. Families have opportunities to prepare and eat healthy recipes and participate in physical activity while learning about the importance of daily exercise as a part of good health. Families also learn and practice ways to save money on groceries. The program consists of twenty-four 15-to-20-minute mini-lessons clustered into six units. Lessons occur in the family's home and mix instruction and activities, including games, exercise, reading, and tasting demonstrations. Although no published evaluation information is available, the program's directors report 340 families participated in a pilot evaluation. They report that children then consumed more fruits and vegetables, and families increased both their physical activity and their understanding of healthy eating (Caskey et al., 2018). (Contact: Mary Krentz, krentoo1@umn.edu)

5.4.2   *Early Childhood Education*

Early childhood educators play a key role in young children's well-being. Sixty percent of children ages three to five years in the United States spend an average of thirty-six hours a week in center-based childcare (Mamedova & Redford, 2019). Quality childcare is linked to children's cognitive development and overall well-being, and as such opportunities for educators to expand their knowledge and skills relevant to early childhood care is critical (Donoghue, 2017).

An environmental scan of early childhood professional development programs offered within the Extension system indicated that Extension played an essential role in providing professional development opportunities for early childhood professionals (Durden et al., 2013). Extension personnel often collaborated with multiple organizations within their states. Various partners such as Child Care Resource and Referral agencies, Health and Human Services, Head Start and Early Head Start, the Department of Education, Offices of Early Learning and Development, and the National Association for the Education of Young Children are engaged in working with Extension staff to support and enhance the quality of early childhood services. Extension personnel provided early childhood educators with a variety of training classes and online resources. Below are examples of programs and resources offered by Extension on the topic of early childhood education.

Better Kid Care, Penn State Extension. Penn State's Better Kid Care (BKC) has been providing online, evidence-informed professional development via its customized learning management system, OnDemand, since July 2011. Prior to 2011, BKC reached clientele through postal mail. Better Kid Care offers educational programming in a wide variety of topics including child growth and development; curriculum and learning experiences, health, safety, and nutrition; and organization and administration. The OnDemand system currently has 317 courses. Better Kid Care serves learners from all fifty states and more than sixty countries. Since 2011, more than 600,000 professionals have completed more than 2,370,000 courses, which equals approximately six million professional development hours. One study evaluating the impact of BKC indicated promising results. In in-depth interviews, most participants (79 percent) described specific, useful knowledge or skills (e.g., behavior management, communication with parents, environments for learning, and safety) they had gained from the programs. Eighty-five percent of respondents also described specific improvements they had made in their early care and education programs as a result of BKC (Ostergren et al., 2011). (Contact: Jill Cox, jnc14@psu.edu)

Infant Toddler Child Development Associate (CDA) Training and Coaching Program, University of Nevada, Reno Extension. The Infant Toddler CDA Training and Coaching Program is designed to improve the care and education of infants and toddlers. The program also increases career advancement opportunities for teachers completing the program and receiving the CDA credential from the national Council for Professional Development. The grant-funded program provides 120 hours of coursework across eight specific content areas through training and online modules, and bi-monthly coaching sessions with a knowledgeable, experienced coach to practice skills and discuss challenges. To earn the full credential, participants must also complete 480 hours of work in an infant/toddler classroom, assemble a professional portfolio, distribute and collect parent questionnaires from a majority of the families in their classroom, pass a comprehensive exam, and undergo teaching observation by a Child Development Associate Professional Development Specialist.

To determine the impact of the program, the CLASS (Classroom Assessment Scoring System), an observation instrument, has been used to assess the quality of teacher–child interactions. Findings suggest positive and significant gains in responsive caring among providers in infant classrooms between pre- and post-tests, and positive and significant gains in emotional and behavioral support and engaged support for learning among educators in the toddler classrooms. Teachers participating in the program reported that their teaching practices were strengthened, and that they had gained the skills and tools needed to be more confident and intentional teachers. (Contact: Teresa A. Byington, byingtont@unr.edu)

Early Care and Education Projects, University of Arkansas Cooperative Extension Service. Arkansas Cooperative Extension Service facilitates four, grant-funded childcare provider training programs that are free to the public. These training programs include Best Care, which is ten hours of face-to-face training created by state faculty and staff and facilitated by county extension agents who train around 2,400 childcare providers, foster parents, and teachers annually. Best Care Connected and Best Care Out-of-School-Time are each five hours online, created by state faculty and staff and presented in five one-hour modules. These programs target teachers and childcare providers. The Guiding Children Successfully program provides 2,000 participants with up to thirty-eight hours of online or correspondence training. The correspondence training is especially helpful for participants who live in areas with limited Internet access or who do not have access to computers or are uncomfortable using them. Approximately 6,000 childcare providers participate in these programs each year. (Contact: Brittany Schrick, bschrick@uaex.edu)

Passport to Early Childhood Education and Essentials Child Care Preservice, Iowa State University Extension and Outreach. Iowa State University Extension offers many different programs for early childhood professionals. These programs include the Passport to ECE Program Administrators course that provides online instruction in the observation of teaching practice, giving effective feedback, and supporting ongoing professional development. The three-week (six-hour) online course uses quick video mini-lessons that easily fit within busy schedules and include chat discussions with other program administrators. The curriculum is accessible by computer, tablet, or smartphone. The Passport to Early Childhood Education for Teachers and Staff online course introduces the basic skills and knowledge to teach and care for children in center-based programs. Teachers quickly learn through video lessons how to create support for early learning and build positive relationships. This eleven-hour online, self-paced curriculum is free, available 24/7, can be implemented immediately, and is designed to easily fit within early childhood professional's busy schedules.

The Essentials Child Care Preservice course is composed of twelve online sessions and must be completed by all beginning childcare providers in the state of Iowa. The course provides helpful answers to many questions about creating a safe and healthy early childhood environment, preparing for an emergency, transporting children, preventing and controlling infectious diseases, handling and storing hazardous materials, giving medication, managing food allergies, creating a safe sleep environment for infants, preventing shaken baby syndrome, understanding child development, supporting cultural diversity, and understanding homelessness. Over 11,000 early childhood professionals complete this course each year. (Contact: Lesia Oesterreich, loesterr@iastate.edu)

5.4.3   Recent and Evolving Trends in Early Childhood

Several new topics relevant to early childhood well-being are emerging within Extension. Examples of emerging issues include an increasing awareness of the need to address mental health and well-being among early childhood caregivers and educators, the use of technology in innovative ways to reach new audiences and provide valuable information to families, and the need for programming to address equity, diversity, and inclusion. The world continues to change and evolve. As such, it is critical that Extension professionals are open and responsive to addressing emerging issues that affect the well-being of young children. Below are examples of recently emergent programming.

5.4.3.1   Mindfulness Education

There is increasing evidence that mindfulness and reflective practices are promising and practical ways to prevent and reduce the stress of early childhood teachers. Saltzman (2011) defines mindfulness as paying attention to your life, here and now, with kindness and curiosity. Because of the resulting lower levels of depression and workplace stress, early childhood teachers who formally practice mindfulness may experience higher quality relationships with children in the classroom (Becker et al., 2017).

Cultivating Healthy Intentional Mindful Educators (CHIME), Nebraska Extension. CHIME is a program designed to provide education and guidance on how to incorporate mindfulness, self-compassion, and reflective practice into the daily routines, teaching, and caregiving to foster healthy and adaptive emotion regulation skills among early childhood (Hatton-Bowers et al., 2022). Engaging in mindfulness and reflective practice has many benefits for health and well-being of both early childhood professionals and young children, including reduced stress, improved emotion management, better sleep quality, increased focus and attention, and enhanced relationships. CHIME program consists of a two-hour introduction followed by seven weekly CHIME sessions on topics that include mindfulness in breathing, listening, emotions, speech, gratitude, and compassion. CHIME aims to support early childhood educators in enhancing and improving their well-being so they can be more effective as caregivers. The program helps to facilitate each participant's thinking to become present in one's personal and professional life, and to find the space to care for children with more calm and sensitivity, even during difficult and stressful moments. (Contact: Holly Hatton, hattonb@unl.edu)

5.4.3.2   Innovations with Technology

The CES has historically been a leader in using innovations to improve community health outcomes. Extension professionals have used a broad range of strategies, including using technology in innovative ways to support their work in early childhood. Using social media platforms, new content delivery vehicles, and innovative measurement, Extension professionals constantly strive to reach their audiences in a variety of ways. Technology is a powerful tool in the expansion of Extension programming. For example, in the *Parenting: Behind the Behavior* video series, educators from the University of Wisconsin-Madison/Extension Human Development and Relationship Institute (HDRI) have aired short, weekly Facebook videos about positive parent–child relationships. The goal of these videos is to reach a wide range of parents and caregivers to increase applicable parenting skills and build knowledge of Extension resources statewide. The series engages Extension specialists, faculty, and county educators, each speaking in short three-to-five-minute videos about specific parenting and child interaction skills. Topics range from emotion coaching to outdoor play and talking to children about racism. Many of the viewers have indicated this was their first exposure to Extension programming.

Another example of using new methods of delivery is the Science of Parenting (SOP) podcast that was launched in 2019. Accessible in video and audio formats, the wide availability and rapid turnaround of podcasting allowed the team to add COVID-specific information to their line-up. An impact report from October of 2020 indicates listeners downloaded the podcast over 11,000 times, and the Facebook video podcast episodes reached approximately 30,000 views over the series of thirty episodes.

Technology can also be an innovative way to collect and use data to motivate participants to take up evidence-based strategies to support child development. A program at Iowa State University called Small Talk utilizes LENA Start™, a universal preventative intervention from the LENA® Research Foundation. The package includes the curriculum and access to a cloud-based program and data-management system (LENA® Online). This plug-and-play curriculum is designed to interactively teach caregivers how to talk to and read more with their children and why those activities are essential, and to provide participants with quantitative linguistic feedback (Suskind et al., 2013) about their talk and conversation habits. During each week of the program, the participant places a wearable digital language processor on a child to complete a sixteen-hour recording of their talk and conversation with the focus on child. A cloud-based system processes the recordings. The following week, participants receive a printed report that details the number of adult words (AW) and the number of conversational turns (CT) with the target child. Additionally, the system includes automatic text messages that ask parents to report on the number of reading minutes for the week. The evaluation study used a quasi-experimental comparison design to examine the changes in talk relative to participants who regularly visit the library but did not participate in the program. Findings demonstrated statistically significant growth in weekly estimates in adult language input to children, conversational turn-taking, and child vocalizations for the intervention group but not for the comparison group (Beecher & Van Pay, 2020).

5.4.3.3 *Increased Focus on Data and Evaluation*

Researchers and evaluators have acknowledged that evaluation methods and tools used in Extension programs can benefit from improved sophistication and rigor (Nichols et al., 2015). In the published studies on Extension, most effectiveness studies reported evidence of outcomes beyond participation level. However, few studies include long-term outcomes or follow-ups (Tompkins et al., 2014). There is increasing recognition among scholars and practitioners that Extension would benefit from increasing efforts in a variety of outcome measures, including longitudinal studies that track long-term impact, and studies that can inform evidence-based practice (e.g., see Monk, this volume). Rigorous evidence is critical to effective demonstration the public value of early childhood Extension programming and communicating public value of Extension. Although such types of evaluation can be expensive and require significant commitment by Extension faculty, collaborations with other university partners, and incorporation of innovative technology may make such efforts more feasible.

5.4.3.4 *Addressing Equity, Diversity, and Inclusion*

There is an ongoing need to create and offer programming that addresses issues related to equity, diversity, and inclusion. Rhian Evans Allvin, Chief Executive Officer of the National Association for the Education of Young Children (NAEYC), stated that "children are best understood and supported in the context of family, culture, community, and society" and that "we must confront biases that create barriers and limit the potential of children, families, and early childhood professionals" (Allvin, 2018, n.p.). NAEYC (2019) has released a position statement on Advancing the Equity in Early Childhood Education that calls for inclusive teaching approaches and equitable access to learning environments within the field of early childhood. Everyone, including Extension personnel, is challenged to "seek information from families and communities about their social and cultural beliefs and practices" to inform the development of programming that is responsive to the audience it serves (NAEYC, 2019). Extension professionals are encouraged to work with "community leaders and public officials to address barriers" and create systems that support the diversity of the children and families served and to provide equitable access to all programming (NAEYC, 2019). Although Extension is engaging in programming and research that promotes childcare quality that is culturally responsive, there is a need for greater attention to reconceptualization of quality programming to include, identify, leverage, and support the rich cultural and linguistic backgrounds of diverse families (Souto-Manning et al., 2019).

Implications for Extension professionals working in Early Childhood program areas. Extension personnel offering early childhood programming must examine their programming through a social equity lens, identify biases, and seek greater input from culturally diverse, underserved audiences. It is time to listen and learn more about meeting the unique needs of today's families. Yesterday's programming may no longer be relevant to the current issues faced by families that have endured a global pandemic, societal prejudices, and social unrest. Additionally, researchers have called for the effectiveness of family enrichment programs to be examined with populations with low resources, underserved populations, and culturally diverse communities (Johnson, 2012). In the United States, children from multiple races represent the fastest growing demographic group today (Vespa et al., 2020). When early childhood professionals and/or parent educators come from a cultural background different from that of the families or communities they serve, more training or information on the cultural implications is necessary to successfully engage with diverse families and communities (Timmons & Dworkin, 2020).

Extension professionals are charged with being nimble and seeking feedback from stakeholders and community members to determine how best to serve and educate today's families. One way to strengthen cultural capital and engagement with diverse communities is to create ways to share or gather contributions to programs from these diverse audiences when designing programming, training, or curriculum, instead of trying to add surface-level diversity in the form of representation after programs have been created (Timmons & Dworkin, 2020).

One example of responsive programming is the Including All of Us program, which trains early childhood professionals on diversity, equity, and inclusion in early childhood. The program helps participants learn to understand individual and group identity and their own worldview, learn about antibias education and cultural competency, and develop strategies to collaborate with families to promote diversity, equity, and inclusion. The Including All of Us training is an intensive six-hour experience led by a cross-racial facilitation team. To promote sharing and full participation, training groups are limited to twenty-five participants. This training goes beyond merely receiving information by using self-reflection and group discussions to scaffold learning around diversity, equity, and inclusion. Twenty-two early childhood professionals participated in the pilot program. Program evaluation reported changes in knowledge and attitudes surrounding diversity, equity, and inclusion, including greater understanding about differences. Participants also indicated planned behavior changes, such as implementing antibias techniques and lessons. (Contacts: Kylie Rymanowicz, rymanow1@msu.edu; Vivian Washington, washi138@msu.edu)

5.5   Conclusions and Recommendations

Fostering young children's healthy development is critical to the development of future productive citizens and the vitality and health of communities. Supporting children's health and well-being requires a collaborative effort to create the optimal environment for their development. The CES is well positioned to lead the way toward enhancing the well-being of children in the domains of physical, psychological, cognitive, social, and economic well-being; and has implemented numerous cutting-edge responses that engage numerous partners and a range of approaches. Despite the considerable contributions of the CES, there is more to be done. Extension personnel should continue to build new partnerships and address community needs by engaging in deep listening with diverse voices from underrepresented populations. Extension has had a long history of helping underrepresented populations build networks and gain social capital (see Do & Zoumenou, this volume). This can be beneficial in the building of partnerships but also can reinforce privileged identities and homogenous groups.

> Social capital is a multilevel concept regarding the quality of personal relationships, such as personal and community networks, sense of belonging, and civic engagement. It includes social norms of reciprocity and trust, which impacts the quality of life, including well-being (Putnam, 2000).

Putnam (2000) notes that social capital can be a critical component of social and psychological support to members of the in-group but can also negatively lead to antagonism toward out-group individuals. Extension should continue to look for ways to diversify the workforce and seek to engage and support the cultural capital of historically underserved and marginalized populations. The concept of helping families build their social capital is an interdisciplinary approach that could impact well-being in a broader scope. For instance, a recent study found many forms of family social capital were associated with reducing or negating the effects of childhood adversity when it was present at multiple ecological levels (Kysar-Moon, 2021). Relatedly, research and educational offerings that promote childcare and parenting quality with culturally responsive, sustained, and relevant pedagogy are scarce. This lack is particularly critical considering the recent emphasis on reconceptualizing high quality to be inclusive of historically underserved and marginalized teachers, children, and families (Souto-Manning et al., 2019). Given Extensions' vast network and long history of responding to community needs, the potential to be a leader in this highly needed work is an opportunity for Extension to team with community partners to promote the health, well-being, and quality of life for our communities and particularly the lives of young children.

References

Allvin, R. E. (2018, November). Making connections. Toward equity. *Young Children*, 73(5). www.naeyc.org/resources/pubs/yc/nov2018/toward-equity

APLU Task Force on the New Engagement Planning Team. (2016). *The New Engagement: Exploring the Issues Across a Spectrum—A framework for thought and action by the Task Force on The New Engagement.* Accessed from www.aplu .org/wp-content/uploads/the-new-engagement-exploring-the-issues-across-a-spectrum.pdf

Beecher, C. C., & Van Pay, C. K. (2020). Investigation of the effectiveness of a community-based parent education program to engage families in increasing language interactions with their children. *Early Childhood Research Quarterly*, 53, 453–463. https//10.1016/j.ecresq.2020.04.001

Bornstein, M. H. (2003). Positive parenting and positive development in children. In R. Lerner, F. Jacobs, & D. Wertlieb (Eds.), *Handbook of applied developmental science: Promoting positive child, adolescent, and family development through research, policies, and programs: Vol. 1. Applying developmental science for youth and families: Historical and theoretical foundations* (pp. 187–209). Sage.

Bronfenbrenner, U. (2005). *Making human beings human: Bioecological perspectives on human development.* Sage.

Brophy-Herb, H. E., Moyses, K., Shrier, C., Rymanowicz, K., Pilkenton, A., Dalimonte-Merckling, D., … Mitchell, K. (2021). A pilot evaluation of the Building Early Emotional Skills (BEES) curriculum in face-to-face and online formats. *Journal of Community Psychology*, 49(5), 1505–1521. https://doi.org/10.1002/jcop.22478

Burkhart-Kriesel, C., Weigle, J. L., & Hawkins, J. (2019). Engagement to enhance community: An example of extension's land-grant mission in action. *Social Sciences*, 8(1), 27.

Caskey, M., Kunkel, K., Krentz, M., & Schroeder, M. (2018). *Nutrition in early childhood makes a difference*. University of Minnesota Extension.

DeVoe, J. E., Geller, A., & Negussie, Y. (Eds.). (2019). *Vibrant and healthy kids: Aligning science, practice, and policy to advance health equity*. The National Academies Press. https://doi.org/10.17226/25466

Donoghue, E. A. (2017). Quality early education and child care from birth to kindergarten. *Pediatrics*, 140(2), e20171488. https://doi.org/10.1542/peds.2017-1488

Durden, T. R., Mincemayor, C. C., Gerdes, J., & Lodl, K. (2013). Extension's capacity to deliver quality early childhood professional development. *Journal of Extension*, 51(5).

Gould, F. I., Steele, D. & Woodrum, W. J. (2014). Cooperative Extension: A century of innovation. *Journal of Extension*, 52, 1COM1. www.joe.org/joe/2014february/comm1.php

Hatton-Bowers, H., Clark, C., Parra, G., Calvi, J., Bird, M. Y., Avari, P., Foged, J., & Smith, J. (2022). Promising findings that the Cultivating Healthy Intentional Mindful Educators' program (CHIME) strengthens early childhood teachers' emotional resources: An iterative study. *Early Childhood Education Journal*, 1–14. https://doi.org/10.1007/s10643-022-01386-3

Huston, A. C., & Bentley, A. C. (2010). Human development in societal context. *Annual Review of Psychology*, 61, 411–437. https://doi.org/10.1146/annurev.psych.093008.100442

Kim, Y. B. (2016). Evaluating an integrated nutrition and parenting education program for preschoolers and their parents. *Journal of Extension*, 54(5), 5RIB5.

Kim, Y. B., Bowers, J. R., Martin, S., Ebata, A., Lindsey, S. C., Nelson, P. T., & Ontai, L. (2015). Process monitoring evaluation of an online program for parents. *Journal of Extension*, 53(2), 2RIB2.

Korjenevitch, M., Dunifon, R., & Kopko, K. (2010). *Outcomes of participants in Cornell Cooperative Extension Magic Years parent education program*. Accessed from www.human.cornell.edu/sites/default/files/PAM/Parenting/results%20by%20county/ORANGE-COUNTY-OUTCOMES_FINAL2011.pdf

Kysar-Moon, A. (2021). Adverse childhood experiences, family social capital, and externalizing behavior problems: An analysis across multiple ecological levels. *Journal of Family Issues*, 43(12), 3168–3193. https://doi.org/10.1177/0192513X211042849

Learning for Justice. (n.d.). *What is a family?* Accessed from www.learningforjustice.org/classroom-resources/lessons/what-is-a-family

Leung, C. Y., & Suskind, D. L. (2020). What parents know matters: Parental knowledge at birth predicts caregiving behaviors at 9 months. *The Journal of Pediatrics*, 221, 72–80. https://doi.org/10.1016/j.jpeds.2019.12.021

Loes, M. J., Huber, E. C., Bowne, M., Stluka, S., Wells, K., Nelson, T., ... Meendering, J. (2015). iGrow Readers: A literature-based nutrition and physical activity program for young children. *Journal of Nutrition Education and Behavior*, 47(4), S31. https//doi.org/10.1016/j.jneb.2015.04.084

Mamedova, S., & Redford, J. (2019). *Early childhood program participation, From the National Household Education Surveys Program of 2012 (NCES 2013-029.REV2)*. National Center for Education Statistics, Institute of Education Sciences, U.S. Department of Education. Retrieved from https://nces.ed.gov/pubsearch

McCartney, K., Wood, G., Gabbert, K., & Poffenbarger, M. (2019). P74 Impact of the WV Kids Market Program on children's knowledge, attitudes and consumption of fruits and vegetables. *Journal of Nutrition Education and Behavior*, 51(7), S65–S66. https://doi.org/10.1016/j.jneb.2019.05.450

Moeller, M., McKillip, A., Wienk, R., & Cutler, K. (2016). In pursuit of child and family well-being: Initial steps to advocacy. *Social Sciences*, 5(3), 30. https://doi.org/10.3390/socsci5030030

National Association for the Education of Young Children. (2019). *Advancing equity in early childhood education: A position statement*. www.naeyc.org/resources/position-statements/equity

Neumann, M. M., Hood, M., Ford, R. M., & Neumann, D. L. (2012). The role of environmental print in emergent literacy. *Journal of Early Childhood Literacy*, 12(3), 231–258. https://doi.org/10.1177/1468798411417080

Nichols, A., Blake, S. M., Chazdon, S., & Radhakrishna, R. (2015). From farm results demonstrations to multistate impact designs: Cooperative Extension navigates its way through evaluation pathways. *Journal of Human Sciences and Extension*, 3(2), 7. https://doi.org/10.54718/DNHS3672

Ostergren, C. S., Riley, D. A., & Wehmeier, J. M. (2011). Better Kid Care program improves the quality of child care: Results from an interview study. *Journal of Extension*, 49(6), 6.

Pew Charitable Trusts. (2009). *Workforce competitiveness & economic sustainability starts with young children*. Accessed from www.uschamberfoundation.org/sites/default/files/publication/edu/Pre-K_Krupicka_Pew%20Center%20on%20the%20States.pdf

Pollard, E. L., & Lee, P. D. (2003). Child well-being: A systematic review of the literature. *Social Indicators Research*, 61(1), 59–78.

Prenatal-to-3 Policy Impact Center. (2021). *Why do we focus on the prenatal-to-3 age period? Understanding the importance of the earliest years*. Child and Family Research Partnership, Lyndon B. Johnson School of Public Affairs, University of Texas at Austin. B.001.0121. https://pn3policy.org/resources/why-do-we-focus-on-the-prenatal-to-3-age-period-understanding-the-importance-of-the-earliest-years

Putnam, R. D. (2000). *Bowling alone: The collapse and revival of American community*. Simon & Schuster.

Romeo, R. R., Segaran, J., Leonard, J. A., Robinson, S. T., West, M. R., Mackey, A. P., … Gabrieli, J. D. (2018). Language exposure relates to structural neural connectivity in childhood. *Journal of Neuroscience*, 38(36), 7870–7877. https://doi.org/10.1523/JNEUROSCI.0484-18.2018

Rowe, M. L. (2017). Understanding socioeconomic differences in parents' speech to children. *Child Development Perspectives*, 12(2), 122–127. https://doi.org/10.1111/cdep.12271

Saltzman, A. (2011). *Mindfulness: A guide for teachers*. The Center for Contemplative Mind in Society. Retrieved from www.contemplativemind.org/Mindfulness-A_Teachers_Guide.pdf

Souto-Manning, M., Falk, B., López, D., Barros Cruz, L., Bradt, N., Cardwell, N., … Rollins, E. (2019). A transdisciplinary approach to equitable teaching in early childhood education. *Review of Research in Education*, 43(1), 249–276. https://doi.org/10.3102/0091732X18821122

Statham, J., & Chase, E. (2010). Childhood wellbeing: A brief overview. *Loughborough: Childhood Wellbeing Research Centre.*

Suskind, D., Leffel, K. R., Hernandez, M. W., Sapolich, S. G., Suskind, E., Kirkham, E., & Meehan, P. (2013). An exploratory study of "Quantitative Linguistic Feedback": Effect of LENA feedback on adult language production. *Communication Disorders Quarterly*, 34(4), 199–209. https://doi.org/10.1177/1525740112473146

Swick, K., & Williams, R. (2006). An analysis of Bronfenbrenner's bio-ecological perspective for early childhood educators: Implications for working with families experiencing stress. *Early Childhood Education Journal*, 33(5), 371–378. https://doi.org/10.1007/s10643-006-0078-y

Timmons, J., & Dworkin, J. (2020). A literature review of family engagement with African immigrant and refugee families. *Journal of Human Sciences and Extension*, 8(2), 10. https://doi.org/10.54718/UTKS2303

Tompkins, S. A., Rosa, J. D., Henry, K. L., & Benavente, J. (2014). Outcomes of a multi-component family enrichment project: 12-month follow-up. *Journal of Human Sciences and Extension*, 2(1). https://doi.org/10.54718/YLWB9857

Vespa, J., Medina, L., & Armstrong, D. M. (2020). *Demographic turning points for the United States: Population projections for 2020 to 2060*. US Census Bureau. Accessed from www.census.gov/content/dam/Census/library/publications/2020/demo/p25-1144.pdf

CHAPTER 6

Supporting Youth through Family Engagement
Opportunities for Extension

Jodi Dworkin

Before beginning a conversation about the role of Extension in the integration of youth and family development, it is essential to position this chapter. Bronfenbrenner's bioecological theory would suggest that both context and proximal processes impact child development. More specifically, a bioecological perspective is one that focuses on the complex relationships between a developing individual and the multiple levels of their ecology (Bronfenbrenner, 2001, 2005). This suggests that understanding family is essential to understanding youth development. Further, it requires embedding development within the historical time and space in which it is happening (Bronfenbrenner, 2001, 2005).

In 2020, the United States and the world experienced the COVID-19 global pandemic and a time of racial reckoning, protests, calls for police reform, and the Black Lives Matter movement. The COVID-19 pandemic and resulting trauma for families (which has disproportionately affected families of color) presented a unique, unexpected, and unwelcome opportunity to see how families would respond to a crisis, and the effects on families when their in-person supports shut down and when young people's physical learning spaces (schools and out-of-school-time programs) closed. Although some schools and programs moved online, with physical spaces no longer available to allow parents to go to work while feeling comfortable knowing their children were safe and fed during the day, online learning was not enough. Without those physical supports, families needed basic coverage. The limited learning spaces that remained open were just that, limited with reduced capacity. Further, those who are immunocompromised or living with someone who is immunocompromised or who has other health vulnerabilities were left without any in-person options, and that continued for years.

The pandemic provided an opportunity to look back and reflect on what programs, communities, and Extension had been doing in terms of youth and family development. With programs forced to either stop or change their delivery, there was space to reflect on what had been working, what had not been working and why. This was also a time when families had experienced many traumas – illness and death, food insecurity, reduced and limited employment and income, closed school buildings, closed out-of-school-time spaces, and some in-person programs moved online – access to reliable Internet and devices created a greater digital divide, and some families had an increased need for out-of-home care and learning because parents were forced to work from home. This was the first example of many in which this pandemic had completely shifted our thinking. Previously, we would have argued that parents need children in school and programs so that parents can go to work. While that remains true, it is now clear that the *work* – not the *location* of the work – demands childcare. The closure of schools and afterschool programs, the two contexts in which youth were inherently away from family, living and learning and growing was particularly difficult for families. Although we have yet to fully realize the outcomes of these disruptions, they offer an important opportunity for reflection. With youth and families spending an increasing amount of time at home, would family relationships be strengthened in a way that reduces the perceived need for out-of-school-time activities? Alternatively, now that families have seen on a daily basis the negative effect of the loss of in-person school and other activities, will we see a renewed appreciation for development that occurs outside the family through those in-person interactions?

In this chapter, I will present a case for integrating youth and family development and, more specifically, for recognizing the family as one critical context for youth development. Although there are challenges to this work, Extension is uniquely positioned to create intentional spaces to support positive youth development and well-being through family engagement. Extension has skills and expertise in building community partnerships, working with and on behalf of families and communities, and working together to develop new models for partnership.

6.1 Using a Positive Youth Development (PYD) Framework

The collaborative of twenty-one federal departments and agencies supporting youth (including USDA), the Interagency Working Group on Youth Programs, has defined Positive Youth Development (PYD) as such:

> PYD is an intentional, prosocial approach that engages youth within their communities, schools, organizations, peer groups, and families in a manner that is productive and constructive; recognizes, utilizes, and enhances

young people's strengths; and promotes positive outcomes for young people by providing opportunities, fostering positive relationships, and furnishing the support needed to build on their leadership strengths. (youth.gov, n.d.b)

Consistent with this approach, youth development programs provide youth with many supports and opportunities which range from basic support like supervision, safety, and food, to providing support for higher order needs like academic support, social emotional development, mentoring, and social support. There are two particularly well-established and validated frameworks of Positive Youth Development: the 5C Framework and the Developmental Assets Framework. Both frameworks reflect family development and provide an important context for considering the challenges and opportunities of integrating family development into youth development programming.

Lerner and Lerner (n.d.) developed the 5C framework of PYD, designed around positive development and the skills and characteristics young people need to be healthy and productive citizens. When young people have opportunities for meaningful youth development experiences, the likelihood that they will experience these five outcomes increases significantly: competence, confidence, connection, character, and caring/compassion. Once a young person has developed fairly well in these five areas, space is created for a sixth C: contribution to self, community, and the larger society. Two of the six Cs give particular attention to family systems: the third C, "Connection: Positive bonds with people and institutions – peers, family, school, and community – in which both parties contribute to the relationship," and the sixth C, contribution to self, community, and the larger society.

The Search Institute (2021) developed the Developmental Assets Framework, which includes forty supports that young people need to be successful. These forty assets are focused on four conceptual domains: support, empowerment, boundaries and expectations, and constructive use of time. The framework presents five assets specific to families: family support, family communication, parent engagement with school, family boundaries, high expectations, and time at home.

6.1.1 *Integrating Youth and Family Development*

Making the case for integrating family engagement into positive youth development initiatives is not new. I will highlight three prominent approaches to integrating youth and family development that began nearly forty years ago. First, in 1983 the Harvard Family Research Project (which became the Global Family Research Project in 2017) was initiated. The Global Family Research Project recognizes an ecology of learning, where the benefits of family engagement are recognized across the different spaces (school, afterschool programs, childcare, etc.) where youth are learning and growing (Global Family Research Project, 2021).

Next, in 2002, Eccles and Gootman released the pivotal report, *Community Programs to Promote Youth Development*. They identified "Integration of Family, School, and Community Efforts" as one of just eight features of positive developmental settings. They defined this feature as: "Concordance; coordination; and synergy among family, school, and community." The other seven features include: physical and psychological safety, appropriate structure, supportive relationships, opportunities to belong, positive social norms, support for efficacy and mattering, and opportunities for skill building. Although there are eight features, Eccles and Gootman (2002) acknowledge that no single program can incorporate all of them into positive youth development, and in fact that is not the objective. Programs differ in their goals and outcomes, and they serve different youth, families, and communities. Programs must remain nimble enough to respond to the many facets of youth development as well as the diversity of the youth, families, and communities that they serve. They must flex to respond to the needs of the youth and families they are seeing in their program at each moment.

Finally, a third approach to PYD that recognizes the role of family is the 2008 Ready by 21 initiative launched by the Forum for Youth Investment (The Forum for Youth Investment, n.d.). This work is described as: "Ready by 21: the Forum is committed to helping leaders change the odds that all children and youth are ready for college, work and life." These efforts toward readiness happen in many ways, one of which is recognizing not just youth but also families as change agents, and consequently working to improve not just the quantity but also the quality of family, school, and community supports. There are twelve Ready by 21 principles that are considered "The key ingredients that help leaders think differently, act differently and act together to achieve equity, engagement, quality and readiness." These twelve principles are: leadership, families, development, evidence, environment, assets, advocacy, adults, identity, partnership, alignment, and agency. Their work is sensitive to the understanding that youth grow up in families and communities and despite the fact that they spend a lot of hours during the week in schools and programs, that is not where they are growing up. Further, young people show up to schools, programs, and other learning spaces with the culture, experiences, and support they got from family and community. Family, school, and community supports are depicted in their theory of change as the gear in between leadership accountability and children and youth outcomes.

Consistent with these approaches to PYD, and slightly different (but not divergent) ways of articulating the integration of family development into PYD, there are different strategies for integrating youth and family development in programs. This may require redefining what integrating family engagement with youth development means; for instance, moving beyond family involvement to family engagement is a first step. There is perhaps a continuum of integrated activities/behaviors, some which may happen intentionally and strategically within programs, and others that may happen simply because parents are the decision-makers, coordinators, and funders in family systems.

Family engagement may simply be honoring parents as the drivers, or payers, or even the person that signs their child up or approves their participation in the activity. Families are generally responsible for the more mundane factors like cost, transportation, and scheduling. In addition, families are critical to determining the spaces in which youth learn by choosing neighborhoods, schools, or activities. Parents register their children for activities; this could be an activity that fits with the family's schedule, an activity in which the child is interested in participating, an opportunity to interact with friends or other peers to whom the parent wants the child connected, an activity in which the parent would like the child to be interested, or merely determine whether the child has interest in an activity. In stark contrast, families may be involved as key partners in program development, management, and advisory work.

6.1.2   Barriers to Family Engagement in Positive Youth Development

Although often identified as integral to PYD, the realities of engaging families into youth development programs are much harder. The idea of increased family engagement in youth development is not a new suggestion, and it has not gotten any easier over the years. As a result of the challenges of engaging parents and families in youth development programs, family engagement has become a convenient feature for programs to ignore, and it may be the first program component to be dropped when resources (time and money) are tight. There are also challenges with staff time and training when staff are focused on youth development. Family engagement can be the area where staff feel the least prepared because their own training and experiences perhaps did not address family development, and specifically how to integrate family development into youth development work.

Some of those challenges are logistical in that youth are physically present at the program and family members are often not, generally dropping children off at the program location so they can go to work, care for other children or family members, or run errands. Program staff may see some family members regularly at drop-off and/or pick-up times, and they may rarely or never see other family members who are not coming into the physical space for drop-off or pick-up or may be in a hurry during those busy times of the day. Parents may not want to be engaged and are perhaps less eager learners than the children. It is not uncommon that a parent or family engagement component is the hardest program component to implement successfully and consistently, and thus, when family engagement is part of a program, it can be a barrier to reaching implementation fidelity.

There has been research on barriers to family involvement and engagement, but that scholarship has primarily focused on the school context; there is less research on out-of-school-time learning contexts (Horowitz & Bronte-Tinkew, 2007). Thus, it is not surprising that a Google search on the integration of youth and family development reveals information about schools and even more specifically often focuses on students with disabilities or school safety. More specifically, there is a focus on early childhood and early childhood education, with the expectation that young people become independent as they get older and families and teens are experiencing individuation during adolescence. There seems to be a faulty assumption that family engagement in youth development programs runs counter to adolescents developing independence, but that is not necessarily true. Appropriate family engagement can support positive development and allow young people to seek independence in a safe context, with the opportunity to return to family when they need support or advice (Youniss & Smollar, 1985).

The US Department of Education (n.d.) has noted that raising young people is a "shared responsibility" and that family engagement is essential to education reform. Epstein and Salinas (2004) define a school learning community as a community that "includes educators, students, parents, and community partners who work together to improve the school and enhance students' learning opportunities (para. 1–2)." It is an organized approach to school, family, and community partnerships that are explicitly linked to the goals for the school. Programs intentionally designed in this way have been found to increase student success, and strengthen family and community support (Epstein, 2001; Henderson & Mapp, 2002; Sheldon, 2003). Building on this approach, we might envision an out-of-school-time learning community. This would include a program of partnerships including youth workers, young learners, parents, and community partners with activities linked directly to the out-of-school-time learning goals.

Although we can certainly learn from the research on school settings, there also needs to be an openness to thinking about how nonschool learning contexts are different and provide unique opportunities for family engagement. For example, Black parents are generally labeled by schools as unengaged (Bridges, Awokoya, & Messano, 2012; Roberts, 2011). Research has shown that teachers hold lower expectations and provide poorer quality instruction to Black students compared with their White counterparts (Roberts, 2011), and most Black parents report that their student is not getting the quality of education they need to achieve their future goals (Bridges et al., 2012). This history can lead families to have limited trust in teachers and school staff, and to not want to show up to the school building or participate in school events. Lower family visibility in school can in turn be incorrectly assumed by officials to mean that parents and families are not engaged in their students' learning, rather than recognizing that the context of the school space is not welcoming to diverse families; the structures and systems need to change, including adopting culturally appropriate measures of engagement (Bridges et al., 2012). In contrast, families may not have the same history of experiences with nonschool contexts, as these are more likely to be chosen spaces in which families feel welcome. As a result, nonschool contexts may provide a unique opportunity for family engagement, without the expectations of state education standards and rules that often come with the context of school buildings. Out-of-school-time programs can generally be more creative in their programming than schools, and youth workers can have learning expectations for their students that may be quite different from classroom teachers and very consistent with family expectations (for instance, a shared goal of college attendance and life-skill development).

Whereas youth development and youth work have a deep history, and there is a vast accompanying body of research exploring youth development and even unique and innovative youth development strategies, there is not the same history of developing, implementing, or evaluating integrated youth/family programming. Programmatically, an integrated approach may appear as starting from scratch because there is an evaluation gap, as we know less about what has worked and not worked, and under what conditions.

Extension is uniquely positioned to overcome some of these barriers and act strategically and intentionally to integrate youth and family into outreach and engagement work. However, there are structural challenges in place that often make this work extremely difficult and success unlikely. For instance, in many states Extension is structured such that youth and family development are separate units or centers, and Specialists/Faculty and Educators/Agents are assigned to work in one area, either youth or family, but typically not both. When there is a promotion system in place for Educators/Agents, rewards are based on individual work, and one's work is evaluated against one's job description. As a result, doing work outside of one's expectations may not only not be rewarded; one may be penalized in the promotion process for focusing outside the scope of what is explicitly stated in one's job description. This is true with promotion and tenure systems for campus faculty as well; team science and collaboration can be hard to reward as it can be difficult to articulate one's unique contribution to a project or program. Barriers and challenges do not mean this work should not be happening.

6.2   Why Extension Should Be Doing Integrated Work

Extension was founded on a mission to serve the citizens and residents of each individual state. Specifically, land-grant institutions were developed as part of an agreement to serve the citizens of the state in exchange for land, with the original directive focused on farm families. The United States Department of Agriculture, National Institute of Food and Agriculture articulates the history:

> The Smith Lever Act formalized extension in 1914, establishing USDA's partnership with land-grant universities to apply research and provide education in agriculture. Congress created the extension system to address exclusively rural, agricultural issues. At that time, more than 50 percent of the U.S. population lived in rural areas, and 30 percent of the workforce was engaged in farming. (USDA-NIFA, n.d.)

In the more than 100 years since Extension was formalized, state demographics, family structure, the communities in which land-grant institutions are located, and youth and family needs have undoubtedly changed. Agriculture, farming, industry, and family employment have also experienced dramatic shifts (see Table 6.1).

These contemporary trends undoubtedly impact Extension and require Extension to be nimble and adapt quickly (see Do & Zoumenou, this

Table 6.1 *Demographic shifts over the past decade*

Demographic	Year	
Black (Social Explorer Dataset, 1920)	1920	9.9%
(Social Explorer Tables, 2010)	2010	12.6%
Immigration	1911–1920	5,735,811 immigrants arrive in the US
(Social Explorer Dataset, 1920)		
(Social Explorer Tables, 2010)	2001–2010	13,900,000 immigrants arrive in the US
Women in US labor force	1920	20%
(US Department of Labor, 2020)		
	2020	47%
Wives contributions to family earnings	1970	26.6%
(Bureau of Labor Statistics, 2014)		
	2011	37%
Divorce (Wang, 2020)	1960	9.2%
	2019	14.9% (after a peak of 22.6% in 1980)
Education	1990	Enrollment rate for young adults ages 18–19: Secondary: 15% Postsecondary: 43%
(The Condition of Education, 2016)		
	2014	Enrollment rate for young adults ages 18–19: Secondary: 20% Postsecondary: 49%
Rural (Social Explorer Dataset, 1920)	1920	48.8%
(Social Explorer Tables, 2010)	2010	19.3%

volume). I contend that these contemporary trends require that adaptation include greater focus on the intersection of youth and family. Some examples of trends for consideration include migration and the shifting demographic landscape, accelerating information/Internet access, and growing socioeconomic gaps. For instance, there are significantly more parents working outside the home today, same-sex marriage is now legal, and divorce and co-parenting relationships look different. Even perspectives on divorce have changed, with now a stronger push toward co-parenting and ensuring that children have continued access to both parents when it is both safe and healthy for children to do so (e.g., Berman & Daneback, 2020). In addition, there are larger populations of immigrant and refugee communities that are inherently more collectivist than US-born families (see Table 6.1). This means that the way in which we consider family must shift, as talking about parents without recognizing kin, siblings, grandparents, aunts, and uncles may be exclusionary.

Extension is uniquely positioned to take on the opportunity for more relevant and integrated programming because it offers both campus and field faculty who have deep expertise in research and practice around both youth and family development; this is rare as youth programs are focused on youth development programming and family programs are focused on family development, and there is often minimal overlap. Youth programs are designed to support youth in many different capacities but that generally does not translate into staff having all of the necessary skills, capacity, or expertise in working with families or parents. Simultaneously, many youth and family professionals have training that is often needed in human development and family-studies programs (names vary from HDFS to child development and family studies to similar iterations), and these programs typically require training in both theories and methods of human/child development and family studies. Although individuals can and do choose to specialize in child development or family studies, they still come equipped with the background in both. There is a demand for ensuring Extension programs and resources are accessible and reach youth and families who may not have been previously reached by Extension.

In addition to expertise, and equally important, Extension is skilled at building bridges and linkages. Extension often has a community reputation as a builder/connector, creating pathways and linkages between universities and communities, youth and programs, and families and programs. For example, the University of Minnesota Extension mission is "Making a difference by connecting community needs and University resources to address critical issues in Minnesota" (University of Minnesota Extension, 2021). Connection is at the core of the work.

6.2.1   The How: Implications for Practice

When youth are receiving the same positive and support messages from multiple places (programs and family in this case), those messages are more likely to be internalized. When parents are aware of what is happening in programs and can be partners in learning, there are better outcomes for youth (Horowitz & Bronte-Tinkew, 2007; Rosenberg, Wilkes, & Harris, 2014). Designing, creating, or implementing a program that integrates both youth and family development must be part of the program process from the beginning. Taking an integrated approach requires advance planning and involving key stakeholders in decision-making, design, planning, and reflection.

6.2.1.1 Program Examples

Logic models are pictorial descriptions of program components: inputs, outputs, short-, medium-, and long-term outcomes or impacts, as well as the assumptions and external factors that need to be recognized. Although the names of these components can shift slightly, the overall logical model depiction and process is the same (University of Wisconsin Extension, 2021). Program development must begin with a logic model that includes youth outcomes and a pathway towards those outcomes that could be through parent or family inputs and outputs. The family must not be relegated to being considered an external factor or negative assumption. Frameworks and conceptual models that are from both family studies and youth development disciplines should be considered, as this approach will better allow the visual depiction of alternative theories of change.

Theories of change are "a comprehensive description and illustration of how and why a desired change is expected to happen in a particular context" (The Annie E. Casey Foundation, 2021). There are multiple ways in which an integrated youth/family approach can show up in a theory of change. For instance, a program focused on life skills or academic achievement should recognize family as part of the context in which young people are learning, practicing, and developing these skills. Family should also be recognized as a support in that family members are able to reinforce the skills, show support for developing those skills, provide opportunities for youth to practice those skills, and show praise and appreciation for the effort to work on those skills. Family members often will also be the first to recognize when hard work and success happen. Family support and engagement should be a key part of the pathway to youth outcomes.

Both within and outside Extension, there are many guides and programmatic attempts designed to support family involvement in children's learning and development. Despite the existence of tools and strategies, most educators will tell you that integrated programming still does not happen enough, that it is hard to deliver with fidelity, and that when decisions need to be made to reduce programming because of limited time or resources or both, family initiatives are the first to go. However, this is also the time when integrating family into youth development is needed most; as families continue to change, as the contexts of family development continue to change, communities are increasingly diverse in terms of culture and language, and at this moment are differentially experiencing the short- and long-term effects of COVID-19 and the traumas that has created for families.

Statewide and locally across the United States, there are solid examples of how and why "engaging" and "bringing" families into out-of-school-time

programming is essential to meet the needs of families and also support
youth development; however, sustained involvement and ultimately
engagement takes time (Horowitz & Bronte-Tinkew, 2007). Rosenberg
et al. (2014) argue that both families and out-of-school-time learning are
critical to youth development. Further, support by parents is also critical to children's learning and development during out-of-school time.
They share three examples of programs that do the work of integrating
family into youth development programs. However, while there is general agreement that families matter, strategies for engagement vary quite
dramatically, from offering literacy support to bringing families into program planning, to having youth and parents co-engage in learning. For
example, the federally funded out-of-school-time programs, 21st Century
Community Learning Centers, which are authorized under the Elementary
and Secondary Education Act, offer literacy programs and other educa-
tionally focused supports to families. Appropriation has increased from
$40 million in 1998 when the program first started to $1.25 billion in 2020
(Afterschool Alliance, n.d.).

There are also multiple examples of Extension programs that have incorporated a family engagement component to improve youth outcomes, and they
use different approaches, providing a diverse set of models to inform future
programming efforts. To provide a glimpse into some of the innovations
and efforts that are currently in place across the country, Table 6.2 highlights
three program examples, one focused on Somali youth, one focused on the
educational success of Latino youth, and one focused on military families.

6.2.1.2   Guiding Principles for Family Engagement
The existing literature suggests that there are nine key principles that
should guide this work and can contribute to the successful integration of
youth and family development.

1.   Start with the assumption that families and programs have the
     same goals: positive youth development and positive outcomes for
     young people. They may have slightly different ideas about how
     to get there because of cultures, values, and experiences, but those
     differences can be a strength.
2.   Recognize family as an essential component in positive youth
     development, evolving the approach from consideration of *either*
     youth or family to that of *both* youth and family.
3.   Redefine family engagement to be inclusive of all families and the
     many ways in which families may show up that are impacted by
     family values and culture, community, and programming.

Table 6.2 *Examples of programs that integrate family development into youth development programs*

Program name/URL	State	Partners	Program description	Program outcomes
Takeoff 4-H STEAM Club www.kajoog.org/the-takeoff/	Minnesota	University of Minnesota Extension Urban 4-H Youth Development and Kajoog, a Somali nonprofit committed to "enriching the lives of Somali American youth" (Rising Impact, 2021).	A culturally appropriate educational program for Somali youth that engages the parents to bridge the gap between generations (Rising Impact, 2021).	Increases in on-time graduation and enrollment in postsecondary education (Rising Impact, 2021), increased workforce and higher education preparation (Skuza, 2019), and youth reported parents as the primary influencer of their educational goals including aspiring to be doctors to support family values (Tzenis, 2019).
Juntos https://juntosnc.com/	North Carolina	Extension's 4-H and FCS agents, school and college administrators and staff, and other community volunteers (Behnke et al., 2020).	Developed "to help Latino students achieve high school graduation and attend higher education." Family engagement is one of four components in what is described as an intensive, long-term program to support students' educational success (Behnke et al., 2020).	Improvements in academics, college readiness, parent engagement, and community engagement (Behnke et al., 2020).

Table 6.2 (cont.)

Program name/URL	State	Partners	Program description	Program outcomes
Military Teen Adventure Camps http://fcs-hes.ca.uky.edu/ MTAC	Kentucky	Initiated through a partnership between the Department of Defense and USDA, the National Institute of Food and Agriculture in partnership with Purdue University. University of Kentucky Family and Consumer Sciences Extension agents incorporated parents into the model (Ashurst, Weisenhorn, & Atkinson, 2021).	Developed to offer high-adventure camps for military teens. Building on models of family reintegration among military families, parents were engaged and service member parents were able to attend camp with their teens (Ashurst et al., 2021).	Significant increases in resilience for service members and youth as well as elevated youth outcomes in the areas of problem solving and connecting with others (Ashurst et al., 2021).

Note: This table was not designed as a comprehensive list. These programs were selected to present a few different models of meeting the needs of diverse youth using different strategies for family/parent engagement.

4. Full engagement by families does not require that they always show up to a physical space when you want them to do so. Engagement happens in many ways and in many places.

5. Family needs to be present in logic models as input, output, and outcomes, not only as external factors and assumptions. Sometimes programs engage families; at other times, families can engage programs.

6. Center family and recognize that whatever is happening in the family (positive, negative, or neutral) will impact youth development processes and outcomes.

7. Use culturally relevant and responsive approaches to teaching and learning. This method is critical to building engagement with families and creating space for families to engage with programs.

8. The program needs to explicitly and intentionally incorporate ways to engage parents/families/guardians through family activities, newsletters, websites, and program policies. This could be incorporated during regular program time or integrated into existing programming; it could require extended programming in terms of time or activities (youth.gov, n.d.a).

9. This work requires having professionals with expertise and training in both youth and family development. There needs to be diverse leadership, spaces that are welcoming to diverse audiences (images, location, cost, food options, etc.), and recruitment materials that encourage diverse youth and families to engage (The Forum for Youth Investment, n.d.).

6.3 Conclusion: A Commitment to Diversity, Equity, and Inclusion

This chapter was initiated in the midst of a global pandemic, when some young people had been out of a school building for more than 400 days. It was and continues to be a time of racial reckoning in the United States, when we have seen the murder of unarmed Black men and boys by law enforcement, and communities reliving this trauma all too frequently. Extension responded in many ways to these crises (see de Guzman & Hatton, this volume). In the years to come, we will see whether these events will result in longer-term changes, to what extent Extension will commit to integrating trauma-informed approaches into their youth and family development work, and whether Extension will commit to diversifying its workforce to better reflect the population of the states and communities being served. Anecdotally, across the country and on my own campus are countless examples of an increasingly diverse Extension work-force and a clear commitment to diversity. For instance, there are positions like Director of Diversity, Equity, and Inclusion emerging across Extension systems. When these positions sit outside of one program area, they present an exciting opportunity for a cross-disciplinary perspective.

States are grappling with changing demographics and shifting family needs: seeking staff that better reflect the communities they are serving, working to strengthen critical partnerships and build new partnerships, and pivoting their programming to adapt to those changes. This pivot could include a move to online services, a shift in programming hours to accommodate changes to the virtual or in-person school day, a need to reduce costs and increase food availability because families have lost or reduced income and employment, or a need to shift programming to accommodate greater family needs (such as an increased need for homework help and technology support because of distance learning or a need for a greater focus on managing stress and strong emotions). To prepare for and perform this critically important and demanding work, we must engage in and contribute to the development of culturally sensitive conceptualizations of parent and family engagement (Roberts, 2011), responding to and engaging with families in their diverse forms.

Engaging diverse youth and families as partners in building integrated programs that honor equity and inclusion must be built from the ground up. This is a unique generation of youth, with higher levels of civic engagement and advocacy than previous generations (Wray-Lake, 2019). They are particularly outspoken and strong advocates for social justice and change, demanding accountability. Youth are leaders and change makers, and are ready to engage with their families and adults in their community to impact change. Extension can be a space for young people to learn and build those skills and that efficacy. The future of Extension and its ability to meet the needs of diverse family systems will be forecasted by Extension's response to these dramatic demographic shifts.

References

Afterschool Alliance. (n.d.). *21st Century community learning centers*. www.afterschoolalliance.org/policy21stcclc.cfm

Ashurst, K., Weisenhorn, D., & Atkinson, T. (2021). Extension Military Parent–Teen Camp experiences: Family resilience building in action. *Journal of Extension*, 58(2). https://tigerprints.clemson.edu/joe/vol58/iss2/14

Behnke, A. O., Urieta, D. M., Duan, S., & Lewis, Z. (2020). Evaluation of Juntos 4-H: A wraparound program helping Latinx high schoolers succeed. *Journal of Extension*, 58(2). https://joe.org/joe/2020april/rb8.php

Berman, R., & Daneback, K. (2020). Children in dual-residence arrangements: A literature review. *Journal of Family Studies*, 28(4), 1448–1465. https://doi.org/10.1080/13229400.2020.1838317

Bridges, B. K., Awokoya, J. T., & Messano, F. (2012). *Done to us, not with us: African American parent perceptions of K-12 education*. Frederick D. Patterson Research Institute, UNCF.

Bronfenbrenner, U. (2001). The bioecological theory of human development. In N. J. Smelser & P. B. Baltes (Eds.), *International encyclopedia of the social and behavioural sciences* (pp. 6963–6970). Elsevier.

Bronfenbrenner, U. (Ed.). (2005). *Making human beings human: Bioecological perspectives on human development*. Sage.

Bureau of Labor Statistics, U.S. Department of Labor, The Economics Daily. (2014). *Working wives in married-couple families, 1967–2011*. www.bls.gov/opub/ted/2014/ted_20140602.htm

Eccles, J., & Gootman, J. A. (Eds.). (2002). *Community programs to promote youth development*. National Academy of Sciences – National Research Council.

Epstein, J. L. (2001). *School, family, and community partnerships: Preparing educators and improving schools*. Westview Press.

Epstein, J. L., & Salinas, K. C. (2004). Partnering with families and communities. *Schools as Learning Communities*, 61(8), 12–18.

Global Family Research Project. (2021). *Family engagement*. https://globalfrp.org/Our-Work/Family-Engagement

Henderson, A. T., & Mapp, K. L. (2002). *A new wave of evidence: The impact of school, family, and community connections on student achievement*. Southwest Educational Development Laboratory.

Horowitz, A. & Bronte-Tinkew, J. (June 2007). *Building, engaging and supporting family and parental involvement in out-of-school time programs*. Child Trends: Research to Results, #2007-16. www.childtrends.org/wp-content/uploads/2007/06/Child_Trends-2007_06_19_RB_ParentEngage.pdf

Lerner, R. M., & Lerner, J. V. (n.d.). *The five Cs model of positive youth development*. Retrieved from http://exploresel.gse.harvard.edu/frameworks/52

Rising Impact: Kajoog. (2021). *The takeoff*. Retrieved from www.kajoog.org/the-takeoff/

Roberts, S. O. (2011). *Reconsidering parental involvement: Implications for Black parents*. Online Publication of Undergraduate Studies. Retrieved from https://wp.nyu.edu/steinhardt-appsych_opus/reconsidering-parental-involvement-implications-for-black-parents/

Rosenberg, H., Wilkes, S., & Harris, E. (2014). Bringing families into out-of-school time learning. *The Journal of Expanded Learning Opportunities*, 1(1), 1–6. Retrieved from https://youthtoday.org/wp-content/uploads/sites/13/2017/04/Bringing-Families-into-the-OST.pdf

Search Institute. (2021). *The developmental assets framework*. www.search-institute.org/our-research/development-assets/developmental-assets-framework/

Sheldon, S. B. (2003). Linking school-family-community partnerships in urban elementary schools to student achievement on state tests. *Urban Review*, 35(2), 149–165.

Skuza, J. A. (2019). Teens in the Somali diaspora: An evaluative program study. *Journal of Youth Development*, 14(2). https://doi.org/10.5195/jyd.2019.703

Social Explorer Dataset (SE), Census 1920, Digitally transcribed by Inter-university Consortium for Political and Social Research. Edited, verified by Michael Haines. Compiled, edited and verified by Social Explorer.

Social Explorer Tables (SE), Census 2010, Census Bureau; Social Explorer.

The Annie E Casey Foundation. (2021). *Theory of change*. Retrieved from www.aecf.org/resources/theory-of-change/

The Condition of Education. (2016). *Enrollment trends by age*. Retrieved from https://nces.ed.gov/programs/coe/pdf/coe_cea.pdf

The Forum for Youth Investment. (n.d.). *What is ready by 21?* Retrieved from www.readyby21.org/what-ready-21

Tzenis, J. A. (2019). Understanding youths' educational aspirations in the Somali diaspora. *Journal of Youth Development*, 14(2). https://doi.org/10.5195/jyd.2019.717

United States Department of Agriculture, National Institute of Food and Agriculture. (USDA-NIFA). (n.d.). *Cooperative Extension history*. Retrieved from https://nifa.usda.gov/cooperative-extension-history

University of Wisconsin Extension. (2021). *Logic models*. Retrieved from https://fyi.extension.wisc.edu/programdevelopment/logic-models/

University of Minnesota Extension. (2021). *What we do*. Retrieved from https://extension.umn.edu/about-extension/what-we-do

U.S. Department of Education. (n.d.). *Family and community engagement*. Retrieved from www.ed.gov/parent-and-family-engagement

U.S. Department of Labor. (2020). *History: An overview 1920–2020*. Retrieved from www.dol.gov/agencies/wb/about/history

Wang, W. (2020, November 10). *The U.S. divorce rate has hit a 50-year low*. Retrieved from https://ifstudies.org/blog/the-us-divorce-rate-has-hit-a-50-year-low

Wray-Lake, L. (2019). How do young people become politically engaged? *Child Development Perspectives*, 13(2), 127–132. https://doi.org/10.1111/cdep.12324

Youniss, J., & Smollar, J. (1985). *Adolescent relationships with mothers, fathers, and friends*. University of Chicago Press.

youth.gov. (n.d.a). *Positive youth development*. Retrieved from https://youth.gov/youth-topics/positive-youth-development

youth.gov. (n.d.b). *Interagency working group on youth programs develops common language on positive youth development*. Retrieved from https://youth.gov/feature-article/interagency-working-group-youth-programs-develops-common-language-positive-youth

CHAPTER 7

The Application of Social Science in 4-H Youth Development

Theresa M. Ferrari and Mary E. Arnold

4-H, the largest youth-serving organization in the United States, reaches an estimated six million young people annually. At the beginning of the twentieth century, educators organized rural youth clubs that formed the foundation of what is now the 4-H program (Wessel & Wessel, 1982). Although 4-H and its four-leaf clover emblem are often associated with county fairs and agriculture, 4-H, in fact, is so much more. Today, youth in 4-H pursue projects in a wide range of areas including robotics, mental health, photography, performing arts, dog training, and civic engagement, to name just a few. Ranging in age from five to eighteen years old, 4-H members participate in clubs, camps, school classrooms, and after-school programs that can be found in rural communities, small towns, suburbs, big cities, and US military bases throughout the world. The 4-H concept has been adapted around the world, where similar independent, country-led programs can be found in more than eighty countries (Archibald et al., 2021; Brinn, 2020).

From its inception, 4-H has been firmly rooted in empirical research, particularly in the field of the social sciences. The 4-H pledge itself embodies attention to the developmental needs of youth – head (clearer thinking), heart (greater loyalty), hands (larger service), and health (better living) – and to the nested environments in which they participate (e.g., their clubs, their communities, their country, and the world). Thus, although the term *positive youth development* (PYD) did not emerge until the 1990s (Roth & Brooks-Gunn, 2016), 4-H programs were already being developed and implemented in support of the developmental and psychological needs of youth as championed by the likes of Gertrude Warren, a 4-H national program leader from 1917 to 1952 (Wessel & Wessel, 1982).

In this chapter, we write about 4-H as a research-informed program from a unique vantage point. Collectively, we have experience as 4-H professionals at the local, state, and national levels over a period of more than forty years – from 1980 to the present. We can write about the

recent historical development and incorporation of social science within
the 4-H program because we have been part of its evolution. One of us
(Mary) was a 4-H member; one of us (Theresa) has been a county educator. We are both now state specialists at our respective land-grant universities and have each been in these positions for 20+ years. Mary has
worked in one state (Oregon); Theresa has worked in four states (Maine,
Michigan, Florida, and Ohio). Both of us have served in national roles:
Theresa was on loan for a year in 2008 to 4-H National Headquarters
to work with 4-H military programs; Mary is currently on loan as the
Director of Youth Development Research and Practice with the National
4-H Council. In these roles, we have designed, implemented, and evaluated programs; conducted volunteer and in-service training; carried
out research projects and given scholarly presentations; written curriculum, grant proposals, reports, and publications; served on national
committees; mentored teens, undergraduate and graduate students, and
colleagues; and held leadership roles in 4-H's professional association.
Perhaps most relevant to this chapter's topic, we have been champions
of the science of youth development that forms the foundation of 4-H
practice, and we have worked consistently to elevate this science across
the 4-H system.

The story of 4-H's early years has been told many times and is documented in several sources (e.g., Rasmussen, 1989; Reck, 1950; Wessel &
Wessel, 1982). Therefore, in this chapter, we aim to tell a different story.
We discuss *why* and *how* 4-H goes about implementing its programs,
right up until the present time. We begin by describing several PYD
frameworks that have guided 4-H as developmental science evolved in
the 1990s and early 2000s. We identify ongoing challenges to translating the science into practice where it means the most – at the point of
service, where youth participants are engaged – that persist despite our
efforts and those of others in the 4-H system past and present. We then
describe the 4-H Thriving Model, and how 4-H has taken major steps
toward embracing a comprehensive theory of change that makes meaningful connections between context, content, and outcomes. Recent
developments in understanding the science of learning and development
and efforts to translate PYD research into practice are promising. We
conclude with next steps for 4-H to position itself to take full advantage
of these recent developments. Based at land-grant universities across the
United States and working with national and local partners, we believe
4-H is well positioned to capitalize on these developments and to intentionally apply them in practice.

7.1 The Application of Social Science in 4-H: Program Context, Content, and Outcomes

4-H is unique among youth development organizations across the United States. It is embedded within the national Cooperative Extension system, which is housed within the vast US land-grant university system. It is connected to federal agencies, in particular the US Department of Agriculture, which is the location of the 4-H National Headquarters. 4-H professionals thus have direct access to cutting-edge research conducted in universities across the country, as well as the resulting deep, research-based content knowledge that provides the subject-matter foundation of 4-H projects and experiences. Programs operate at local, state, and national levels, but at its core, 4-H is based in the community and thus is pivotal to accomplishing the Extension mission of "taking the university to the people" (Rasmussen, 1989, p. vii).

4-H is delivered in a wide range of settings and in the form of various educational experiences designed to achieve learning goals – projects, which consist of a series of planned learning experiences that culminate in a tangible product; workshops and clinics; conferences and trips; camps; domestic and international exchanges; and fairs. Although subject-matter content is important, as it is generally what attracts and hooks a young person to get involved in a program, content alone is not enough. 4-H's educational approach emphasizes the development and mastery of life skills within the context of self-directed, hands-on learning experiences reflected in the 4-H slogan "learn by doing" and the motto "to make the best better." These educational experiences are intended to foster transferable skills such as teamwork, communication, and leadership. 4-H curriculum developers have focused on intentionally building on an experiential learning model (Dewey, 1938; Kolb, 1984) and embedding life skills along with a project's subject-matter content. For example, an activity in a nutrition project (the subject matter) might involve reading food labels and ranking foods based on their sodium content (the project-specific skill) as one way to develop the life skills of critical thinking and making healthy lifestyle choices that transcend the project and are transferable to other settings.

Offering novelty and challenge, educational experiences in 4-H often take young people out of their comfort zone, but also expand their horizons. Young people meet others who share their interests, and they often develop lifelong friendships. They meet adults who can offer them instrumental and emotional support and social capital as they navigate their pathway through childhood and adolescence. Regardless of delivery mode or program setting, the goal is to optimize young people's healthy development and empower them to reach their full potential (US Department of Agriculture and National 4-H Council, 2017).

The importance of evaluating educational programs to assess whether resources have been used wisely and that these efforts are having their intended impacts has been broadly recognized in the scholarly community (Hatry, 2013; Roth & Brooks-Gunn, 2016). Once skills are identified, they can be measured to evaluate the program's impact, which became particularly important as the pressure for accountability increased at the end of the twentieth century (Arnold, 2015; Arnold & Cater, 2011; Peterson et al., 2001; see also Monk, this volume). However, youth programs presented a particular challenge to evaluators: to use an Extension agricultural analogy, how a crop grows depends on a variety of environmental factors, but unlike a crop of corn that is planted and harvested the same year, these people (i.e., youth) have a long growing season. It is precisely this involvement across time that contributes to the impact, but as has been pointed out by Roth and Brooks-Gunn (2016) and experienced directly by us and our counterparts, it also makes it difficult to tie this impact to one specific project, program, event, or experience. Despite this challenge, the impact of 4-H has been borne out by current members and alumni, who have put skills they gained through 4-H into practice in school, work, and community settings (e.g., Anderson, 2020; Anderson et al., 2010; Bates et al., 2020; Digby & Ferrari, 2007; Ferrari et al., 2009; Fox et al., 2003).

7.1.1   PYD Frameworks Commonly Used in 4-H

A paradigm shift occurred in the late 1980s when youth-serving organizations, informed by theories of human ecological development and resilience, began to take a strengths-based approach rather than one based on simply keeping youth out of trouble or narrowly focused on fixing problem behaviors (Blyth, 2011; Damon, 2004; Roth & Brooks-Gunn, 2016). As youth development emerged as a field of research and practice, a second shift occurred as scholars and practitioners grappled with what distinguished a program as a youth development program, what constituted program quality, and how to measure impact (Roth & Brooks-Gunn, 2003, 2016; Roth et al., 1998). Evidence supporting the link between high-quality programs and youth outcomes mounted (e.g., Vandell et al., 2015). As important as it was to ascertain program outcomes, *how* programs produced the outcomes was also of interest to researchers and practitioners (e.g., Larson et al., 2019; Larson et al., 2011). Clearly, attention to what can be described as the program context, climate, or environment is paramount. This current focus on processes and youth programs as a context for development is part of the third wave in the youth development field (Roth & Brooks-Gunn, 2016). Unlike outcomes, these elements are "front loaded"; that is, they must be an intentional part of program design, and as such, are within the control of adult program leaders and are key determinants of program quality. This third wave also encompasses consideration of program evaluation methods and measures, better research designs that take individual differences and context into account, and longitudinal research (Roth & Brooks-Gunn, 2016).

Many complimentary forces were at work that advanced the practice of youth development during these years (Blyth, 2011). 4-H was influenced by and had an influence on the evolution of youth development as a field. For example, the National Association of Extension 4-H Agents (known since 2020, as the National Association of 4-H Youth Development Professionals), 4-H's professional association, established a Research and Evaluation Committee under its Vice President for Research, Evaluation, and Programs. After several years of discussion and planning by committee members, in 2006 the association launched the *Journal of Youth Development* with the intention of bridging developmental science and practice, not just for 4-H, but for the field more broadly. Both of us have served the journal in various capacities during its formation and in the ensuing years.

Conceptual frameworks provide a lens with which to view a topic of interest and show how concepts are related; they bring order to complex issues. Space does not permit an exhaustive review of all the various frameworks that have guided 4-H programs over the years, so we refer the reader to other sources for such reviews (Arnold & Silliman, 2017; Heck & Subramaniam, 2009; Lerner et al., 2011). Here we limit our discussion to four PYD frameworks prominent in 4-H during a time that parallels the expansion of the youth development field more broadly (late 1990s to early 2000s): critical elements from the National 4-H Impact Study (Peterson et al., 2001), program features identified by the National Research Council (Eccles & Gootman, 2002), Kress's (2003) four essential elements, and the Five Cs model from the National 4-H Study of PYD (Lerner et al., 2005).

Summarized in Table 7.1, Kress's (2003) essential elements are best characterized as developmental needs, 4-H critical elements (Peterson et al., 2001) and those of the National Research Council (Eccles &

Table 7.1 *Alignment of common youth development frameworks used in 4-H*

4-H Essential Elements (Kress, 2003)	4-H Impact Study (Peterson et al., 2001)	National Research Council (Eccles & Gootman, 2002)	Five Cs (Lerner et al., 2005)
Belonging	Positive relationship with a caring adult	Supportive relationships	Connection
	Physically and emotionally safe environment	Physical and psychological safety	
	Inclusive, welcoming environment	Opportunities to belong	
Mastery	Engagement in learning Opportunity for mastery	Opportunities for skill building	Competence
Independence	Opportunity for self-determination	Support for efficacy and mattering	Confidence
	Opportunity to see oneself as an active participant in the future		
Generosity	Opportunity to value and practice service to others		Caring
		Appropriate structure	
		Positive social norms	Character
		Integration of family, school, and community efforts	

Note: Adapted from Cochran et al., 2007.

Gootman, 2002) are features that define quality programs, and the Five Cs (Lerner et al., 2005) are outcomes of participation. Collectively they are aligned, even though each framework describes just a piece of an overall program theory. For example, to address the need young people have for developing mastery, adult program leaders provide engaging opportunities for skill building; in turn, such involvement leads to developing competence.

Roth et al. (1998) noted that effective youth development programs share some commonalities – intentional inclusion of youth development principles, opportunities for youth–adult relationships to flourish, and activities that allow for young people's active participation and skill development. The National 4-H Impact Study (Peterson et al., 2001) identified critical elements similar to those in work commissioned by the National Research

Council to identify features exhibited in high-quality programs (Eccles & Gootman, 2002). Dr. Cathann Kress, who from 2002 to 2008 was the Director of Youth Development at 4-H National Headquarters, recast the four elements of belonging, independence, mastery, and generosity from the Native American Circle of Courage (Brendtro et al., 1991; 2005) as the four essential elements of 4-H (Kress, 2003). Along with the eight elements from the national impact study, these four elements continue to guide 4-H programming and frame program evaluation (e.g., Archibald et al., 2021; Bikos et al., 2014; Hensley et al., 2020; Lile et al., 2021; Martz et al., 2009; Wahle et al., 2019). These frameworks were important steps forward, but they did not go far enough.

As the realization grew that structured youth programs had great, but untapped, potential to support PYD, there was an increasing awareness among researchers and scholars of the need to understand that participation was more than just showing up; that to achieve positive youth outcomes, program participants had to become more fully engaged (e.g., Dawes & Larson, 2010; Larson, 2000; Saito & Sullivan, 2011). By far one of the most significant steps toward illuminating the science underpinning 4-H programs came with the advent of the 4-H Study of PYD, an eight-year multiwave study started in 2002 by Richard Lerner and colleagues at Tufts University (Lerner et al., 2005, 2013). The results of this study elucidated a more refined model of youth development that articulated the connection between youth and their ecological assets, to developmental outcomes, and ultimately, over time, to increased positive youth contribution and reduction of risk behaviors (Bowers et al., 2015). The PYD outcomes tested in the 4-H study were comprised of what has come to be known as the Five Cs model of youth development: competence, confidence, character, caring, and connection, leading to the sixth C – contribution. Although only a portion of the more than 7,000 study participants were also in 4-H, the study revealed some key programmatic impacts that were unique to those who did. For example, youth in 4-H programs, especially girls, displayed higher engagement in citizenship activities. 4-H youth also reported higher academic competence and higher school engagement at various grade levels than non-4-H participants, as well as greater engagement in science, engineering, and computer technology programs (Lerner et al., 2013). Altogether, results of the 4-H study are too numerous to describe fully here, as they are published in more than eighty-eight scholarly articles, fifty-one book chapters, four books or monographs, and eight special journal issues or sections (Institute for Applied Research in Youth Development, 2019). The Five

Cs model has been used to frame 4-H curriculum and programming outcomes (e.g., Bowers et al., 2013; Robinson et al., 2012; Worker et al., 2019)
and to frame studies of youth development programs across the United
States and internationally (Lerner, Tirrel, et al., 2019; Mercier et al., 2019).

The Five Cs model is quite robust, and it was widely adopted. Despite
the success of the national study in establishing the Five Cs model, important critiques of the study were brought forth. One such critique com-
mended the scope of the study, affirming that such important work was
long overdue, yet pointed out the underrepresentation of minority youth in
the study, and the associated concerns for the implications of the research
on practice, policy, and further research (Spencer & Spencer, 2014). Other
critiques pointed to the lack of specificity related to translating the results
into effective youth development practice in general, and 4-H programs
specifically (Arnold & Silliman, 2017; Heck & Subramaniam, 2009).
Lacking specificity for translating the research into practice meant that,
despite the far-reaching impact of the Five Cs model in youth development research, its practical adoption in 4-H programs remained underuti-
lized (Arnold, 2018).

7.1.2   Challenges to Adopting a Consistent
Framework to Guide Programming

These four PYD frameworks, used with considerable consistency across the
4-H program, reflected the emerging awareness of the science underlying
the practice of 4-H. Despite a general understanding of and support for the
frameworks, several aspects of how 4-H is organized and implemented have
worked against adopting a consistent framework to guide programming.

1. *Decentralized system across multiple institutions in fifty states and
    territories and variation even within states* – The decentralized nature
    of 4-H's multilevel organizational structure is both an advantage
    and disadvantage. The advantage is that programs can be tailored to
    meet local needs, often thought to be one of the overall strengths of
    Extension programs. The disadvantage is that lacking an organizing
    theoretical framework and with the wide variety of possible
    programs, assessing outcomes across similar programs, across a state,
    and across the country presents challenges.
2. *Program variety* – The wide variety and types of programs
    conducted by 4-H and the tendency to make local adaptations
    are a challenge to implementation fidelity and standardized

reporting, which have made it difficult to assess outcomes on a comprehensive scale. Conversely, this variety may be the reason why 4-H appeals to its members.

3. *Varying academic backgrounds of field staff* – Not all 4-H professionals (which encompasses various titles such as agent, educator, program coordinator, and program assistant) come to their positions with a background in youth development and with skills in program planning, evaluation, and research. Onboarding and in-service training vary from state to state, in large part due to the decentralized system mentioned above, which leads to wide variations in knowledge of the science underlying PYD.

4. *Programs delivered largely by volunteers* – Although there is oversight by 4-H professionals, 4-H clubs are facilitated by volunteer leaders and many 4-H programs use a teens-as-teachers model as well (Worker et al., 2019), which adds another level of complexity and needs to be considered when building PYD capacity.

5. *Time demands of the day-to-day aspects* – 4-H professionals generally juggle multiple administrative and organizational aspects of their positions that require their immediate attention. These concerns may overshadow the big picture and constrain the focus on the more abstract theoretical issues that may seem removed from the daily jumble of tasks.

6. *Disconnected from research* – Despite being situated at land-grant universities, 4-H is often not integrated into academic departments and thus may be disconnected from research conducted at these institutions and from contributing to the research agenda. Practitioners' knowledge may not be valued within the research community.

7. *Lost in translation* – Lack of translating theories into practical strategies limits their application at the point of service, where it is most needed.

In addition, there would usually be some confusion when a new framework was introduced. Did this new framework replace the previous one? Were 4-H professionals supposed to revamp their programming to align with the new framework, and if so, how? The translation of theory and research findings to practice was one missing link. The frameworks each provided some conceptual pieces, but each had limitations, the most notable being that some models had limited or no empirical evidence to support their use (Arnold & Silliman, 2017;

Heck & Subramaniam, 2009). In fact, frameworks such as the essential elements were developed with program implementation in mind. Their swift uptake and adoption indicated that 4-H professionals were seeking frameworks to guide their programs. A comprehensive theory of change, that is, an explanation of why a particular way of working will be effective in leading to desired outcomes, was needed. Roth and Brooks-Gunn (2016) identified a focus on program context, coupled with what was in the programming "black box," as necessary for moving the field of youth development forward.

7.1.3   *Bringing It All Together: The 4-H Thriving Model*

To build on the national 4-H study and improve the translation of research to practice, Arnold (2015, 2018) articulated a theory of change for 4-H youth development. Entitled the 4-H Thriving Model, it consists of three elements: (a) 4-H programs as developmental settings for youth characterized by youth sparks, a safe physical environment and positive emotional climate, and developmental relationships; (b) indicators of youth thriving that reflect social, emotional, cognitive, and behavioral development; and (c) developmental outcomes, which are indicators of PYD, including academic motivation and success, social competence, responsibility, connection with others, and contribution to others. Youth engagement is what is "driving the thriving" along a developmental pathway to outcomes. The developmental outcomes, in turn, lead to long-term outcomes that are realized in adulthood (Arnold & Gagnon, 2020; see Figure 7.1).

Thus, the 4-H Thriving Model addresses the need to show how programs provide the developmental context (Roth & Brooks-Gunn, 2016), connects concepts from previous frameworks, and serves as the bridge between the program context and the developmental outcomes thought to result from participation. The three elements of the model form a predictive theory of change for 4-H programs (Arnold, 2018), the first time such a testable model had been put forward. Arnold and Gagnon (2019) tested and confirmed a full mediational model, in which youth thriving mediates the effect of the quality of the program setting (developmental context) on developmental outcomes. In other words, the effect of developmental context is important, but indirect. Prior to this point, 4-H had used developmental science largely to describe and frame what it did, but it never had a theory of change that articulated how the various aspects were connected. The importance of such a model is its potential

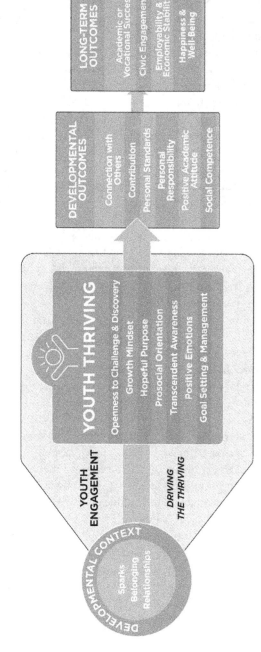

Figure 7.1 The 4-H Thriving Model.

to influence practice because "by focusing on the processes through which PYD is promoted in 4-H programs, the purpose of program activities can be more clearly defined and thus implemented with greater intention" (Arnold & Gagnon, 2019, p. 44).

The 4-H Thriving model met a conceptual and practical need by providing a logical path that connected what 4-H professionals did every day with desired youth development outcomes. Because it was purposely presented in this manner, it made sense to 4-H professionals, and they could situate their work easily in the model. Many expressed renewed pride in their work and in the connection of 4-H to the land-grant university and the Extension mission. As interest in the 4-H Thriving Model grew organically across the national 4-H system, so did the requests from state 4-H programs for professional development and training materials for 4-H professionals and volunteers. These growing needs led to the development of the Advancing the 4-H Thriving Model Task Force, which in 2019 was chartered by the national 4-H Program Leaders Working Group (Arnold & Gagnon, 2020). Establishment of the task force represented a major step toward embracing the model and legitimizing its systemwide adoption, and this work has continued to advance the foundation of science within 4-H.

7.1.4   Progress of the 4-H Thriving Model

Arnold and Gagnon (2020) provided an update on the work of the 4-H Thriving Model Task Force, sharing the advances that had been made as interest in the model increased and spread across the 4-H system. This paper rearticulated the importance of and need for a theoretical model to ensure that 4-H stays true to its research-based mission and to ensure that 4-H programs are based on the latest science related to youth development. The authors also pointed out the need for a theoretical model to ensure high-quality program evaluation – appraisal that needs to evolve beyond outcomes measures alone to include measures of program quality and the processes that lead to those outcomes (Arnold & Cater, 2016; Lerner et al., 2016; Roth & Brooks-Gunn, 2016).

The establishment of a research-based theory of change for 4-H (as articulated in the 4-H Thriving Model) and its alignment with the science of learning and development principles (which are discussed in Section 7.2) have contributed to 4-H being more scientifically based than perhaps at any point in its history. Furthermore, researchers outside of 4-H have recognized 4-H's position as a leader in science-based youth development practice. In his commentary on the advancement of the 4-H Thriving Model, Lerner (2020) pointed out that the 4-H Thriving Model exemplifies a "creative and richly theoretically and empirically informed vision for promoting youth development" (p. 147). Lerner goes on to support the model as "an exemplar of how theoretically predicated and cutting-edge developmental science and the enactment of youth programs can be mutually informative."

In a related commentary, Moroney (2020) supported the 4-H Thriving Model as an excellent example of the application of developmental science in youth development practice. Moroney goes on to state that the translation alone, although commendable, is not enough. Rather, if 4-H is going to move forward with strengthening the scientific base of its youth development practice, the organization as a whole must achieve a level of readiness for systemwide implementation. Three factors are crucial for successful implementation: motivation, general capacity, and content-specific knowledge (which Moroney portrays as $R = MC^2$, where R represents implementation readiness). Despite the work that still lies ahead, Moroney affirmed that the work the 4-H Thriving Model Task Force has done to foster organizational learning and development to implement science-based programming in 4-H is critical to implementing sound youth development practices that are based on a scientific body of evidence.

Although the support of the scientific community related to youth development, and the general enthusiasm and interest in the 4-H Thriving Model as a theory of change for 4-H, has been positive for moving the model forward, further translation of the model into practical application was necessary before 4-H could intentionally and consistently implement programs based in science. As this work moved forward, it became clear that the scientific theory of change embodied in the model must be expressed differently across different levels of the 4-H system. One of the most important levels is the practitioner level, the professionals who are the individuals in 4-H who design and implement programs at the local, state, and national level. Frontline 4-H professionals view themselves as practitioners of youth development, not developmental scientists. As such, they may not need to know the detailed body of evidence related to youth development, but they do need to understand the basic theory, and most of all, how to put the science into practice effectively (Arnold, 2015; Arnold & Cater, 2016). They, in turn, must be able to explain it in a way that makes sense to the volunteers and stakeholders with whom they work.

7.2 The Next Wave: The Science of Learning and Development

Simultaneously with the advancement of the 4-H Thriving Model as a theory of change for the 4-H program, significant advances in the science of learning and development (SoLD) were taking place. SoLD is a holistic view of developmental processes that has emerged from multidisciplinary strands of research to form a comprehensive understanding of how young people learn, grow, and develop (Cantor et al., 2019, 2021; Osher, Cantor et al., 2020). Findings from this emerging field underscored the dynamic and interactional effects of context, relationships, environments, and social structures on development, and the importance of a "whole-child" approach to learning. Of particular importance are the multiple contexts that shape who youth are, how they learn, and their experiences. One of the initial results of this work was the identification of eight key findings of how youth learn and develop:

1. Potential – every child, no matter their background, has the potential to succeed.
2. Malleability – young brains are highly malleable and resilient in learning new concepts and overcoming challenges.
3. Individuality – every child learns and develops differently.
4. Context – experiences, environments, and cultures are the most critically defining influences on development.
5. Relationships – strong and trust-filled relationships are essential for learning and development.
6. Integration – learning is accelerated and enhanced when it is intentionally integrated across learning environments.
7. Continuum – youth learn and develop continually in progression, but not necessarily in a linear fashion.
8. Meaning making – learning happens most effectively when connections to prior experiences and knowledge are made. (Science of Learning and Development Alliance, 2020)

The findings from SoLD were translated into five guiding principles for an equitable whole-child approach to educational design. These five principles are (a) positive developmental relationships; (b) environments filled with safety and belonging; (c) rich learning experiences and knowledge development; (d) development of skills, habits, and mindsets; and (e) integrated support systems (Learning Policy Institute & Turnaround for Children, 2021; see Figure 7.2). The outer ring of the figure has five additional overarching concepts that are embodied in the principles: that

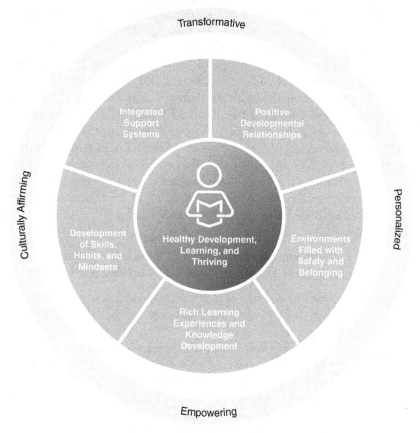

Figure 7.2   Guiding principles for equitable whole-child design.
Note: Learning Policy Institute & Turnaround for Children, 2021. Used with permission.

learning environments, relationships, and support systems will be transformative, personalized, empowering, and culturally affirming.

Although presented in the context of formal education (i.e., referring to classrooms and students), the key design principles derived from the SoLD findings align directly with best practices identified in the youth development research literature. As a result, leading youth development researchers were quick to embrace the SoLD findings, pointing out the coalescing of theory, research methods, and related implications for application in youth development practice (Lerner, Geldhof, et al., 2019). The initial SoLD findings align well with established youth development theory, perhaps most importantly with respect to the critical influence of mutually beneficial person <–> context relations on youth development and thriving (Lerner et al., 2003). The findings also align with cutting-edge research methods in youth development that increasingly focus on individual analysis, charting idiopathic, rather than average, developmental pathways (Nesselroade, 2019; Rose, 2016). Such nonreductionist advances in research methods are consistent with holistic and individual child development emphasized in the SoLD findings (Lerner, Geldhof, et al., 2019). In terms of application for youth development practice, the SoLD findings underscore the importance of the specificity principle articulated by Bornstein (2019), which informs youth development practice by emphasizing the importance of determining the specific ways in which a program works, with what specific groups of youth, and under what specific conditions (Bronfenbrenner, 1979; Lerner, 2020).

7.3   Convergence: SoLD Design Principles, Youth Development Theory, and the 4-H Thriving Model

The SoLD scholarship (Cantor et al., 2019; Osher, Cantor, et al., 2020) began to emerge at the same time as the development of the 4-H Thriving Model. Direct alignments can be drawn between the five SoLD design principles, youth development theory and research, and the elements of the 4-H Thriving Model (see Table 7.2). Specifically, the developmental context element of the 4-H Thriving Model describes the ingredients for a high-quality 4-H program: sparks, belonging, and relationships. Additional elements of 4-H programs that are important to a high-quality developmental setting are those identified by Peterson et al. (2001) and Eccles and Gootman (2002), among which include psychological and physical safety. All these elements align with the SoLD design principle of environments filled with safety and belonging. Fostering developmental relationships (Pekel, 2019; Roehlkepartain et al., 2017) is a key element of the 4-H Thriving Model, which aligns with the SoLD principle of positive developmental relationships.

The rich learning experiences design principle is reflected in the 4-H Thriving Model with its emphasis on youth sparks (Benson & Scales, 2011) and youth engagement, which center the 4-H learning experience in what a young person finds most interesting and most meaningful. 4-H has long embraced a youth-centered approach to learning and knowledge development that reflects the SoLD principle of productive instructional strategies. 4-H begins with a young person's interests and builds a program of learning and development that is centered on that spark. An emphasis on

Table 7.1 Alignment of the 4-H Thriving Model to the SoLD principles of equitable whole-child design and youth development scholarship

SoLD whole-child design principle	Design principles summary	Supporting youth development research	4-H Thriving Model element
Positive developmental relationships	Fostering developmental relationships through structures and practices that allow for caring, continuous, and secure youth–adult relationships	*Developmental Relationships* • Express care • Challenging growth • Providing support • Sharing power • Expanding possibilities (Pekel, 2019; Roehlkepartain et al., 2017)	Developmental Relationships
Environments filled with safety and belonging	Providing physical, psychological, cultural, and identity-safe learning environments where you experience safety, belonging, and inclusion	*Youth Program Quality Features* • Physical and psychological safety • Appropriate structure • Opportunities to belong • Positive social norms • Support for efficacy and mattering (Eccles & Gootman, 2002)	Belonging
Rich learning experiences and knowledge development	Providing learning opportunities that are relevant, engaging, and inquiry based	*Sparks* (Benson & Scales, 2011) *Experiential Learning* (Dewey, 1938; Kolb, 1984)	Sparks Youth Engagement
Development of skills, habits, and mindsets	Integrating cognitive, social, and emotional learning that build resilience, a growth mindset, hope, purpose, social awareness, and self-regulation	*Whole Child Development, Learning, and Thriving* Leading to the development of skills; knowledge; and academic, social, and emotional outcomes (Devaney, 2015; Durlak et al., 2010; Osher, Pittman, et al., 2020)	Indicators of Youth Thriving: • Growth mindset • Openness to challenge and discovery • Hopeful purpose • Prosocial orientation • Transcendent awareness • Positive emotionality • Goal setting and management
Integrated support systems	Supporting youth health and mental health; providing social services and opportunities to build on interests and passions	*Grounding, Well-Being, and Agency* (Damon, 2004; Osher, Pittman, et al., 2020)	Sparks Youth Engagement

learning by doing (i.e., experiential learning; Dewey, 1938; Kolb, 1984), which intentionally helps youth apply learning to novel settings, leads to the development of problem-solving and metacognitive skills.

The thriving indicators identified in the 4-H Thriving model represent the critical social, emotional, cognitive, and behavioral learning and habits of mind articulated in the SoLD design principles. Research shows that regular participation in high-quality youth development programs contributes to the social and emotional development of young people (Devaney, 2015; Durlak et al., 2010; Osher, Pittman, et al., 2020). Supporting the development of these thriving indicators along with rich content learning experiences leads to transformative learning for youth (Osher, Pittman, et al., 2020).

The alignment between the integrated support systems design principle and the 4-H Thriving Model is not as direct as the others primarily due to the principle's roots in formal education, with the intent of emphasizing that meeting the ancillary needs of students is essential to academic success. Even so, 4-H practice reflects this understanding when considering the ultimate well-being and personal agency of young people, especially through a multitiered systems of support (e.g., 4-H volunteers, professional 4-H educators, parents, and other adults working with 4-H youth). Focusing on youth sparks, for example, supports positive youth identity, sense of purpose, and hope, all key aspects of mental health and PYD (Damon, 2004). Likewise, youth engagement and empowerment through strong relationships and leadership opportunities promote youth agency (Larson, 2011; Larson & Angus, 2011), another important indicator of youth well-being. Throughout their 4-H career, youth are encouraged to explore applications for their interests, with a particular emphasis on developing transferable life skills and college and career connections (e.g., Anderson, 2020; Cochran & Ferrari, 2009; Digby & Ferrari, 2007; Ferrari et al., 2008; Horrillo et al., 2021).

The social and emotional development identified in the SoLD whole-child design model (Figure 7.2) aligns directly with the indicators of youth thriving in the 4-H Thriving Model (Figure 7.1). These seven indicators of thriving reflect social, emotional, cognitive, and behavioral learning that is critical for youth to form the positive habits and mindsets for success identified in the SoLD whole-child design principles. Finally, 4-H youth development program design and practice methods embody the systems of supports identified in the SoLD principles and the opportunities for extended in-depth learning – long a hallmark of 4-H's approach to youth development. In short, the current scientific body of evidence for how youth learn and develop is in alignment with youth development scholarship and is reflected in the 4-H Thriving Model, which illustrates the translation of the research into 4-H practice.

7.3.1 Application: 4-H Practice Principles

To meet the need to put the science into practice, six principles guide the alignment of 4-H practice at all levels of the system. These six principles translate science into practice by emphasizing that all 4-H programs:

- are based on the science of PYD;
- combine learning, teaching, and the promotion of youth thriving for life-changing (transformative) learning;
- promote robust equity to ensure thriving and opportunity for all youth (robust equity is "the intentional counter to inequality, institutionalized privilege and prejudice, and systemic deficits and the intentional promotion of thriving across multiple domains for those who experience inequity and injustice"; Osher, Pittman, et al., 2020, p. 3);
- prioritize youth voice, leadership, and civic engagement;
- facilitate the creation of pathways for youth leading to actionable postsecondary plans; and
- make continual investments in professional and volunteer capacity building to ensure that those responsible for planning and implementing 4-H programs have the knowledge, skills, and capacity to ensure that 4-H programs are grounded in science, while they are informed by practice.

Translation of the SoLD findings into the whole-child design principles was a key step in translating the findings into practice. Likewise, aligning the principles with the 4-H Thriving Model connected the PYD theory to the science, and the 4-H practice principles guide practitioners as they plan 4-H programs based on science.

Building the capacity of 4-H professionals to implement 4-H programs grounded in science requires both translation and application. Although these six principles provide the foundation for translating the science of youth development into 4-H practice, it is important to underscore that as the science evolves, the *how* and the *why* of 4-H practice remain the same (Arnold, 2020). In other words, the science that is translated into the six principles must have real-world, authentic application in the everyday work of 4-H professionals to be fully adopted. Here is where the long-standing 4-H pedagogy and science intersect. Take, for example, 4-H camp counselor training programs, which are ubiquitous across the 4-H system. In many states, 4-H camp counselors are teens who lead and work with small groups of younger campers in a residential camp experience, typically held over three to five days. For the 4-H professional, the camp experience has two audiences that they must plan for: camp counselors and campers (Ferrari & McNeely, 2007). While every counselor must be trained for their role in ensuring a safe and fun camp for every camper, purposeful attention to these six principles when designing the camp counselor training program ensures that teen counselors are not only being prepared for a summer job; they are also receiving a transformational experience that is grounded in the science of youth development. For example, they are empowered when adult leaders entrust them to carry out their leadership position responsibly (Digby & Ferrari, 2007; Ferrari & Arnett, 2011; Ferrari & McNeely, 2007). Applying these principles ensures that the campers' experience will be positive as well (e.g., Wahle et al., 2019).

7.4   Serious about the Science: What Comes Next for 4-H?

Outlining the alignment between developmental science and 4-H practice through the 4-H Thriving Model has advanced the scientific base of 4-H youth development practice considerably. The 4-H Thriving Model elucidates the necessary ingredients of effective 4-H program settings and opens the "black box" of 4-H program processes that lead to outcomes (as recommended by Roth & Brooks-Gunn, 2016). Arguably, this work has illuminated the science behind the practice more so than at any time in the history of the 4-H program. However, as Arnold (2018) pointed out, providing professional development to ensure the science is practiced across the 4-H system is a critical and daunting next step, requiring a commitment to building organizational learning at all levels of the 4-H organization.

But perhaps the moment has come for 4-H to get even more serious about the science. One way to do this is to address barriers that may affect 4-H professionals' use of research evidence, such as locating and assessing what is available and having the skills to interpret and apply findings (Bikos et al., 2011). Further, because of its unique home within the land-grant university system, it is incumbent upon 4-H to be a leader in bridging research and practice – with research informing practice and practice informing research – and to ensure that there is research *about* practice and that it involves *practitioners*. It is not always easy to do such research, and it can be messy, as we and those who have done it can attest (e.g., Agans et al., 2020). As well, when research describes how practitioners achieve their aims, it can go far in validating good practice, as Burrow et al. (2020) did in their recent study exploring 4-H as a context for developing youth's sense of purpose. When practice validates the theory, we have come full circle.

Organizationally, the 4-H program is poised to take a pronounced step forward in building the connection between science and practice. The coalescing of cutting-edge developmental science and the 4-H Thriving Model has resulted in an organic groundswell of interest across the 4-H system, a departure from the historical national-to-local level approach of instigating change. Instead of being directed from a national 4-H office, a team of 4-H professionals from across the 4-H system has worked together for the past several years to advance the 4-H Thriving Model and its grounding in the SoLD. This task force is providing leadership, training, and resources to support frontline 4-H professionals and is working to build professional capacity from the ground up.

Developmental science is alive and well in 4-H. As we started writing this chapter, the first-ever 4-H PYD Academy brought together more than 900 4-H professionals from around the country. This three-day virtual academy was designed with the sole purpose of connecting developmental science to applied practice, with a focus on understanding theory, creating effective developmental settings, and ensuring equity and opportunity for all youth. Unlike the approach in most 4-H professional development opportunities, the 4-H PYD Academy did not focus on any particular program content, but rather on the *science* of PYD. The virtual PYD Academy is one step on a long road of organizational change that lies ahead if 4-H is to get serious about the science of PYD. As Moroney (2020) stated:

> The diverse 4-H system now has the ultimate challenge of adopting and implementing the principles presented in their theory of change (…) to implement a model into practice, the real and human factors of implementation readiness are key to success, which means that 4-H must align resources; coordinate professional learning; and get the adults, or implementers, bought in and up to speed on the theory of change and associated practices. (pp. 162–163)

4-H is ready and up to the task. After the successful 4-H PYD Academy, a 4-H Thriving Champions Regional Network was formed. These individuals, representing thirty-six land-grant universities, are charged with advancing the consistent use of the 4-H Thriving Model as the theory of PYD used in 4-H. Note the important difference between the standard use of the *model* versus using a standard 4-H *program*, as such program standardization would run counter to SoLD principles (Lerner, 2020). The thriving champions will focus primarily on capacity building efforts for 4-H professionals and volunteers, with a special focus on consistent orientation for onboarding new 4-H professionals (thereby addressing challenges previously confronting model adoption).

We must also acknowledge that we have been writing this chapter in the middle of a global pandemic, the impact of which on a generation of youth and youth organizations will become more and more apparent in the coming months and years. We are surrounded by insistent calls for racial and social justice, borne of frustration and anger at the relentless inequities that not only persist, but are exacerbated by the pandemic and ongoing political and ideological strife. The message brought forth by the science of learning of development, however, is one of hope. It is a message that reveals how every young person has the potential to learn, grow, develop, and thrive given the right supports and opportunities. Ensuring that 4-H practitioners not only understand the science but also use it to plan and implement 4-H programs is key to helping today's youth find a successful pathway forward.

Perhaps the beauty of this moment is the realization that 4-H is already practicing the science – just as it has for more than 120 years. 4-H has always provided safe and structured contexts for youth, where belonging, mattering, and skill building were emphasized, even if we did not use those exact words to describe it. Since the beginning, youth's positive relationships with caring adults and the promotion of social, emotional, and cognitive skills have been woven into the fabric of everyday 4-H practice. 4-H has endured, despite its shortcomings and challenges, because as an organization it strives to walk the talk: to "learn by doing" and "to make the best better" when it comes to keeping pace with developments in science and applying them in practice, learning and improving along the way. 4-H must "do the work" if it is to reach its ambitious goals, including a more diverse membership and workforce (Fields, 2020; Sumner et al., 2018; U.S. Department of Agriculture and National 4-H Council, 2017). The 4-H Thriving Model and the resulting work it has catalyzed represent how 4-H has advanced as the science has advanced; it continues to influence and to be influenced by developmental science, and to bridge research and practice. All these recent developments are now part of the next chapter in 4-H's continuing story.

By continuing to apply what the best of science has to offer, we, as a 4-H organization, can ensure that as young people navigate their developmental pathway and write their own story, their 4-H experience is anchored upon a firm foundation.

References

Agans, J. P., Burrow, A. L., Kim, E. S., Garbo, C., Schroeder, M., Graf, S., & Davis, T. (2020). "You're going to burn some bridges if you come at it the wrong way": Reflecting on the realities of research-practice partnerships. *Community Development*, 51(1), 36–52. https://doi.org/10.1080/15575330.2020.1714686

Anderson, B. L. (2020). Exploring the impacts of state 4-H council service on career readiness. *Journal of Youth Development*, 15(6), 136–146. https://doi.org/10.5195/jyd.2020.800

Anderson, J., Bruce, J., & Mouton, L. (2010). 4-H made me a leader: A college-level alumni perspective of leadership life skill development. *Journal of Leadership Education*, 9(2), 35–49. https://doi.org/10.12806/V9/I2/RF3

Archibald, T., Guisse, B. K., Ndiaye, A., Kane, F., Diouf, F., & Jamison, K. (2021). Positive youth development in Senegal: A case study of 4-H Senegal. *Journal of Youth Development*, 16(2–3), 344–362. https://doi.org/10.5195/jyd.2021.1054

Arnold, M. E. (2015). Connecting the dots: Improving Extension program planning with program umbrella models. *Journal of Human Sciences and Extension*, 3(2), Article 5. https://doi.org/10.54718/JNCI4860

Arnold, M. E. (2018). From context to outcomes: A thriving model for 4-H youth development programs. *Journal of Human Sciences and Extension*, 6(1), Article 11. https://doi.org/10.54718/NBNL5438

Arnold, M. E. (2020). America's moment: Investing in positive youth development to transform youth and society. *Journal of Youth Development*, 15(5), 16–36. https://doi.org/10.5195/jyd.2020.996

Arnold, M. E., & Cater, M. (2011). From then to now: Emerging directions for youth program evaluation. *Journal of Youth Development*, 6(3), 80–92. https://doi.org/10.5195/jyd.2011.176

Arnold, M. E., & Cater, M. (2016). Program theory and quality matter: Changing the course of Extension program evaluation. *Journal of Extension*, 54(1), Article 28. https://tigerprints.clemson.edu/joe/vol54/iss1/28

Arnold, M. E., & Gagnon, R. J. (2019). Illuminating the process of youth development: The mediating effect of thriving on youth development program outcomes. *Journal of Human Sciences and Extension*, 7(3), 24–51. www.jhseonline.com/article/view/901

Arnold, M. E., & Gagnon, R. J. (2020). Positive youth development theory in practice: An update on the 4-H Thriving Model. *Journal of Youth Development*, 15(6), 1–23. https://doi.org/10.5195/jyd.2020.954

Arnold, M. E., & Silliman, B. (2017). From theory to practice: A critical review of positive youth development frameworks. *Journal of Youth Development*, 12(2), 1–20. https://doi.org/10.5195/jyd.2017.17

Bates, S., Anderson-Butcher, D., Ferrari, T., & Clary, C. (2020). A comparative examination of how program design components influence youth leadership skill development. *Journal of Youth Development*, 15(6), 91–155. https://doi.org/10.5195/jyd.2020.868

Bikos, L. H., Haney, D. M., Kirkpatrick-Husk, K., & Hsia, S. (2014). A qualitative evaluation of the 4-H record book in light of PYD concepts: Belonging, mastery, independence, and generosity. *Journal of Youth Development*, 9(2), 99–115. https://doi.org/10.5195/jyd.2014.63

Bikos, L. H., Kocheleva, J. A., Campbell, T., Daryani, R., Chahil, S., Brown, T., Winberg, Y., & Pavese, L. (2011). Investigating the utilization of research evidence in the 4-H youth development program. *Journal of Youth Development*, 6(2), 24–38. https://doi.org/10.5195/jyd.2011.185

Benson, P. L., & Scales, P. C. (2011). Thriving and sparks. In R. J. R. Leveque (Ed.), *Encyclopedia of adolescence* (pp. 2963–2976). Springer.

Blyth, D. A. (2011). The future of youth development: Multiple wisdoms, alternate pathways and aligned accountability. *Journal of Youth Development*, 6(3), 168–182. https://doi.org/10.5195/jyd.2011.182

Bornstein, M. H. (2019). Fostering optimal development and averting detrimental development: Prescriptions, proscriptions, and specificity. *Journal of Applied Developmental Science*, 23(4), 340–345. https://doi.org/10.1080/10888691.2017.1421424

Bowers, E. P., Geldhof, G. J., Johnson, S. K., Hilliard, L. J., Hershberg, R. M., Lerner, J. V., & Lerner, R. M. (2015). Applying research about adolescence in real-world settings: The sample case of the 4-H study of positive youth development. In E. P. Bowers, G. J. Geldhof, S. K. Johnson, L. J. Hilliard, R. M. Hershberg, J. V. Lerner, & R. M. Lerner (Eds.), *Promoting positive youth development: Lessons from the 4-H study* (pp. 1–20). Springer. https://doi.org/10.1007/978-3-319-17166-1_1

Bowers, E. P., Napolitano, C. M., Arbeit, M. R., Chase, P., Glickman, S. A., & Lerner, R. M. (2013). On a pathway towards thriving: Evaluating effectiveness of tools to promote positive development and intentional self regulation in youth. *Journal of Youth Development*, 8(3), 4–31. https://doi.org/10.5195/jyd.2013.82

Brendtro, L. K., Brokenleg, M., & Van Bockern, S. (2005). The circle of courage and positive psychology. *Reclaiming Children and Youth*, 14(3), 130–136.

Brendtro, L. K., Brokenleg, M., Van Bockern, S., & Blue Bird, G. (1991). The circle of courage. *Beyond Behavior*, 2(2), 5–12. www.jstor.org/stable/44707005

Brinn, J. (2020, May 15). *4-H around the world: Africa*. Michigan State University Extension. www.canr.msu.edu/news/4_h_around_the_world_africa

Bronfenbrenner, U. (1979). *The ecology of human development: Experiments by nature and design*. Harvard University Press.

Burrow, A. L., Ratner, K., Porcelli, S., & Sumner, R. (2020). Does purpose grow here? Exploring 4-H as a context for cultivating youth purpose. *Journal of Adolescent Research*, 37(4), 471–500. https://doi.org/10.1177/0743558420942477

Cantor, P., Lerner, R. M., Pittman, K., Chase, P. A., & Gomperts, N. (2021). *Whole-child development, learning, and thriving: A dynamic systems approach.* Cambridge University Press. https://doi.org/10.1017/9781108954600

Cantor, P., Osher, D., Berg, J., Steyer, L., & Rose, T. (2019). Malleability, plasticity, and individuality: How children learn and develop in context. *Journal of Applied Developmental Science*, 23(4), 307–337. https://doi.org/10.1080/1088 8691.2017.1398649

Cochran, G., Arnett, N., & Ferrari, T. M. (2007). Adventure Central: Applying the "demonstration plot" concept to youth development. *Journal of Higher Education Outreach and Engagement*, 11(4), 55–75. https://openjournals.libs .uga.edu/jheoe/article/view/541

Cochran, G., & Ferrari, T. M. (2009). Preparing youth for the 21st century knowledge economy: Youth programs and workforce preparation. *Afterschool Matters*, 8, 11–25. www.robertbownefoundation.org/pdf_files/2009_asm_spring.pdf

Damon, W. (2004). What is positive youth development? *The ANNALS of the American Academy of Political and Social Science*, 591(1), 13–24. https://doi .org/10.1177/0002716203260092

Dawes, N. P., & Larson, R. (2010). How youth get engaged: Grounded-theory research on motivational development in organized youth programs. *Developmental Psychology*, 47(1), 259–269. https://doi.org/10.1037/a0020729

Devaney, E. (2015). *Supporting social and emotional development through quality afterschool programs.* American Institutes for Research. www.air.org/ sites/default/files/downloads/report/Social-and-Emotional-Development-Afterschool-Programs.pdf

Dewey, J. (1938). *Experience and education.* Simon & Schuster.

Digby, J. K., & Ferrari, T. M. (2007). Camp counseling and the development and transfer of workforce skills: The perspective of Ohio 4-H camp counselor alumni. *Journal of Youth Development*, 2(2), 103–122. https://doi.org/10.5195/ jyd.2007.349

Durlak, J. A., Weissberg, R. P., & Panchan, M. (2010). A meta-analysis of after-school programs that seek to promote personal and social skills in children and adolescents. *American Journal of Community Psychology*, 45, 294–309. https:// doi.org/10.1007/s10464-010-9300-6

Eccles, J., & Gootman, J. A. (Eds.). (2002). *Community programs to promote youth development.* The National Academies Press. https://doi.org/10.17226/10022

Ferrari, T. M., & Arnett, N. (2011). Implementing a work-based-learning approach to 4-H camp counseling. *Journal of Youth Development*, 6(4), 17–31. https://doi.org/10.5195/jyd.2011.161

Ferrari, T. M., Arnett, N., & Cochran, G. (2008). Preparing teens for success: Building 21st century skills through a 4-H work-based learning program. *Journal of Youth Development*, 3(1), 27–44. https://doi.org/10.5195/jyd.2008.317

Ferrari, T. M., Lekies, K. S., & Arnett, N. (2009). Opportunities matter: Exploring youths' perspectives on their long-term participation in an urban 4-H youth development program. *Journal of Youth Development*, 4(3), 22–40. https://doi.org/10.5195/jyd.2009.249

Ferrari, T. M., & McNeely, N. N. (2007). Positive youth development: What's camp counseling got to do with it? Findings from a study of Ohio 4-H camp counselors. *Journal of Extension*, 45(2), Article 16. https://tigerprints.clemson .edu/joe/vol45/iss2/16

Fields, N. I. (2020). Exploring the 4-H thriving model: A commentary through an equity lens. *Journal of Youth Development*, 15(6), 171–194. https://doi .org/10.5195/jyd.2020.1058

Fox, J., Schroeder, D., & Lodl, K. (2003). Life skill development through 4-H clubs: The perspective of 4-H alumni. *Journal of Extension*, 41(6), Article 10. https://tigerprints.clemson.edu/joe/vol41/iss6/10

Hatry, H. P. (2013). Sorting the relationships among performance measurement, program evaluation, and performance management. In S. B. Nielsen & D. E. K. Hunter (Eds.), Performance management and evaluation. *New Directions for Evaluation*, 137, 19–32. https://doi.org/10.1002/ev.20043

Heck, K. E., & Subramaniam, A. (2009). *Youth development frameworks* [Monograph]. University of California 4-H Center for Youth Development. http://4h.ucanr.edu/Resources/Research/

Hensley, S. T., Kent, H. C., Broaddus, B. A., Ellison, S., Michael, S. T., & Spero, V. (2020). 4-H volunteer attainment of quality positive youth development practices. *Journal of Youth Development*, 15(4), 87–96. https://doi.org/10.5195/jyd.2020.882

Horrillo, S. J., Smith, M. H., Wilkins, T. R., Diaz Carrasco, C. P., Caeton, N. W., McIntyre, D., & Schmitt-McQuitty, L. (2021). A positive youth development approach to college and career readiness. *Journal of Youth Development*, 16(1), 74–99. https://doi.org/10.5195/jyd.2021.966

Institute for Applied Developmental Research in Youth Development. (2019, November). *The 4-H Study of PYD: Publications as of November 1, 2019.* https:// sites.tufts.edu/iaryd/files/2021/01/The-4-H-Study-of-PYD-Publications.pdf

Kolb, D. A. (1984). *Experiential learning: Experience as the source of learning and development*. Prentice-Hall.

Kress, C. (2003). The circle of courage in practice: The 4-H club study. *Reclaiming Children and Youth*, 12(1), 27.

Larson, R. W. (2000). Toward a psychology of positive youth development. *American Psychologist*, 55(1), 170–183. https://doi.org/10.1037//0003-066X.55.1.170

Larson, R. W. (2011). Adolescents' conscious processes of developing regulation: Learning to appraise challenges. In R. M. Lerner, J. V. Lerner, E. P. Bowers, S. Lewin-Bizan, S. Gestsdóttir, & J. B. Urban (Eds.), Thriving in childhood and adolescence: The role of self-regulation processes. *New Directions for Child and Adolescent Development*, 133, 87–97. https://doi.org/10.1002/cd.306

Larson, R. W., & Angus, R. M. (2011). Adolescents' development of skills for agency in youth programs: Learning to think strategically. *Child Development*, 82(1), 277–294. https://doi.org/10.1111/j.1467-8624.2010.01555.x

Larson, R., McGovern, G., & Orson, C. (2019). Youth development programs: Supporting self-motivation in project-based learning. In K. Renninger & S. Hidi (Eds.), *The Cambridge handbook of motivation and learning* (pp. 111–138). Cambridge University Press. https://doi.org/10.1017/9781316823279.007

Larson, R. W., Perry, S. C., Kang, H., & Walker, K. C. (2011). New horizons: Understanding the processes and practices of youth development. *Journal of Youth Development*, 6(3), 156–166. https://doi.org/10.5195/jyd.2011.181

Learning Policy Institute & Turnaround for Children. (2021). *Design principles for schools: Putting the science of learning and development into action*. https://learningpolicyinstitute.org/sites/default/files/product-files/SoLD_Design_Principles_REPORT.pdf

Lerner, R. M. (2020). A roadmap for youth thriving: A commentary on the Arnold and Gagnon vision for positive youth development. *Journal of Youth Development*, 15(6), 147–161. https://doi.org/10.5195/jyd.2020.1056

Lerner, R. M., Dowling, E. M., & Anderson, P. M. (2003). Positive youth development: Thriving as the basis of personhood and civil society. *Journal of Applied Developmental Science*, 7(3), 172–180. https://doi.org/10.1207/S1532480XADS0703_8

Lerner, R. M., Geldhof, G. J., & Bowers, E. P. (2019). The science of learning and development: Entering a new frontier of human development theory, research, and application. *Journal of Applied Developmental Science*, 23(4), 305–306. https://doi.org/10.1080/10888691.2019.1630995

Lerner, R. M., Lerner, J. V., Almerigi, J., Theokas, C., Phelps, E., Gestsdóttir, S., Nadeau, S., Jelicic, H., Alberts, A., Ma, L., Smith, L. M., Bobek, D. L., Richman-Raphael, D., Simpson, I., Christiansen, E. D., & von Eye, A. (2005). Positive youth development, participation in community youth development programs, and community contributions of fifth grade adolescents: Findings from the first wave of the 4-H Study of Positive Youth Development. *Journal of Early Adolescence*, 25(1), 17–71. https://doi.org/10.1177/0272431604272461

Lerner, R. M., Lerner, J. V., Brown, J., & Zaff, J. (2016). Evaluating programs aimed at promoting positive youth development: A relational development systems-based view. *Applied Developmental Science*, 20(3), 175–187. https://doi.org/10.1080/10888691.2015.1082430

Lerner, R. M., Lerner, J. V., & colleagues. (2013). *The positive development of youth: Comprehensive findings from the study of positive youth development*. National 4-H Council.

Lerner, R. M., Lerner, J. V., Lewin-Bizan, S., Bowers, E. P., Boyd, M. J., Mueller, M. K., Schmid, K. L., & Napolitano, C. M. (2011). Positive youth development: Processes, programs, and problematics. *Journal of Youth Development*, 6(3), 38–62. https://doi.org/10.5195/jyd.2011.174

Lerner, R. M., Tirrell, J. M., Dowling, E. M., Geldhof, G. J., Gestsdóttir, S., Lerner, J. V., King, P. E., Williams, K., Iraheta, G., & Sim, A. T. R. (2019). The end of the beginning: Evidence and absences studying PYD in a global context. *Adolescent Research Review*, 4(1), 1–14. https://doi.org/10.1007/s40894-018-0093-4

Lile, J. R., Weybright, E. H., & Watson, P. (2021). Using the 4-H essential elements to evaluate teen programming. *Journal of Youth Development*, 16(1), 55–73. https://doi.org/10.5195/jyd.2021.906

Martz, J., Mincemoyer, C., McNeely, N. N., & contributing authors Bledsoe, L. P., Dart, P. C., Johannes, E., Arnould, A., Gressley, K., Jones, K.,

Lerner, J. V., McDonald, D., & Worthington, K. (2009). *Essential elements of 4-H youth development programs: Key ingredients for program success.* National 4-H Council.

Mercier, J., Powell, C., Langdon-Pole, G., Finau, D., Hicks, K., Bourchier, L., & Hampton, J. (2019). The five Cs of positive youth development in an Aotearoa/ New Zealand program context. *Journal of Youth Development,* 14(4), 36–58. https://doi.org/10.5195/jyd.2019.774

Moroney, D. A. (2020). From model to reality: The role of implementation readiness. *Journal of Youth Development,* 15(6), 162–170. https://doi.org/10.5195/ jyd.2020.1057

Nesselroade, J. R. (2019). Developments in developmental research and theory. *Applied Developmental Science,* 23(4), 346–348. https://doi.org/10.1080/1088869 1.2017.1421426

Osher, D., Cantor, P., Berg, J., Steyer, L., & Rose, T. (2020). Drivers of human development: How relationships and context shape learning and development. *Applied Developmental Science,* 24(1), 6–36. https://doi.org/10.1080/10888691.2 017.1398650

Osher, D., Pittman, K., Young, J., Smith, H., Moroney, D., & Irby, M. (2020). *Thriving, robust equity, and transformative learning and development: A more powerful conceptualization of the contributors to youth success.* American Institutes for Research and Forum for Youth Investment. https://forumfyi.org/wp-content/ uploads/2020/07/Thriving.Equity.Learning.Report.pdf

Pekel, K. (2019). Moving beyond *Relationships Matter*: An overview of one organization's work in progress. *Journal of Youth Development,* 14(4), 1–13. https:// doi.org/10.5195/jyd.2019.909

Peterson, B., Gerhard, G., Hunter, K., Marek, L., Phillips, C., & Titcomb, A. (2001). *Prepared and engaged youth serving American communities: The national 4-H impact assessment project.* National 4-H Headquarters. http://4h .ucanr.edu/files/13698.pdf

Rasmussen, W. D. (1989). *Taking the university to the people: Seventy-five years of Cooperative Extension.* Iowa State University Press.

Reck, F. (1950). *The 4-H story.* Iowa State College Press.

Robinson, A. M., Esters, L. T., Dotterer, A., McKee, R., & Tucker, M. (2012). An exploratory study of the five Cs model of positive youth development among Indiana 4-H youth. *Journal of Youth Development,* 7(1), 82–98. https:// doi.org/10.5195/jyd.2012.154

Roehlkepartain, E., Pekel, K., Syvertsen, A., Sethi, J., Sullivan, T., & Scales, P. (2017). *Relationships first: Creating connections that help young people thrive.* Search Institute. www.search-institute.org/wp-content/uploads/2017/12/2017-Relationships-First-final.pdf

Rose, T. (2016). *The end of average: How we succeed in a world that values sameness.* HarperOne.

Roth, J. L., & Brooks-Gunn, J. (2003). What exactly is a youth development program? Answers from research and practice. *Applied Developmental Science,* 7(2), 94–111. https://doi.org/10.1207/S1532480XADS0702_6

Roth, J. L., & Brooks-Gunn, J. (2016). Evaluating youth development programs: Progress and promise. *Applied Developmental Science*, 20(3), 188–202. https://doi.org/10.1080/10888691.2015.1113879

Roth, J., Brooks-Gunn, J., Murray, L., & Foster, W. (1998). Promoting healthy adolescents: Synthesis of youth development program evaluations. *Journal of Research on Adolescence*, 8(4), 423–459. https://doi.org/10.1207/s15327795jra0804_2

Saito, R. N., & Sullivan, T. K. (2011). The many faces, features and outcomes of youth engagement. *Journal of Youth Development*, 6(3), 107–123. https://doi.org/10.5195/jyd.2011.178

Science of Learning and Development Alliance. (2020). *How the science of learning and development can transform education: Initial findings*. www.soldalliance.org/what-weve-learned

Spencer, M. B., & Spencer, T. R. (2014). Invited commentary: Exploring the promises, intricacies, and challenges to positive youth development. *Journal of Youth and Adolescence*, 43(6), 1027–1035. https://doi.org/10.1007/s10964-014-0125-8

Sumner, R., Turner, A., & Burrow, A. L. (2018). Diversity and inclusion as essential elements of 4-H youth development programs. *Journal of Youth Development*, 13(4), 68–80. https://doi.org/10.5195/jyd.2018.586

U.S. Department of Agriculture and National 4-H Council. (2017). *Strategic plan: 4-H youth development a 2025 vision*. https://nifa.usda.gov/sites/default/files/resources/National%204-H%20Strategic%20Plan%202017.pdf

Vandell, D. L., Larson, R. W., Mahoney, J. L., & Watts, T. W. (2015). Children's organized activities. In M. H. Bornstein, T. Leventhal, & R. M. Lerner (Eds.), *Handbook of child psychology and developmental science: Ecological settings and processes* (pp. 305–344). John Wiley & Sons.

Wahle, A., Owens, M. H., & Garst, B. A. (2019). Strengthening the 4-H essential elements of positive youth development at camp. *Journal of Extension*, 57(5), Article 8. https://tigerprints.clemson.edu/joe/vol57/iss5/8

Wessel, T., & Wessel, M. (1982). *4-H: An American idea 1900–1980*. National 4-H Council.

Worker, S. M., Iaccopucci, A. M., Bird, M., & Horowitz, M. (2019). Promoting positive youth development through teenagers-as-teachers programs. *Journal of Adolescent Research*, 34(1), 30–54. https://doi.org/10.1177/0743558418764089

CHAPTER 8

Promoting Healthy Behaviors and Communities through Food, Nutrition, and Health Extension Efforts

Lisa Franzen-Castle, Michelle Krehbiel, and Jean Ann Fischer

For over a hundred years, the United States (US) Cooperative Extension Service (CES) has provided research/science-based food, nutrition, and health (FNH) education to support the health and well-being of children, youth, and families across the country. This role is especially important today, with current elevated levels of FNH-related chronic health issues such as cardiovascular disease, type 2 diabetes, and obesity. More than half of adults in the US today have one or more diet-related chronic disease (United States Department of Agriculture [USDA] and United States Department of Health and Human Services [DHHS], 2020; National Center for Chronic Disease Prevention and Health Promotion [NCCDPHP], 2021a) and chronic diseases are now one of the leading drivers of the nation's $3.8 trillion in annual health care costs (NCCDPHP, 2021b).

Environmental factors and personal behaviors that contribute to the development of chronic diseases include a combination of the following elements: levels of physical activity, dietary patterns, medication use, food and physical activity environment, education and skills, and food marketing and promotion (NCCDPHP, 2021a). Food-insecure individuals and populations with limited resources face more challenges in meeting optimal dietary choices and levels of physical activity because of systemic environmental and financial barriers (Chang & Kim, 2017; Leung et al., 2012; Nguyen et al., 2015). Addressing these health issues and systemic barriers requires complex problem-solving and creative solutions. The FNH CES focus area, since its inception, has partnered with businesses, health care professionals, nonprofit organizations, and communities to improve the quality of life for individuals and families across settings in which they live, learn, work, play, and gather.

The goal of this chapter is to provide an overview of the work conducted within the focus area of FNH. FNH programming has evolved in its delivery, coverage, and approach over time despite constancy in the overall goal to support the health and well-being of constituents. This chapter will explore the relevant policies, legislations, and demographic trends that have contributed to such shifts alongside advancing research, evaluation tools, national guidelines and recommendations, and technology. FNH CES has also evolved to meet the changing needs of clientele (e.g., heightened rates of chronic disease) and in recognition of the need for more inclusive and equitable responses to its constituents. Additionally, we discuss current national CES frameworks that guide FNH-related programming, and their implications. We end the chapter with recommendations for future directions based on current trends and projections that are relevant to FNH programming.

8.1   Historical Context, Background, and Foundations

The Smith–Lever Act of 1914 initiated the CES as a partnership between USDA and state land-grant colleges. Earlier federal legislation that laid the groundwork for CES included the Morrill Acts of 1862 that established land-grant instruction, and 1890 that established the historically black colleges and universities; as well as the 1887 Hatch Act that provided funding to land-grant colleges to create a series of agricultural experiment stations (National Research Council, 1995). At its inception, CES was intended to help people in rural settings live healthier lives by translating and delivering information generated by research conducted in land-grant colleges and the USDA (USDA-National Association of State Universities and the Land-Grant Colleges (NASULGC) Study Committee, 1968). As the US population grew and more individuals and families moved away from farms and rural areas, CES began shifting educational efforts to include all geographic locations, and thus now includes audiences in rural, urban, and suburban settings.

FNH education has been present since the beginning of the CES. Throughout its history, FNH CES programming has been provided directly to audiences by personnel from land-grant colleges, delivering educational resources aimed at addressing various physical, psychological, and economic well-being issues of families (Rasmussen, 1989). In the early years of CES, these professionals were known as Home Demonstration Agents (HDAs) who taught in the field of home economics. A key mission for HDAs during the World Wars and the Great Depression was to help rural families save money and maintain financial stability to keep their family farms (Babbitt, 1993; Frysinger, 1932, USDA, 1951). HDAs provided education around food preservation (e.g., canning), sanitation, and child feeding; they also contributed to the establishment of lunch programs in schools.

With increased popularity of CES programming across the country, HDAs started engaging volunteers to expand the reach of their educational efforts. HDAs began training local community groups on various FNH topics such as production and preservation of food (Frysinger, 1932). In turn, volunteers would share information with neighbors, family, and friends. The result of this expansion was tremendous. In 1950, CES Director M. L. Wilson stated that over 3,500 county home economists and assistants, together with 450,000 volunteers, encouraged more than three million families to make improvements to family living (Rasmussen, 1989). To further keep up with increasing demand, HDAs began to distribute information and education through mass communication outlets, such as newspaper and radio, and continued to rely on homemakers' clubs and volunteers.

The 1960s was a period of marked shifts in focus for CES programming with the introduction of influential federal legislation, such as the 1965 Housing and Urban Development Act, as well as the 1964 Food Stamp Act (Rasmussen, 1985). Population growth, increasing diversity in family structures (e.g., more single-parent homes), and accelerated movement from rural to urban areas further contributed to such shifts. In 1968, *A People and a Spirit* was published by the Joint USDA (NASULGC) Study Committee on CES. This report called for CES to serve all families regardless of residence and to support their well-being and quality of life by addressing such topics as food, clothing, housing, and social and psychological issues – factors noted in the report as necessities for living, human dignity, and personal fulfillment. The committee recommended that the CES "fully commit their staffs to work on the problems of the disadvantaged" (p. 61) by carrying out programming to all, especially to "disadvantaged youth, potential school dropouts, young families, unemployed out of school young adults" (p. 68) and adults with limited financial resources or living in substandard housing (USDA-NASULGC Study Committee, 1968).

The 1968 report helped pave the way for national programs such as the Expanded Food and Nutrition Education Program (EFNEP), which was launched in 1969 by USDA and the National Institute of Food and Agriculture (NIFA) as the first nutrition Extension program for low-income populations (USDA, n.d.). For over fifty years, EFNEP has reached diverse populations in rural and urban locations with the program goal of supporting individuals with limited financial resources to build self-sufficiency and improve nutritional health and well-being (USDA, n.d.).

8.2 Current FNH Programming and Initiatives

The contemporary CES in the field of FNH supports well-being among children, youth, adults, and families in two ways. First, CES engages audiences to adopt healthy practices through educational programs and resources addressing nutrition and food preparation, physical activity and healthy lifestyles, food security, food safety, chronic disease prevention and management, and health literacy (Battelle, 2015). These educational programs and resources engage a broad range of approaches that include both in-person and web-based instruction in a variety of settings/venues. Second, CES addresses the contextual and systemic issues that affect health. CES does so by striving to intentionally co-identify and cocreate resources with nonuniversity partners to address policy, system, and environmental (PSE) factors that facilitate or inhibit healthy lifestyle choices. CES addresses these PSE factors through programs targeting sectors of influence (e.g., public health and health care, education, media, community design, and agriculture), establishing infrastructure that advances healthy living, and by working at the policy level to introduce broad changes that promote a healthier society. Section 8.2.1 highlights examples of federal nutrition programs that illustrate CES direct education and outreach to a diversity of audiences, as well as efforts toward systemic impacts through collaborations at local and national levels to achieve sustained and broad-reaching improvements in the nutrition and health of families.

8.2.1 *Expanded Food and Nutrition Education Program*

EFNEP is the nation's first nutrition education program for populations with lower resources and it continues to lead nutrition education efforts to decrease food insecurity of families and youth living in homes with lower resources. EFNEP utilizes direct education, a combination of hands-on learning and applied science to support participants' well-being, self-reliance, and nutritional health. EFNEP originally started in 1964 as a pilot program in a few states, arising out a need to equip families in poverty with tools and knowledge to combat hunger and to increase food security. After five years of success, Congress allocated funding from NIFA within the USDA to implement the program nationally (EFNEP, 2021). EFNEP currently operates through the 1862 and 1890 land-grant universities (LGUs) in every state, the District of Columbia, and the six US territories. Funding is allocated directly to LGUs' CES, so EFNEP is a uniquely Extension program (USDA-NIFA, 2017). Since 1969, EFNEP has reached more than thirty-three million families and youth with limited resources. Nationally, over 71 percent of all EFNEP adults identify as an ethnic minority (2020 Impacts: EFNEP NIFA National Data Report; EFNEP, 2021). As such, EFNEP not only has tremendous reach but also specifically addresses the needs of underserved populations across the country.

Rooted in the USDA and located within the LGU system, EFNEP is positioned to not only deliver programming and outreach, but also contribute to the advancement of the field of nutrition education. EFNEP has a nationally coordinated evaluation strategy, including the use of assessment tools for adult and youth audiences. Evaluation data indicate that EFNEP influences the nutrition and physical activity behaviors of limited-resource families, especially those with young children, through community-based and relationship-driven direct education. EFNEP participants improve their lives in four core categories for healthy living: diet quality and physical activity, food resource management, food safety, and food security (EFNEP Program Polices, 2017). Fifty years of empirical data indicate impressive results, with longitudinal studies suggesting not just positive behavior change and lifetime maintenance of health-related skills among EFNEP clientele but also that such gains impact families across generations (EFNEP Impacts, 2020).

8.2.2   Supplemental Nutrition Assistance Program (SNAP-Ed)

SNAP-Ed (formerly known as the Family Nutrition Program and Food Stamp Nutrition Education) is a federally funded grant program that supports evidence-based nutrition education and obesity prevention interventions and projects for persons eligible for SNAP (formerly known as food stamps). The program began in 1988 through a partnership between CES in Brown County, WI, University of Wisconsin Extension staff, and the state SNAP agency. In 1992, seven states conducted SNAP-Ed, and by 2004 the program was implemented throughout the country (USDA-NIFA, n.d.). Prior to 2013, funding for SNAP-Ed was limited to direct education for SNAP-eligible participants. However, amended legislation increased the reach and capacity of SNAP-Ed programming to work in the PSE strategy and intervention space (FNA, Section 28, amended by

Healthy, Hunger-Free Kids Act of 2010 [HHFKA] and SNAP: Nutrition Education and Obesity Prevention Grant Program Final Rule, adopted amended interim rule published April 5, 2013, to implement SNAP-Ed provisions of HHFKA). The rule also implemented a provision of the Agricultural Act of 2014 to authorize physical activity promotion in addition to promotion of healthy food choices as part of this nutrition education and obesity prevention program (USDA-FNS).

SNAP-Ed is an example of how CES uses direct and indirect education as well as multilevel PSE programming to reach audiences and help make the healthy choice the easier choice at the individual and environmental levels (SNAP-Ed Plan Guidance FY2022). SNAP-Ed is delivered by multiple providers across the nation, of which CES is the largest, reaching more SNAP-eligible families than all other SNAP-Ed providers combined (Battelle, 2015). In 2017, SNAP-Ed was delivered to more than 60,000 low-resource community locations nationwide (USDA Education and Administration Reporting System, personal communications, 2017). In 2018, programming reached 3.8 million people through direct education, the most of any USDA nutrition education program (US Government Accountability Office, 2019). Part of SNAP-Ed's success is because of its community-based orientation. Land-grant universities work closely with state and local public and private entities to strategically deliver SNAP-Ed using methods and locations most suitable or effective for SNAP-eligible populations (USDA, NIFA).

Evidence of positive results from SNAP-Ed programming have included positive changes in attitudes, self-efficacy, and behaviors regarding fruit and vegetable preparation and consumption; increases in long-term food security; and maintenance of behavior changes six months post-program completion (Dannefer et al., 2015; Hersey et al., 2020; Koszewski et al., 2011; Rivera et al., 2016, 2019). Rivera et al. (2019) also stated that with the recent focus on PSE sectors, SNAP-Ed may potentially expand its reach and impact by supporting interventions and resources from which all community members may benefit, even those not eligible or directly participating in the program (Rivera et al., 2019). Burke et al. (2022) looked at how states planned to use PSE change strategies in SNAP-Ed from 2014 to 2016 and found a 22 percent increase in states that included PSEs as a statewide goal and a 42 percent increase in states that planned to implement at least 1 PSE strategy, with the most common settings being places where people learn (92 percent), live (90 percent), and work (83 percent) (Burke et al., 2022). Through Extension's implementation of EFNEP, SNAP-Ed, and other programs in nutrition, it is likely that nutrition and health efforts in

CES reach more people with nutrition education than any other source in the US (Battelle, 2015).

8.3   Leveraging Partnerships to Creating Change

Whereas direct engagement with clientele has traditionally been a strength of FNH programming, CES also targets PSE-level change through a range of initiatives. Such work acknowledges the multiple levels of influence that surround individuals, as is depicted in the nested contexts of the Social Ecological Model (SEM) (Kilanowski, 2017). The SEM is a theory-based, interdisciplinary, and broadly applied paradigm, highlights how multiple factors interact to impact population behaviors at complementary spheres of influence: individual, environmental settings, sectors, and social/cultural norms and values (USDHHS, 2015). SEM suggests the critical need to identify leverage points, intentionally layer interventions, use reinforcing strategies, and engage multiple sectors to achieve sustainable population-level results (Naja-Riese et al., 2019). In order to engage multiple sectors and layer interventions, partnerships within and outside of CES are critical components of success. The following examples show how CES, public agencies, and nonprofit and local communities worked together to address health issues and disparities.

Reaching audiences in more equitable and inclusive ways and working with a variety of national, state, and local partners to reach target populations have been a focus for many CES in recent years. For example, Kaiser et al. (2015) showed that a partnership between California CES, the University of California-Davis, and rural communities in California's Central Valley was able to develop a culturally tailored obesity prevention program appropriate for Mexican-origin parents with young children living in low-income homes. Another example from Kentucky CES, by using a mixed-methods study, identified areas of opportunity for improving cultural sensitivity when working with Hispanic/Latino participants and delivering nutrition education programs (Durr, 2018). Kentucky's findings supported the inclusion of culturally sensitive and relevant program materials and resources, emphasizing the relationship of unique dietary habits and chronic disease development, and including cultural values in the curriculum and training (Durr, 2018). When a culturally responsive curriculum is implemented, program participants are more likely to retain knowledge and gain skills needed to make positive behavior changes, and program staff are more likely to be effective in program delivery (Blank, 1997; Jones, Nobles, & Larke, 2006).

Outreach programs that integrate community-based research, education, and collaboration among committed partners hold promise in finding effective strategies to sustain health-related community changes (CSREES, 2006; EFNEP, 2006; TDSHS, 2005; USDHHS, 2006). For example, a Texas CES EFNEP engaged with community partners to generate solutions for reducing obesity among primarily African American and Hispanic audiences through the Healthy Weigh (HW) program (Dart, Frable, & Bradly, 2008). In HW, community partners worked together to find solutions for reducing obesity, family members learned about their roles in guiding and evaluating the intervention, and university students (nursing, nutrition/dietetics, social work, kinesiology, and medicine) learned effective ways of engaging with families with limited literacy and English skills (Dart, Frable, & Bradly, 2008). HW illustrates the feasibility of positioning an EFNEP intervention in a medical clinic setting to support pediatric obesity prevention, thus expanding reach to address the needs of more families with limited resources (Shilts et al., 2021).

The following are examples of programs, initiatives, and strategies that include a combination of direct education and/or PSE approaches to improve behaviors and environments for youth and/or adult audiences. Multiple states participated in each of these efforts.

Voices for Food. A transdisciplinary team of specialists in nutrition, agriculture, youth, community development, evaluation, and researchers from the CES North Central Region developed *Voices for Food (VFF)* (Stluka et al., 2018). VFF is an intervention designed to enhance food security in diverse rural communities with high rates of poverty. It utilizes community coaches to develop new or provide support to existing food councils and encourages policy changes in local food pantries that increase the availability of healthy foods (Stluka et al., 2018). Community coaches address food-system issues by focusing on local food policy, establishing community gardens, expanding food pantries by obtaining more space, and working on other issues related to food security (Tusha, 2019). Community coaches, who were primarily Extension educators/field staff during the development and testing phases, work collaboratively with food pantries to help them transition from food distribution (prepackaged or boxed) to a client-choice model also known as MyChoice. Additionally, community coaches offer the VFF Ambassador's training, which includes nutrition education, cultural competency training, and food safety training primarily to food pantry staff/volunteers (Remley et al., 2019).

VFF has been tested in twenty-four (twelve treatment, twelve comparison) rural, high-poverty counties in South Dakota (including two reservation communities), Indiana, Missouri, Michigan, Nebraska, and Ohio in partnership with researchers and Extension personnel and has reached approximately 1,600 food pantry clients (USDA, SNAP-Ed Toolkit). Treatment and comparison communities both received VFF resources (e.g., food pantry toolkit, food council guide, and opportunity to apply for mini-grant funds), but only treatment communities had a community coach (Stluka et al., 2018). Participating communities had a high percentage of people who identified as Hispanic/Latino, American Indian, Black, or African. A longitudinal, matched-intervention evaluation design was used to examine how well VFF served the target audience and community setting (Stluka et al., 2018). Results showed that the VFF intervention was effective in helping communities develop new or strengthen existing food councils. Additionally, MyChoice Scorecard scores differed significantly between treatment and comparison food pantries at mid- and postintervention, indicating treatment communities were more likely to transition to a client-choice food distribution model (McCormack et al., 2019).

iCook 4-H. The iCook 4-H program was designed to reach the following objectives: increase cooking skills and culinary self-efficacy, improve openness to new foods, increase frequency and/or quality of mealtime with family members, and decrease sedentary time. It is intended for out-of-school settings with the goal of promoting healthy lifestyles for nine- and ten-year-old youth and the adults who prepare their meals (White et al., 2019). iCook 4-H consists of eight two-hour sessions that each includes food preparation, physical activity, family engagement and communication, and goal setting (Franzen-Castle et al., 2019). Primary settings for the program were community centers, Extension offices, and schools; with the target audience being low-income, rural, and/or diverse audiences. Collaborators for the iCook 4-H Study were from Maine, Nebraska, South Dakota, Tennessee, and West Virginia (Franzen-Castle et al., 2019). Because the scope of the project spanned five states, there was a strong partnership between academic researchers and CES professionals (e.g., specialists, educators, assistants) and additional community partners with representation of expertise in positive youth development, nutrition education, exercise physiology, 4-H youth-development programing, web design and development, technology, and graphic design and formatting (Franzen-Castle et al., 2019).

iCook 4-H was designed with intention to test and evaluate sustainability strategies to ensure the key ingredients of the program were in place after researchers were removed from program implementation (Franzen-Castle et al., 2019). A benefit of iCook 4-H is the inclusion of tools for leaders to use with both youth and adults to assess program success and identify any areas of needed improvements. Such tools can help instructors measure program effectiveness and can be collected by administrators for more widespread monitoring of program goals (Mathews et al., 2019). Other features of this program include a tool to assess fidelity, as well as a ripple effects mapping assessment to help participants understand the program's impact not only on themselves but also their families and communities (Olfert et al., 2019). The program has now also been adapted to address food security for Burundian and Congolese refugee families using a community-based cultural adaption process (McElrone et al., 2021).

Well Connected Communities (WCC). The goal of the WCC initiative is to address life-long health and well-being by intentionally forging connections, building capacity, and taking action in communities and across the CES network. Extension's WCC initiative is an illustrative example of achieving these goals by helping to build diverse, multigenerational, cross-sector coalitions that can recognize and address systemic health inequities (Rodgers & Vinlaun, 2018). WCC is a CES effort in partnership with the National 4-H Council and support from the Robert Wood Johnson Foundation (WCC, 2021). As a result of WCC, seventeen LGUs have committed to creating healthier, more sustainable places to live, work, and play in forty-six communities (fifteen urban and thirty-one rural settings), five of which are tribal communities (WCC, 2021).

The original intention of WCC was to engage five LGUs for Wave One, but due to widespread interest, eight additional universities joined the launch phase (Rodgers & Lovelace, n.d.). The Wave One effort involved four key strategies: (1) applying 4-H's Youth Leadership Model, in which youth will work alongside community members, local public health, and nonprofit organizations, businesses, and government entities to address top public health priorities; (2) leveraging the applied research foundation of CES; (3) engaging expert community volunteers; and (4) extending impact through technical assistance – by spreading innovation and impact to more communities. Wave Two is focused on supporting health equity by developing and supporting PSE change in communities and throughout the CES. WCC is helping local health coalitions use combined youth-adult voice and action to recognize and address systemic health inequities in their communities. Across the Extension System, successful innovations from WCC work are being scaled up and making institutional shifts to catalyze changes at the local, state, and national levels (WCC, 2021).

The previous examples illustrate the multitiered approach that CES uses to achieve sustained and meaningful change, from direct-education programs to implementation of strategies that address PSEs. This work is being done with a variety of collaborators and partners at all levels of the SEM, with examples spanning individual-, community-, and society-level changes. The SEM framework can be used to help identify factors that impact health behaviors, integrate elements of other theories and models, and help develop comprehensive health-promotion or disease-prevention programs or policies.

8.4   Utilizing Technology to Expand Reach

Although traditionally many CES direct-education efforts were conducted in face-to-face settings with youth and adult audiences, in recent years it has become more challenging to recruit and sustain regular or sizable attendance with adult audiences. The way in which people seek out and consume information has shifted, with Extension audiences turning more to internet-based media for information (Whitaker, Leggette, & Barbeau, 2018). In response, CES programs have increasingly been offered online with the use of video conferencing, password-protected web pages, and learning-management platforms (Elliott-Engel, Crist, & James, 2022). To better reach audiences where they are, FNH Extension programming has also developed an online presence using social media (e.g., open and closed/private groups) (Brinkman, Kinsey, & Henneman, 2017; Franzen-Castle et al., 2015; Franzen-Castle & Henneman, 2014; Garcia et al., 2018), websites (Colgrove, Henneman, & Franzen-Castle, 2014; Henneman, Franzen-Castle, Colgrove, & Singh, 2016), and electronic newsletters (Henneman, Franzen-Castle, Wells, & Colgrove, 2016; Henneman & Franzen-Castle, 2014) to promote, market, and/or provide live and archived educational content. Direct contact and follow-up communication (e.g., text messages, emails, social media apps) for additional outreach and programming have also become easily available (Beecher & Hayungs, 2017; DePhelps & Lawrence, 2020; Gharis et al., 2014).

Research has shown that access to nutritional education may be limited by social determinants of health. Low-income families face several barriers to attending and/or sustaining multisession participation in nutrition-education programming, including transportation difficulties, family responsibilities, and schedule conflicts (Richardson et al., 2003). During and soon after the COVID-19 pandemic, some nutrition-education programs were moved online, which ultimately helped circumvent some of the previously identified challenges to participating in traditional, face-to-face programming (McGoron et al., 2018). Online educational modules may be an easy, low-touch intervention to address this important problem, especially with Internet access becoming more universal even among low-income populations (McGoron et al., 2018; Smith, 2015; Stotz et al., 2019). An example of how transitioning in-person cooking classes to a virtual platform was beneficial for a SNAP-Ed audience includes the Poe Center for Health Education in North Carolina (SNAP-Ed Connection, 2021). When COVID-19 prevented face-to-face education, the Center, with the help of community-partner support and supplemental funding, modified traditional in-person cooking classes for a virtual format targeted at youth and adults. Advantages noted by educators included reaching more participants than in-person programming, people were more comfortable with their own kitchen, and the entire household, rather than only primary participants joining programming (SNAP-Ed Connection, 2021).

8.5 Guiding Principles for Future Programming

To help communities implement science-based information, FNH-Extension professionals and volunteers should utilize the following frameworks and principles to inform how they go about improving the health of individuals and families. Future programming should be guided by one or more of the following examples, which all align with the layered and multicomponent approach of the SEM.

Cooperative Extension's National Framework for Health Equity and Well-Being. This Framework was released on July 2021 and was produced by the Extension Committee on Organization and Policy Health Innovation Task Force. The Framework focuses on the core themes of health equity, SDOH, and working through coalitions to increase community health assets to advance CES's portfolio of work focused on improving population health and equity (Burton et al., 2021). The following recommendations resulted from the work of the task force and included: (1) Advance health equity as a core system value to ensure that all people have a fair and just opportunity to be as healthy as they can be; (2) Utilize community assessment processes that integrate data science and resident voice to identify and address health inequities with greater precision; (3) Invest in the success and visibility of Extension's health-related professionals, programs, and initiatives; (4) Establish partnerships with academic units, government agencies, corporations, nonprofit organizations, and foundations that share a commitment to reducing or eliminating health inequities; and (5) Utilize a community development approach to advance the work of coalitions focused on influencing the SDOH (Burton et al., 2021).

Healthy People 2030. According to Healthy People 2030, SDOH, which include economic stability, education access and quality, health care access and quality, neighborhood and built environment, and social and community context, are environmental conditions that affect a wide range of health, functioning, and quality of life outcomes and risks. Addressing health determinants at the local, state, national, and global levels combined with a variety of agencies, community partners and policymakers, and communities can eliminate health disparities, thus giving more children, individuals, and families an opportunity to maintain healthy lifestyles. Reducing health disparities is a major public health goal, and achieving health equity, eliminating disparities, and improving the health of all US population groups is a foundational principle of Healthy People 2030 (USDHHS, Office of Disease Prevention and Health Promotion).

Culture of Health Action Framework. The Robert Wood Johnson Foundation, in partnership with the RAND Corporation, and with input from more than 1,000 experts, community members, and global leaders, developed the Culture of Health Action Framework to catalyze a national movement toward improved health, well-being, and equity. Drawn from rigorous research and analysis of systemic barriers to health in the US, this framework invites individuals, communities, and organizations to find entry points for better health that are unique to their own needs and goals. Based on ten underlying principles, it connects health and social, economic, physical, and environmental factors. After organizing these principles into conceptual clusters, the team created logic models to determine how they would connect, then reviewed them with diverse stakeholders across the country. These resulting clusters became the core structure of the framework: (1) Make health a shared value; (2) Foster cross-sector collaboration; (3) Create healthier, more equitable communities; (4) Strengthen integration of health services and systems; and (5) Improve population health, well-being, and equity.

8.6   Summary

FNH CES is an example of programming that has had wide reach and documented impact in meeting the needs of underserved populations. It serves as a model for Extension in research and science-based education, with approaches rooted in national frameworks and principles, tailored to state and local needs. Several promising frameworks to guide Extension programming in FNH exist, including the CES National Framework for Health Equity and Well-Being, Healthy People 2030 and Culture of Health Framework, in combination with community-based research, education, and collaboration among committed partners to foster and sustain positive health-related community change.

Relevant to programming around FNH, several other contributors to this volume have noted critical components of contemporary Extension programming. First, using evidence-based needs assessments to determine local needs is essential in increasing relevance of programming, as well as to better understand our audiences and thus increase cultural awareness, competence, and sensitivity of future and existing programming. Second, given the demographic landscape of current Extension clientele (see also Do and Zoumenou, this volume) attention to issues around diversity (e.g., in race, gender, religion, sexual orientation, ethnicity, nationality, socioeconomic status, language, (dis)ability, age, religious commitment, or political perspective), equity (e.g., justice, impartiality and fairness with procedures, processes, and distribution of resources by institutions or systems), and inclusion (i.e., ensure those that are marginalized, minoritized and underserved feel and/or are welcomed) are crucial components of program planning, delivery, and assessment. Finally, the rapidly shifting information landscape makes it necessary for FNH CES and the broader Extension enterprise to continue to explore web-based and electronic delivery, as well as new and innovative ways of disseminating and communicating with audiences, as technology will undoubtedly evolve.

Overall, key elements of FNH CES have stayed consistent over the years, but the methods of engagement, funding priorities, and other elements of programming have shifted. Furthermore, efforts are no longer limited to providing resources to clientele but has moved into promoting quality of life and disease prevention and involving more rigorous and in-depth methods of assessment. Extension has consistently adapted and innovated FNH CES to meet specific local needs and improve well-being among clientele. Maintained focus in this direction will continue to ensure that all families and individuals have opportunities for healthy lives.

References

Babbitt, K. (1993). The productive farm woman and the extension home economist in New York State, 1920–1940. *American Rural and Farm Women in Historical Perspective*, 67(2), 83–101. www.jstor.org/stable/3744051

Battelle. (2015). *Analysis of the value of family and consumer sciences extension in the North Central Region.* Directors of Cooperative Extension, North Central Region. www.nccea.org/battelle-teconomy-reports/

Beecher, C., & Hayungs, L. (2017). Getting your message across: Mobile phone text messaging. *Journal of Extension*, 55(5), 5TOT1. https://archives.joe.org/joe/2017october/pdf/JOE_v55_5tt1.pdf

Blank, R. M. (1997). *It takes a nation.* Princeton University Press.

Brinkman, P., Kinsey, J., & Henneman, A. (2017). Increasing the capacity of social media to extend your outreach. *Journal of Extension*, 55(1), Article 6, www.joe.org/joe/2017february/tt4.php

Burke, M., Gleason, S., Singh, A., & Wilkin, M. (2022). Policy, systems, and environmental change strategies in the Supplemental Nutrition Assistance Program-Education (SNAP-Ed). *Journal of Nutrition Education and Behavior*, 54(4), 320–326. https://doi.org/10.1016/j.jneb.2021.09.008

Burton, D., et al. (2021). *Cooperative extension's national framework for health equity and well being.* [Report of the Health Innovation Task Force] Extension Committee on Organization and Policy: Washington, DC, available at www.aplu.org/members/commissions/foodenvironment-and-renewable-resources/board-on-agriculture-assembly/cooperative-extensionsection/ecop-members/ecop-documents/2021%20EquityHealth%20Sum.pdf

Chang, S. H., & Kim, K. (2017). A review of factors limiting physical activity among young children from low-income families. *Journal Exercise Rehabilitation*, 13(4), 375–377.

Colgrove, K., Henneman, A., & Franzen-Castle, L. (2014). Using a food-themed calendar to engage the public and promote Extension from field to fork. *Journal of Extension*, 52(2), 2IAW3. www.joe.org/joe/2014april/iw3.php

Dannefer, R., Abrami, A., Rapoport, R., Sriphanlop, P., Sacks, R., & Johns, M. (2015). A mixed-methods evaluation of a SNAP-Ed farmers' market-based nutrition education program. *Journal of Nutrition Education and Behaviors*, 47, 516–525.

Dart, L., Frable, P., & Bradly, P. (2008). Families and community partners learning together to prevent obesity. *Journal of Extension*, 46(1), 1IAW2.

DePhelps, C., & Lawrence, M. (2020). *Idaho's Cultivating Success program increases digital outreach to small farms.* University of Idaho Extension. https://sitecore03l.its.uidaho.edu/-/media/UIdaho-Responsive/Files/Extension/admin/Impacts/2020/47-20-cdephelps-digital-outreach.pdf?la=en&hash=7A6331DFFFEEF33C0A1AC838BCEC13CCEBA61604

Durr, A. (2018). *Cultural sensitivity in Cooperative Extension Nutrition Education Programming in Kentucky.* (2018). Theses and Dissertations – Dietetics and Human Nutrition. 63. https://uknowledge.uky.edu/foodsci_etds/63

Elliott-Engel, J., Crist, C., & James, G. (2022). The power of extension: Research, teaching, and outreach for broader impacts. In D. Westfall-Rudd, C. Vengrin, & J. Elliott-Engel (Eds.), *Teaching in the university: Learning from graduate students and early-career faculty.* Virginia Tech College of Agriculture and Life Sciences. https://doi.org/10.21061/universityteaching. License: CC BY-NC 4.0.

Expanded Food and Nutrition Education Program. *National Institute of Food and Agriculture, Capacity Grants.* Accessed June 15, 2021 https://nifa.usda.gov/program/expanded-food-and-nutrition-education-program-efnep

Expanded Food and Nutrition Education Program Impacts. (2020). *Improving nutritional security through education.* Prepared by NIFA. Retrieved June 15, 2021 from https://nifa.usda.gov/sites/default/files/2020%20EFNEP%20National%20Data%20Reports.pdf

Franzen-Castle, L., Colby, S., Kattelmann, K., et al. (2019). Development of the iCook 4-H Curriculum for Youth and Adults: Cooking, eating, and playing together for childhood obesity prevention. *Journal of Nutrition Education and Behavior*, 51(3S), S60–S68. https://doi.org/10.1016/j.jneb.2018.11.006

Franzen-Castle, L., & Henneman, A. (2014). Pinning for success: Using Pinterest as the hub of simple and successful food-related social media campaigns. *Journal of National Extension Association of Family & Consumer Sciences*, 9, 122–128. http://media.wix.com/ugd/c8fe6e_71e72b6d633c44528decd28bad4dbadf.pdf

Franzen-Castle, L., Henneman, A., Colgrove, K., & Wells, C. A. (2015). Successful team approach to social networking. *Journal of National Extension Association of Family & Consumer Sciences*, 10, 100–108.

Frysinger, G. E. (1932, March 16). *National farm and home hour.* Produced by the United States Department of Agriculture.

Garcia, A., Dev, D., McGinnis, C., & Thomas, T. (2018). Impact of an extension social media kit on audience engagement. *Journal of Extension*, 56(2), 2RIB1.

Gharis, L., Bardon, R., Evans, L., Hubbard, W., & Taylor, E. (2014). Expanding the reach of Extension through social media. *Journal of Extension*, 52(3), 3FEA3. https://archives.joe.org/joe/2014june/pdf/JOE_v52_3a3.pdf

Henneman, A., & Franzen-Castle, L. (2014). Changing food behavior through an email newsletter. *Journal of Nutrition Education and Behavior*, 46(3), 221–223.

Henneman, A., Franzen-Castle, L., Colgrove, K., & Singh, V. (2016). Successfully changing the landscape of information distribution: Extension food website reaches people locally and globally. *Journal of Human Sciences and Extension*, 4(1), 78–88.

Henneman, A., Franzen-Castle, L., Wells, C., & Colgrove, C. (2016). Are you overlooking the power of email newsletters? *Journal of National Extension Association of Family & Consumer Sciences*, 11, 832.

Hersey, J. C., Cates, S. C., Blitstein, J. L., & Williams, P.A. (2020). *SNAP-Ed can improve nutrition of low-income Americans across life span* (RTI Press publication No. RR-0023-1406). www.rti.org/rtipress. Accessed December 8, 2020.

Jones, W., Nobles, C., & Larke, A. (2006). The effectiveness of a public nutrition education and wellness system program. *Journal of Extension*, 44(3), RIB5.

Kaiser, L., Martinez, J., Horowitz, M., Lamp, C., Johns, M., Espinoza, D., et al. (2015). Adaptation of a culturally relevant nutrition and physical activity program for low-income, Mexican-origin parents with young children. *Preventing Chronic Disease*, 12, 140591. https://doi.org/10.5888/pcd12.140591

Kilanowski, J. (2017). Breadth of the Socio-Ecological Model. *Journal of Agromedicine*, 22(4), 295–297. https://doi.org/10.1080/1059924X.2017.1358971

Koszewski, W., Sehi, N., Behrends, D., & Tuttle, E. (2011). The impact of SNAP-ED and EFNEP on program graduates 6 months after graduation *Journal of Extension*, 49, 1–8.

Leung, C. W., Ding, E. L., Catalano, P. J., Villamor, E., Rimm, E. B., & Willett, W. C. (2012). Dietary intake and dietary quality of low-income adults in the Supplemental Nutrition Assistance Program. *Am J Clin Nutrition*, 96(5), 977–988, 10.3945/ajcn.112.040014

Mathews, D., Kunicki, Z., Colby, S., et al. (2019). Development and testing of program evaluation instruments for the iCook 4-H curriculum. *Journal of Nutrition Education and Behavior*, 51, S21–S29. https://doi.org/10.1016/j.jneb.2018.10.014

McCormack, L., Eicher-Miller, H., Remley, D., Moore, L., & Stluka, S. (2019). The development and use of an assessment tool to capture changes in the food pantry nutrition environment and system of food distribution. *Translational Behavioral Medicine*, 9(5), 962–969. https://doi.org/10.1093/tbm/ibz114

McGoron, L., Hvizdos, E., Bocknek, E., Montgomery, E., & Ondersma, S. (2018). Feasibility of internet-based parent training for low-income parents of young children. *Children and Youth Services Review*, 84, 198–205. www.ncbi.nlm.nih.gov/pmc/articles/PMC5931387/

Naja-Riese, A., Keller, K., Bruno, P., Foerster, S. B., Puma, J., Whetstone, L., MkNelly, B., Cullinen, K., Jacobs, L., & Sugerman, S. (2019). The SNAP-Ed Evaluation Framework: Demonstrating the impact of a national framework for obesity prevention in low-income populations. *Translational Behavioral Medicine*, 9(5), 970–979. https://doi.org/10.1093/tbm/ibz115

National Center for Chronic Disease Prevention and Health Promotion. (2021a). *Adult chronic diseases*. Centers for Disease Control and Prevention. Retrieved from www.cdc.gov/chronicdisease/about/index.htm

National Center for Chronic Disease Prevention and Health Promotion. (2021b). *Health and economic costs of chronic diseases*. Centers for Disease Control and Prevention. Retrieved from www.cdc.gov/chronicdisease/about/costs/index.htm

National Research Council. (1995). *Colleges of agriculture at the land grant universities: A profile*. The National Academies Press. https://doi.org/10.17226/4980

Nguyen, B. T., Shuval, K., Bertmann, F., Yaroch, A. L. (2015). The Supplemental Nutrition Assistance Program, Food Insecurity, Dietary Quality, and Obesity Among U.S. *Adults. Am J Public Health*, 105(7):1453–1459, 10.2105/AJPH.2015.302580.

Office of Disease Prevention and Health Promotion. *Social Determinants of Health from Healthy People 2030 – objectives and data*. Accessed April 25, 2021 via Social Determinants of Health – Healthy People 2030 | health.gov

Olfert, M. D., King, S. J., Hagedorn, R. L., Barr, M. L., Baker, B. A., Colby, S. E., Kattelmann, K. K., Franzen-Castle, L., & White, A. A. (2019). Ripple effect mapping outcomes of a childhood obesity prevention program from youth and adult dyads using a qualitative approach: iCook 4-H. *Journal of Nutrition Education and Behavior*, 51(3S), S41–S51. https://doi.org/10.1016/j.jneb.2018.08.002

Remley, D. T., Rapp, B., Contreras, D., Duitsman, P., Moore, L., Rauch, J., Franzen-Castle, L., & Stluka, S. (2019). *Voices for food: Food pantry toolkit.* SDSU Extension, October, 2019. https://extension.sdstate.edu/sites/default/files/2019-11/P-00106-02.pdf

Rasmussen, W.D. (1985). *90 years of rural development programs.* Rural Development Perspectives, v2 n1 p2–9. PDF (usda.gov)

Rasmussen, W.D. (1989). *Taking the university to the people: Seventy Five Years of Cooperative Extension.* Iowa State University: Ames, IA.

Richardson, J., Williams, J., & Mustian, R. D. (2003). Barriers to participation in Extension expanded foods and nutrition programs. *Journal of Extension,* 41(4), 4FEA6.

Rivera, R., Maulding, M., Abbott, A., Craig, B., & Eicher-Miller, H. (2016). SNAP-Ed (Supplemental Nutrition Assistance Program-Education) increases long-term food security among Indiana households with children in a randomized controlled study. *Journal of Nutrition,* 146, 2375–2382.

Rivera, R., Maulding, M., & Eicher-Miller, H. (2019). Effect of Supplemental Nutrition Assistance Program-Education (SNAP-Ed) on food security and dietary outcomes. *Nutrition Reviews,* 77(12), 903–921. https://doi.org/10.1093/nutrit/nuz013. PMID: 31077323

Rodgers, M., & Lovelace, N. (n.d.). *Building a culture of health: Well-connected communities.* Cooperative Extension and National 4-H Council. www.aplu.org/members/commissions/food-environment-and-renewable-resources/board-on-agriculture-assembly/cooperative-extension-section/ecop-members/ecop-documents/Well%20Connected%20Communities%20Wave%201.pdf

Rodgers, M., & Vinlaun, M. (2018). Closing thoughts: On the power of youth and system change. *Journal of Youth Development,* 13(3), 284–290.

Shilts, M., Rios, K., Panarella, K., Styne, D., Lanoue, L., Drake, C., Ontai, L., & Townsend, M. (2021). Feasibility of colocating a nutrition education program into a medical clinic setting to facilitate pediatric obesity prevention. *Journal of Primary Care & Community Health,* 12, 1–13. https://doi.org/10.1177/21501327211009695

Smith, A. (2015). *US smartphone use in 2015.* Retrieved from www.pewinternet.org/2015/04/01/us-smartphone-use-in-2015/. Accessed February 1, 2021.

SNAP-Ed. National Institute of Food and Agriculture. USDA. Accessed June 15, 2021 via https://nifa.usda.gov/program/supplemental-nutrition-education-program-education-snap-ed

SNAP-Ed Connection. (2021). *Transitioning cooking classes for a virtual audience.* US Department of Agriculture (USDA). https://snaped.fns.usda.gov/success-stories/transitioning-cooking-classes-virtual-audience. Accessed March 4, 2021.

SNAP-Ed Plan Guidance and Templates FY2022. *SNAP-Ed Connection.* US Department of Agriculture. Accessed June 15, 2021.

Stluka, S., Moore, L., Eicher-Miller, H. A. et al. (2018). Voices for food: Methodologies for implementing a multi-state community-based intervention in rural, high poverty communities. *BMC Public Health,* 18, 1055. https://doi.org/10.1186/s12889-018-5957-9

Stotz, S., Lee, J., Rong, H., & Murray, D. (2019). E-learning nutrition education program for low-income adults: Perspectives of key stakeholders. *Journal of Extension*, 57(1), v57–1rb5. www.joe.org/joe/2019february/rb5.php. Accessed January 29, 2021.

Tusha, K. (2019). *The role of a community coach in rural food councils in six Midwestern states*. Electronic Theses and Dissertations. 3131. https://openprairie.sdstate.edu/etd/3131

United States Department of Agriculture. (1951). *The Home demonstration agent [Brochure]*. https://naldc.nal.usda.gov/download/CAT87791369/PDF

United States Department of Agriculture and United States Department of Health and Human Services (USDHHS). (2020). *2015–2020 dietary guidelines for Americans*. 8th ed. Office of Disease Prevention and Health Promotion. Retrieved January 5, 2019 from https://health.gov/dietaryguidelines/2015/guidelines/

US Department of Agriculture – National Institute of Food and Agriculture [USDA-NIFA]. (2017). *The expanded food and nutrition education program policies*. US Department of Agriculture. Retrieved from https://nifa.usda.gov/sites/default/files/program/EFNEP-Policy-December-2017-Update.pdf

US Department of Agriculture and US Department of Health and Human Services. *Dietary guidelines for Americans, 2020–2025*. 9th ed. December 2020. Available at DietaryGuidelines.gov

US Government Accountability Office. (2019). *Nutrition education: USDA actions needed to assess effectiveness, coordinate programs, and leverage expertise*. US Government Accountability Office. www.gao.gov/assets/710/700489.pdf. Accessed September 20, 2020.

USDA-FNS. Implementation of the Healthy Hunger Free Kids Act, 2010. SNAP-Education Provision. Implementation of the Healthy, Hunger-Free Kids Act of 2010, SNAP Education Provision | USDA-FNS

USDA-NASULGC Study Committee. (1968). *A people and a spirit*. https://eric.ed.gov/?id=ED029195 (Colorado State University).

USDHHS and Office of Disease Promotion and Health Promotion. Available at https://health.gov/healthypeople

Well-Connected Communities. (2021). Retrieved from https://wellconnected communities.org/https://wellconnectedcommunities.org/

Whitaker, H., Leggette, H. R., & Barbeau, S. (2018). A marketing standpoint: What marketers can teach extension professionals about internet-based media. *Journal of Extension*, 56(6), Article 24. https://doi.org/10.34068/joe.56.06.24

White, A., Colby, S., Franzen-Castle, L., et al. (2019). The iCook 4-H Study: An intervention and dissemination test of a youth/adult out-of-school program. *Journal of Nutrition Education and Behavior*, 51(3S), S2–S20.

CHAPTER 9

Youth Entrepreneurship Education
Insights from Social Science Research[*]

Surin Kim, Maria Rosario T. de Guzman, Claire Nicholas,
Yunqi Wang, Irene Padasas, and Olivia Kennedy

Contemporary entrepreneurship education in the United States traces its roots to the first instructional courses conducted near the start of the twentieth century, including classes offered at the University of Michigan in the 1920s and the seminal entrepreneurship class taught by Myles Maces at Harvard University in 1947 (Katz, 2003; Princeton Staff Review, 2014). Since then, there has been growing recognition of the potential of entrepreneurial activities to uplift individuals, families, and communities by spurring economic opportunities. Consequently, there has been heightened interest in implementing entrepreneurship education across the country. Katz (2003) opined that after over fifty years of growth and development, entrepreneurship education (mostly referring to higher education in business programs) has now reached maturity, with a substantial footprint in the teaching and research realms, as well as outside the academe. Further, he posits that given the continued and increasing demands in both education and industry for entrepreneurship education, this field will continue to grow in the years to come.

Entrepreneurship education within Extension is somewhat newer but rapidly gaining traction, and there are now several curricula, programs, and entrepreneurship resources offered through various state Extension entities. In this chapter, we examine youth entrepreneurship education in Extension and draw insights from the rich body of scholarship from the social and behavioral sciences to develop best practices and identify future directions. We will propose the following: (a) that entrepreneurship is indeed a promising endeavor in spurring economic opportunities, particularly in rural contexts and among underserved populations that Extension serves; (b) that clarity is needed in the approach and goals

[*] This work is supported by Agricultural and Food Research Initiative Grant No. 2017-08327/ Accession no.1015511 from the USDA National Institute of Food and Agriculture and a Research and Extension grant from the Rural Futures Institute.

for programming; (c) that consequently, evaluation needs to align with the goals and the approach of the program; and (d) that Extension entrepreneurship education needs to be contextualized – taking into account the features of the immediate (e.g., local) and broader settings (e.g., rural versus urban) in which it is implemented and the specific needs, characteristics, and resources of its audience. To illustrate these points, we describe UpStarts: From Classroom to Boardroom, a federally funded Extension program for high school youth. In developing this program, we drew from the scholarship in entrepreneurship and youth development to contribute to participants' well-being and connections to their communities. UpStarts is an example of how Extension evolves – responsive to the emerging needs and demands of its clientele through information dissemination and program development that involves developing solutions and innovative products to support its constituents.

9.1   Definitions, Myths, and the Reality of Entrepreneurship

The term "entrepreneur" often evokes notions of a person who has started their own business, perhaps with an innovative idea upon which they have staked substantial risk that resulted in a successful enterprise. The stereotypical entrepreneur might have had their start after dropping out of college, is tech savvy, and has innate skills and talents that set them apart from their peers (Hunter, 2012; Raible & Williams-Middleton, 2021).

The reality of entrepreneurship may not be as glamorous, or as heroic as has been mythologized in the current zeitgeist. In fact, approximately half of new businesses started by entrepreneurs fail within the first five years; and nearly two-thirds of new businesses end by the ten-year mark (Carter, 2019). Furthermore, although several studies indicate that entrepreneurs experience higher positive emotions compared to peers who are employees, likely because of their greater sense of autonomy and ownership of their enterprise, research also suggests higher levels of stress and potential for negative emotions among entrepreneurs (Lerman et al., 2021; Shir et al., 2019; Stephan et al., 2023). Indeed, entrepreneurship offers numerous benefits at the personal level but can also pose stresses, challenges, and risks.

The definition of entrepreneurship itself has varied and evolved over time and there is still no singular and unanimously agreed upon description of the term. Early definitions narrowly conceptualized entrepreneurship as the process of creating and launching new businesses (Cooper, 1973; Kent et al., 1983). Conceptualizations have shifted to now encompass its various components and generally focus on entrepreneurship as a process that variably includes opportunity identification, value creation, and innovation (see

Ratten, 2023). This broader definition, which focuses on an approach rather than a product is reflected in emergent subdomains within entrepreneurship scholarship (e.g., social entrepreneurship, corporate entrepreneurship, academic entrepreneurship), thus extending the boundary of entrepreneurship education. The clarity in the definitions of entrepreneurship is critical in program development, a point to which we will return later in this paper.

9.2　Entrepreneurship Efforts in Extension

Despite the competing perspectives surrounding entrepreneurship, scholars and policymakers agree that encouraging entrepreneurial endeavors can have substantial value for individuals, organizations, and communities (Luke et al., 2007). Entrepreneurial activity generally yields net economic gains and has the potential to help alleviate poverty by generating employment opportunities, introducing innovations, fostering creative ideas, and developing new products and services that can result in profits (Stel, Carree, & Thurik, 2005; van Praag & Versloot, 2007). Entrepreneurship can have transformative impacts for communities and engaging in such activities can help individuals gain a host of positive personal outcomes. The impacts of entrepreneurship may be especially beneficial to underserved populations (e.g., immigrants) as a path toward upward mobility for individuals and communities (Portes & Zhou, 1999). Substantial evidence exists for how promoting entrepreneurship helps individuals and communities address economic issues, including extreme poverty (see Sutter et al., 2019).

Extension programs in agriculture, food production, and rural communities. Within Extension, the potential for entrepreneurship to spur economic activity has been recognized for decades. Initiatives that support various aspects of the entrepreneurship process and/or focus on specific industries have been in place across the country for years. One example of an agriculture-focused initiative is Mississippi State University Extension's multidisciplinary workshop series that is aimed at helping agriculture and food producers and entrepreneurs enhance their businesses and maximize profitability by providing resources and professional development opportunities (Crist & Canales, 2020). This program involves a one-day face-to-face workshop that is supplemented with other resources (e.g., webinars) and addresses such topics as risk mitigation, finance and regulations (e.g., licenses), and marketing. Similarly aimed at helping current but relatively new agriculture business owners and entrepreneurs, Cornell University implemented a program that made "profit teams" available to participants (Rangarajan et al., 2019). Profit teams are groups of consultants and/or experts who can aid and/or provide resources to participants regarding businesses, including examining various features of participants' farms and providing feedback and suggestions. Both programs report promising findings.

With sparse populations, distance to production and distribution sites, and sometimes gaps in infrastructure, rural communities face unique challenges as settings for entrepreneurship and growth-oriented business operations (Kim et al., 2018). Many of the entrepreneurship programs within Extension are intended to address such issues and spur economic activity in small towns and communities across the country. For example, the University of Wyoming's recently launched Rural Entrepreneurship Center is an Extension website that features a plethora of resources on agriculture- and food-related production for entrepreneurs. Informational materials on the site cover a wide range of topics including beekeeping and practices around direct marketing for beef producers.

Other programs and Extension initiatives are aimed at supporting entrepreneurship by fostering networks and connections that are beneficial (if not critical) to successful entrepreneurship. One example is Connecting Entrepreneurial Communities (CEC) – an annual conference held by Michigan State University Extension. Connecting Entrepreneurial Communities began in 2012 and is designed to highlight and support local businesses and encourage entrepreneurial activities. In this conference, professional development opportunities (e.g., talks, workshops) are held within various local stores and shops, thus drawing much-needed attention to small and local enterprises. This conference and its unique design have now been adopted in at least four other states, namely Nebraska, South Dakota, North Dakota, and Minnesota (Northrop et al., 2022). Similarly aimed at fostering connections and building networks, the University of Wisconsin has recently launched an entrepreneurship program that will provide professional development for potential and current entrepreneurs, foster access to resources, and build linkages and connections among various individuals (Call, 2022). Finally, Rise29 from East Carolina University, is a program that involves an advisory board that supports new and hopeful entrepreneurs through mentorship and provides other resources to launch a business (e.g., helping identify resources). Rise29 connects expertise and resources from the university with budding entrepreneurs, recognizing that successful business development often necessitates human capital and the resources represented within networks (Paynter et al., 2020).

Another approach to fostering entrepreneurship within Extension goes beyond the specific entrepreneur and potential partners to instead reach out to equip stakeholders and leaders who may have a substantial influence on the contexts in which businesses are embedded. The Ohio State University's Building an Entrepreneur-Friendly Community program is a set of resources and curricula designed to help community leaders gain information about supporting local businesses and helping build an ecosystem in which small enterprises can thrive. Research suggests the critical role that ecosystems play in successful entrepreneurship endeavors, and the importance of supportive contexts and stakeholders in business success (Bischoff, 2021; Malecki, 2018). Programs that focus on supporting settings and the influential entities therein are intended to contribute to these systems.

Extension programs for underserved populations. With the potential for entrepreneurial activity to uplift individuals, families, and communities, various Extension systems have also developed resources to aid nascent and current business owners from underserved or underrepresented communities. One example of such an effort is programming conducted in Nebraska by the Rural Prosperity Network (RPN) that delivers workshops, provides individual consulting, and generates educational materials to help immigrants and ethnic minorities develop and launch their business ideas (Nebraska Extension, 2023; Shaffer, 2022). Although the RPN focuses broadly on fostering positive quality of life and the viability of rural communities, entrepreneurship and supporting economic development is a key area of emphasis. Another resource is from the University of Arkansas that includes training materials, curricula, and workshops to support Hispanic and Latino entrepreneurs (Abreo et al., 2014). Catering specifically to Latinx women, the University of Reno has also launched a program to provide professional development opportunities to support entrepreneurship. Among points of emphasis, the program is intended to build connections between aspiring entrepreneurs and current business owners, as well as provide educational resources on business development (Nevada Today, 2023). Finally, *Handcrafted*: Business and Community Building, from the University of Nebraska-Lincoln, is both a series of workshops and a curriculum facilitator guide that is intended to support entrepreneurship endeavors among immigrants. The program model is designed to foster connections among immigrants and longer-term residents by bringing them together around textiles-related projects upon which they can collaborate, share experiences, and collaboratively build businesses and/or community-focused activities to share their works (Chincoa, 2019; Nebraska Extension, n.d.).

The range of programs and resources that Extension has developed to support entrepreneurial endeavors has thus ranged widely across the country in their emphases (e.g., helping increase profit), audience, and approach. Each program reflects the local contexts, needs, and populations that state Extension systems serve and utilize effective practices documented in the broader literature.

9.3 Entrepreneurship Education and Applying Lessons from the Social Sciences

Given the empirical evidence that indicates its promising impacts, preparing youth and young adults to engage in entrepreneurship has thus been the focus of many educational institutions around the world. For instance, the European Union's European Education Area, an entity that promotes collaboration among EU members for high-quality education, has identified entrepreneurship as a key competency that is essential for all EU citizens. They now provide opportunities for learning through long-standing programs (e.g., Erasmus Mundus) as well as tools to support educators in promoting entrepreneurship (European Education Area, 2023; Lackéus, 2015). Large international organizations have also highlighted the value of entrepreneurship. The United Nations, to reach its sustainable development goal of inclusive and equitable education, aims that by 2030, there would be a substantial increase in "the number of youth and adults who have relevant skills, including technical and vocational skills, for employment, decent jobs and entrepreneurship" (Department of Economic and Social Affairs, United Nations, 2019).

In Extension specifically, there are a handful of curricula, after-school programs, and school enrichment activities on the topic of entrepreneurship for children and youth. Several of these programs are intended to spur entrepreneurial activities by providing learners with experiences and resources to build out and launch their business ideas. Topics covered in such programs include ideation, estimating profits and costs, developing marketing plans, and mapping out operations. Other programs are focused on helping youth understand business operations and include such topics as entrepreneurial career exploration and entrepreneurial skill development that are often combined with other leadership programs. Finally, other instructional classes focus on specific aspects of the entrepreneurship process, for instance, helping youth develop and think through innovative ideas and communicate their propositions through pitch competitions. Table 9.1 highlights several examples of youth entrepreneurship programs and resources within Extension from across the country.

Youth entrepreneurship education is gaining substantial interest in Extension. This growth follows decades of research and programming in

Table 9.1 *Examples of youth entrepreneurship education programs in Extension*

Name of program	Description
Entrepreneurship Investigation (University of Nebraska-Lincoln)	Curriculum and program for middle and high school students designed to help learners gain knowledge about entrepreneurship. The program utilizes experiential learning to guide participants through the "ideation and creation of a business and marketing plan."
YE$ Youth Entrepreneurship (University of Tennessee)	Curriculum for high school age youth that can be implemented in a range of settings. The program focuses on various topics around entrepreneurship (e.g., definitions, real world exemplars), career exploration, and various aspects of business development and implementation.
Alabama Youth Entrepreneurial Initiatives and Workforce Development (Tuskegee University)	A program and resource comprised of curricula and educational materials to support entrepreneurial education for youth and young adults.
Be the E: Entrepreneurship (National 4-H)	Curriculum that is comprised of various activities including simulations to guide participants in developing business plans. The curriculum can be applied in a range of settings including after-school programs and clubs.
4-H Cloverpreneur (University of Missouri)	Resource site for various youth entrepreneurship education materials that can be used by 4-H members in Missouri.
Equity in Youth Entrepreneurship (West Virginia University Extension)	One-year strategic planning process that ensures rural and low-income youth (grades 6–12) in underserved communities have equal access to programs and resources that reinforce entrepreneurship.

entrepreneurship education in higher education and in nonformal settings from around the world. As such, it is worth capitalizing upon learnings from scholarship and other settings to apply insights to guide the growing Extension efforts in entrepreneurship education. We propose several key lessons that can be gleaned from the now large body of literature on entrepreneurship education from around the world:

First, in developing and implementing entrepreneurship education, it is critical to clarify program definitions and instructional approaches. Lackéus (2015), writing for the OECD, notes that there are three general approaches to entrepreneurship education. One approach is to teach "about" entrepreneurship, with the goal of helping learners gain knowledge on entrepreneurship and the processes involved therein. Teaching "for" entrepreneurship is intended to foster skills and knowledge among learners, thus preparing them to become entrepreneurs in the future. Finally, teaching "through" entrepreneurship utilizes the experiential and hands-on nature of entrepreneurial processes to gain skills and knowledge that may or may not pertain specifically to value creation or business development. The goal for this last approach might be for learners to gain better problem-solving skills or decision-making, not necessarily applied to business development.

Clarifying the program's definition of entrepreneurship education is also critical and has important implications for designing objectives, goals, and instructional activities. A narrow definition characterizes the instructional experience as helping learners gain "opportunity identification, business development, self-employment, venture creation and growth," with the goal then of helping develop future entrepreneurs (Lackéus, 2015, p. 9). In contrast, a broader definition of entrepreneurship education focuses on "personal development, creativity, self-reliance, initiative taking, action orientation," which are skills related to being entrepreneurial that can be applied in a broad range of settings (Lackéus, 2015).

Second, evaluation outcomes need to reflect the approach and goals of the program. For example, two popular ways of assessing the impact of entrepreneurship education are to measure learners' intentions to engage in entrepreneurship in the future (i.e., "entrepreneurial intentions") and/or to measure actual entrepreneurial activity postprogramming (e.g., how many of the learners started a business) (Kim et al., 2020). No doubt, these measures can serve as important markers of program impact, however, may not be appropriate if the course takes a "wide" view of entrepreneurship education (and thus the goal of fostering personal development, etc.) and/or takes the "through" or "about" entrepreneurship approach wherein the intent is not necessarily to cultivate entrepreneurs. Thus, as with any other program, the evaluation measures of entrepreneurship education programs need to reflect the goals and approaches of the instructional activity (Kim et al., 2020; Luke et al., 2007).

Third, attention to contextual characteristics is important in developing and implementing entrepreneurship education in Extension. A substantial body of literature indicates several contextual factors that impact entrepreneurial activity and success, for instance, the physical and structural features of settings (e.g., population density), population characteristics (e.g., general economic levels of the community), national/local/regional policies, and the "culture" around entrepreneurship and readiness to support new enterprises (Leitch, Hazlett, & Pittaway, 2012; Walter & Dohse, 2012). Developing or implementing entrepreneurship programs should similarly consider or at least acknowledge such factors.

A somewhat new but growing body of literature has been looking at "entrepreneurial ecosystems," or elements of the context that contribute to or hinder entrepreneurial endeavors and success. Although this field of study is still in developing, evidence suggests the utility of the entrepreneurial ecology concept in representing not just contextual factors but how they work together as a system to support or limit entrepreneurial successes (Stam & van de Ven, 2021). Fewer studies have looked at contextual factors in entrepreneurship education, nonetheless, scholars are beginning to acknowledge the need to take context into account when developing and implementing programs (Larty, 2021).

The fourth and final point that can be gleaned from current research and established entrepreneurship programs around the world is the value of building capacity among nascent entrepreneurs, particularly their access to resources. Returning to our earlier discussion of the mythological entrepreneur, another stereotypical notion is that heroic entrepreneurs attained their successes through sheer grit and determination. There is, for example, the "start-up garage" myth, made popular by such stories as Steve Jobs and Steve Wozniak developing Apple computers in their garages, as well as other tech companies that emerged out of pure hard work and innate brilliance of their founders (Gann & Dodgson, 2016). In reality, social capital, access to resources, and personal networks generally play a significant role in entrepreneurial activity and success (Martinez & Aldrich, 2011 McKeever et al., 2014). Social connections can serve as a form of capital upon which individuals can draw support, mentorship, and instrumental assistance. And as for the mythical start-ups that were borne out of hard work in the proverbial garage, in fact many of the successful entrepreneurs in tech start-ups had access to important resources such as university laboratories, research equipment, and experts with whom to consult (Gann & Dodsgon, 2016).

The value of not just helping learners gain skills but also helping them build capacity is already reflected in many Extension programs for entrepreneurs. Though not always explicitly noted, several of the programs described earlier in this paper are intended to foster connections between nascent entrepreneurs and the broader community and key stakeholders (e.g., CEC, Rise29). Entrepreneurship activities do not occur in a vacuum and this reality should be acknowledged. The importance of building networks and capital of various forms is critical to incorporate into programming so that learners understand the multiple factors associated with entrepreneurship.

9.4   UpStarts: From Classroom to Boardroom

We offer one example of programming that our team has developed around entrepreneurship education to illustrate the points noted above. UpStarts is an entrepreneurship education curriculum designed for high school aged youth. We developed this program in response to several broad issues including declining rural populations and a gap in youth entrepreneurship programming that is specifically suited to rural locales. Within the broader aim of contributing to the quality of life and well-being in rural communities, we intended to develop a program that would support youth development including a positive attachment to place and community, a sense of connection and contribution to others, and an entrepreneurship mindset which we defined here as a set of socio-cognitive skills that include a focus on value creation, recognizing opportunities, adaptability and resilience, evidence-based decision-making, and perspective-taking (Daspit et al., 2023). Whereas the history of the scholarly efforts to define entrepreneurial mindset and measure its effects is relatively short, early findings suggest that youth with an entrepreneurial mindset also display critical thinking, perceptions of future career success, and escalation of commitment regardless of outcomes of venture creation (Daspit et al., 2023; Kuratko et al., 2021; Rodriguez & Lieber, 2020).

In building the program, we recognized that there is growing interest and engagement in entrepreneurship education for youth, but that nonetheless, two gaps exist. First, most preexisting programs that provide vocational and entrepreneurial training have been designed in and for large communities and are not specifically attuned to the unique context of rural locales. They do not explicitly consider such issues as a lack of growth-oriented start-ups and entrepreneurs who can serve as role models, as well as a lack of experiential educational contents with methodologies that are designed for growth-oriented business models appropriate to the rural context. Moreover, scholars have noted that it is critical for youth programs and educational opportunities to be locally relevant, so that youth are able to connect higher level skills, education, and job prospects to the communities in which they are situated (Howley, 2006; Haas & Nachtigal, 1998).

Second, few entrepreneurship programs engage youth in ways that maximize their potential not just for personal development but as agents of change for their broader community, which is a key developmental task for adolescents and may help foster a better sense of attachment to community. In other words, few youth entrepreneurship programs exist that link such skills as problem-solving, citizenship, communication, iterative design, decision-making, risk management, and analytical skills as potentially helpful beyond the business realm – for example, to solve real-world issues that may or may not be directly linked to economic gains. UpStarts was developed to address these gaps.

The resulting program is a curriculum and program that can be adapted to a range of settings (e.g., after-school clubs, classrooms) and timelines (e.g., three days, six weeks, twelve weeks), and can be taught as a standalone program or in conjunction with other targeted instructional goals (e.g., STEAM). As the main premise, the program engages youth in pairs or teams and partners them with local businesses or organizations which pose an authentic challenge they are facing. Youth and their partnering organization or business then engage with UpStarts to dissect the problem and generate/test/iterate potential solutions over the course of the program. The youth participants learn about business operations through deep engagement with their partners, including the realities (and often less glamorous) sides of running a business. Partnerships also foster a sense of connection between youth and their business partners. Facilitators are given tools to set up the program, including guidelines for helping business partners develop appropriate challenges and manage expectations regarding youth. We now have implemented three versions of the program – one in which youth propose and create mock-ups of their final products, one in which they build out the solutions, and another that builds out the solutions using STEAM (e.g., developing a web application). UpStarts has reached over 150 learners across ten communities, including both rural and urban areas in Nebraska, one community in Wyoming, and even one high school and one technical college in Krakow, Poland. Eleven cohorts have undergone the program thus far.

Our website (http://upstartsacademy.com) details examples of the issues that businesses and organizations have posed for youth teams and the solutions and products that youth have developed. We highlight a few examples here. In one case, a therapist from a small community approached UpStarts to help generate traffic for her budding equine therapy practice. Youth conducted extensive research about customer needs and identified one key challenge – some potential clients were hesitant in seeking information due to uncertainty about pricing and trepidations around initial contact. The team's eventual solution was a website that was streamlined, utilizing images that represented the practice, and an information page in which potential clients could easily input information to generate an estimate for cost.

In one of our first cohorts that was implemented utilizing the STEAM component, a food processing business posed the challenge of a somewhat high chance of human error in recording various aspects of operations. For example, when a product must be weighed, a person jots down the reading and manually enters this onto a computer. Done dozens or even hundreds of times a day, there was a significant chance for human error. Conducted over twelve weeks, this cohort was one that included a STEAM (i.e., science, technology, engineering, art, and math) component where youth had college student coaches and an instructor who guided them through developing apps, coding, and other procedures. The youth team developed an automated process that linked the measuring devices (e.g., a scale) directly to a minicomputer (i.e., raspberry pi) that removed one step and minimized the potential for human error.

Finally, in one case, a new art gallery was seeking ways to engage customers, which was challenging given the small size of their immediate community. The student team conducted research to identify and understand potential markets and generated ideas on how to engage other potential customers who may or may not be residing nearby. Their resulting solution was to engage the local alumni association to incorporate a silent auction as part of yearly homecoming events. They proposed a partnership with the alumni association that organized this yearly event that was thus in touch with an untapped market that came into the community yearly.

It should be noted here that companies and organizations partnering with the youth are not necessarily engaging with UpStarts with the expectation of a professional-level solution. These entities partner with the program to engage with youth, though in some cases they are truly seeking out assistance for their authentic challenges. They understand that youth solutions may or may not be immediately usable. However, in many cases, they can benefit from insights and ideas from the products that youth develop from their unique perspectives.

UpStarts illustrates several of the insights and best practices that can be gleaned from the current literature regarding youth entrepreneurship education. First, clarity in definitions and approach is critical. In UpStarts, we take a "teaching through" entrepreneurship approach primarily, and a "teaching for" approach secondly. Whereas youth gain skills that will prepare them to engage in entrepreneurial activities, including potentially starting their own businesses in the future; the main goal of UpStarts is to address youth development issues including a sense of contribution to others, a sense of connection with the broader community, and other socio-cognitive skills (e.g., problem-solving, decision-making). Understanding this approach guided program development and is communicated in the curriculum.

Second, the evaluation of UpStarts reflects the goals of the program. We are employing a mixed methods design to assess shifts in decision-making skills, sense of teamwork, technology efficacy, quality of relationships with others, sense of community, and entrepreneurial mindsets. Our assessments and refinement of instruments are ongoing. However, we have reported preliminary findings for both the program and the corresponding train-the-trainer workshop (Kim et al., in press; Kim & de Guzman, 2020; Padasas et al., 2020). Our initial findings are indicating promising results regarding participants' perceptions of what they are gaining from the program, including a sense of efficacy and connection with others.

Finally, to our third and fourth points about context and building capacity, UpStarts not only recognizes but also capitalizes on context. We developed UpStarts specifically to address features of rural communities and to help highlight potential opportunities for youth in their proverbial backyards. The program itself can be customized and applied in a range of settings – both urban and rural. However, we avoided activities that necessitated access to resources that may be challenging in rural settings, such as finding and engaging with high-growth businesses or testing solutions in person with a certain number of targeted respondents.

UpStarts is also designed to foster positive relations between youth and supportive adults in their communities and to address an issue that scholars suggest is a specific challenge for rural youth: that is, the need to have a positive link between attachment to place and strong future aspirations. Attachment to place is generally linked to favorable outcomes. For rural youth, however, it has been associated with lower educational and vocational aspirations. Our own research indicated that youth from rural towns see their own communities as hindering their future aspirations, with respondents expressing the belief that in order to pursue their goals of entrepreneurship, they need to leave their communities (Kim et al., 2018). Many rural youth must contend with the challenging task of weighing career and educational goals against the desire to be near their families and the communities in which they are raised (Howley, 2006). Thus, youth who want to remain or return to rural communities tend to lower their educational and/or career goals because they do not perceive further education and skills as relevant to available opportunities in their rural communities (Howley, 2006; Jamieson, 2000). Hektner (1995) describes this long-standing dissonance between higher aspirations and staying in rural locales as the phenomenon of "moving up implies moving out" and needs to be understood and considered when developing programs for youth in small towns and communities (see also, Parsons, 2022).

The paradox of community attachment and lowered educational/career aspirations is problematic at the individual level because educational and career aspirations are strong predictors of actual attainment, and as such many rural youth may be sacrificing their full potential in order to remain in their communities (Beal & Crockett, 2010). At the community level, the outmigration of talented youth contributes to human capital decline and exacerbates rural–urban economic gaps and further decline of rural contexts, even though this may be what youth perceive as necessary for individual upward mobility (Parsons, 2022; Paul & Seward, 2016). For these reasons, we designed UpStarts as a place-based curriculum, fostering a positive connection to one's community and highlighting opportunities and connections that can be found therein.

Education can and should be made relevant to rural contexts so that youth understand how advanced skills and training can make available opportunities in their own communities and not just relevant in urban centers (Howley, 2006; Nachtigal & Haas, 1998). This ensures that vocational training and educational goals are consistent with the desire to remain in rural communities. By making programs relevant to local rural contexts, Paul and Seward (2016) suggest that educational experiences become investments in the youth and community rather than further fueling young people's departures. Additionally, they recommend a Place-Based Investment Model in rural contexts and five pathways for fostering youth talent: (1) providing enrichment (nonschool) activities; (2) advancing learning opportunities; (3) fostering human connections; (4) teaching entrepreneurial thinking; and (5) providing specialized guidance. UpStarts is designed to reflect each of these tenets.

9.5   Conclusions

Entrepreneurship education has reached "maturity" after decades of implementation, particularly within colleges and universities (Katz, 2003). Within Extension, entrepreneurship programming has been in place for decades. However, entrepreneurship education for youth in Extension is in its infancy. Only a handful of curricula and initiatives are currently in place but there is increasing interest in providing more opportunities in this realm. Research from around the world suggests strong potential for entrepreneurship education to impact the lives of youth both as a means of spurring economic activity and as an instructional tool to reach other developmental outcomes. Fortunately, as we advance in our efforts around entrepreneurship education, we do not have to start from scratch. We have substantial research and rich empirical evidence upon which to draw as we move forward with programming.

The growing field of entrepreneurship education for youth serves as an example of how Extension can serve as a powerful agent to translate research into action and to glean insights from scholarship for the benefit of its constituents. Extension has already been supporting entrepreneurs for decades, especially in rural settings. And as entrepreneurship education continues to grow outside of the university context, there is strong potential for Extension to lead the way in supporting entrepreneurship education that is innovative, impactful, and meaningful to both program participants and the communities of implementation.

References

Abreo, C., Miller, W., Farmer, F., & Moon, Z. (2014). Training materials developed for Latino Entrepreneurs. *The Journal of Extension*, 52(4), 27. https://doi.org/10.34068/joe.52.04.27

Beal, S. J., & Crockett, L. J. (2010). Adolescents' occupational and educational aspirations and expectations: Links to high school activities and adult educational attainment. *Developmental Psychology*, 46(1), 258.

Bischoff, K. A. (2021). A study on the perceived strength of sustainable entrepreneurial ecosystems on the dimensions of stakeholder theory and culture. *Small Business Economics*, 56, 1121–1140. https://doi.org/10.1007/s11187-019-00257-3

Call, M. (2022, January 12). *New extension program supports rural entrepreneurship*. University of Wisconsin-Madison. News from Extension. https://fyi.extension.wisc.edu/news/2022/01/12/new-extension-program-supports-rural-entrepreneurship/

Carter, P. (2019, July 5). 11 reasons why most entrepreneurs fail. *Forbes*. www.forbes.com/sites/forbescoachescouncil/2019/07/05/11-reasons-why-most-entrepreneurs-fail/?sh=5ad7201e1b7b

Chincoa, A. (2019, April 12). Textiles department to showcase female entrepreneurship Nebraska history. *The Daily Nebraskan*. www.dailynebraskan.com/news/textiles-department-to-showcase-female-entrepreneurship-nebraska-history/article_b76f3e64-5cbc-11e9-94f6-9b0203132df3.html

Cooper, A. C. (1973). Technical entrepreneurship: What do we know? *R&D Management*, 3(2), 59–64.

Crist, C., & Canales, E. (2020). Multidisciplinary program approach to building food and business skills for agricultural entrepreneurs. *The Journal of Extension*, 58(3), Article 12. https://doi.org/10.34068/joe.58.03.12

Daspit, J. J., Fox, C. J., & Findley, S. K. (2023). Entrepreneurial mindset: An integrated definition, a review of current insights, and directions for future research. *Journal of Small Business Management*, 61(1), 12–44, https://doi.org/10.1080/00472778.2021.1907583

Gann, D., & Dodgson, M. (2016, November 3). Forget the start-up garage myth. We need golden triangles and super clusters. *World Economic Forum*. www.weforum.org/agenda/2016/11/the-startup-garage-myth/

Haas, T., & Nachtigal, P. (1998). *Place value: An educator's guide to good literature on rural lifeways, environments, and purposes of education*. ERIC Clearinghouse on Rural Education and Small Schools, PO Box 1348, Charleston, WV 25325-1348.

Hektner, J. M. (1995). When moving up implies moving out: Rural adolescent conflict in the transition to adulthood. *Journal of Research in Rural Education*, 11(1), 3–14.

Howley, C. W. (2006). Remote possibilities: Rural children's educational aspirations. *Peabody Journal of Education*, 81(2), 62–80.

Hunter, M. (2012). On some of the misconceptions about entrepreneurship. *Economics, Management, & Financial Markets*, 7(2), 55–104.

Jamieson, L. (2000). Migration, place and class: Youth in a rural area. *The Sociological Review*, 48(2), 203–223.

Katz, J. A. (2003). The chronology and intellectual trajectory of American entrepreneurship education: 1876–1999. *Journal of Business Venturing*, 18(2), 283–300. https://doi.org/10.1016/S0883-9026(02)00098-8

Kent, C. (1983). Business education for women entrepreneurs. *The Journal of Business Education*, 59(1), 28–33.

Kent, C. A., Sexton, D. L., & Vesper, K. H. (1982). *Encyclopedia of entrepreneurship*. University of Illinois at Urbana-Champaign's Academy for Entrepreneurial Leadership Historical Research Reference in Entrepreneurship.

Kim, D., Lee, W. J., & Joung, S. (2020). The effect of youth entrepreneurship education programs: Two large-scale experimental studies. *SAGE Open*, 10(3), 1–21. https://doi.org/10.1177/2158244020956976

Kim, S., & de Guzman, M. R. T. (2020). *Rural communities in flux: Cultural shifts and programmatic responses to address economic and population decline*. Symposium presented at the annual meeting of the Society for Cross-Cultural Research, Seattle, WA.

Kim, S., Taylor, S., & de Guzman, M. R. T. (2018). Addressing declining rural communities through youth entrepreneurship education. *Journal of Extension*, 56(6).

Kuratko, D. F., Fisher, G., & Audretsch, D. B. (2021). Unraveling the entrepreneurial mindset. *Small Business Economics*, 57, 1681–1691. https://doi.org/10.1007/s11187-020-00372-6

Lackéus, M. (2015). *Entrepreneurship in education: What, why, when, how (Entrepreneurship background paper)*. OECD.

Larson, A. (in press). Upstarts T3: An asynchronous and cohort-based entrepreneurship train-the-trainer program. *Journal of Extension*.

Larty, J. (2021). Towards a framework for integrating place-based approaches in entrepreneurship education. *Industry and Higher Education*, 35(4), 312–324. https://doi.org/10.1177/0950422221102153I

Leitch, C., Hazlett, S. A., & Pittaway, L. (2012). Entrepreneurship education and context. *Entrepreneurship & Regional Development*, 24(9–10), 733–740. https://doi.org/10.1080/08985626.2012.733613

Lerman, M. P., Munyon, T. P., & Williams, D. W. (2021). The (not so) dark side of entrepreneurship: A meta-analysis of the well-being and performance consequences of entrepreneurial stress. *Strategic Entrepreneurship Journal*, 15(3), 377–402. https://doi.org/10.1002/sej.1370

Luke, B., Verreynne, M., & Kearins, K. (2007). Measuring the benefits of entrepreneurship at different levels of analysis. *Journal of Management and Organization*, 13(4), 312–330. https://doi.org/10.5172/jmo.2007.13.4.312

Malecki, E. J. (2018). Entrepreneurship and entrepreneurial ecosystems. *Geography Compass*, 12(3), e12359. https://doi.org/10.1111/gec3.12359

Malloy, M. (2023, April 7). Extension launches program to connect and support Latina entrepreneurs. Nevada Today. www.unr.edu/nevada-today/news/2023/latina-entrepreneur-breakfast-series

Martinez, M. A., & Aldrich, H. E. (2011). Networking strategies for entrepreneurs: Balancing cohesion and diversity. *International Journal of Entrepreneurial Behavior & Research*, 17(1), 7–38. https://doi.org/10.1108/13552551111107499

McKeever, E., Anderson, A., & Jack, S. (2014). Entrepreneurship and mutuality: Social capital in processes and practices. *Entrepreneurship & Regional Development*, 26(5–6), 453–477. https://doi.org/10.1080/08985626.2014.939536

NDSU Agricultural Communication. (2019, April 7). NDSU Extension helps vitalize rural communities. Morning Ag Clips. www.morningagclips.com/ndsu-extension-helps-vitalize-rural-communities/

Northrop, C. A., Jamieson, K. M., Jones, P. B., Reilly, M. A., & Augst, T. (2022). Unique conference design showcases small towns, highlights entrepreneurs, and strengthens capacity. *The Journal of Extension*, 60(2), Article 12. https://doi.org/10.34068/joe.60.02.12

Padasas, I., Kennedy, O., Kim, S., de Guzman, M. R. T., Guru, A., & Nicholas, C. (2020). *Youth Entrepreneurship Clinics: An experimental approach to encourage youth connection to rural communities and developing entrepreneurial mindsets.* Paper presented at the annual meeting of the Society for Cross-Cultural Research, Seattle, WA.

Parsons, R. (2022). Moving out to move up: Higher education as a mobility pathway in the rural South. *Russell Sage Foundation Journal of the Social Sciences*, 8(3), 208–229. https://doi.org/10.7758/RSF.2022.8.3.09

Paul, K. A., & Seward, K. K. (2016). Place-based investment model of talent development: A proposed model for developing and reinvesting talents within the community. *Journal of Advanced Academics*, 27(4), 311–342.

Paynter, S. R., Harris, M. L., & Barber, D. (2020). Regional Advisory Councils to Support Nascent Rural Entrepreneurs. *The Journal of Extension*, 58(3), Article 5. https://doi.org/10.34068/joe.58.03.05

Portes, A., & Zhou, M. (1999). Entrepreneurship and economic progress in the 1990s: A comparative analysis of immigrants and African Americans. *Immigration and Opportunity: Race, Ethnicity, and Employment in the United States*, 143–171.

Princeton Staff Review. (2014, September 15). The oldest entrepreneurship programs in America. *Entrepreneur.* www.entrepreneur.com/leadership/the-oldest-entrepreneurship-programs-in-america/237387

Raible, S. E., & Williams-Middleton, K. (2021). The relatable entrepreneur: Combating stereotypes in entrepreneurship education. *Industry and Higher Education,* 35(4), 293–305. https://doi.org/10.1177/09504222211017436

Rangarajan, A., McCarthy, K., & Welch, D. (2019). Improving the viability of new farmers' operations through the use of profit teams. *The Journal of Extension,* 57(5), Article 18. https://doi.org/10.34068/joe.57.05.18

Ratten, V. (2023). Entrepreneurship: Definitions, opportunities, challenges, and future directions. *Global Business and Organizational Excellence,* 42(5), 79–90. https://doi.org/10.1002/joe.22217

Rodriguez, S., & Lieber, H. (2020). Relationship between entrepreneurship education, entrepreneurial mindset, and career readiness in secondary students. *Journal of Experiential Education,* 43(3), 277–298. https://doi.org/10.1177/1053825920919462

Shaffer, R. (2022, July 6). Latino Small Business Program gains momentum. *Nebraska Today.* https://news.unl.edu/newsrooms/today/article/latino-small-business-program-gains-momentum/

Shir, N., Nikolaev, B. N., & Wincent, J. (2019). Entrepreneurship and well-being: The role of psychological autonomy, competence, and relatedness. *Journal of Business Venturing,* 34(5), 105875. https://doi.org/10.1016/j.jbusvent.2018.05.002

Stam, E., & Van de Ven, A. (2021). Entrepreneurial ecosystem elements. *Small Business Economics,* 56, 809–832. https://doi.org/10.1007/s11187-019-00270-6

Stel, A. V., Carree, M., & Thurik, R. (2005). The effect of entrepreneurial activity on national economic growth. *Small Business Economics,* 24, 311–321. https://doi.org/10.1007/s11187-005-1996-6

Stephan, U., Rauch, A., & Hatak, I. (2023). Happy entrepreneurs? Everywhere? A meta-analysis of entrepreneurship and wellbeing. *Entrepreneurship Theory and Practice,* 47(2), 553–593. https://doi.org/10.1177/10422587211072799

Sutter, C., Bruton, G. D., & Chen, J. (2019). Entrepreneurship as a solution to extreme poverty: A review and future research directions. *Journal of Business Venturing,* 34(1), 197–214. https://doi.org/10.1016/j.jbusvent.2018.06.003

United Nations. Department of Economic and Social Affairs. (2018). *World youth report: Youth and the 2030 agenda for sustainable development.* United Nations Publications. http://hdl.voced.edu.au/10707/503451

van Praag, C. M., & Versloot, P. H. (2007). The economic benefits and costs of entrepreneurship: A review of the research. *Foundations and Trends in Entrepreneurship,* 4(2), 65–154. https://doi.org/10.1561/0300000012

Walter, S. G., & Dohse, D. (2012). Why mode and regional context matter for entrepreneurship education. *Entrepreneurship & Regional Development,* 24(9–10), 807–835.

PART III

Looking Ahead: Emerging Issues and Trends

CHAPTER 10

Cooperative Extension and Diversity
Supporting Children, Youth, and Families amid Demographic and Social Change

Kieu Anh Do and Virginie Zoumenou

The contemporary Cooperative Extension System (CES) plays a critical role in the land-grant system of the United States. More than 100 years after its inception, the core mission of Extension remains the same – to disseminate information and knowledge gathered through research to enhance the well-being of individuals and families across the nation (Warner & Christenson, 2019). However, the United States as we know it today has changed dramatically since the early 1900s when Extension was established. In this chapter, we explore the demographic shifts in the United States and the increasing diversity of the population that have significant implications for Extension. We also examine how CES has adapted to keep pace with these changes and the extent to which existing efforts are adequately meeting the emerging needs of children, youth, and families representing diverse populations in the country today.

10.1 Demographic Changes in the United States since the Establishment of the Land-Grant System

The United States has experienced several notable sociodemographic transformations. The nation's population has grown in size and diversity, tripling in size since the 1920s (U.S. Census Bureau, 1930; 2021b). Whereas the population was mostly White in the early 1900s when Extension began its outreach work (89.7 percent; U.S. Census Bureau, 1930), today the country is much more racially/ethnically diverse (76.3 percent being White/Caucasian, 18.5 percent Hispanic/Latino, 13.4 percent Black/African American, 5.9 percent Asian, and 1.3 percent Native Americans; U.S. Census Bureau, 2021a). Changes in the demographic composition is most evident among those under eighteen years of age, of whom almost 53 percent today are non-White and specifically a quarter of whom are Hispanic/Latino (Johnson, 2021).

Much of the changes in the ethnic composition of the country have resulted from the influx of people who immigrated to the United States from different parts of the world. Although the overall proportion of the foreign-born population has not changed much since the 1920s (13.2 percent vs. 13.6 percent; U.S. Census Bureau, 1930; 2021b), the dispersion of countries of origin has. A century ago, over 85 percent of the foreign-born population came from Europe, primarily England, Scotland, Germany, and Poland (U.S. Census Bureau, 1930). However, the passage of the 1965 Immigration Act removed discriminatory immigration restrictions from countries other than those of European origin and changed existing patterns of migration (Kohut, 2019). Today, the proportion of immigrants from Europe has dropped to 10.4 percent, whereas the percentage of those from Central/South America (40.3 percent), Asia (31.4 percent), and Africa (5.5 percent) has risen (U.S. Census, 2019a). This rise in racial and ethnic diversity in the United States is especially pronounced in the western and southern part of the country (Johnson, 2021) and also in many urban communities where the non-White population has become the majority in some counties (Parker et al., 2018). The U.S. Census Bureau (2013) projects that by the early 2040s, the United States will become a "minority-majority" country, such that no single ethnic group will make up a majority of the nation's population.

Rural communities across the country have also undergone major transitions (Parker, 2018). In the 1920s, roughly equal proportions of people resided in urban and rural areas (51.4 percent vs. 48.6 percent, respectively; U.S. Census Bureau, 1930). However, young adults today are moving out of small towns into metropolitan centers for better job opportunities and amenities. Currently, only about 19 percent of the total US population are living in rural areas (Slack & Jensen, 2020). The rate of out-migration in some communities has been offset by flows of in-migration from Central and South America, driven mostly by job opportunities in the agricultural and meat-packing industries (Lichter & Johnson, 2020). Although the size of many rural communities has generally declined, in some regions the population has become more diverse.

Another demographic change with important implications for Extension programming relates to family composition. In the 1920s, more than half of all persons fifteen years and older were married, with less than 1 percent of people divorced (U.S. Census Bureau, 1930). These proportions were somewhat similar across different racial/ethnic groups at the time. Today, the rate of marriage has gone down to under 50 percent, while the rate of divorce has gone up to over 30 percent, for those who are twenty years and older who have ever been married (Mayol-Garcia, Gurrentz, & Kreider, 2021).

Changes in rates of marriage and divorce give rise to diverse family configurations. Children living with two biological parents are no longer the norm. The number of children living in a single-parent household increased from 9 percent in 1960 to 26 percent in 2014, and they are also more likely to be living with cohabitating parents who are not married, with 15 percent living in blended or stepfamilies (Pew Research Center, 2015).

Diverse family forms also emerged as a result of two prominent court cases. In 1967, the Supreme Court ruling in Loving v. Virginia, legalized interracial marriages (Livingston & Brown, 2017). Since then, the rate of marriage across racial lines has gone up. The largest share of interracial marriages is between White and Hispanic couples (42 percent), followed by White and Asian (15 percent), and White and Black couples (11 percent) (Livingston & Brown, 2017). An increasing number of children born today are of diverse racial/ethnic backgrounds, with one in ten babies who resided in a two-parent household in 2015 identified as multiethnic or multiracial (Livingston, 2017).

The second historical case was the 2015 ruling on Obergefell v. Hodges, which federally recognized same-sex marriages (Masci, Brown, & Kiley, 2019). Gallup reported that as of 2016, 4.1 percent of adults in the United States identified as lesbian, gay, bisexual or transgender (LGBT), equating to more than ten million people nationwide (Gates, 2017). Rates of same-sex marriage have increased after the Supreme Court passed its decision. Recent estimates showed that there are approximately 543,000 same-sex couples who are married, and 469,000 who are cohabitating or living with a same-sex partner (U.S. Census Bureau, 2019b). Of these numbers, 191,000 have children living in the household. This means that Extension professionals are more likely to be working with LGBTQ individuals and children from same-sex families today than in the past.

In addition to changes in family forms and compositions, the US population is also aging. In the 1920s, the age structure of the country was younger, with 41 percent being nineteen years or under, 38.4 percent between twenty and forty-four years of age, and 20.8 percent were forty-five years and older (U.S. Census Bureau, 1930). Today, the percentages have flipped, with only a quarter of the population being nineteen years or younger, and the highest proportion (41.8 percent) being forty-five years or older (U.S. Census Bureau, 2021a). The changes are more pronounced in the older age groups (i.e., those sixty-five years or older). Just four decades ago, about 10 percent of the US population were sixty-five years or older (Urban Institute, 2021). Today, it has gone up to 16.3 percent and is projected to increase to 20.4 percent by the year 2040 (Urban Institute, 2021). Shifts are largely due to changes in life expectancy, which increased from an average of fifty-one to fifty-eight years in the early 1900s, to eighty-one and eighty-four years today (for men and women, respectively; Urban Institute, 2021).

In summary, the contemporary Extension system serves a remarkably different population today than that of the early 1900s when it was first established. The population is much bigger, more diverse, more urban, and proportionately older. Families are also more diverse in racial/ethnic identity, composition, and structure. Changing families and communities constitute changing service needs and require different working approaches. For example, lesson plans that focus on traditional family structure might not be applicable to different family configurations. A strong focus on youth development might overshadow the needs of older adults. Whether Extension continues to be relevant and able to serve the nation of today is a question that the system continues to grapple with.

10.2   Federal Initiatives to Reach and Serve Diverse Audiences

Views on whether Extension remains relevant in today's world vary. Some argue that Extension has been slow to change and that it has not adequately addressed the needs of diverse populations (Fields & Nathaniel, 2015). Some point out that Extension remains predominantly focused on agriculture even as the nation undergoes accelerating urbanization and globalization (McDowell, 2001). In contrast, others argue that Extension has, in fact, progressed – showing sufficient efforts to adapt to demographic shifts (Iverson, 2008; Peterson et al., 2002). We see evidence that Extension has made efforts to evolve but there are places where these efforts need to be accelerated to keep pace with societal changes. In this section, we focus on one aspect of the demographic shifts: racial/cultural diversity. We also examine gaps in service delivery that remain to be addressed.

Extension and the broader land-grant system are aware of and have strived to serve the needs of racially/culturally diverse communities. One significant effort is the land-grant status designation to minority-serving institutions (MSIs). Today, there are nineteen historically Black colleges and universities (HBCUs), thirty-six tribal (TCUs), and 158 Hispanic-serving (HSACUs) institutions of higher education (APLGU, 2020; Brewer II & Stock, 2016; CFR, 2021). Extension systems exist in many of these institutions. Moreover, there are several federal youth development (e.g., 4-H) and family and consumer sciences programs geared towards addressing emerging issues and reaching underserved populations, along with the Expanded Food and Nutrition Education Program (EFNEP), the Supplemental Nutrition Assistance Program Education (SNAP-Ed), and the Children, Youth and

Families at Risk (CYFAR) program. In this section, we review the development of various federal initiatives, including those that aim to reach underserved populations and those that foster workforce development for broad community outreach.

10.2.1   *Extension at Historically Black Colleges and Universities (HBCUs)*

In the 1850s, Vermont Representative Justin Smith Morrill proposed a bill to provide 30,000 acres of land to establish land-grant institutions to provide professional learning to the public in agriculture and industry (Allen & Jewell, 2002). This bill was passed by Congress in 1859 but initially vetoed by President Buchanan. Seizing a new opportunity with the onset of the Civil War, Morrill added education in military tactics to this bill to garner legislative support. Congress passed the bill, and President Lincoln subsequently signed it into law in 1862. Thus, it came to be known as the Morrill Act of 1862 (Comer et al., 2006).

After the Civil War ended in 1865, the United States entered the Jim Crow era, in which Black/African Americans were segregated and barred from participation as full citizens of the United States through the passage of various local, state, and federal laws (Howard University School of Law, n.d.). Against the backdrop of segregation, Congress passed the second Morrill Act in 1890, providing federal funding to establish colleges specifically for Black/African Americans (Hughes, 1990). The bill supported the creation of seventeen HBCUs, and two were later added. As such, HBCUs are commonly referred to as the 1890 land-grant institutions and are primarily located in the southeastern states (APLGU, 2020).

Besides these legislative and institutional establishments, a key figure in expanding Extension's reach to broader audiences was Seaman Knapp, also known as "the Father of Extension." To disseminate best practices in agriculture, Knapp engaged farmers to demonstrate methods and techniques for their peers. Extending this work further, Booker T. Washington and George Washington Carver at Tuskegee Institute (now known as Tuskegee University) designed and implemented the "movable school," where they identified the needs of Black farmers and brought information about new farming practices directly to those who needed them. Tuskegee had been conducting outreach work across twenty-eight states and abroad even prior to the official establishment of the CES in 1914 (Comer et al., 2006). The practice of disseminating information to farmers and end users through direct engagement and demonstration continues to be an important means of delivering information to individuals, families, industries, and communities today.

10.2.2   Extension at Tribal Colleges and Universities (TCUs)

In 1994, Congress passed the Equity in Educational Land-Grant Status Act that added twenty-nine tribal colleges and universities (TCUs) to the land-grant system (Croft, 2019). Seven more TCUs have been established since then. Extension programs were then brought on Native American reservations and areas under tribal jurisdiction to address the specific needs of tribal members and families (Hiller, 2005). These programs were originally called the National Extension Indian Reservation Program and later renamed as Federally-Recognized Tribes Extension Program (FRTEP) (NIFA, 2021a).

Extension on Native American reservations remains sparse (Hiller, 2005). There are currently 562 Native American tribes and 314 federally recognized reservations, yet only thirty-six Extension programs exist under FRTEP (Brewer II & Stock, 2016). The 1994 institutions carry out similar programs as the rest of CES, including a strong focus on agriculture and natural resource management, as well as entrepreneurship and business development, along with tribal youth development through 4-H (NIFA, 2021a).

10.2.3   Extension at Hispanic-Serving
Agricultural Colleges and Universities

The newest member of the land-grant system are Hispanic-serving agricultural colleges and universities (HSACUs). These institutions were certified by the passage of the 2008 Food, Conservation and Energy Act (NIFA, 2021b). There are currently 158 Hispanic-serving institutions (HSIs) that are part of the HSACUs, many located in California and Texas (CFR, 2021). Hispanic-serving institution designation requires that the institution have accredited agriculture-related degree programs and a minimum of 25 percent full-time enrolled undergraduates who are of Hispanic origin (CFR, 2021; Croft, 2019). Due to the recency of the designation, not much has been written about these land-grant institutions or the Extension programs that they conducted.

10.2.4   National Extension Initiatives to Address
Underserved and Minoritized Populations

Several large-scale national programs and initiatives within Extension address economically and racially diverse populations. Responding to the needs of families in poverty has been one of the biggest initiatives within Extension across the country. The Expanded Food and Nutrition Education Program (EFNEP) is an example. Initially piloted in Alabama and expanded nationwide in 1969, EFNEP was designed to address poverty and hunger by promoting self-sufficiency, nutritional health, and well-being among families with limited resources (NIFA, 2013). Originally, EFNEP programs worked within 1862 land-grant institutions. It was not until 2006 that the program expanded to include 1890 institutions (EFNEP, 2018). EFNEP is currently operated in seventy-six land-grant universities, serving over 59,000 adults and more than 204,000 youth (EFNEP, 2021). Franzen-Castle and colleagues (this volume) provide details regarding the reach and impact of EFNEP and related programs, such as the Supplemental Nutrition Assistance Program (i.e., SNAP) and SNAP-Ed.

Another example of Extension efforts specifically designed to address the needs of underserved populations is the USDA funding mechanism known as the Children, Youth and Families at Risk (CYFAR). The CYFAR grant provides resources to 1862, 1890, and 1994 land-grant institutions and CES to develop and deliver educational programs to at-risk children, youth, and families (CYFAR, 2020). CYFAR has funded programs in over 2,400 communities to date (NIFA, 2021c), reaching an average of 12,000 participants each year, with approximately 50 percent from ethnic/racial minority backgrounds (CYFAR, 2020). Participants across these programs report positive outcomes, such as higher levels of critical thinking, problem-solving skills, and general life skills (CYFAR, 2018; 2020).

Lastly, starting in the late 1980s, the national CES began exploring the need to address diversity, equity, and inclusion in their organizational structure and programming. The discussions led to the establishment of the Council on Diversity and the publication of several reports focusing on the topic (Iverson, 2008). Toward the end of the 1990s, Extension initiated the Change Agent States for Diversity project to provide support, technical assistance, and training to participating land-grant institutions to address the changing demographics in their regions (Ingram, 2005). The project included four major components. The first was leadership development implemented through a series of workshops for Extension administrators, project coordinators, and other leaders from the participating consortium institutions to identify their state-specific goals. The second component involved the creation of the diversity catalyst team. Each state or consortium member established a state-level work group to coordinate and implement organizational change to address diversity. This team was led by a diversity coordinator who helped to facilitate and manage the change process. The last component consisted of assessments, where each state created a demographic profile and conducted a diversity climate survey every five years to evaluate its progress (Ingram, 2006). The consortium began with seven institutions, including those in Arizona, Colorado, Missouri, New York, North Carolina, North Dakota, and Pennsylvania, with seven additional states joining in 2004 (Ingram, 2006).

One of the consortium members, Washington State University Extension, went on to produce a nationally recognized program, *Navigating Difference* (Deen et al., 2014). The program was designed to foster skills and cultural competencies among Extension professionals to better enable them to respond to and work with clientele of diverse backgrounds. Navigating Difference is comprised of instructional modules aimed to foster cultural awareness, cultural understanding, cultural knowledge, cultural interaction, and cultural sensitivity. The entire curriculum takes eighteen hours to complete but can be delivered in different formats (e.g., three-day workshop or a weekly modules). Numerous states have adopted Navigating Difference and evaluations indicate both short- and long-term changes in attitudes, knowledge, and beliefs about cultural differences (Deen et al., 2014).

10.3   State-Level Extension Initiatives to Address Diversity

As Extension systems are largely delivered at local and state levels, much of the efforts to work with diverse populations occur more locally. After initial successes at local levels, many of these initiatives are adopted for use across state lines. We highlight three examples here to illustrate the range of responses to diversity, equity, and inclusion issues; and in Extension's efforts to address the needs of specific populations. These programs are the Coming Together for Racial Understanding (CTRU) workshop, California's professional development model to promote intercultural competence, and Juntos 4-H with Latinx youth and their families.

10.3.1   Coming Together for Racial Understanding (CTRU)

Whereas systemic oppression and racial inequities are intertwined with the history of the United States, events in the early 2020s highlighted the unresolved challenges that the country continues to grapple with. Recognizing Extension's role in addressing societal needs even prior to the tumultuous summer of 2020, the Extension Committee on Organization and Policy partnered with Michigan State University Center for Regional

Food Systems, the Southern Rural Development Center (SRDC), and several other organizations in 2016 to facilitate open dialogues and build diversity, equity, and inclusion capacity within CES (Weiss & Mensch, 2020). With the end goal of improving race relations in Extension and in the local and national community, the resulting program was a week-long, train-the-trainer workshop called Coming Together for Racial Understanding or CTRU (SRDC, n.d.; Walcott et al., 2020). CTRU engages participants in fourteen hours of work to promote racial under-standing and fourteen hours of guided experiential practice in engaging in civil dialogue, along with guided planning and ongoing support to take the training and implement it in their respective states (SRDC, n.d.). As of 2019, twenty-six states have participated in CTRU (Weiss & Mensch, 2020). Evaluation data suggest that those who complete the training report positive growth across sixteen competencies, including being able to communicate effectively with someone from a different racial/ethnic background, organizing a community dialogue, and engaging racially diverse audiences (SRDC, n.d.).

10.3.2   *California's Statewide Professional Development Model*

The second example of a state-level initiative to address diversity comes from the 4-H Youth Development Program (4-H YDP) in California (Moncloa et al., 2019). The California team created a professional development model to strengthen intercultural competence among 4-H professionals. Those enrolling in the program complete an assessment to measure their prepro-gram levels of intercultural competence, then meet with program staff to create a professional development plan based on their assessment results. Participants also attend monthly meetings over the course of three years to learn more about intercultural practices. The model has been institutional-ized within the California 4-H YDP. Preliminary evaluation results show that the program improved staff and educators' intercultural competence. Consequently, it also increased enrollment of diverse youth in 4-H YDP (Moncloa et al., 2019).

10.3.3   *Juntos and Positive Youth Development*

Finally, Extension programs across the country implement numer-ous initiatives to address the needs of specific minoritized populations. Efforts include adapting existing programs to address the needs of spe-cific populations and developing new programs for particular groups. One successful example of the latter approach is the Juntos program (Behnke & Kelly, 2011; see also Dworkin, this volume). In 2007, a team from North Carolina State University collaborated with 4-H to develop the program to tackle high rates of school dropout and low college attainment among Latinx youth (Behnke et al., 2019). Juntos is designed to engage parents in supporting their youth and guide families in learning more about higher education (e.g., understand mechanisms of loans and scholarships), help youth further their skills that underlie success (e.g., decision-making), and to foster parent–child positive relationships. Program components include family workshops, after-school 4-H club meetings, monthly success coaching and mentoring sessions with a 4-H coordinator, wrap-around activities to involve the family, and summer programming (Behnke et al., 2020). Several studies that explore the impact of Juntos suggest positive effects among participants such as higher aspirations around further education, improved attendance, increased parental educational engagement, and a higher sense of connection among youth to their communities (Behnke et al., 2019, 2020; López-Cevallos et al., 2020).

10.4   Lingering Challenges Facing Cooperative Extension and Charting the Path Forward

Extension continues to exist to leverage expertise and resources generated in the land-grant institutions of higher learning, and research and experimental stations toward positively impacting the lives of individuals, families, and communities. The demographic makeup of local communities and of the country, however, has experienced dramatic shifts. As this review suggests, Extension has in fact made significant strides toward addressing the changing needs that result from such shifts. At the national, state, and local levels, Extension experts have developed numerous programs to address the needs of specific underserved and minority populations; and there has been growing recognition for the need for Extension personnel to develop skills that make for more effective interaction with people of diverse backgrounds (e.g., Navigating Difference). Nonetheless, challenges continue to exist that merit attention from Extension to continue to be relevant in today's changing social context.

First, although Extension programs have been developed to directly address the needs of ethnic, racial, and culturally diverse populations, programs designed for other minoritized populations, such as sexual and gender minority youth (Murray et al., 2020), individuals with disabilities or special needs (Peterson et al., 2012), homeless youth and families (Weigel & Myer, 1990), stepfamilies (Adler-Baeder, 2002), military families (Ames et al., 2011), or aging families (Yelland et al., 2019) remain limited. Strategies to increase efficiency and effectiveness in working with all aspects of diversity require two tracks – one focusing on providing relevant programs and the other focusing on professional development. These two tracks must go hand-in-hand, and both no doubt require time and significant resources.

Second, Extension has traditionally been supply driven, such that the role of Extension experts and educators is to bring resources to the clientele who are then expected to be recipients of the information. However, another potentially effective process for knowledge transfer is to exchange expertise and partnership with community stakeholders. The role of local partners and the community in driving programming and their inclusion in program development can be promising in best addressing their needs (Reed et al., 2015). Extension has been effective in leveraging such partnerships to address various issues including the nutritional needs of clientele (e.g., see Franzen-Castle et al., this volume). Such an approach may be especially effective for minoritized populations that may be harder to reach and for whom building initial trust is necessary. Extension also needs to build expertise regarding who is in their service area and conduct regular needs assessment to create, align, and update program offerings to fill programming gaps with traditionally underserved populations.

Client-informed programming is an approach already adopted by some Extension systems and may be especially helpful in working with diverse or new populations. For instance, Erbstein and colleagues (2017) developed assessments tools to guide 4-H program development among Latino youth in California. Their resources include an *Engagement Resource Chart* that can be used to better understand their targeted Latino populations' ecosystems (e.g., spaces they frequent, cultural events they hold), an *Engagement Resource Log* to guide the identification of resources already used by the targeted clientele, and a *Key Informant Interview Protocol* that can be used to engage partners and stakeholders in dialogue to gain in-depth and broad understanding of their population of interest. By working with clientele to understand various aspects of their learners' ecosystems and engaging stakeholders in the process of program development, Extension can better understand populations with whom they have limited familiarity and engage in true partnership.

A second challenge facing Extension is in the need to recruit and retain a diverse workforce that is representative of the changing demographics of the country (Ingram, 2005; Schauber & Castania, 2001). For example, in a survey of youth development professionals, Evans et al. (2009) found that 4-H workers were less diverse than workers from other youth-serving organizations. Considerable evidence from the field of education suggests benefits of ethnic diversity of instructors, including matching ethnicity for teachers and students (Egalite, Kisida, & Winters, 2015; Redding, 2019). For example, minority students in classrooms taught by teachers of similar racial/ethnic backgrounds performed better in subjects such as math and reading (Dee, 2004). Those who attended schools and districts with better racial/ethnic representation among teachers were less likely to drop out and more likely to pass state standardized tests (see Grissom, Kern, & Rodriguez, 2015). One of the reasons is that professionals who share similar backgrounds with their clients are more likely to understand the nuances of the group they serve and are less likely to have negative perceptions of different behaviors (Gershenson, Holt, & Papageorge, 2016; Redding, 2019). They are also more likely to advocate for the specific needs of their clients (Grissom et al., 2015).

Third, training to prepare Extension professionals to address the needs of diverse populations needs further development. Although several programs are in place to support professional development among Extension personnel to work with diverse audiences, training of professionals prior to entry into the Extension workforce is generally lacking (see Donaldson, this volume). Thus, professional preparation to work with diverse audiences is similarly learned on the job. Providing diversity training for current employees is a good first step; however, a comprehensive approach that allows Extension professionals to have an action plan to be implemented in their day-to-day work with colleagues and clients would be more promising (Regan et al., 2007). Participants in programs such as Coming Together for Racial Understanding reported feeling isolated and alone in their attempts to address racial equity at their institutions or geographical areas of programming (Walcott et al., 2020). Many do not feel that they are prepared or adequately trained to engage in diversity-related work. One reason is that diversity efforts are often implemented as an add-on to existing programming rather than an integrated approach to community outreach. Additionally, Extension professionals may face pushback or resistance in their attempts to implement inclusive programming, such as youth clubs that include discussions of LGBTQ topics (Elliott-Engel, 2018; Ingram, 2005). As such, explicit institutional and administrative commitment to equity and inclusion are critical to support the professional development opportunities available to Extension professionals (Soule, 2017; Walcott et al., 2020).

Finally, limited funding is a reality that challenges almost all aspects of Extension, but particularly attempts to reach diverse populations (Harder, Lamm, & Strong, 2009). Increasing efforts to address diversity and understanding and meeting the needs of a changing audience place additional pressures on a system that is already taxed (Harder et al., 2009). Extension professionals are experiencing high levels of burnout and staff turnover (Harder et al., 2009). Needless to say, additional resources are needed to support staffing and programming needs. Sharing best practices among members of the Extension system and strengthening professional development may help to alleviate some of these issues.

Extension and the land-grant system are also steeped in a complicated history of inequity in funding that needs to be acknowledged and addressed. When it comes to diversity, the missions of MSLGIs have always been to provide educational opportunities for those who otherwise would not have had these opportunities, specifically communities of color who have been excluded from mainstream programs and institutions. However, these institutions continuously have had to justify their existence and are being measured against their 1862 counterparts (Ambler, 2005; Esters & Strayhorn, 2013). Such a comparison is problematic given inequitable funding levels for teaching, research, and Extension across institutions (Harris & Worthen, 2004; Lee & Keys, 2013; Toldson, 2016). For instance, the Equity in Education Land-Grant Status Act of 1994 authorized $50,000 to each land-grant TCU for educational programming each year, but each institution only received an average of about $32,000 (Phillips, 2003). Additionally, funding for some initiatives at the MSIs are often channeled through the in-state 1862 institutions. For example, in 1977, Congress passed the Food and Agricultural Act of 1977 to strengthen Extension programs at 1890 institutions. However, to receive these funds, these institutions had to work with their 1862 counterparts to develop statewide Extension programs (Harris & Worthen, 2004) and much of the administrative oversights were often assigned to the 1862 institutions. In contrast, it is rare for 1862 institutions to be mandated to collaborate with their 1890 counterparts to secure funding.

Harris and Worthen (2004) argued that the legacy of funding inequities is setting in place several trajectories and development of the 1862, 1890, and 1994 institutions. One such trajectory is the struggle for MSLGIs to maintain their infrastructures, such as constructing new facilities or updating dilapidated buildings (Esters & Strayhorn, 2013; Phillips, 2003). They also have a harder time recruiting and retaining faculty and Extension professionals because they are unable to offer competitive pay in comparison to their 1862 counterparts (Phillips, 2003). These challenges limit the scope of Extension programming at the MSLGIs. Consequently, they are unable to fully carry out their mission and many community problems go unaddressed (Bain, Harden, & Heim, 2020).

Despite these challenges, MSLGIs have persevered. There are numerous examples of fruitful and equitable partnerships among the 1862, 1890, and 1994 institutions, which paves a sustainable way forward. One such example is the Woodlands Wisdom Confederation, where six 1994s and one 1862 institution came together to address health challenges within the

Native American community (Hassel et al., 2001). MSLGIs, such as the 1994s, have a comprehensive understanding of the unique communities they serve, while 1862 institutions have a deep connection to research and more established programming. Each institution also has its own strengths, which need to be explored and built upon (Hughes, 1990). However, entering into a partnership should be by choice and should be mutually beneficial. Power, resources, and decision-making should be shared among all members in the partnership (Phillips, 2003).

10.5   Conclusion

In conclusion, the United States has been and continues to experience demographic changes. Extension is at a critical junction of maintaining its ability to fulfill its goals of supporting the well-being of its constituents amid a rapidly shifting demographic landscape. Nonetheless, Extension continues to be uniquely positioned with its mission and history to reach children, youth, and families from diverse backgrounds. Programs and initiatives have been implemented to adapt to the new social realities, but several challenges remain. Partnership will be the key to overcoming these challenges. This includes partnerships between different land-grant institutions to share best practices, as well as meaningful collaborations with community programs and services to leverage existing resources. Within institutions, partnerships between Extension and non-Extension personnel are needed to fully maximize the potential of LGUs.

To be effective and continue to be relevant today and for the foreseeable future, Extension must focus on the "reach" aspect of their outreach mission. As a system created to bring to bear the innovations and insights from LGUs and agriculture experiment stations to individuals, families, and communities, Extension needs to continue evaluating whether it is truly reaching all its constituents and serving the changing needs of the ever-changing population that it serves.

References

Adler-Baeder, F. (2002). Understanding stepfamilies: Family Life Education for community professionals. *Journal of Extension*, 40, 6IAW2.

Allen, W. R., & Jewell, J. O. (2002). A backward glance forward: Past, present, and future perspectives on historically Black colleges and universities. *Review of Higher Education*, 25, 241–261. https://doi.org/10.1353/rhe.2002.0007

Ambler, M. (2005). Tribal colleges redefining success. *Journal of American Indian Higher Education*, 16, 8–11.

Ames, B., Smith, S., Holtrop, K., Blow, A., & Hamel, J., MacInnes, M., & Onaga, E. (2011). Meeting the needs of national guard and reserve families: The vital role of Extension. *Journal of Extension*, 49, 5FEA7.

Association of Public & Land-Grant Universities (APLGU). (2020). *History of APLU.* www.aplu.org/about-us/history-of-aplu

Bain, J., Harden, N., & Heim, S. (2020). Decision-making tree for prioritizing racial equity in resource allocation. *Journal of Extension*, 58, v58–5tt2.

Behnke, A. O., Bohenhamer, A., McDonald, T., & Robledo, M. (2019). The impact of the Juntos program: A qualitative evaluation. *Hispanic Journal of Behavioral Sciences*, 41, 63–84. https://doi.org/10.1177/073998631882048

Behnke, A. O., & Kelly, C. (2011). Creating programs to help Latino youth thrive at school: The influence of Latino parent involvement program. *Journal of Extension*, 49, 1FEA7.

Behnke, A. O., Urieta, D. M., Duan, S., & Lewis, Z. (2020). Evaluation of Juntos 4-H: A wraparound program helping Latinx high schoolers succeed. *Journal of Extension*, 58, v58–2rb8.

Brewer II, J. P., & Stock, P. V. (2016). Beyond Extension: Strengthening the Federally Recognized Tribal Extension Program (FRTEP). *Journal of Agriculture, Food System, & Community Development*, 6, 91–102. https://doi.org/10.5304/jafscd.2016.063.007

Children, Youth and Families At-Risk (CYFAR). (2018). *2017 annual report.* National Institute of Food and Agriculture. https://nifa.usda.gov/resource/2017-cyfar-annual-report

Children, Youth and Families At-Risk (CYFAR). (2020). *2018 annual report.* National Institute of Food and Agriculture. https://nifa.usda.gov/resource/2018-cyfar-annual-report

Code of Federal Regulations (CFR). (2021). *Part 3434 – Hispanic-serving agricultural colleges and universities certification process.* National Archives and Records Administration. https://ecfr.federalregister.gov/current/title-7/subtitle-B/chapter-XXXIV/part-3434

Comer, M. M., Campbell, T., Edwards, K., & Hillison, J. (2006). Cooperative Extension and the 1890 land-grant institution: The real story. *Journal of Extension*, 44, 3FEA4.

Croft, G. H. (2019). *The U.S. land-grant university system: An overview.* Congressional Research Service Report R45897. https://crsreports.congress.gov/product/pdf/R/R45897

Dee, T. S. (2004). Teachers, race, and student achievement in a randomized experiment. *The Review of Economics and Statistics*, 86, 195–210.

Deen, M. Y., Parker, L. A., Hill, L. G., Huskey, M., & Whitehall, A. P. (2014). Navigating difference: Development and implementation of a successful cultural competency training for Extension and outreach professionals. *Journal of Extension*, 52, 1FEA2.

Egalite, A. J., Kisida, B., & Winters, M. A. (2015). Representation in the class-room: The effect of own-race teachers on student achievement. *Economics of Education Review*, 45, 44–52. https://doi.org/10.1016/j.econedurev.2015.01.007

Elliott-Engel, J. (2018). *State administrators' perceptions of the environmental challenges of Cooperative Extension and the 4-H program and their resulting adaptive leadership behaviors*. [Doctoral dissertation]. Virginia Polytechnic Institute and State University.

Erbstein, N., Moncloa, F., Olagundoye, S. S., & Diaz-Carrasco, C. (2017). Engaging Latino communities from the ground up: Three tools. *Journal of Extension*, 55, 4TOT3.

Esters, L. L., & Strayhorn, T. L. (2013). Demystifying the contributions of the public land-grant historically black colleges and universities: Voices of HBCU presidents. *Negro Educational Review*, 64, 119–134.

Evans, W. P., Sicafuse, L. L., & Killian, E. (2009). 4-H youth worker characteristics: Comparisons with workers from other youth-serving organizations. *Journal of Extension*, 47, 6RIB4.

Expanded Food and Nutrition Educational Program (EFNEP). (2018). *2017 Impacts: Expanded Food and Nutrition Education Program (EFNEP)*. National Institute of Food and Agriculture. https://nifa.usda.gov/resource/efnep-2020-national-reports

Expanded Food and Nutrition Educational Program (EFNEP). (2021). *2020 Impacts: Expanded Food and Nutrition Education Program (EFNEP)*. National Institute of Food and Agriculture. https://nifa.usda.gov/resource/efnep-2020-national-reports

Fields, N. I., & Nathaniel, K. C. (2015). Our role in and responsibility toward social justice. *Journal of Extension*, 53, v53-5comm2.

Gates, G. (2017, January 11). *In U.S., more adults identifying as LGBT*. Gallup. https://news.gallup.com/poll/201731/lgbt-identification-rises.aspx

Gershenson, S., Holt, S. B., & Papageorge, N. W. (2016). Who believes in me? The effect of student-teacher demographic match on teacher expectations. *Economics of Education Review*, 52, 209–224. https://doi.org/10.17848/wp15-231

Grissom, J. A., Kern, E. C., & Rodrigez, L. A. (2015). The "representative democracy" in education: Educator workforce diversity, policy outputs, and outcomes for disadvantaged students. *Educational Researcher*, 44, 185–192. https://doi.org/10.3102/0013189X15580102

Harder, A., Lamm, A., & Strong, R. (2009). An analysis of the priority needs of Cooperative Extension at the county level. *Journal of Agricultural Education*, 50, 11–21.

Harris, R. P., & Worthen, H. D. (2004). Working through the challenges: Struggle and resilience within the historically black land grant institutions. *Education*, 124, 447–455.

Hassel, C., O'Kelley, K., Gailfus, P., Brummel, A., Ramczyk, L., Wold, A., & Price, M. (2001). Woodlands Wisdom: Tribal colleges take action to improve community health across North America. *Tribal College Journal*, 13, 36–38.

Hiller, J. (2005). *The National Extension Indian Reservation Program (EIRP)*. University of Arizona. https://cals.arizona.edu/landandpeople/spring2005/article3_1&p.pdf

Howard University School of Law. (n.d.). *Jim Crow Era*. Howard University. https://library.law.howard.edu/civilrightshistory/blackrights/jimcrow

Hughes, L. R. (1990). The future of the 1890's. *Journal of Extension*, 28, 4FUTI.

Ingram, P. D. (2005). A snapshot of the Change Agent States of Diversity Project. *Journal of Extension*, 43, 1FEA5.

Ingram, P. D. (2006). A Change Agent States for Diversity Project: The catalyst team approach. *Journal of Extension*, 44, 5FEA1.

Iverson, S. V. (2008). Now is the time for change: Reframing diversity planning at land grant universities. *Journal of Extension*, 46, 1FEA3.

Johnson, K. (2021, October 6). *New census reflects growing U.S. population diversity, with children in the forefront*. University of New Hampshire, Carsey School of Public Health. https://carsey.unh.edu/publication/new-census-reflects-growing-US-population-diversity

Kohut, A. (2019, September 20). *From the archives: In '60s, Americans gave thumbs-up to immigration law that changed the nation*. Pew Research Center. www.pewresearch.org/fact-tank/2019/09/20/in-1965-majority-of-americans-favored-immigration-and-nationality-act-2/

Lee, J. M., & Keys, S. W. (2013). *Policy brief: Land-grant but unequal state one-to-one match funding for 1890 land-grant universities* (Report No. 3000-PB1). Association of Public and Land-Grant Universities. www.aplu.org/library/land-grant-but-unequal-state-one-to-one-match-funding-for-1890-land-grant-universities/file

Lichter, D. T., & Johnson, K. M. (2020). A demographic lifeline? Immigration and Hispanic population growth in rural America. *Population Research & Policy Review*, 39, 785–803.

Livingston, G. (2017). *The rise of multiracial and multiethnic babies in the US*. Pew Research Center. www.pewresearch.org/fact-tank/2017/06/06/the-rise-of-multiracia…

Livingston, G., & Brown, A. (2017). *Intermarriage in the U.S. 50 years after Loving v. Virginia*. Pew Research Center. www.pewresearch.org/social-trends/2017/05/18/intermarriage-in-the-u-s-50-years-after-loving-v-virginia/

López-Cevallos, D. F., Young, A. W., Gomez-Diazgrandados, A., Reyes, Y., Garcia, J. R., Sherman, J., & Galaviz-Yap, G. (2020). Improving parental engagement for Latino youths' educational success: Lessons from Juntos Oregon. *Journal of Extension*, 58, v58–4rb5.

Masci, D., Brown, A., & Kiley, J. (2019). *Five facts about same-sex marriage*. Pew Research Center. www.pewresearch.org/fact-tank/2019/06/24/same-sex-marriage/

Mayol-Garcia, Y., Gurrentz, B., & Kreider, R. M. (2021, April 22). *Number, timing, and duration of marriages and divorces: 2016*. United States Census Bureau. www.census.gov/library/publications/2021/demo/p70-167.html

McDowell, G. R. (2001). *Land-grant universities and extension into the 21st century: Renegotiating or abandoning a social contract*. Iowa State University Press.

Moncloa, F., Horrillo, S., Espinoza, D., & Hill, R. (2019). Embracing diversity and inclusion: An organizational change model to increase intercultural competence. *Journal of Extension*, 57, 6FEA1.

Murray, K., Trexler, C. J., & Cannon, C. E. B. (2020). Queering agricultural education research: Challenges and strategies for advancing inclusion. *Journal of Agricultural Education*, 61, 296–316. https://doi.org/10.5032/jae.2020.04296

National Institute of Food and Agriculture (NIFA). (2013). *The Expanded Food and Nutrition Education Program policies*. National Institute of Food and Agriculture. https://nifa.usda.gov/sites/default/files/program/EFNEP%20Program%20Policies%20(onscreen%20version).pdf

National Institute of Food and Agriculture (NIFA). (2021a). *Federally-Recognized Tribes Extension Program (FRTEP)*. United States Department of Agriculture. https://nifa.usda.gov/program/federally-recognized-tribes-extension-grant-program

National Institute of Food and Agriculture (NIFA). (2021b). *Hispanic-serving agricultural colleges and universities (HSACU)*. United States Department of Agriculture. https://nifa.usda.gov/hispanic-serving-agricultural-colleges-and-universities-hsacu

National Institute of Food and Agriculture (NIFA). (2021c). *Children, Youth and Families at Risk (CYFAR)*. United States Department of Agriculture. https://nifa.usda.gov/program/children-youth-and-families-risk-cyfar

Parker, K. (2018). *America is changing demographically. Here's how your county compares*. Pew Research Center. www.pewresearch.org/fact-tank/2018/05/22/america-is-changing-demographically-heres-how-your-county-compares/

Parker, K., Horowitz, J. M., Brown, A., Fry, R., Cohn, D., & Igielnik, R. (2018). *What unites and divides urban, suburban and rural communities*. Pew Research Center. www.pewresearch.org/social-trends/2018/05/22/what-unites-and-divides-urban-suburban-and-rural-communities/

Peterson, D. J., Betts, S. C., & Richmond, L. S. (2002). Diversity in children, youth, and family programs: Cooperative Extension. *Journal of Family & Consumer Sciences*, 94, 58–65.

Peterson, R. L., Grenwelge, C., Benz, M. R., Zhang, D., & Resch, J. A. (2012). Serving clientele with disabilities: An assessment of Texas FCS agents' needs for implementing inclusive programs. *Journal of Extension*, 50, 6FEA7.

Pew Research Center. (2015). *Parenting in American: Outlook, worries, aspirations are strongly linked to financial situation*. www.pewresearch.org/wp-content/uploads/sites/3/2015/12/2015-12-17_parenting-in-america_FINAL.pdf

Phillips, J. L. (2003). A tribal college land grant perspective: Changing the conversation. *Journal of American Indian Education*, 42, 24–35.

Redding, C. (2019). A teacher like me: A review of the effect of student-teacher racial/ethnic matching on teacher perceptions of students and student academic and behavioral outcomes. *Review of Educational Research*, 89, 499–535. https://doi.org/10.3102/0034654319853545

Reed, A. S., Swanson, L., & Schlutt, F. (2015). Timberline Manifesto: Seven concepts linking Extension and engagement. *Journal of Extension*, 53, 4COM1.

Regan, C., Swisher, M., Barnett, R., Luzar, J., & Mastrodicasa, J. (2007). *Diversity training: A way to increase organizational support for sexual minority adolescents (FCS 2268)*. University of Florida IFAS Extension. https://ufdcimages.uflib.ufl.edu/IR/00/00/23/30/00001/FY87500.pdf

Schauber, A. C., & Castania, K. (2001). Facing issues of diversity: Rebirthing the Extension Service. *Journal of Extension*, 39, 6COM2.

Slack, T., & Jensen, L. (2020). The changing demography of rural and small-town America. *Population Research & Policy Review*, 39, 775–783. https://doi .org/10.1007/s11113-020-09608-5

Soule, K. E. (2017). Creating inclusive youth programs for LGBTQ+ communities. *Journal of Human Sciences and Extension*, 5, 103–125.

Southern Rural Development Center (SRDC). (n.d.). *Coming together for racial understanding*. http://srdc.msstate.edu/civildialogue/index.html

Toldson, I. A. (2016). The funding gap between historically black colleges and universities and traditionally white institutions needs to be addressed. *The Journal of Negro Education*, 85, 97–100. https://doi.org/10.7709/ jnegroeducation.85.2.0097

United States Census Bureau. (1930). *Statistical abstract of the United States: 1930*. www.census.gov/library/publications/1930/compendia/statab/52ed.html

United States Census Bureau. (2013). *International migration is projected to become primary driver of U.S. population growth for first time in nearly two centuries*. www.census.gov/newsroom/archives/2013-pr/cb13-89.html

United States Census Bureau. (2019a). *Place of birth for the foreign-born population in the United States (ACSDT1Y2016.B05006)*. https://data.census.gov/cedsci/ table?tid=ACSDT1Y2019.B05006&q=ACSDT1Y2016.B05006

United States Census Bureau. (2019b). *U.S. Census Bureau releases CPS estimates of same-sex households*. www.census.gov/newsroom/press-releases/2019/same-sex-households.html

United States Census Bureau. (2021a). *Quick facts: United States*. www.census .gov/quickfacts/fact/table/US/PST045219

United States Census Bureau. (2021b). *U.S. and world population clock*. www .census.gov/popclock/

Urban Institute. (2021). *The U.S. population is aging*. www.urban.org/policy-centers/cross-center-initiatives/program-retirement-policy/projects/ data-warehouse/what-future-holds/us-population-aging

Walcott, E., Raison, B., Welborn, R., Pirog, R., Emery, M., Stout, M., Hendrix, L., & Ostrom, M. (2020). We (all) need to talk about race: Building extension's capacity for dialogue and action. *Journal of Extension*, 58, v58-5comm1.

Warner, P., & Christenson, J. A. (1984, 2019). *The Cooperative Extension Service: A national assessment*. Routledge.

Weigel, D. J., & Myer, P. A. (1990). Homeless families: Extension's role. *Journal of Extension*, 28, 1IAW3.

Weiss, A., & Mensch, L. (2020). *Building diversity, equity, and inclusion capacity for extension educators across the United States*. Michigan State University Center for Regional Food System.

Yelland, E. L., Benson, J. J., Litzelman, K., Gerstenecker, C. B., & Bartholomae, S. (2019). An analysis of aging-related needs and programming across the Extension North Central region. *Journal of Extension*, 57, 27.

CHAPTER II

Reaching and Serving Underrepresented Families
The Necessity of Engaging Fathers in Extension Programming

Kerrie Fanning, Jiwon Yoon, and Margaret L. Kerr

Despite continued efforts to diversify participation, many children, families, and communities remain underrepresented and underserved in research and family programming (National Institutes of Health [NIH], 2020). Community-based scholarship consists of research and program development, implementation, and practice in community-engaged frameworks that must engage underrepresented and underserved communities. Such engagement is paramount to ensuring program relevance, acceptance, and community benefits and for addressing community-generated concerns (Strand et al., 2003). The NIH (2020) designates underrepresented and hard-to-reach populations to include socioeconomically disadvantaged, rural, and structurally and historically marginalized communities, including Black/African American, Hispanic and Latinx, Asian and Asian American, American Indian and Alaskan Native, Native Hawaiian and Pacific Islander, sexual and gender minorities, and individuals with disabilities. Given the inequitable impacts the COVID-19 pandemic continues to have on underrepresented and underserved families, it is crucial to identify effective and sustainable ways to promote family and community well-being among these communities (Millett et al., 2020). With Extension's unique physical location and relational position within communities, Extension programs possess many of the necessary tools for engaging and supporting hard-to-reach families.

For many families, experiences of poverty exacerbate inequitable representation in research and programs. In 2019, the US Census Bureau reported poverty rates to be higher among Black/African American individuals (19 percent), Hispanic individuals (16 percent), and individuals living outside metropolitan settings (13 percent) (Semega et al., 2020). These disproportionate rates of poverty are particularly stark among different constellations of families, with 22 percent of single, mother-headed households and 12 percent of single, father-headed households living in poverty compared to 4 percent of households headed by married couples (Semega et al., 2020). Families living in poverty are also more likely to experience homelessness (Bassuk, 2010; Park et al., 2011), parental incarceration (Murphey & Cooper, 2015), and child welfare system involvement (Kim & Drake, 2018). Living in poverty coupled with these other life challenges can make it difficult for Extension programs and resources to reach these families; however, there are also great opportunities.

Supporting fathers is one effective pathway for Extension to reach underrepresented families and those living with lower resources. There are many unique and positive ways that fathers contribute to child and family well-being (Cabrera et al., 2014). In general, children with more engaged fathers exhibit higher academic achievement, fewer challenging behaviors, and better psychological outcomes (Barker, Iles, & Ramchandani, 2017; Kim & Hill, 2015; Lee & Schoppe-Sullivan, 2017). Indeed, fathers' engagement may buffer the impacts of adversities for vulnerable children (e.g., Choi & Pyun, 2014). Thus, supporting father–child relationships within vulnerable families is crucial for child and family well-being. To ensure that programming for underrepresented families is appropriate and effective, understanding the barriers to and opportunities for fathers' engagement becomes critical. In this chapter, we review relevant literature on fathers' participation in family-based research and programming, examining common obstacles to fathers' participation, emerging opportunities, and innovative approaches to father-centric programming in Extension.

11.1 Fathers and Families

Until recently, fathers were largely absent in family-based programming and research (Panter-Brick et al., 2014), which is unsurprising given gendered, heteronormative expectations of fathers (e.g., father as "breadwinner") (Roy, 2014). However, fathers' contributions to child and family well-being beyond financial and in-kind resources are now well documented (see Fitzgerald et al., 2020 for a review). Research demonstrates that fathers' parenting behaviors qualitatively differ from mothers (Cabrera et al., 2014), where fathers often encourage children's risk taking, hands-on or "rough-and-tumble" play, and support them in navigating difficult, novel, or scary situations (Amodia-Bidakowska et al., 2020). Furthermore, fathers' contributions exceed the father–child relationship to include benefits to the father–partner relationship and family system. For example, greater support from fathers is associated with lower parenting stress in mothers (Harmon & Perry, 2011) and fathers' sensitive and involved parenting buffers maternal depression's effects on child outcomes and family cohesion (Mezulis et al., 2004; Vakrat et al., 2018). For fathers in same-sex couples, nonresident father engagement relates to partners' increased feelings of accomplishment as parents (Barrett & Tasker, 2001).

Despite advances in our understanding of fathers' roles and unique contributions within families, scholarship on supporting fathers' well-being and subsequent family engagement has lagged behind (Palkovitz & Hull, 2018; Roy, 2014). The experiences of many fathers, especially those contending with greater adversities, continue to be overlooked, and many fathers remain underserved by parenting and family programming. This is especially true for nonresidential fathers. Despite facing unique challenges compared to residential fathers (Wilson, 2006), Goldberg et al. (2009) reported only one in four journal articles on fatherhood focused on nonresidential fathers, presenting a serious gap in scholarship. Supporting fathers' positive engagement with their children and families is particularly important in vulnerable families, including single-parent and low-income households, where fathers' engagement has been shown to be especially important for family well-being and child development (e.g., Choi & Pyun, 2014; Lee & Schoppe-Sullivan, 2017; Miller et al., 2020).

Supporting and engaging fathers present an avenue through which Extension programming and research can serve as a model to support other underrepresented groups. For example, supporting fathers who are incarcerated exemplifies how Extension can reach an underserved population. In the United States, nearly five million children experience parental incarceration, and the vast majority of incarcerated parents are fathers (Sykes & Pettit, 2014). Due to structural racism and discriminatory policing, many families impacted by parental incarceration are families of color and living in poverty (Murphey & Cooper, 2015). Paternal incarceration relates to a host of negative outcomes for children and families, ranging from children's increased challenging behaviors and later child psychopathology and criminal justice involvement (Poehlmann-Tynan & Turney, 2021). There can also be disruptions in caregiving routines and resources resulting in coparenting relationship strain with the incarcerated parent, substantial financial and in-kind resource loss, and increased risk for eviction and homelessness (Arditti & McGregor, 2019); all of which can lead to adverse outcomes for a caregiver's mental health. Importantly, supporting incarcerated fathers' well-being and involvement with their children and family during their incarceration and upon returning to the community predicts positive outcomes for parents, children, and families, including positive parent–child and parent–caregiver relationships, reduced recidivism, and increased family cohesion and stability (Peterson et al., 2019). Extension can conduct critical work with incarcerated fathers because of their relationships with community partners, such as local governments and criminal legal agencies (e.g., jails, community re-entry programs). There is an opportunity for Extension to use these community partnerships to reach other underserved audiences as well, such as building relationships with local children's hospitals, medical respite programs, or occupational therapy to provide programming for families who have children with disabilities or other special health care needs.

11.2   Barriers to Father Program Engagement

Despite fathers' desire to be involved with their children and interest in parenting and family programming, significant barriers to their engagement persist (Panter-Brick et al., 2014). In general, few evidence-based father-centric programs exist (Kramer Holmes et al., 2020). Although fathers are not explicitly excluded from most parent education classes, most programs are designed for mothers and contain little information specific to fathers or fatherhood, such as the transition to fatherhood, peer fatherhood support, rights and responsibilities (e.g., custody laws), fathers' roles, and awareness of the importance of their involvement in their children's lives (Henry et al., 2020; Lechowicz et al., 2019; Panter-Brick et al., 2014). In these mother-centric programs, fathers report feeling out of place or uninvited (e.g., Panter-Brick et al., 2014). Furthermore, many facilitators of family programs may be unaware of the importance of father engagement or ways to effectively involve them (e.g., McBride et al., 2017; Tully et al., 2018).

Given the variety of ways fathering and perceptions of fatherhood are conceptualized by different cultures, fathering programs that do exist may be irrelevant, provide conflicting messages regarding fathering, or be disrespectful to fathers from different cultures (Concha et al., 2016; Lechowicz et al., 2019; Lee et al., 2011). Some fathers of color may mistrust research and programming, potentially due to feeling misunderstood or disrespected by the study or program providers (Stahlschmidt et al., 2013). Many gay and plurisexual fathers report feeling out of place at traditional family-based programming (Carroll, 2018). Furthermore, Carbone et al. (2004) describe how many fathers in high-risk contexts often balance "competing needs," where "survival" needs (e.g., working; obtaining housing) outweigh program attendance.

One important barrier to fathers' engagement in their children's lives and family programming is maternal gatekeeping, or the ways that mothers and other caregivers consciously and unconsciously discourage fathers' engagement with their children (Austin et al., 2013). Many fathers report that their relationship with their child's mother is a significant source of conflict or tension that impedes their ability to engage with their children (e.g., Schoppe-Sullivan et al., 2008), and numerous previous studies evidence the relations between maternal gatekeeping and father parenting behaviors and quality (e.g., Altenburger et al., 2018). Indeed, studies find increased father engagement when father–mother coparenting relationships are more positive (e.g., Fagan, 2014; Roberts et al., 2014).

Further, many societal structures (e.g., legal system, children's health care, family leave) are inherently based on traditional gendered expectations of mothers and fathers which subsequently bolster gatekeeping through policy and practices. For example, many nonresident fathers report feeling ostracized by the legal and child welfare systems, given its design to favor mothers regarding child custody and placement (e.g., Coady et al., 2013; Costa et al., 2019). For fathers experiencing homelessness, a woefully underserved group, many family shelter policies prohibit men from staying at the shelter, often requiring them to stay at a men's only shelter or be unsheltered (e.g., car, outside), separated from their family (Rollins & Boose, 2021). Numerous studies document gay and plurisexual fathers' experiences of "othering" in their children's schooling and parenting groups (e.g., Goldberg et al., 2020), and much of children's health care focus on engaging mothers, with fathers reporting feeling lost in their child's health care (Allport et al., 2018; Davison et al., 2017). These strategies limit outreach, undermine the value of inherently father-centric programs, and systematically discourage and prohibit the engagement of fathers, especially more marginalized fathers. Addressing gatekeeping and mother-centered practices along with other barriers to fathers' engagement is necessary for successful development and implementation of fatherhood programs.

11.3   The Promise of Father-Centric Programs

Several studies have examined effective recruitment and retention strategies for fathers, a key aspect of successful father programming. Based on a review of programs and research, Bronte-Tinkew et al. (2012) identified ten characteristics defining high-quality fatherhood programs and program engagement strategies, each of which has since been corroborated by further research (e.g., Panter-Brick et al., 2014), and align with best practice principles in community-based scholarship outlined by Strand et al. (2003). Specifically, the authors emphasize collaboration with fathers and other key community stakeholders during the development, implementation, and evaluation of programs, tailoring location, timing, content, and delivery format of programs specifically to fathers, and ensuring trainers have comprehensive training and are prepared to work with fathers specifically.

When fatherhood programs align with these best practice principles to support fathers' well-being and engagement, there are positive spill over effects for the family system (Panter-Brick et al., 2014). A recent meta-analysis of programs for low-income, nonresident, and never married fathers revealed significant positive effects on fathers' involvement, parenting behaviors, and coparenting alliance with their child's mother (Kramer Holmes et al., 2020). Of note, the strongest effects were for father–mother coparenting relationships. Although the authors reported nonsignificant effects on fathers' employment and child support payments, it is likely additional barriers exist (e.g., employment opportunities, systemic inequalities) that are not addressed by fatherhood programs, but rather require systemic changes at the community and socio-political levels. Nevertheless, these programs present promise for supporting fathers and families.

A successful example of a father-centric program is the Alameda County Father Corps in Alameda, California, aiming to support and engage fathers and advocate for father-friendly practices. In part, this program is successful because it draws upon seven principles for best practice in father-centric work (Alameda County Father Corps, 2014). Similar to those identified by Bronte-Tinkew et al. (2012), these include intentional recruitment and hiring of men and fathers in leadership roles, setting and modeling a clear admiration of the importance of fathers and expectations for fathers' engagement in programming, and explicit outreach efforts aiming to portray programming as celebrating and welcoming fathers. Importantly, these principles also align well with the diversity tenets of working with families presented by the Irving Harris Foundation (2018), including reflecting on one's own culture and cultural basis for the program and program content, embracing nondominant ways of knowing and knowledge held by communities, and honoring families' and communities' values, beliefs, languages, and cultures in which they live and thrive.

In practice, however, developing and implementing effective fatherhood programming aligned with these tenets and principles can be challenging. Program implementation requires an immense amount of resources, including establishing authentic relationships with community partners, engaging stakeholders, and piloting and evaluating programs (Panter-Brick et al., 2014). The Cooperative Extension network, however, can be well positioned to implement these principles and meet the needs of vulnerable and underserved audiences, such as fathers.

11.4 The Role of Extension

The Cooperative Extension System is a national network of professionals connected to over 100 land-grant colleges and universities, consisting of over 32,000 university- and county-based professionals, and are described in-depth in Chapters 1 and 2 of the current volume. Extension specialists and educators partner with community organizations to better serve families through coordination of community-based workshops, events, and programs. Partners include but are not limited to schools, libraries, courts, and family-serving agencies. Extension programming broadly covers family well-being, youth development, child development, finances, and agriculture, with program options varying dramatically by location.

A handful of fatherhood initiatives currently exist in Extension. However, these programs offer a piecemeal approach to supporting and engaging fathers. In contrast to how Extension programs have addressed mothers' and overall family needs, few Extension programs to date have implemented a multipronged, holistic approach to reaching and serving fathers, especially those from marginalized communities. For example, Utah State University Extension recently received a Department of Health and Human Services grant funding fatherhood and relationship-based programs, beginning with programs for incarcerated fathers and later expanding to coparenting programs. Similarly, partnering with Minnesota Department of Corrections, University of Minnesota Extension offers parenting classes for incarcerated fathers. Alabama Cooperative Extension offers evidence-based, online fatherhood courses, covering a wide range of topics. Although the examples noted above and expanded on below are important starting points, father-centric programming in Extension is an area of great growth and opportunity.

Due to Extension's location within communities and established relationships with university and community partners, many Extension programs have access to the resources needed to implement father-centric programs based on the principles and activities described above. These well-established connections and trust within the community make Extension well positioned for collaboration and the development of innovative ways to reach fathers; particularly in connecting communities to the university community. For example, Extension programs have access to university-based resources that facilitate program creation and evaluation, including access to existing evidence-based programs, research resources, and program evaluation experts. Extension networks also currently partner with many key community stakeholders, including organizations directly serving and advocating for men and fathers specifically (e.g., the National Fatherhood Initiative). Furthermore, many of the programs already systematically provided by Extension networks target needs similar to those fathers have expressed (e.g., employment, parenting) and may prove easily adaptable to better address fathers' specific needs. Through systematic coordination of these existing programs, with modifications and additions made unique for fathers, and expansion to include unaddressed needs, Extension has the capacity to provide a holistic approach to supporting fathers and fatherhood scholarship. This inherent "infrastructure" of Extension programs provides a foundation for which fatherhood initiatives could flourish.

11.5   Existing Work with Fathers in Extension

In response to recent calls for father-focused programming (e.g., Fisher, 2017; Palkovitz & Hull, 2018) and emerging community needs, there has been an increase across Extension networks to engage and serve fathers, which includes reading programs, relationship and parenting education, and programs specific to incarcerated fathers. In 2019, University of Wisconsin-Madison, Division of Extension (UW-Extension) launched a statewide initiative aiming to better serve Wisconsin fathers. Section 11.5.1 describes this in detail, including a multipronged needs assessment and initial efforts toward father-centric programming.

11.5.1   Wisconsin Statewide Needs Assessment

UW-Extension's Human Development & Relationships Institute recognizes parents' importance for child and family well-being and provides parenting programs to families across Wisconsin. Despite these efforts, several county-based educators identified limited approaches and resources for supporting fathers in Wisconsin, often resulting in one-on-one case management with little guidance. To better meet community needs, in 2020 UW-Extension conducted a statewide, multimethod needs assessment to identify the specific needs of Wisconsin fathers and engage Extension colleagues and father-serving organizations in programming, advocacy, and partnerships to improve outcomes for fathers and families.

The multipronged needs assessment included: (1) a review of the literature on the impacts of fathers' involvement and engagement on children's development; (2) interviews with personnel in agencies and organizations working with children and families in Wisconsin; and (3) focus groups with fathers residing in Wisconsin. The Fatherhood Team conducted eleven interviews and six surveys with informants from key family-serving organizations (e.g., county social services, county jail, and county family resource center) and six focus groups consisting of approximately twenty-eight fathers across the state. Relevant findings are presented below to highlight how this multipronged approach can be an informative way to create programming that uniquely meets the needs of local communities.

11.5.1.1 Stakeholder Interviews

Stakeholder interviews were designed to investigate community partners' views on fathers' needs, existing programs, and remaining program gaps in Wisconsin. Interviews consisted of twelve questions, with the key topics being: (1) "What are the major issues or concerns that you hear about fathers in the community," (2) "What are the biggest barriers that prevent fathers from being involved or engaged with their children," and (3) "What gaps in programs or services for fathers exist in the community?" Stakeholder interviews yielded four broad categories: (1) information and resources pertaining to basic life skills, (2) parenting support, (3) systems approach to reduce gendered norms and stigma, and (4) justice-involved father support.

Many interviewees reported lack of support for meeting fathers' basic needs, including housing, finances, fathers' own mental and physical health, substance use, and accessing quality childcare. Meeting basic needs is essential for fathers' own well-being, for fulfilling their parenting role, and for parenting program participation. Similarly, interviewees expressed that fathers may need general parenting skills support. Stakeholders explained that some fathers find nurturing and child-rearing challenging, which may result from a lack of father figures or role models in fathers' own lives, or lack of knowledge on the influence of fathers' parenting behaviors on children. Suggestions for programming ranged from more general (e.g., parenting behaviors, child development) to more specific topics (e.g., coparenting, communication).

Many stakeholders emphasized the need to increase father inclusivity and address gendered stigma and stereotypes. Some community partners acknowledged that family-serving organizations and fathers themselves might hold gendered beliefs toward fatherhood, which operates as a barrier to fathers' seeking support or programming. These gender stereotypes may devalue fathers' importance in children's lives and further discourage them from seeking support. Further, existing community resources are predominantly mother oriented, focused on mothers, and led by women. Several stakeholders identified the need for more father-led programming or more programming that is specific to fathers and their needs. Lastly, supporting justice-involved fathers' navigation of the legal systems emerged as a critical unmet need, including child custody, child support, and criminal justice involvement. For these fathers, their experiences during incarceration, custody limitations, and gatekeeping barriers with their child(ren)'s mother presented additional challenges to engaging with their children.

In conclusion, interviews with stakeholders consistently revealed that fathers have unique needs and challenges currently unmet by family support services, likely affecting fathers' participation in programs. Overall, these findings were in line with the tenets and principles for best practices in engaging fathers, detailed earlier in this chapter. It is critical that existing programs serving families throughout Wisconsin reevaluate their scope to intentionally engage fathers and their specific needs. Several stakeholders underscored being inclusive of all fathers, including single fathers, grandparents, and LGBTQ+ fathers; a crucial direction for innovative programming. Examined next, father-based focus group consultation can provide information regarding modifications to existing and development of new programming in this regard.

11.5.1.2 *Father Focus Groups*

Along with stakeholder interviews, the fatherhood team conducted six focus groups with Wisconsin fathers. In addition to identifying fathers' needs and challenges in fulfilling their father roles, the focus groups aimed to uncover specific strategies for attracting fathers to existing programs. To ensure group cohesion and active participation, each focus group consisted of fathers with shared experiences. Thus, fathers were grouped by parenting situation; fathers with primary or sole custody, with shared custody, nonresidential fathers, and justice-involved fathers. An additional focus group with Latino fathers was offered in Spanish. All focus groups were conducted virtually, lasting ninety minutes. Facilitators utilized twelve discussion prompts, including: (1) "What are some of the most challenging things about being a father," (2) "What services or organizations do you know about that could support you as a parent," (3) "What kind of supports/services would you want to receive," and (4) "How would you like to get information?"

Preliminary findings reflect similar themes from the stakeholder interviews, such as needing support with basic needs, parenting education or support, coparenting, and navigating the justice system. These needs varied across focus groups (e.g., coparents, fathers with sole custody), and fathers' specific situations (e.g., incarcerated, living far from children), but common themes arose as well. For example, nearly all fathers indicated the desire for peer groups and programming specific to or exclusively for fathers. Fathers conveyed the desire for opportunities to build relationships with other fathers or a father network to learn from each other and share their experiences with other fathers. Specifically, many fathers discussed the desire to have a father-exclusive space because they do not always feel comfortable or included in mother-dominated spaces. Fathers also commonly mentioned the need for child-focused activities that are free or low cost. Using focus groups as an approach to obtain information from fathers increases understanding of their own needs and ensures their voices inform how Extension can deliver father-centric programming. Extension's dedication to community-based research supports Extension in understanding the unique needs of underserved families in their communities allowing them to provide timely and authentic responses through programming and resources.

In line with previous fatherhood scholarship, the present needs assessment confirmed fathers' general and unique needs as parents and expanded by recommending father-specific peer groups to build networks and share information. Despite father-targeted initiatives addressing these gaps, these findings demonstrate tremendous need for continued work and advocacy, especially at institutional and sociopolitical levels. As described above, Extension's infrastructure and resources enable collaboration and advocacy surrounding father-centered programs, and these findings provide recommendations for strengthening Extension's impact. Next, we detail current programs supporting fathers within UW-Extension.

11.5.2   *Examples of Fatherhood Efforts in Extension*

Alongside the ongoing needs assessment, several father-specific efforts exist within UW-Extension. Described in detail below, these examples demonstrate various implementation strategies and how these efforts serve other underrepresented audiences in Extension (e.g., justice-involved families, single-parent families). A consistent finding from our needs assessment, fathers desire programs tailored to and exclusive to fathers. In response, examples are presented in two groups: *father-centric programs*, programs developed exclusively for fathers, and *father-relevant programs*, programs with content readily adaptable to fathers.

11.5.2.1　Father-Centric Programs

Focus on Fathers. During the focus groups, fathers reported feeling unwelcome at mother-dominated programs and felt they had different topics to discuss and learn about. Fathers were looking for social connections with other fathers that did not emerge naturally through other events, such as participating in their children's schooling. In response to this emerging need, UW-Extension is currently developing *Focus on Fathers*, a parent cafe-modeled peer group specific to fathers. The program incorporates UW-Extension's Raising Caring Kids[1] curriculum, a social/emotional skills-focused parenting program, to provide brief parenting education (another expressed need) while also providing a starting point for fathers' discussion. During each one-hour session, the first ten to fifteen minutes are spent engaging the fathers in the day's topic which is then followed by open discussion.

　　Anywhere Dads Podcast. Another in-progress effort by UW-Extension, *Anywhere Dads*, is a podcast series aiming to connect science-based parenting information to fathers in jail or otherwise separated from their children. This series of eleven 15-minute podcasts combines fathers' voices and experiences with experts in parenting, child development, and incarceration. Fathers at local jails were interviewed about their parenting experiences and being separated from their children. Excerpts of these interviews are included in each podcast, alongside an interview with a topic area expert. Topics include parenting styles, play and reading, communicating and staying connected to your child, and returning home. These podcasts are free to download[2] through UW-Madison Extension and have been shared with local jails throughout Wisconsin. Podcast creation and listening has skyrocketed over the last twenty years (Casares, 2022), with around 75 percent of Americans reporting familiarity with the podcast medium (Edison Research & Triton Digital, 2020). They are an effective and accessible tool for sharing information, research findings, and educational programming (e.g., Hew, 2009; Kelly et al., 2022). Podcasts have been used to

---

[1]　https://parenting.extension.wisc.edu/raising-caring-kids/
[2]　https://parenting.extension.wisc.edu/anywhere-dads/

supplement evidence-based programming, such as the Triple P: Positive Parenting Program (Morawska et al., 2014). The affordability, convenience, and accessibility of podcasts make them an area of opportunity for Extension to disseminate research-based information and support the well-being of underserved audiences in their communities.

11.5.2.2   Father-Relevant Programs

The Literacy Link. UW-Extension has devoted significant efforts to supporting justice-involved families, a highly underrepresented and vulnerable group. Because men are incarcerated at exceedingly higher rates than women (Sykes & Pettit, 2014), these efforts primarily target fathers. In 2017, UW-Extension launched *The Literacy Link*, a program providing evidence-informed literacy opportunities to young children (ages 0–8) with parents involved in local correctional systems (UW-Extension, n.d.). UW-Extension partners with jails and prisons, criminal justice organizations, libraries, and others to (1) promote language and literacy skills in children by creating literacy rich experiences in jail and justice settings that extend into the home, and (2) foster healthy family relationships by promoting positive literacy-focused interactions between children and their justice-involved parents and caregivers.

The Literacy Link program accomplishes these goals through four key strategies: (1) creating child-friendly, learning-rich visit spaces for incarcerated parent–child visits through significant physical space changes (e.g., repainting, offering books and child-friendly activities during visits); (2) creating connecting jailed parents and their children virtually through Making Reading Memories, recorded opportunities for incarcerated parents to read stories for their children; (3) offering free literacy-focused video visits for children and jailed parents through TeleStory, often hosted through a local library; and (4) offering a variety of parent education and support for jailed parents and families, such as parenting information on tablets for incarcerated parents, reading and coaching workshops, and evidence-based parenting programs (e.g., Parenting Inside Out; Eddy et al., 2019). Initial evaluation data of the Literacy Link is promising. In early 2020, over 2,000 high-quality children's books were distributed to justice spaces across Wisconsin. Out of the 123 families who participated, 90 percent of caregivers reported that the program helped maintain their child's relationship with their parent in jail. Further, 57 percent of caregivers reported reading to their children more often and 43 percent said their children looked at books more often at home. Fifty-three parents in local jails also participated in a Literacy Link provided reading workshop and of those, 96 percent reported that the workshop taught them how to create new learning experiences for their children, 96 percent said it increased their knowledge of child development, and 89 percent said it increased their confidence in reading to their children.

Coparenting Programs. Each year, more than 14,000 Wisconsin children experience their parents' divorce or separation. This transition can be easier for children when their parents have a cooperative coparenting relationship (Amato et al., 2011). Over the last three decades, UW-Extension educators across the state have worked with family court officials to provide education for divorcing or separating parents with minor children. Wisconsin's family courts can require divorcing parents complete up to four hours of coparenting education. Using the Parents Forever^{TM} (University of Minnesota Extension, n.d.) research-informed curriculum from the University of Minnesota Extension, educators guide parents in supporting themselves and their children through this time of change. Topics include preventing children's witnessing of parental conflict, avoiding involving children in adult matters, improving communication, and supporting the other parent's role in the child's life. Educators support parents in creating a "parenting plan," including how to revise the plan as children grow. Several studies have emerged that support program effectiveness (e.g., Becher et al., 2018), and recent evaluation data from UW-Extension found that of 523 parents who participated in 2020, 91 percent of parents reported increased coparenting cooperation, 87 percent argued less in front of their children, and 12 percent reported involving the children in adult issues less often.

Acknowledging technology's ever-increasing role in family interactions, UW-Extension county educators and state specialists developed a text messaging series titled *eParenting®: Co-Parenting*[3] to help parents learn positive coparenting methods. Text messages are a low-cost communication method with the potential to reach a high number of adults. Text messages supplement classroom coparenting education and extend the duration coparents are engaged in relevant child development topics. The messages also address how digital media can be used to enhance parenting skills and build connection between children and all their parents and caregivers. The texts include a brief topic introduction with a short URL link to the full *eParenting®: Co-Parenting* article online. Of the 287 parents that received these text messages in 2019 and 2020, 91 percent remained engaged throughout the eight-week program (only 9 percent opted out of

[3] https://fyi.extension.wisc.edu/eparenting/category/coparenting/

the text messages), and 70 percent of parents indicated the text messages helped increase their knowledge or improve their coparenting skills.

Although not focused exclusively on fathers, these and other coparenting programs serve as avenues for connecting fathers with other Extension programs and resources. Because coparenting courses are often mandatory for divorcing parents, families who may not otherwise seek out programming are therefore connected with Extension; thus presenting one path for extending Extension's reach to underserved audiences. Further, supplemental text message programs, such as *eParenting®: Co-Parenting*, following mandatory coparenting classes provide an opportunity for continued program engagement. For fathers specifically, text message based interventions are a promising emerging strategy for reaching fathers, as they overcome several barriers to father engagement (e.g., stigma) (Fletcher et al., 2017).

In summary, UW-Extension has recognized the importance of engaging fathers and the downstream impact this has on serving other underserved audiences. The needs assessment and newer programs offer a promising future for more systematically and intentionally engaging fathers in parenting and family programming in Extension. Further, these examples exemplify how programs can integrate the father-friendly principles and best practices outlined by fatherhood scholarship (e.g., Alameda County Father Corps, 2014; Bronte-Tinkew et al., 2012).

11.6   Future Directions and Next Steps

In the past, fathers have been portrayed as uninvolved and at times irrelevant. This image is changing, however, with emerging evidence documenting fathers' importance for child and family well-being. As new father-centric initiatives develop within university and community contexts, gaps remain in supporting father well-being and father engagement. Yet, the inherent strengths of Extension networks provide one promising avenue through which systematic and holistic father-centric scholarship can effectively address these gaps.

11.6.1   Future Opportunities for Fathers and Extension

One important step forward in this work may be stronger dissemination of fatherhood-specific efforts in Extension. Although several individual Extension agencies across the country provide father-specific programs, a search of the *Journal of Extension* using keywords "father," "fathers," and "fatherhood" found only four articles in the last twenty years that were specific to father-centric programming. More widespread publication and dissemination of father-specific efforts across Extension may help educators and specialists learn from each other and spark multistate collaborations. Similarly, interviews with family-serving agencies as part of our needs assessment revealed that stronger outreach efforts are needed to share research on fathers' importance for child development to influence change in cultural norms around the role of and importance of fathers. This may be one avenue where Extension can thrive, given their strong connections with community service providers and government agencies (e.g., courts).

In a broader approach to supporting fathers, programs must also address the role of mothers in encouraging and discouraging fathers' family engagement and well-being. For example, Fagan et al. (2021) evaluated pilot data for the Understanding Dad™ program (Fagan et al., 2015), a program designed to support mothers in understanding the importance of father engagement for their children and the ways they may intentionally and unintentionally discourage father engagement. Results from the evaluation indicated that following the intervention, mothers reported increased confidence in their ability to engage fathers, decreased disagreements, and used less behavior that undermined a father's relationship with their child.

In addition to considering new father-specific programs, there are several ways that Extension can adapt existing programs to be more inclusive of and welcoming to fathers. For example, results from our needs assessment and other existing research (Bronte-Tinkew et al., 2012) highlight the importance of father-led programming. Many family service providers are women and engaging more men in this work is an area of opportunity for Extension and family services more broadly. One way to accomplish this and gain access to more fathers may be to partner with community organizations that already serve fathers. For example, in Wisconsin, there are several agencies that already work with men and fathers, such as Urban League, Just Dane, and the Milwaukee Fatherhood Initiative. As Extension establishes its father-specific programming, it may benefit from engaging partners that are already doing this work.

11.6.2   Expanding Extension's Reach toward Marginalized Communities

As described in this chapter, father-centric programming presents only one of the many possible pathways through which Extension networks can reach and serve historically marginalized and underserved communities. Many additional pathways for reaching other audiences remain underdeveloped. Extension programs should continue to expand their efforts in reaching underserved audiences, including communities of color, LGBTQ+ communities, and disability communities. Though described in this chapter through the lens of fathers, many of the foundational principles, diversity tenets, and community-based research approaches presented throughout this chapter may prove effective in supporting and authentically engaging other diverse groups. Extension's inherent strengths, access to resources, and community-based location position it well to implement holistic and systematic programming based on these principles for other underserved communities, including engaging relevant stakeholders and community partners, relying on community wisdom and ways of knowing, and ensuring community representation in leadership roles. This and additional work supporting underserved and underrepresented communities are crucial areas for Extension's continuous expansion and improvement in the years to come.

References

Alameda County Father Corps. (2014). *Father-friendly principles for agencies and organizations in Alameda county.* www.first5alameda.org/files/Fathers_Corps/Alameda_County_Fathers_Corps_-_Father_Friendly_Principles_Sheet.pdf

Allport, B. S., Johnson, S., Aqil, A., Labrique, A. B., Nelson, T., KC, A., Carabas, Y., & Marcell, A. V. (2018). Promoting father involvement for child and family health. *Academic Pediatrics, 18*(7), 746–753. https://doi.org/10.1016/j.acap.2018.03.011

Altenburger, L. E., Schoppe-Sullivan, S. J., & Kamp Dush, C. M. (2018). Associations between maternal gatekeeping and fathers' parenting quality. *Journal of Child and Family Studies, 27*, 2678–2689. https://doi.org/10.1007/s10826-018-1107-3

Amato, P. R., Kane, J. B., & James, S. (2011). Reconsidering the "good divorce." *Family Relations, 60*(5), 511–524. https://doi.org/10.1111/j.1741-3729.2011.00666.x

Amodia-Bidakowska, A., Laverty, C., & Ramchandani, P. G. (2020). Father-child play: A systematic review of its frequency, characteristics and potential impact on children's development. *Developmental Review, 57*, 100924. https://doi.org/f79v

Arditti, J., & McGregor, C. M. (2019). A family perspective: Caregiving and family contests of children with an incarcerated parent. In J. M. Eddy & J. Poehlmann-Tynan (Eds.), *Handbook on children with incarcerated parents* (2nd ed., pp. 117–130). Springer. https://doi.org/10.1007/978-3-030-16707-3_9

Austin, W. G., Fieldstone, L., & Pruett, M. K. (2013). Bench book for assessing parental gatekeeping in parenting disputes: Understanding the dynamics of gate closing and opening for the best interests of children. *Journal of Child Custody, 10*(1), 1–16. https://doi.org/10.1080/15379418.2013.778693

Barker, B., Iles, J. E., & Ramchandani, P. G. (2017). Fathers, fathering and child psychopathology. *Current Opinion in Psychology*, 15, 87–92. https://doi.org/gdrbbs

Barrett, H., & Tasker, F. (2001). Growing up with a gay parent: Views of 101 gay fathers on their sons' and daughters' experiences. *Educational and Child Psychology*, 18(1), 62–77.

Bassuk, E. L. (2010). Ending child homelessness in America. *American Journal of Orthopsychiatry*,80(4),496–504.https://doi.org/10.1111/j.1939-0025.2010.01052.x

Becher, E. H., Mcguire, J. K., McCann, E. M., Powell, S., Cronin, S. E., & Deenanath, V. (2018). Extension-based divorce education: A quasi-experimental design study of the Parents Forever program. *Journal of Divorce & Remarriage*, 59(8), 633–652. https://doi.org/f8rq

Bronte-Tinkew, J., Burkhauser, M., & Metz, A. J. R. (2012). Elements of promising practices in fatherhood programs: Evidence-based research findings on interventions for fathers. *Fathering*, 10(1), 6–30. https://doi.org/10.3149/fth.1001.6

Cabrera, N. J., Fitzgerald, H. E., Bradley, R. H., & Roggman, L. (2014). The ecology of father-child relationships: An expanded model. *Journal of Family Theory & Review*, 6(4), 336–354. https://doi.org/10.1111/jftr.12054

Carbone, S., Fraser, A., Ramburuth, R., & Nelms, L. (2004) *Breaking cycles, building futures. Promoting inclusion of vulnerable families in antenatal and universal early childhood services: A report on the first three stages of the project.* Victorian Government Department of Human Services.

Carroll, M. (2018). Gay Fathers on the margins: Race, class, marital status, and pathway to parenthood. *Family Relations*, 67(1), 104–117. https://doi.org/10.1111/fare.12300

Casares, D. R., Jr. (2022) Embracing the podcast era: Trends, opportunities, & implications for counselors. *Journal of Creativity in Mental Health*, 17(1), 123–138. https://doi.org/10.1080/15401383.2020.1816865

Choi, J., & Pyun, H. (2014). Nonresident fathers' financial support, informal instrumental support, mothers' parenting, and child development in single-mother families with low income. *Journal of Family Issues*, 35(4), 526–546. https://doi.org/f79w

Coady, N., Hoy, S., & Cameron, G. (2013). Fathers' experiences with child welfare services. *Child and Family Social Work*, 18(3), 275–284. https://doi.org/f45sp2

Concha, M., Villar, M. E., Tafur-Salgado, R., Ibanez, S., & Azevedo, L. (2016). Fatherhood education from a cultural perspective: Evolving roles and identities after a fatherhood intervention for Latinos in South Florida. *Journal of Latinos and Education*, 15(3), 170–179. https://doi.org/10.1080/15348431.2015.1099532

Costa, L. L. F., Esteves, A. B. D., Kreimer, R., Stuchiner, N., & Hannikainen, I. (2019). Gender stereotypes underlie child custody decisions. *European Journal of Social Psychology*, 49(3), 548–559. https://doi.org/10.1002/ejsp.2523

Davison, K. K., Charles, J. N., Khandpur, N., & Nelson, T. J. (2017). Fathers' perceived reasons for their underrepresentation in child health research and strategies to increase their involvement. *Maternal and Child Health Journal*, 21(2), 267–274. https://doi.org/f9ttd9

Eddy, J. M., Kjellstrand, J., Martinez, C. R., Jr., & Newton, R. (2019). Theory-based multimodal parenting intervention for incarcerated parents and their families. In J. M. Eddy & J. Poehlmann (Eds.), *Children of incarcerated parents: A handbook for researchers and practitioners*. Urban Institute Press.

Edison Research and Triton Digital. (2020). *The infinite dial 2020*. www .edisonresearch.com/wp-content/uploads/2020/03/The-Infinite-Dial-2020-from-Edison-Research-and-Triton-Digital.pdf

Fagan, J. (2014). Adolescent parents' partner conflict and parenting alliance, fathers' prenatal involvement, and fathers' engagement with infants. *Journal of Family Issues*, 35(11), 1415–1439. https://doi.org/10.1177/0192513X13491411

Fagan, J., Cherson, M., Brown, C., & Vecere, E. (2015). Pilot study of a program to increase mothers' understanding of dads. *Family Process*, 54, 581–589. https://doi.org/f79x

Fagan, J., Henson, A., & Pearson, J. (2021). Low-income mothers' participation in the Understanding DadsTM intervention and changes in self-reported coparenting. *Journal of Family Social Work*, 24(3), 199–218. https://doi.org/f79z

Fisher, S. D. (2017). Paternal mental health: Why is it relevant? *American Journal of Lifestyle Medicine*, 11(3), 200–211. https://doi.org/10.1177/1559827616629895

Fitzgerald, H. E., Klitzing, K. V., Cabrera, N. J., Scarano de Mendonça, J., & Skjøthaug, T. (Eds.). (2020). *Handbook of fathers and child development: Prenatal to preschool*. Springer. https://doi.org/10.1007/978-3-030-51027-5

Fletcher, R., May, C., Lambkin, F., Gemmill, A. W., Cann, W., Nicholson, J. M., Rawlinson, C., Milgrom, J., Highet, N., Foureur, M., Bennett, E., & Skinner, G. (2017). SMS4dads: Providing information and support to new fathers through mobile phones—a pilot study. *Advances in Mental Health*, 15(2), 121–131. https://doi.org/f792

Goldberg, A. E., Allen, K. R., & Carroll, M. (2020). "We don't exactly fit in, but we can't opt out": Gay fathers' experiences navigating parent communities in schools. *Journal of Marriage and Family*, 82(5), 1655–1676. https://doi .org/10.1111/jomf.12695

Goldberg, W. A., Tan, E., & Thorsen, K. L. (2009). Trends in academic attention to fathers, 1930–2006. *Fathering*, 7(2), 159–179. https://doi.org/10.3149/fth.0702.159

Harmon, D. K., & Perry, A. R. (2011). Fathers' unaccounted contributions: Paternal involvement and maternal stress. *Families in Society*, 92(2), 176–182. https://doi.org/ggk4jw

Henry, J. B., Julion, W. A., Bounds, D. T., & Sumo, J. N. (2020). Fatherhood matters: An integrative review of fatherhood intervention research. *Journal of School Nursing*, 36(1), 19–32. https//10.1177/1059840519873380

Hew, K. F. (2009). Use of audio podcast in K-12 and higher education: A review of research topics and methodologies. *Educational Technology Research and Development*, 57, 333–357. https//doi.org/10.1007/s11423-008-9108-3

Irving Harris Foundation. (2018). *Diversity-informed tenets for work with infants, children and families.* https://diversityinformedtenets.org/the-tenets/english/

Kelly, J. M., Perseghin, A., Dow. A. W., Trivedi, S. P., Rodman, A., & Berk, J. (2022). Learning through listening: A scoping review of podcast use in medical education. *Academic Medicine, 97*(7), 1079–1085. https://doi.org/10.1097/ACM.0000000000004565

Kim, H., & Drake, B. (2018). Child maltreatment risk as a function of poverty and race/ethnicity in the USA. *International Journal of Epidemiology, 47*(3), 780–787. https://doi.org/gcxzsq

Kim, S. W., & Hill, N. E. (2015). Including fathers in the picture: A meta-analysis of parental involvement and students' academic achievement. *Journal of Educational Psychology,* 107(4), 919–934. https://doi.org/10.1037/edu0000023

Kramer Holmes, E., Egginton, B. R., Hawkins, A. J., Robbins, N. L., & Shafer, K. (2020). Do responsible fatherhood programs work? A comprehensive meta-analytic study. *Family Relations, 69*(5), 967–982. https://doi.org/10.1111/fare.12435

Lechowicz, M. E., Jiang, Y., Tully, L. A., Burn, M. T., Collins, D. A. J., Hawes, D. J., Lenroot, R. K., Anderson, V., Doyle, F. L., Piotrowska, P. J., Frick. P. J., Moul, C., Kimonis, E. R., & Dadds, M. R. (2019). Enhancing father engagement in parenting programs: Translating research into practice recommendations. *Australian Psychologist,* 54(2), 83–89. https://doi.org/10.1111/ap.12361

Lee, J., & Schoppe-Sullivan, S. J. (2017). Resident fathers' positive engagement, family poverty, and change in child behavior problems. *Family Relations,* 66(3), 484–496. https://doi.org/gfkk55

Lee, S. J., Yelick, A., Brisebois, K., & Banks, K. L. (2011). Low-income fathers' barriers to participation in family and parenting programs. *Journal of Family Strengths,* 11(1), 1–16. https://digitalcommons.library.tmc.edu/jfs/vol11/iss1/12

McBride, B. A., Curtiss, S. J., Uchima, K., Laxman, D. J., Santos, R. M., Weglarz-Ward, J., Dyer, W. J., Jeans, L. M., & Kern, J. (2017). Father involvement in intervention: Exploring the gap between service providers' perceptions and practices. *Journal of Early Intervention,* 39(2), 71–87. https://doi.org/10.1177/1053815116686118

Mezulis, A. H., Hyde, J. S., & Clark, R. (2004). Father involvement moderates the effect of maternal depression during a child's infancy on child behavior problems in kindergarten. *Journal of Family Psychology,* 18(4), 575–588. https://doi.org/dxk22g

Miller, D. P., Thomas, M. M. C., Waller, M. R., Nepomnyaschy, L., & Emory, A. D. (2020). Father involvement and socioeconomic disparities in child academic outcomes. *Journal of Marriage and Family,* 82(2), 515–533. https://doi.org/10.1111/jomf.12666

Millett, G. A., Jones, A. T., Benkeser, D., Baral, S., Mercer, L., Beyrer, C., Honermann, B., Lankiewicz, E., Mena, L., Crowley, J. S., Sherwood, J., & Sullivan, P. S. (2020). Assessing differential impacts of COVID-19 on black communities. *Annals of Epidemiology,* 47, 37–44. https://doi.org/10.1016/j.annepidem.2020.05.003

Morawska, A., Tometzki, H., & Sanders, M. R. (2014). An evaluation of the efficacy of a Triple P – Positive Parenting Program podcast series. *Journal of Developmental & Behavioral Pediatrics*, 35(2), 128–137. https://doi.org/10.1097/DBP.0000000000000020

Murphey, D., & Cooper, P. M. (2015). Parents behind bars: What happens to their children? *Child Trends*. www.childtrends.org/publications/parents-behind-bars-what-happens-to-their-children

National Institutes of Health. (2020). *Underrepresented populations in the U.S. biomedical, clinical, behavioral and social sciences research enterprise*. https://diversity.nih.gov/about-us/population-underrepresented

Palkovitz, R., & Hull, J. (2018). Toward a resource theory of fathering. *Journal of Family Theory & Review*, 10(1), 181–198. https://doi.org/10.1111/jftr.12239

Panter-Brick, C., Burgess, A., Eggerman, M., McAllister, F., Pruett, K., & Leckman, J. F. (2014). Practitioner review: Engaging fathers – Recommendations for a game change in parenting interventions based on a systematic review of the global evidence. *Journal of Child Psychology and Psychiatry*, 55(11), 1187–1212. https://doi.org/10.1111/jcpp.12280

Park, J. M., Fertig, A. R., & Metraux, S. (2011). Changes in maternal health and health behaviors as a function of homelessness. *Social Service Review*, 85(4), 565–586. https://doi.org/10.1086/663636

Peterson, B., Cramer, L., & Fontaine, J. (2019). Policies and practices for children of incarcerated parents: Summarizing what we know and do not know. In M. J. Eddy & J. Poehlmann-Tynan (Eds.), *Handbook on children with incarcerated parents* (2nd ed., pp. 331–343). Springer. https://doi.org/10.1007/978-3-030-16707-3_22

Poehlmann-Tynan, J., & Turney, K. (2021). A developmental perspective on children with incarcerated parents. *Child Development Perspectives*, 15(1), 3–11. https://doi.org/f8rr

Roberts, D., Coakley, T. M., Washington, T. J., & Kelley, A. (2014). Fathers' perspectives on supports and barriers that affect their fatherhood role. *SAGE Open*, 4(1), 1–10. https://doi.org/10.1177/2158244014521818

Rollins, L., & Boose, T. (2021). Engaging and working with African American fathers experiencing homelessness. In. L. S. Rollins (Ed.), *Engaging and working with African American fathers: Strategies and lessons* (1st ed., pp. 122–131). Taylor & Francis.

Roy, K. M. (2014). Fathers and fatherhood. In J. Treas, J. Scoot, & M. Richards (Eds.), *The Wiley Blackwell companion to the sociology of families* (1st ed., pp. 424–443). John Wiley & Sons.

Schoppe-Sullivan, S. J., Brown, G. L., Cannon, E. A., Mangelsdorf, S. C., & Sokolowski, M. S. (2008). Maternal gatekeeping, coparenting quality, and fathering behavior in families with infants. *Journal of Family Psychology*, 22(3), 389–398. https://doi.org/dkxdnb

Semega, J., Kollar, M., Shrider, E. A., & Creamer, J. F. (2020). *Income and poverty in the United States: 2019*, Current Population Reports, U.S. Census Bureau, U.S. Government Publishing Office. www.census.gov/library/publications/2020/demo/p60-270.html

Stahlschmidt, M. J., Threlfall, J., Seay, K. D., Lewis, E. M., & Kohl, P. L. (2013). Recruiting fathers to parenting programs: Advice from dads and fatherhood program providers. *Children and Youth Services Review*, 35(10), 1734–1741. https://doi.org/f5drjx

Strand, K., Marullo, S., Cutforth, N. J., Stoecker, R., & Donohue, P. (2003). Principles of best practice for community-based research. *Michigan Journal of Community Service Learning*, 9(3), 5–15. https://digitalcommons.du.edu/rms_faculty/36

Sykes, B. L., & Pettit, B. (2014). Mass incarceration, family complexity, and the reproduction of childhood disadvantage. *The Annals of the American Academy of Political and Social Science*, 654(1), 127–149. https://doi.org/10.1177/0002716214526345

Tully, L. A., Collins, D. A. J., Piotrowska, P. J., Mairet, K. S., Hawes, D. J., Moul, C., Lenroot, R. K., Frick, P. J., Anderson, V. A., Kimonis, E. R., & Dadds, M. R. (2018). Examining practitioner competencies, organizational support and barriers to engaging fathers in parenting interventions. *Child Psychiatry and Human Development*, 49(1), 109–122. https://doi.org/10.1007/s10578-017-0733-0

University of Minnesota Extension. (n.d.). *Parents Forever^{TM} Curriculum*. Retrieved April 26, 2021, from https://extension.umn.edu/divorce-and-other-family-transitions/parents-forevertm-curriculum

University of Wisconsin-Madison, Division of Extension. (n.d.). *The Literacy Link: Connecting children and parents in justice-involved families*. Retrieved April 26, 2021, from https://theliteracylink.extension.wisc.edu/

Vakrat, A., Apter-Levy, Y., & Feldman, R. (2018). Fathering moderates the effects of maternal depression on the family process. *Development and Psychopathology*, 30(1), 27–38. https://doi.org/10.1017/S095457941700044X

Wilson, G. B. (2006). The non-resident parental role for separated fathers: A review. *International Journal of Law, Policy and the Family*, 20(3), 286–316.

CHAPTER 12

Preparing the Next Generation
of Extension Professionals

Joseph L. Donaldson

How does the Cooperative Extension System prepare the next generation of Extension professionals who will support the well-being of tomorrow's children, youth, and families? Continuing to have a strong, competent, and engaged workforce is essential for the sustainability of Cooperative Extension in the years to come. This chapter addresses this question via five parts. Part 1 presents a synopsis of career development research highlighting how a person identifies and advances in a profession as well as different Extension careers to demonstrate the multiple pathways and roles in Extension organizations. Part 2 provides a discussion of competencies and skills needed for successful contemporary Extension professionals. These competencies include diversity and inclusion; leadership; teaching and learning; program planning, delivery, and implementation; and interpersonal skills, among others. Parts 3–5 explore each of the primary mechanisms for preparing the next generation of Extension professionals, including discussions around relevant, (a) college curriculum; (b) career development activities such as internships, externships, and job shadowing; and (c) onboarding, continuing professional development, and other organizational factors that will empower Extension professionals to succeed.

Preparing the next generation of Extension professionals is a multidimensional topic and is the collective responsibility of students, educators, and Extension organizations. Individual students seeking careers in Extension are responsible for preparing, obtaining, and advancing in an Extension professional position. Higher education institutions and the faculty therein are obligated to provide curricula and instructional opportunities that foster core competencies for Extension professions among the students they serve. Additionally, the Cooperative Extension System is responsible for recruiting and retaining a high performing workforce that stays on the cutting edge in each of their fields in service to individuals, families, farmers, and communities. This chapter provides insights specific to each of these vantage points.

12.1 Part 1: Career Development in Extension – Challenges and Opportunities

Careers in Cooperative Extension can be extremely fulfilling. Every day is different, and the best days end with someone thanking you for providing information and resources that will have a positive impact on their life. (Gornish et al., 2018, p. 540)

Cooperative Extension careers can be both rewarding and challenging. Careers in Extension can involve working long hours and the constant need to multitask (Seevers & Graham, 2012). Extension professionals engage in multifarious work that involves addressing questions from clients; recruiting, providing education for, and utilizing volunteers; and conducting needs assessment, program planning, marketing, and evaluation (Gutter & Stephenson, 2016; Russell et al., 2018). Extension professionals may encounter demanding schedules, challenging clients and emotionally charged situations, and oftentimes, high pressure work (Bradley et al., 2012). Yet, the Extension profession remains a gratifying career from both personal and professional standpoints (Arnold & Place, 2010). Extension professionals are inextricably linked to the community, and the work of community engagement affords opportunities to help people improve their lives (Donaldson, 2020a). In general, how does one identify, secure, and advance in a career? And for those interested in pursuing a career in Extension, what are the potential positions, roles, and career pathways?

12.1.1 *Synopsis of Career Development Research*

Career development is an important field to understand because of its many implications for individuals and institutions. Similarly, this is critical for Cooperative Extension. Researchers have worked to understand the dominant factors that explain how a person gains and advances in a fulfilling career and have identified such factors as one's aptitude, personality, and maturity all influence career development (Hackett & Lent, 1992).

How Does One Identify and Advance in a Career? McDonald and Hite (2015) noted that the past twenty years have been "turbulent for careers" due to "…economic fluctuations, amazing advances in technology, globalization, and demographic shifts…" (p. 36). One major contemporary view on career choice is reflected in the Social Cognitive Career Theory (SCCT), which is an outgrowth of Social Cognitive Theory. SCCT focuses on three factors that determine a career path, namely, self-efficacy, outcome expectations, and personal goals. When a person has useful career experiences and the aptitude to succeed in a particular career, they develop a positive perception that they will be successful in that given career and may then pursue a job in that field (Lent, 2008). Career counselors may be helpful, and assessments that career counselors use elucidate interests, needs and values, abilities and skills, personality, and decision-making, self-efficacy, and maturity (Swanson & Fouad, 2010).

Regarding career development, Holland's Theory of Personality and Environmental Types (Swanson & Fouad, 2010) delineates six personality types (realistic, investigative, artistic, social, enterprising, and conventional) and corresponding work environments that best fit those personalities. Optimal for career development is a match between personality type and work environment. As an illustration, Holland describes people of the "social" personality type as those who are concerned for the welfare of others, among other traits. People with the "social" personality trait would enjoy teaching others, solving problems, and providing mental health services, among many other work activities (Harmon et al., 2005).

Cooperative Extension work is often interdisciplinary and focused on addressing complex social, economic, and environmental issues through education. Therefore, all personality types can find a place in the various roles and positions within Cooperative Extension. The key for a high school or college student considering a career or a professional considering a career transition is to understand how their personality, academic background, talents, and desires align with the needs of the differing jobs and environments of Cooperative Extension professions.

12.1.2 Different Extension Careers and Pathways

The series of work an individual does or the progression of jobs over their lifetime defines a career pathway (Walker, 1980). For some individuals, this career pathway may encompass a sequence of only a few jobs, and for other individuals this career pathway may encompass many different roles and positions. Career pathways are special in that they must be developed and are somewhat individualized. Career pathways "cannot be purchased off the shelf" (Jenkins & Spence, 2006, p. 2).

Hedge and Rineer (2017) have described various career pathways that one might have, including more traditional career ladders and different dynamics such as dual pathways. A career ladder is a type of highly structured career pathway wherein one position is known to follow another. For example, it is very common for Extension Agent positions to progress from Extension Agent I to Extension Agent II, and then to Extension

Agent III. Extension Agent I denotes the entry-level position, and each successive step describes more expertise and experience. In contrast, a dual career pathway allows the Extension professional to prepare for technical and supervisory roles. This may include both technical training (i.e., in-service professional development in a technical topic) and formal leadership programs (e.g., LEAD21). Cooperative Extension supports both structured career ladders and dual pathways for multiple careers and opportunities within a given position. For example, an Extension Agent working in one or more counties may pursue an advance degree to prepare for the role of Extension Specialist working in a college academic department. An Extension County Director may engage in leadership development programs to prepare for middle and upper management careers in Extension. There is certainly not a one-size-fits-all approach to Extension careers and Extension career pathways. Some of the major Extension positions are as follows:

Extension Program Assistants assist Extension Agents (a.k.a. Educators) in implementing Extension programs. Program Assistants are typically supervised by Extension Agents and/or County Extension Directors. Program assistants serve in all Extension programs such as Expanded Food and Nutrition Education Program (EFNEP), Food Stamp Nutrition Education Program (SNAP-Ed), agricultural programs, 4-H youth development programs, and others. A high school education is always required and a Bachelor's degree is often needed for the program assistant career.

Extension Agents are described as the "heart and soul of Cooperative Extension" (Seevers & Graham, 2012, p. 50). Typically, Extension Agents are assigned to serve one county or geographic area of multiple counties. Extension Agents conduct assessments to identify key needs, assets, and opportunities for the community. Using that information, they set priorities for planning, implementing, and evaluating educational programs. All the programs are based on translating science so that they can provide applied solutions to the home, farm, and community. These positions always require a Bachelor's degree and often require a Master's degree. Extension Agents may have different titles depending on the institution, for instance, Extension Advisor (Gorman, 2019), or Extension Educator (Seevers & Graham, 2012).

Extension Specialists are experts in their fields. Specialists typically have a terminal degree (e.g., PhD) in the academic discipline (Gornish et al., 2018). Within a certain academic discipline, specialists tend to have a niche or specialization. As an illustration, an Extension Specialist may provide specialized, research-based programming in parenting. Whereas their training may be in the broader human development discipline, their scholarship might be specifically directed to parenting research and Extension parenting education programs. Extension Specialists often work 100 percent of their time in providing professional development for Extension Agents, conducting Extension programs in concert with other Extension professionals, conducting applied research, securing extramural funding for Extension programming, answering inquiries from Extension professionals and the public, and interpreting research in the form of Extension publications and educational technologies. Yet, responsibilities vary greatly depending on the institution and the area of specialization. In many cases, specialists work with a "highly specialized industry" such as food processing. Some may also have formal research and/or teaching appointments in their respective academic departments (Seevers & Graham, 2012). Specialists are typically on the university tenure and promotion system whereby their promotion and tenure are based on their scholarly performance.

Extension Administrators may serve in various roles at the county, regional, state, or federal levels. A Regional Extension Director, for example, would supervise, mentor, appraise, and support Extension personnel who work in a defined geographic area, often a multicounty region of the state. State administrators provide leadership, administration, and budgetary oversight for a statewide Extension program (such as Family and Consumer Sciences) or an entire unit (such as the Department Extension Leader for the University Department of Agricultural and Extension Education). Extension administrators at the regional, state, and federal levels need at least a Master's degree and often a doctoral degree.

Organizational Support roles vary greatly and professionals in these positions represent a host of academic disciplines such as program evaluation, public administration, and business management. The careers may include advancement (also known as fund development), information technology, evaluation and program planning, human resources, and organizational learning (also known as staff development). Many Extension organizations have a role for an Organizational Development Leader who supports the professional development of Extension professionals to ensure they are on the cutting edge of technology, social trends, and the latest research in their respective Extension assignments. While these roles vary, they all share a common goal to support Extension personnel in doing their jobs to their fullest capacity.

12.2 Part 2: Competencies and Skills

Competencies collectively describe the knowledge, attitudes, skills, and behaviors encompassed in performing at an exemplary level (Maddy et al., 2002). Extension professional competencies studies have been valuable for informing professional development (Lakai et al., 2014), college curriculum (Harder et al., 2009), job descriptions, individual learning plans, and performance appraisals. The Extension Committee on Organization and Policy (ECOP) examined various studies to discern eleven competencies that all Extension professionals should exhibit:

- Community and social action processes
- Diversity/pluralism/multiculturalism
- Educational programming
- Engagement
- Information and educational delivery
- Interpersonal relations
- Knowledge of the Cooperative Extension organization
- Leadership
- Organizational management such as structures, processes, and monitoring resources
- Professionalism
- Subject matter proficiency (Maddy et al., 2002)

Yet, competencies and skills are not static as technological advances and economic shifts necessitate adjustments in the competencies required for successful Extension job performance (Lakai et al., 2014). In addition to the competencies identified by the ECOP (Maddy et al., 2002), other foundational competencies for Extension professionals have been described in numerous studies, including:

- Communications (DeBord et al., 2003; Harder & Narine, 2019; Scheer et al., 2011)
- Customer service (Cochran, 2009; Scheer et al., 2011)
- Self-direction (Cochran, 2009; Harder et al., 2015; Scheer et al., 2011)
- Technology adoption and application (Cochran, 2009; Harder et al., 2015; Lakai et al., 2014; Moore & Rudd, 2003; Scheer et al., 2011)
- Thinking and problem-solving (Cochran, 2009; Hall & Broyles, 2016; Harder et al., 2015; Moore & Rudd, 2003; Scheer et al., 2011)

Other than technology and subject matter proficiency, these major competencies can be drawn from social science academic disciplines. In the social sciences, there have been shifts in critical skills and competencies in Extension, reflecting contemporary issues:

- Extension competencies now include diversity and cultural competencies (Fox & LaChenaye, 2015; Moore & Rudd, 2003; Scheer et al., 2011), for instance, sensitivity to issues of diversity, speaking consciously, and community outreach (Fox & LaChenaye, 2015; Deen et al., 2014).
- Even prior to the worldwide COVID-19 pandemic, competencies shifted toward community health. Specifically, Extension Family and Consumer Sciences professionals included community health to address complex social needs (Franck et al., 2017).
- Competencies for Extension community development professionals have included "collaborative learning, teamwork, and community engagement leading to practice change" and "systems thinking and action" (Atiles, 2019, p. 112).
- In the context of interpersonal leadership competencies for Extension professionals, studies demonstrate that conflict management and effectively leading groups are key priorities (Hall & Broyles, 2016; Harder & Narine, 2019). Extension professionals prioritized resolving conflict, efficiently managing time, assessing community needs, effectively leading a team, and prioritizing tasks (Hall & Broyles, 2016).
- Gorman (2019) noted how university students participating in an Extension practicum identified group facilitation as a critical Extension professional competency.
- Extension programming changes have also precipitated changes in competencies needed to serve effectively as Extension professionals. One example is the emergence of specializations among frontline Extension educators, including early childhood development and 4-H, to address community issues while also providing another career opportunity for the Extension professional who may not have the academic background to be a generalist (Harris, 2020).

Innovation, or the ability to develop new ideas and products, has been identified as a critical competency for the twenty first century Extension Professional. The ECOP Extension Task Force Innovation

Report (2016) focused on the need to "build expectations for innovation into job descriptions, working documents, and promotion and tenure process" (p. 7). In terms of Extension leadership, the ECOP report stressed the need to focus professional development on critical thinking, managing difficult conversations, experimentation, learning from failure, avoiding groupthink – all for the purpose of promoting innovation as a core competency and a way of doing business in Extension (ECOP, 2016).

12.3   Part 3: College Curriculum

A recent study (see Donaldson et al., 2021b) sought to describe the Extension Education courses taught at colleges and universities across the country by surveying the membership of the American Association for Agricultural Education. The major Extension Education courses offered to graduate students were:

- Program Delivery and Teaching: This course engages students in appropriate teaching techniques, learning theories, curricula, and resources. Emphasis of the course is on teaching and instruction in nonformal/extension and outreach setting.
- Leadership Education: The intent of the course is to introduce theory, principles, ethics, and application of leadership in Extension settings.
- Conducting Needs Assessments: This course focuses on the concept of needs and conducting needs assessment in Extension settings.
- Research Methods: The intent of this course is to introduce methods and procedures of conducting research in Extension.

The major Extension Education courses provided to undergraduate students were:

- History, Philosophy, and Foundations of Extension: The focus of this course is to make an introduction to Land-grant Mission, Cooperative Extension System mission, philosophy, history, organization, structure, administration, and program areas.
- Program Planning, Instructional Design, and Curriculum Development for Extension Education: The intent of this course is to discuss extension program development, extension teaching and delivery methods, and techniques and applications of technology to enhance instruction of agricultural topics.

- Extension Communication: This course covers topics such as technological communication theory, instructional and presentation models, teaching strategies, and multimedia development.
- Adult Education: The contents of this course include identification of basic principles motivating adults to learn and procedures to implement these principles in bringing about changes in adult behavior.
- Diffusion of Innovations: The course contents include the analysis of change models and theories and the application of those in societal changes and technology transfer.
- Volunteer Management: The topics included in this course are principles, theories, concepts, techniques, and applications for leading volunteers in agriculture and life sciences nonprofit, governmental, and community organizations.
- Program Evaluation: The course contents include evaluation principles applied to educational programs in agriculture and life sciences. Students gain a basic understanding of skills in program evaluation processes, concepts, and theories and develop skills needed to design and conduct evaluations of youth and adults in Extension, community, and school-based programs.
- International Agricultural and Extension Education: The intent of this course is an introduction to international agricultural and Extension Education (see Donaldson et al., 2021a).

Yet, as this was just one study of one professional association (i.e., American Association for Agricultural Education), it is likely there are more courses taught across disciplines and more study in this arena is warranted to develop an accurate picture of academic opportunities that prepare Extension professionals. This course list is interesting in the context of Extension professional competencies. By comparing the courses listed above to Extension professional competencies, it is evident that work has aligned the Extension core competencies with Extension Education college courses as Scheer and colleagues (2006) described.

Narine and colleagues (2018) reviewed land-grant university websites and reported nineteen institutions that provided an Extension Education academic program (i.e., offering a major, minor, concentration, program, emphasis, and/or specialization). Twelve institutions offered master's level degrees and five institutions offered doctoral degrees in Extension Education. This review identified eighty-two undergraduate courses and 154 graduate-level courses collectively. The lists of undergraduate courses were the same in the Narine et al. (2018) and Donaldson et al. (2020) studies with two exceptions. The 2018 study found undergraduate Extension Education courses in agricultural leadership and management while the 2020 study found courses in international agricultural and Extension education.

12.3.1 College Extension Education Curriculum

Extension Education courses to prepare future Extension professionals are typically organized in one of the three major ways depending on the institution. First, several universities offer a degree that combines Agricultural Education or Family and Consumer Sciences Education with Extension Education. These degree programs include coursework specific to Extension Education. An example is the Family and Consumer Sciences Education and Extension Master of Science degree program at Utah State University and the Agricultural and Extension Education Bachelor of Science and Master of Science at Tennessee State University. Yet, other universities have organized the Extension Education courses into major and/or minor curricula. A minor in Extension Education aligns well with technical subject matter (e.g., human nutrition, animal science) and provides future Extension professionals with a well-rounded higher education experience. An example is the Extension Education minor offered by the University of Florida, for others see Table 12.1.

Second, other universities provide an Extension Education concentration within a major. Such concentrated study (which may also be known as areas of emphasis or career tracks) within a degree program provides another way by which universities prepare future Extension professionals. See Table 12.2.

Third, several institutions offer minors and concentrations for undergraduates that are similar to the Extension Education curricular tracks and are valuable for preparing future Extension professionals. However, the courses have a focus on a smaller subset of the Extension Education competencies such as:

Table 12.1 *Examples of Extension education programs*

	Undergraduate Minor	Undergraduate Major	Graduate Minor	Graduate Major
North Carolina State University	●	●	●	●
University of Florida	●		●	●
Colorado State University				●
Texas A&M University	●			

Table 12.2 *Examples of Extension education concentrations within degree programs*

	Undergraduate	Graduate	Degree program
Louisiana State University	●		Agricultural and Extension Education, BS
West Virginia University	●		Agricultural and Extension Education, BS
University of Kentucky	●		Family Sciences, BS
Oklahoma State University	●		Bachelor of Science in Agriculture, Agricultural Leadership Program, BSAG
Iowa State University		●	Agricultural and Extension Education Specialization, PhD and MS
New Mexico State University	●		Agricultural Community Development, BS
Ohio State University	●	●	Community Leadership, BS; Community and Extension Education and Leadership, PhD

- Agricultural Communications and Leadership Minor (University of Idaho)
- Leadership Option within the Agricultural Education program (University of Nebraska, Lincoln)
- Community Outreach Area of Emphasis within the Family and Consumer Sciences program (University of Georgia)
- Professional Studies within FCS Education Program (Iowa State University)

These various curricular approaches have an important and perhaps overlooked role. That is, they can provide instruction in adult education, program planning, evaluation, volunteer management, and other courses in such entities as Colleges of Agriculture and Colleges of Human Sciences, which might otherwise not have such coursework that are more typically offered in education or the social sciences. At the same time, inclusion of such coursework and instruction in educational preparation for Extension professionals also has the potential to infuse the social sciences on to applied settings (e.g., Extension) that can foster collaborations and opportunities that might not otherwise be possible.

12.4   Part 4: Internships and other Career Development Opportunities

Experience in Extension may be especially helpful in entering a career therein. College students, recent graduates, and those in career transitions should consider volunteering for Cooperative Extension and/or other public agencies and community organizations where they want to explore careers. Linda Block is an Extension professional working in Arizona, and her volunteerism as a graduate student was key to her employment, as noted below from Block (2007):

> Linda encourages recent graduates to volunteer in a community program where they would like to be employed. Contacting the local Extension Office may lead to these opportunities. While a graduate student, Linda trained for the Master Consumer Advisor program as a volunteer in its first class and now she has responsibility for the program in her family and consumer sciences (FCS) position. The [Pima County Community Health Advancement Partnership] project hires students to work on community projects through paid employment, internships, and volunteer opportunities. These are great opportunities for career exploration, skill development, and involvement with FCS.

Extension internships help students to understand career pathways, gather information, and make career decisions. For Cooperative Extension, internships provide experiential education to explore and learn about the Extension organization and its work with the public, as well as career opportunities therein. In fact, internships are powerful for growing college students' interest in Extension careers and graduate education. In a North Carolina study of thirty Extension interns, the percentage of interns who were very or extremely interested in pursuing a career in Extension increased from 36 percent before the internship to 68 percent after the internship. Likewise, the percentage of interns who were very or extremely interested in pursuing a graduate degree in Extension Education increased from 36 percent before the internship to 45 percent after the internship (Donaldson et al., 2020).

What makes an effective internship program? Internships and other practical experiences for college students vary in terms of duration, responsibilities, and number of academic credits that may be earned for the experience. All are an attempt to help students apply their formal education to real-life issues in the community and understand the role of Extension. Gorman (2019) describes how University students in Ireland are engaged in a two-year placement in an Extension professional role while simultaneously advancing in their studies. This supports reflective practice whereby students can "make sense of difficulties they experience in the first 2–3 months of their professional placement" (pp. 182–183).

A recent study surveyed the Joint Council of Extension Professionals (JCEP) regarding their perspectives on priority courses for future Extension professionals. JCEP is composed of twenty-one members, the president, past president, and president-elect of the seven Extension professional organizations. Respondents identified competencies they believed are critical for Extension career success, noting that a student who pursues Extension Education in college needs to achieve competence in: (a) program development, inclusive of all aspects of program planning, delivery, and evaluation; and (b) teaching and learning, inclusive of how people learn as well as pedagogy and andragogy. Respondents also prioritized competencies in leadership, technology, and communication – again within the college curriculum. JCEP members also felt that college curriculum should provide for internships, job shadowing, practicums, and other practical experiences in Extension careers (Donaldson et al., 2021a).

12.5   Part 5: Onboarding, Professional Development, Other Organizational Resources

12.5.1   Onboarding and Professional Development

Several existing programs are available to Extension professionals to further develop competencies already noted, including several onboarding and professional development opportunities. Onboarding refers to initial orientation to the Extension job or orientation that occurs just after hiring. These onboarding and professional development programs are typically: (a) organized by State Extension entities and often include state-specific information; (b) organized by Extension professional groups; and/or (c) organized via a collaborative approach of state Extension organizations seeking to pool resources for exemplary professional development.

Professional development is key for competent, highly skilled Extension professionals because many Extension professionals enter the profession without the vital competencies needed for professional success (Benge et al., 2020). Onboarding is one professional development effort that has emphasized working with advisory groups, program planning and evaluation, customer service, motivating adult learners, and effective personal contacts (Donaldson, 2019a; 2020b; 2020c).

In Extension, participation in professional organizations and collaborative teams is important for advancing professionalism and staying on the cutting edge of one's field that it is often credited as part of Extension professionals' performance appraisals. Extension professional organizations vary but many focus on programming (e.g., curriculum development, methods expertise) and professional competencies. One example at the national level is the 4-H Professional, Research, Knowledge, and Competencies (4-H PRKC), originally established in 1986 and since then updated multiple times. 4-H PRKC is a taxonomy that identifies the competencies needed by Extension 4-H youth development professionals, and it links these competencies to the available, updated knowledge and research base (Seevers & Graham, 2012). The 2017 PRKC taxonomy, titled *Growing Together*, lists competencies for the major domains of youth development; youth program development; volunteerism; access, equity, and opportunity; partnerships; and organizational systems (USDA NIFA 2017a). An example competency from the access, equity, and opportunity domain is: "Ensures that communication/information meets the cultural, language and literacy levels required for full understanding" (USDA NIFA, 2017b, p. 17).

An example of the collaborative approach to professional development within Extension is LEAD21, a national leadership development program for all institutions delivering research and Extension and the USDA National Institute of Food and Agriculture. Institutions nominate and fund participation in the program which involves various Extension professional roles faculty, specialists, middle managers, program leaders, department heads, and others (Lamm et al., 2016). Program assessments show that the initiative has been successful. For example, in a longitudinal study of LEAD21 graduates, the program improved conflict management capacity, an important leadership skill for achieving organizational outcomes (Lamm et al., 2020). Griffeth et al. (2018) recommended that LEAD21 and other structured leadership development programs would be especially effective for women in the roles of Extension middle managers and administration.

12.5.2 Other Organizational Resources Supporting Career Development

Wellness Programs – Work and health are inextricably linked, and work affects psychological, physical, and socioeconomic wellness. Satisfying work can enhance a person's health, whereas not working or working too much can diminish a person's health (Vondracek et al., 1986). In sixteen focus groups that involved 105 Extension professionals in one state, Donaldson and Franck (2019) found that Extension professionals are motivated to pursue personal health and wellness to be role models for others, to give and receive support from a group, to address a personal health crisis, and to realize health insurance savings.

Mentoring – Mentoring is a form of career development that allows organizations to transfer some of the costs of hiring to developing and retaining a high-performing workforce (Kroth & Christensen, 2009). In professional relationships, a mentor provides "information, advice, opinions, [and] instruction" (Lee & Nolan, 1998, p. 6). In a study of 244 women who were Cooperative Extension administrators in southeastern states, respondents strongly supported professional mentoring. In fact, 85 percent suggested a mentoring program for their state Extension organization (Lee & Nolan, 1998).

Examples of mentoring programs for Extension professionals include Texas A&M AgriLife Extension, which assigns mentors to all newly hired Extension Agents for the first two to three years of employment (Cummings et al., 2015) and University of New Hampshire Cooperative Extension, which assigns mentors to all newly hired Extension professionals for the first year of employment (Townson, 2015).

12.5.3   Resources for Preparing the Next Generation of Extension Professionals

College students, human resource professionals, college faculty, academic advisors, Extension professionals, and others may find the following resources useful in preparing the next generation of Extension professionals.

- **National Job Bank:** https://jobs.joe.org/joejobs/index.php
  National Job Bank is a source for jobs in Extension, outreach, research, and higher education. Job posting represents the diversity of Extension positions across the United States, inclusive of states and territories. Originally, a service of USDA, the Extension Journal, Inc. Board of Directors (who also produce the *Journal of Extension*) provide leadership for the database. This resource is useful for job searching and investigating requirements for different open positions in Extension.
- **eXtension:** https://connect.extension.org/join
  The eXtension Foundation began as a resource for expediently delivering information to the public, and state Extension directors

have now focused eXtension Foundation's work on innovations and professional development (Geith et al., 2018). Connect Extension is open to all Cooperative Extension professionals, and it is an interactive, online platform that supports professional learning, development, and collaboration. The goal of this work is to produce partnerships, innovation, and impact.

- **Research, Education, and Extension Experiences for Undergraduates (REEUs)**
  USDA National Institute of Food and Agriculture funds REEUs, which are typically summer programs where undergraduates engage in career development experiences. One example is the "Explore BiGG Data" REEU at the University of Tennessee that seeks to help women undergraduates develop their skills as researchers and Extension professionals in bioinformatics, genetics, and genomics (Donaldson et al., 2021).
- **University Curriculum**
  Examples of higher education institutions that offer degrees, minors, and certifications in Extension:
  o   University of Florida, Extension Education Minor
  o   North Carolina State University, Extension Education Minor
  o   Texas A& M, Extension Education Minor
  o   West Virginia University, Extension Education Concentration
  o   Colorado State University, Master of Extension Education
  o   University of Kentucky, Family Sciences Cooperative Extension Career Track
  o   University of Georgia, Community Outreach Area of Emphasis within the Family and Consumer Sciences Program
  o   Tennessee State University
  o   Oklahoma State University
  o   Iowa State University, Agricultural Extension Education Specialization (PhD)
  o   New Mexico State University Agricultural and Community Development Degree
  o   Ohio State University: Community and Extension Education Specialization under the Community Leadership Major (undergraduate)
  o   Texas A&M Extension Education Minor (undergraduate)

12.6 Summary

Extension careers present challenges, particularly in terms of work schedules, customer needs, and the interdisciplinary nature of community engagement work. Nonetheless, Extension careers can also be personally and professionally rewarding as it involves helping people help themselves with research-based solutions to individual, family, and community issues. Extension supports multiple career pathways and multiple roles for educators, administrators, and those in organizational support roles. A key question for those interested in an Extension career is – *How does your personality, academic background, talents, and strengths align with the needs of the differing jobs and environments of Cooperative Extension professions?* This question is important for both high school and college students considering Extension careers and experienced professionals considering transitioning to Extension careers.

To prepare for an Extension career, high school and college students should be mindful of opportunities in formal education (e.g., college-level coursework, programs) and internships. Internships and other career development activities are particularly helpful to gain field-based experience in applying concepts from formal instruction. Research has identified core competencies needed for Extension professionals to be successful in their roles. Core competencies include program planning and evaluation, diversity and inclusion, and subject matter knowledge. Efforts to align college instruction, internships, and career development programs with these competencies ensure that the Extension workforce remains on the cutting edge in delivering impactful human sciences programs. Onboarding, wellness programs, and other forms of professional development are key for Extension organizations to amplify the skills and abilities of Extension professionals to serve children, youth, families, and communities.

References

Arnold, S., & Place, N. (2010). Influences on agricultural agents' decisions to remain in an Extension career. *Journal of Agricultural Education*, 51(2), 36–45.

Atiles, J. H. (2019). Cooperative extension competencies for the community engagement professional. *Journal of Higher Education Outreach and Engagement*, 23(1), 107–127.

Baker, S. S., Pearson, M., & Chipman, H. (2009). Development of core competencies for paraprofessional nutrition educators who deliver food stamp nutrition education. *Journal of Nutrition Education and Behavior*, 41, 138–143. https://doi.org/10.1016/j.jneb.2008.05.004

Benge, M., Muscato, A. F., & Beattie, P. N. (2020). Professional development needs of early-career extension agents beyond the first year: Florida county Extension director perspectives. *Journal of Extension*, 58(6). https://joe.org/joe/2020december/rb1.php

Block, L. M. (2007). FCS careers: Cooperative extension. *Journal of Family and Consumer Sciences*, 99(4), 64.

Boyd, H. H. (2009). Ready–made resources for Extension evaluation competencies. *Journal of Extension*, 47(3). www.joe.org/joe/2009june/tt1.php

Bradley, L., Driscoll, E., & Bardon, R. (2012). Removing the tension from Extension. *Journal of Extension*, 50(2).

Cochran, G. R. (2009). *Ohio State University Extension competency study: Developing a competency model for a 21st century Extension organization.* [Unpublished doctoral dissertation]. Ohio State University.

Cummings, S. R., Andrews, K. B., Weber, K. M., & Postert, B. (2015). Developing Extension professionals to develop Extension programs: A case study for the changing face of Extension. *Journal of Human Sciences and Extension*, 3(2), 132–155.

DeBord, K., Dunn, C., Zaslow, S. A., & Smith, P. P. (2003). Identifying competencies needed in FCS Extension staff. *Journal of Family and Consumer Sciences*, 95(4), 99–104.

Deen, M. Y., Parker, L. A., Griner Hill, L., Huskey, L., & Whitehall, A. P. (2014). Navigating difference: Development and implementation of a successful cultural competency training for Extension and outreach professionals. *Journal of Extension*, 52(1). https://joe.org/joe/2014february/a2.php

Donaldson, J. L. (2019a). *Extension programming models.* North Carolina State Extension. https://content.ces.ncsu.edu/extension-programming-models

Donaldson, J. L. (2019b). Case studies for student engagement in undergraduate extension education courses. *NACTA Journal.* Available: www.nactateachers.org/images/TeachingTips/Summer_2019/4_Case_Studies_for_Student_Engagement.pdf

Donaldson, J. L. (2019c, June 18–21). *Innovative practices for using case studies in undergraduate extension education courses.* [Poster presentation]. NACTA Conference Abstracts 63:1. Twin Falls, ID, United States.

Donaldson, J. L. (2020a). *Community engagement for Extension professionals: 21st Century program planning, evaluation, and professionalism.* North Carolina State University.

Donaldson, J. L. (2020b). *Situational analysis/needs assessment for effective community engagement: A guidebook for Extension professionals.* North Carolina State Extension. Available: https://content.ces.ncsu.edu/situational-analysisneeds-assessment-for-effective-community-engagement-a-guidebook-for-extension

Donaldson, J. L. (2020c). *Extension models: Exploring proactive and reactive approaches.* North Carolina State Extension. https://content.ces.ncsu.edu/extension-models-exploring-proactive-and-reactive-approaches

Donaldson, J. L., Dunstan, R., & Jayaratne, K. S. U. (2020, June 16–19). *Using an internship program to build career interest: Implications for student recruitment.*

[Poster presentation]. NACTA Conference Abstracts. NACTA Conference. (Virtual Conference)

Donaldson, J. L., & Franck, K. L. (2019). Promoting healthy lifestyles for Extension employees: An exploratory study. *Journal of Human Sciences and Extension*, 7(3), 92–114. Available: www.jhseonline.com/article/view/906/753

Donaldson, J. L., Graham, D. L., Arnold, S., Taylor, L. K., & Jayaratne, K. S. U. (2021a, May 24–27). *An Extension education needs assessment: Perspectives from professionals in two associations.* [Oral presentation]. American Association for Agricultural Education National Conference, Online Conference.

Donaldson, J. L., Gwinn, K. D., Stephens, C. A., Cregger, M. A., Emrich, S., Frywell, R. T., Greig, J., Hadziabdic, D., Lebeis, S., Olukolu, B.A., Ownley, B. H., & Staton, M. (2021b, February 8–10). *Women undergraduates' leadership and career development in a summer agricultural research program.* [Poster presentation]. Southern Region, American Association for Agricultural Education Conference, Online Conference. http://aaaeonline.org/resources/Documents/Southern%20 Region/2021SouthernConference/ResearchPosterAbstracts.pdf

Extension Committee on Organization and Policy. (2016). *Extension Task Force Innovation Report.* Available: https://4-h.org/wp-content/uploads/2016/10/ Extension-Innovation-Task-Force.pdf

Fox, J. E., & LaChenaye, J. M. (2015). Cultural core competencies: Perceptions of 4-H youth development professionals. *Journal of Human Sciences and Extension*, 3(3), 65–78. www.jhseonline.com/article/view/745

Franck, K., Penn, A., Wise, D., & Berry, A. (2017). Strengthening family and consumer sciences extension professionals through a competency-based professional development system. *Journal of Family and Consumer Sciences*, 109(3), 18–22. https://doi.org/10.14307/JFCS109.3.18

Geith, C., Immendorf, M. C., Griffin, A., & Stiegler, C. T. (2018). Informing innovations through deeper insight on strategic priorities and expansive ideas. *Journal of Extension*, 56(5). https://joe.org/joe/2018september/comm2.ph

Gorman, M. (2019). Becoming an agricultural advisor – The rationale, the plan and the implementation of a model of reflective practice in extension higher education. *The Journal of Agricultural Education and Extension*, 25(2), 179–191. https://doi.org/10.1080/1389224X.2018.1559742

Gornish, E. S., Coffey, P., Tiles, K., & Roche, L. M. (2018). Careers in Cooperative Extension. *Frontiers in Ecology and the Environment*, 16(9), 539–540. https://doi .org/10.1002/fee.1971

Griffeth, L. L., Tiller, L., Jordan, J., Sapp, R., & Randall, N. (2018). Women leaders in agriculture: Data-driven recommendations for action and perspectives on furthering the conversation. *Journal of Extension*, 56(7). www.joe.org/ joe/2018december/a2.php

Gutter, M., & Stephenson, L. (2016). Family and consumer sciences Extension educator pipeline: Career pathway potential. *Journal of Family & Consumer Sciences Education*, 33(1), 8–15. www.natefacs.org/Pages/v33se1/v33se1Gutter.pdf

Hackett, G., & Lent, R. W. (1992). Theoretical advances and current inquiry in career psychology. *Handbook of Counseling Psychology*, 2, 419–452.

Hackett, G., Lent, R. W., & Greenhaus, J. H. (1991). Advances in vocational theory and research: A 20-year retrospective. *Journal of Vocational Behavior, 38*, 3–38. https://doi.org/10.1016/0001-8791(91)90015-E

Hall, J. L., & Broyles, T. W. (2016). Leadership competencies of Tennessee extension agents: Implications for professional development. *Journal of Leadership Education, 15*(3), 187–200. https://doi.org/10.12806/V15/I3/R8

Harder, A., Mashburn, D., & Benge, M. (2009). An assessment of Extension Education curriculum at land–grant universities. *Journal of Agricultural Education, 50*(3), 22–32. 10.5032/jae.2009.03022

Harder, A., & Narine, L. K. (2019). Interpersonal leadership competencies of Extension agents in Florida. *Journal of Agricultural Education, 60*(1), 224–233. www-jae-online-org.prox.lib.ncsu.edu/attachments/article/2207/Harder%20-%2014.pdf

Harder, A., Place, N. T., & Scheer, S. D. (2015). Towards a competency-based Extension education curriculum: A Delphi study. *Journal of Agricultural Education, 51*(3), 44–52. https://doi.org/10.5032/jae.2010.03044

Harmon, L. W., Hansen, J. C., Borgen, F. H., & Hammer, A. C. (2005). *Strong interest inventory: Applications and technical guide.* Counseling Psychology Press.

Harris, T. (2020). *Q&A with Chuck Hibberd, part 2.* Nebraska Farmer. www.farmprogress.com/farm-life/q-a-with-chuck-hibberd-part-2

Hedge, J. W., & Rineer, J. R. (2017). *Improving career development opportunities through rigorous career pathways research.* RTI Press Publication No. OP-0037-1703.RTI Press. https://doi.org/10.3768/rtipress.2017.op.0037.1703

Jenkins, D., & Spence, C. (2006). *The career pathways how-to guide (ED496995).* ERIC. https://files.eric.ed.gov/fulltext/ED496995.pdf

Kroth, M., & Christensen, M. (2009). *Career development basics.* Association for Talent Development.

Lakai, D., Jayarante, K. S. U., Moore, G. E., & Kistler, M. J. (2014). Identification of current proficiency level of Extension competencies and the competencies needed for Extension agents to be successful in the 21st Century. *Journal of Extension and Human Sciences, 2*(1). www.jhseonline.com/article/view/584

Lamm, K., Sapp, L., Lamm, A., & Randall, N. (2020). A longitudinal evaluation of conflict management capacity building efforts in higher education. *Journal of Agricultural Education, 61*(3), 75–85. https://doi.org/10.5032/jae.2020.03075

Lamm, K. W., Sapp, L. R., & Lamm, A. J. (2016). Leadership programming: Exploring a path to faculty engagement in transformational leadership. *Journal of Agricultural Education, 57*(1), 106–120. https://doi.org/10.5032/jae.2016.01106

Lee, J. H., & Nolan, R. E. (1998). The relationship between mentoring and the career advancement of women administrators in Cooperative Extension. *Journal of Career Development, 25*(1), 3–13. https://doi.org/10.1023/A:1022969028052

Lent, R. W. (2008). Understanding and promoting work satisfaction: An integrative view. *Handbook of Counseling Psychology,* 462–480.

Maddy, D., Niemann K., Lindquist, J., & Bateman, K. (2002). *Core competencies for the Cooperative Extension System.* Michigan State University Extension. https://apps.msuextension.org/careers/forms/Core_Competencies.pdf

McDonald, K., & Hite, L. (2015). *Career development: A human resource development perspective* (1st ed.). Routledge. https://doi.org/10.4324/9781315767406

Moore, L. L., & Rudd, R. D. (2003). *Exploring leadership competencies in Extension.* [Paper presentation]. Association of Leadership Educators Annual Conference, Anchorage, AK, United States.

Narine, L., Benge, M., Harder, A., & Albert, B. (2018, May 15–18). *Assessing the availability and academic offerings of Extension education in the United States.* [Poster presentation]. American Association of Agricultural Educators Conference, Charleston, SC, United States. http://aaaeonline.org/resources/Documents/National/FinalCompleteProceedings.pdf

Russell, M. B., Liggans, G. L., & Attoh, P. A. (2018). Job characteristics and employee engagement: A national study of FCS Extension educators. *Journal of Family and Consumer Sciences*, 110(3), 24–31. https://doi.org/10.14307/JFCS110.3.24

Scheer, S. D., Ferrari, T. M., Earnest, G. W., & Conners, J. J. (2006). Preparing Extension professionals: The Ohio State University's model of Extension Education. *Journal of Extension*, 44(4). www.joe.org/joe/2006august/a1.php

Scheer, S. D., Harder, A., & Place, N. T. (2011). Competency modeling in Extension education: Integrating an academic Extension education model with an Extension human resource management model. *Journal of Agricultural Education*, 52(3), 64–74. https://files.eric.ed.gov/fulltext/EJ956089.pdf

Seevers, B., & Graham, D. (2012). *Education through Cooperative Extension* (3rd ed.). University of Arkansas.

Swanson, J. L., & Fouad, N. A. (2010). *Career theory and practice: Learning through case studies.* Sage Publications.

Townson, L. (2015). *Mentoring Program handbook.* University of New Hampshire Cooperative Extension. Available: https://extension.unh.edu/resources/files/Resource002353_Rep3448.pdf%20

USDA National Institute of Food and Agriculture. (2017a). *Growing Together, 4-H Professional Research, Knowledge, and Competency (PRKC).* Fact Sheet. Available: https://nifa.usda.gov/sites/default/files/resources/4-H-PRKC-2017-fact-sheet.pdf

USDA National Institute of Food and Agriculture. (2017b). *Growing Together, 4-H Professional Research, Knowledge, and Competency (PRKC).* Available: https://nifa.usda.gov/sites/default/files/resources/4-H-PRKC-2017-guide.pdf

Vondracek, F. W., Lerner, R. M., & Schulenberg, J. E. (1986). *Career development: A life-span developmental approach.* Lawrence Erlbaum Associates.

Walker, J. W. (1980). *Human resource planning.* McGraw-Hill.

CHAPTER 13

Extending Extension's Outreach and Engagement with Social Media
A Case Study with an Integrated Media Campaign

Jemalyn Griffin and Holly Hatton

In the age of social media, artificial intelligence, and mass communication, the ways by which individuals receive, process, and share information have transformed dramatically. Not only is information more accessible but new technology platforms and the ubiquity of social media now allows any user to be their own creator of content.

Social media refers to digitally mediated platforms by which users can create, exchange, or share information (Chugh & Ruhi, 2020). Information on social media ranges from personal photos, short-video stories, and branded campaigns to news articles written by established outlets providing many creative ways to craft content that is relevant to various audiences (Thompson, 2018). The use of social media has evidenced extraordinary growth in the past decade (Liu et al., 2021) with majority of US adults now getting information and news from these platforms (Gottfried & Shearer, 2016). Within Extension, it is critically important that information and educational content are accessible, meaningful, relevant, and wide-reaching; and this includes social media platforms (Simpson & Donaldson, 2022). Thus, the accelerating shifts in the information landscape, and particularly the increasing use of social media, has significant implications for how Extension delivers information, its role as a reliable source of information, and its continued relevance in the years to come. This chapter is intended to explore these issues.

13.1 Historical Shifts in Communicating Information

The widespread use of social media is preceded by several recent historical shifts related to information communication and mass media. Understanding these historical shifts is important for Extension when thinking about communicating through growing technology, access to data, and mass marketing, all of which have been impacted by generational and cultural shifts in processing information. In the 1960s and 1970s, focus in the field of information communication was on mass production and volume. For example, broadcast communication, particularly with increasing presence of televisions in US households, heralded in growing audiences of various demographics – allowing for unprecedent access and opportunities to share information and reach constituents and consumers (Gewirtz, 2019). In the 1980s, increased channels of communication and mass media allowed for more nuanced targeting of audiences, with greater emphasis on segmenting the market based on demographics and psychographics. Processes and strategies for messaging to specific populations (e.g., rural versus urban) increased in sophistication and focus, for example, cable channels for specific populations emerged that focused on particular groups (e.g., MTV for adolescents and young adults). In perhaps the biggest leap in information communication and dissemination to date, the 1990s marked the entry of mobile communication (e.g., cell phones for individual use) and the Internet – allowing for both broad but even more focused targeting of messages (Gewirtz, 2018).

Since the Internet boom of the 1990s, information dissemination (including marketing) has transformed dramatically – allowing for organizations, agencies, and brands to develop tailored customer relationship management campaigns to target specific audiences. Though to a large extent, there was already targeted communication in earlier days, the current era of communication involves digitization and hyper personalization of everything. For example, in what is dubbed as the "Amazon effect," machine learning drives Amazon's Alexa smart speaker and provides Artificial Intelligence (AI) cloud computing that allows personalized one-on-one interactions between users and technology. Similarly, agencies are increasingly exploring algorithms to select news articles for readers, providing highly individualized selections and filtering out others (Joris et al., 2021). These types of technologies are disrupting the overall user experience of individuals receiving and interpreting information.

13.2   Considerations in Social Media Use

The use of social media to communicate information from even educational institutions has almost become the norm. Nonetheless, it is worth noting that the rapid evolution of how people communicate and interact, as well as the role and use of technology, has impacted generations differently. Baby boomers grew up as television expanded dramatically, changing their lifestyles and connection to the world in fundamental ways. This is the age group that, for the first time, was able to access vivid visuals of on-going events, which their parents had previously relied on newspaper accounts (e.g., Vietnam War). Generation X grew up as the computer revolution was taking hold, and Millennials came of age during the internet explosion (Dimock, 2019). Similarly, there are differences in how various groups of parents, youth, and caregivers use social media which can be important to know in cocreating, designing, and using social media for outreach. Some of these considerations are shared below.

13.2.1 Understanding the Characteristics of the Cohort

Research finds important generational differences in the use and impact of social media use (Liu et al., 2021) and as such Extension should attend to these differences when crafting their outreach and engagement strategies with various social media platforms (see Table 13.1 for descriptions). For example, there are differences in the opinions of Gen Zers and Millennials as compared to older generations with regards to wanting the government involved in solving their problems (Lau & Kennedy, 2023).

Although it is helpful to focus on generations impacted by various historical and social events such as pandemics, wars, and the invention of the Internet, generational thinking should only be used as references points (Dimock, 2023) and that is the intention of discussing generational differences here. If focusing on generational differences in research, it is recommended to include age as a predictor, as age appears to be a salient factor that influences differences in people's beliefs, attitudes, and behaviors. In 2021, a survey administered by the Pew Research Center asked adults if they ever used social media sites and there were notable differences: with 84 percent of adults aged 18 to 29, 81 percent aged 30 to 49, 73 percent aged 50 to 64, and 45 percent aged 65 and older reporting having ever used social media (Auxier & Anderson, 2021). In Table 13.2, social media use is presented by age, income, education, and rurality.

As a case in point, we will focus specifically on Generation Z as they are currently the main group of social media users and may be the most impacted by such aspects as social media fatigue and overload (Liu et al., 2021).

Generation Z and Social Media. Generation Z (also known as Gen Z) includes individuals born between the mid-1990s and 2010, and are referred to as "digital natives" because they grew up in era wherein Internet and digital communication were already broadly available (Mohr & Mohr, 2017). For those in Gen Z, people who hold influence

Table 13.1 *Cohort descriptions*

Generation	Baby Boomer Generation	Generation X	Millennial Generation (also known as Gen Y)	Gen Z Generation
Years Age in 2019	Born: 1946–1964 55–73 years	Born: 1965–1980 39–54 years	Born: 1981–1996 23–38 years	1997 onward 7–22 years
Social Media and Technology Use	Lower in technology proficiency, least likely to access social media through smartphone or purchase an app; prefer Facebook and LinkedIn	Found to use social media platforms approximately seven hours a week; known as multitaskers and have access to computer, tablet, and mobile devices	First generation to adopt social media as their main form of communication	Social media is their main form of entertainment and communication, in one study 44 percent reported checking social media profiles hourly, known as the YouTube generation
General Purpose of Social Media Use	To connect with friends/ family and search information (e.g., share about family [Facebook] or work [LinkedIn]) – have a work/life divide	To connect with friends/ family and search information, value independence so will research information – generation of counter-culture	Will post personal and professional life publicly; are influenced by peers, less trusting of big brands and traditional advertising, have celebrity influencers	More likely to use for entertainment than connecting with friends, love visuals, and reported to have an average attention span of eight seconds

Note: The years for each generation are not conclusive but used a general guideline by the Pew Research Center.
Source: Social Media for Every Generation – PostBeyond.

Table 13.2 *Social media use*

Demographics	Snapchat	Instagram	YouTube	TikTok	Twitter	Facebook	Pinterest
							X (not indicated)
Age 13–17 (2022)	59%	62%	95%	67%	23%	32%	
Age 18–29	65%	71%	95%	48%	42%	70%	32%
Age 30–49	24%	48%	91%	22%	27%	77%	34%
Age 50–64	12%	29%	83%	14%	18%	73%	38%
Age 65+	2%	13%	49%	4%	7%	50%	18%
Less than $30K	25%	35%	75%	22%	29%	70%	21%
$30K–$49,999	27%	45%	83%	29%	22%	76%	33%
$50K–$74,999	29%	39%	79%	20%	34%	61%	29%
More than $75K	28%	47%	90%	20%	34%	70%	40%
High school or less	21%	30%	70%	21%	14%	64%	22%
Some college	32%	44%	86%	24%	26%	71%	36%
College graduate	23%	49%	89%	19%	33%	73%	37%
Urban	28%	45%	84%	24%	27%	70%	30%
Suburban	25%	41%	81%	20%	23%	70%	32%
Rural	18%	25%	74%	16%	18%	67%	34%

Note: Findings come from a nationally representative survey of 1,502 US adults conducted via cellphone and landline telephone January 25 to February 8, 2021 by Pew Research Center. Surveys were weighted to be representative of the US adult population by race, gender, ethnicity, education, and other categories.

Source: Auxier & Anderson (2021). Social Media Use in 2021. Pew Research Center. For the age 13 to 17 years findings, they are from a different survey conducted in April 14 to May 4, 2022 with 1,316 teens. Source: Vogels et al. (2022).

include social media influencers who, since around 2013, have gained public focus and prominence. Through social media, influencers generate conversation, drive engagement, and set cultural trends. Audiences are more receptive to social media influencers than celebrities. Influencers are early adopters of new products and services, creating desire among their audiences and thus have to appear trustworthy and share some similarities with their followers (Lou & Yuan, 2019).

As social media natives, technology advancements in mobile applications and online platforms have greatly impacted the lives and behaviors of Gen Z individuals. More than half of Gen Z uses social media at least four hours a day, more than double the use by other US adults. Additionally, 38 percent of this generation spends more than four hours a day scrolling through their favorite channels and sees a brand every minute (Archrival, 2023). Thus, they have significant exposure to content and marketing.

Such high exposure may cause anxiety, overload, and burn out for this generation online with more than 60 percent reporting that they feel overwhelmed. Unbeknownst to many Gen Zers, corporations have access to tremendous amounts of information that allow for highly targeted messaging and marketing. For example, search engines like Google can have more than 200 factors in their algorithms to deliver targeted content and Gen Z users may not always understand that content to which they are being exposed has already been influenced by AI (Rovira et al., 2021). In comparison to other generations, more than half of Gen Zers report that this type of technology knows their preferences and interests better than their own parents (Archrival, 2023). Having ready access to technology has contributed to Gen Zers being more self-driven in terms of using social media as a learning tool (Seemiller & Grace, 2016).

In a recent survey conducted by Morning Consult (Roberts, 2023), YouTube was the social media platform most frequently used (88 percent) by Gen Z's, followed by Instagram (76 percent), TikTok (68 percent), Snapchat (67 percent), Facebook (49 percent), Twitter (47 percent), Discord (35 percent), Reddit (30 percent), Twitch (24 percent), and BeReal (15 percent). The higher use of YouTube suggests that Gen Zers are interested in social media that provides education, as YouTube is typically used for vlogs, and "how to" videos, as well as for pranks (Roberts, 2023). Attention to the platforms used by the specific cohort or targeted group is critical for Extension. For instance, as of the time this chapter is being written, Extension programming and information dissemination targeting the Gen Z cohort might consider YouTube, Instagram, and TikTok.

In addition to understanding which platforms best reach specific cohorts, it is also important to consider potential challenges that they may pose to the audience. For example, can disseminating information via social media to a particular audience cause distress or overload? For example, during the COVID-19 related lockdown period in the United Kingdom in 2020, Gen Z respondents reported feeling overwhelmed with the information delivered on social media, leading to negative impacts on their psychological well-being and some deciding to discontinue social media use (Liu et al., 2021). A systematic review and meta-analysis of thirty studies similarly found links between digital media use and negative mental health outcomes among youth, however, such effects varied by type of communication during the pandemic. Digital communication that involved self-disclosure and a context of mutual friendships contributed to positive coping, in contrast to overall social and digital media use which were linked to negative outcomes (Marciano et al., 2022).

Thus, as has been the strategy within Extension over the years, understanding one's audience, finding ways to connect with them by building trust, and planning and clearly articulating where, how, and when information will be received is critical. And just as Extension has served as a trusted source of information for over a century, it can serve a critical role in curating information for clients at a time when information communication has become ubiquitous (Liu et al., 2021).

13.2.2 Considering the Context: Rural and Urban Settings

Though social media and digital platforms can reach a broad audience, understanding the specific context of one's audience is helpful in information delivery and effectiveness. Reflecting broader national trends, post-Millennials overwhelmingly reside in metropolitan as opposed to rural areas. Only 13 percent of post-Millennials are in rural areas, compared with 18 percent of Millennials in 2002. By comparison, 23 percent of Gen Xers lived in rural areas when they were ages 6 to 21, as did 36 percent of early Boomers.

In the nation's urban areas and in the Western region of the United States, post-Millennials are at the leading edge of growing racial and ethnic diversity. Two-thirds of post-Millennials living in urban counties are racial or ethnic minorities, with a plurality (36 percent) being Hispanic. Among Millennials, 59 percent who live in cities are racial or ethnic minorities. In rural (nonmetropolitan) counties, only 29 percent of six to twenty-one years old are non-White – still somewhat higher than the share of rural Millennials who are non-White (27 percent). Minorities constitute

43 percent of suburban post-Millennials. Among those living in suburban counties, 39 percent of Millennials, 34 percent of Gen Xers, and 23 percent of Boomers are non-White (Fry & Parker, 2018).

Consideration of rural and suburban differences in use and access to social media platforms is important. For example, rural Americans are less likely to have home broadband as compared to suburban adults, and rural adults report having lower technology ownership; this is in terms of the number of devices and rural residents are less likely to own a tablet (Vogels, 2021). In part, these disparities may be due to limited access to reliable high-speed internet in rural areas, a reality that continues to pose challenges to rural locales today (Read & Wert, 2022). Understanding the clientele regarding relevant demographic factors is critical in reaching audiences for Extension outreach and engagement. Such information can help guide, for example, which social media platforms work better on a mobile phone as compared to a tablet, or whether dissemination may still necessitate face-to-face communication.

13.3   Credibility and Wellness in the Age of Social Media

The ability to disseminate information via social media channels has created a highway of content that puts users in complex situations to decipher what is relevant, accurate, and trustworthy to consume. For the third year in a row, Americans report viewing their family and friends as the most trustworthy sources for accurate news or information and the least likely to spread disinformation (Institute for Public Relations, 2022). Disinformation is a growing concern. In a recent study, seven-out-of-ten Americans said that they believed that disinformation has a negative impact on society and well-being; and that irrespective of political affiliation, 75 percent agreed that disinformation is a threat to democracy, 73 percent said it undermines the election process, and 63 percent said it infringes on human rights. One-quarter (25 percent) of respondents believed that concerns about disinformation are exaggerated while almost half (48 percent) did not. Disinformation also has negative impacts on mental health, with over half (52 percent) agreeing that encountering disinformation makes them feel anxious or stressed (Institute for Public Relations, 2022). Thus, trust is an important component of whether information received will be accepted and utilized.

Social media delivery of parent-, child-, and youth-focused programming and supports appears promising but with important caveats. For example, several studies show positive impacts of online delivery of resources for parents in such areas as nutrition information (Zarnowiecki et al., 2020) and the use of social media for interventions around nutrition and health for youth (Chau et al., 2018). Parents might be more careful in trusting information. In a review of studies examining the potential benefits of support parents receive online, it was found that parents appreciated the convenience and anonymity as well as the information support gained online, but that there were concerns with the credibility of the information (Doty & Dworkin, 2014). Extension professionals need to be aware of the ways in which people trust and use social media to make informed choices as part of their outreach efforts and cannot assume that making information available leads to adoption. It continues to be imperative that Extension partner with trusted community members and take the time to understand how social media can best be used to reach multiple families, youth, and caregivers in effective ways.

Social media and digital platforms are increasingly being used in Extension in promising ways (Simpson & Donaldson, 2022). Nonetheless, a myriad of issues with social media can adversely impact users including contributing to relationship problems, suicide attempts, and physical and mental health problems (Swinton, 2020). As was already noted earlier, COVID-related information via social media was linked to feelings of being overwhelmed and other negative outcomes among those in Gen Z. Taken together, it is imperative that the use of social media as an outreach tool be used with intentionally, thoughtfulness, and responsibly.

13.3.1 *Building Trust and Credibility*

Approximately 81 percent of US consumers say personal vulnerability (around health, financial stability, and privacy) is a reason why brand trust has become more important (Edelman Brand Trust Index). Consumers are more willing to put their trust and purchases in what influencers and advocates say, rather than the brand as a source.

Two-step flow theory (Katz, 1957) of communication states that the flow of information from mass media is greatly impacted by the influence of opinion leaders to their communities and from them to the general masses. This is important to understand when communicating important messages to specific communities. Perspective on influencers within communities and the differences between macro- and micro-influencers are key. Micro-influencers are influencers that are known widely and can be known as a celebrity with millions of followers. Micro-influencers can have a small sphere of influence but can be quite effective in delivering key messages to target audiences, especially when it pertains to niche topics.

These influencers can reach wide and varied audiences as they are not limited by social or geographic restrictions (Yao et al., 2022). Similarly, Extension can reach and engage with audiences worldwide. Some ways to build trust and credibility in these outreach and engagement efforts are adapted from Hughes (2020):

- Post relevant and unique information consistently
- Ensure that information is aligned with the stakeholder, client, and/ or community interests
- Provide information that is helpful (e.g., how-to videos)
- Share positive reviews and feedback regarding programming or the research-based information that is shared
- Have branding that is consistent across social platforms and that is aesthetically professional, clean, and cohesive – consider using a brand style guide
- Increase trust by responding to followers quickly and as often as possible

13.4   A Case Study: Improving Water Quality with an Integrated Communications Campaign

As a successful example that communication can be responsibly used to positively influence youth and family practices, we highlight a case in Nebraska that illustrates a partnership between professionals conducting programming and a social media agency to craft and deliver information. Jacht Agency is a full-service, student-run advertising and public relations agency that provides students opportunities to work collaboratively with a range of clients. Jacht attracts all majors across the University of Nebraska-Lincoln (UNL) campus to sharpen their skills in strategic campaign development and gain confidence in advertising and public relations careers postgraduation. Jacht offers a variety of creative services, including strategic brand development, integrated marketing communications, videography, photography, social media strategy, content creation, print design, and public relations. In every capacity, Jacht provides great opportunities for students to explore the industry and start their careers in an agency setting.

Jacht partnered with the UNL College of Engineering to help the Citizen Science Project with a media campaign to connect with their audience. Citizen Science is focused on water quality, particularly in understanding and testing for water contamination in areas that are near agricultural farms where there is a risk for contamination of water sources.

Citizen Science engaged Jacht to increase their reach to bring awareness to their work, as well as to engage the community to participate in gathering data (i.e., testing their water). College of Engineering and Jacht collaborated on a general approach, strategic branding, messaging, and a video that would teach citizens how to test their water, and a video that would communicate the work that Citizen Science was doing. Examples of messaging include the following:

- Nebraska's multibillion-dollar farm economy depends on groundwater and thankfully, the state has plenty of it for now. But that farming success has come at a cost: The fertilizer used to make those crops grow over the years has contaminated Nebraska's groundwater, the drinking water source for most of the state.
- It's a problem that is quietly costing the state and federal government millions of dollars and changing the way rural residents get water and how much they pay. Health researchers believe nitrate contamination in drinking water could be one cause of Nebraska's higher than average pediatric cancer rate. Nebraska has the seventh-highest pediatric cancer rate in the country and the highest in the Midwest.

We further detail the steps involved in this collaborative partnership.

Community-based participatory approach: The campaign. The first step in preparing for the campaign was to collect information from Nebraskans regarding their perceptions of water quality to inform the social media campaign strategy. The team collected various forms of qualitative data asking participants questions regarding their perception behind water quality, contamination, and the necessity for testing. A series of focus groups were conducted wherein participants discussed and shared their beliefs regarding the accessibility of water testing and their awareness of Citizen Science. From these focus groups, Jacht created a research report for Citizen Science. The results of the focus groups revealed that most people in Nebraska were unaware of the need for water testing and why it can be so important.

Campaign Strategy. Drawing upon the results from the focus groups, a comprehensive brand guide was created for Citizen Science. In part, this included Jacht assisting with developing a clear and concise mission statement. They also supported Citizen Science in developing their brand tone and more effectively understanding their target audience. Another communication strategy was having Citizen Science successfully engage with administrators and teachers so that materials could be effectively disseminated in classrooms.

In addition to communicating the value of the project, a key message that both teams realized was important was how simple it was to participate in the project. One insight that emerged from the focus group was that the initial website was difficult to navigate for learning how to use the water testing kits. In response, Jacht created a short-form video targeted to the comprehension and skill level of seventh-graders and above. The benefit of the short-form instructional video was that it could be used on Instagram Reels and YouTube Shorts, as well as similar platforms like TikTok contributing to the video obtaining virality.

Measuring Success. To measure reach and potential impact, metrics were determined to gauge the level of awareness, the number of kits distributed, and the percentage of engagement on the website. The short-form video impact was measured by number of views, the number of new followers, the number of shares, and the engagement on the social media posts.

Partnerships. Citizen Science illustrates the potential impact of engaging partners in the work of impact-focused and community programming. Entities exist that have expertise in engaging audiences through social media. In the case of Jacht, students who are training to enter into the profession of communication, journalism, and mass media are gaining critical experiences in real world programming so that they can practice what they are learning in real time. Jacht has also partnered with Extension in numerous ways, including providing documentation for Handcrafted – a program that engages immigrants and longer-term residents to foster social connections and entrepreneurship (see Kim et al., this volume), as well as other projects.

13.5   Social Media Brand Tools

There are several articles providing best practices and helpful tips for ways Extension can use social media for outreach and engagement (e.g., Brickman et al., 2017; Christensen et al., 2015; Garcia et al., 2018). Garcia et al. (2018) provide a social media toolkit to use in Family and Consumer Sciences programming. The toolkit provides suggestions for what to post, how to post, where to post, and for collecting evaluation and feedback. Below we highlight some social media platforms and illustrative examples of their use that could be adopted within Extension:

- **TikTok** is a tool that has been used in Extension contexts for multiple purposes such as 4-H Livestock shows, to provide quick demonstrations, and as an engagement strategy to connect with websites, professional learnings, longer educational videos, and to highlight research findings. Simpson and Donaldson (2022) provide a comprehensive list of ideas for using TikTok effectively within Extension.

- **Twitter** can serve as a public platform tool to share information, often serving as a way to follow people whom they do not know in the real world (e.g., celebrities, institutions) (Laor, 2022). The Pew Research Center (Auxier & Anderson, 2021) reported that 23 percent of adults in the United States use Twitter. As an outreach and engagement tool, three schools used Twitter to highlight children's learning with the intention that families would discuss this learning at home, thereby increasing parental engagement in children's learning (Baxter & Dianne, 2023). A finding of this study was that having students be cocreators of the posts and connecting across the home, school, and community environments led to more parental engagement.

- **Snapchat** provides the ability for users to post videos and photos overlaid with theme graphics referred to as "geofilters," which may be helpful at Extension events where people can then become digital advocates of the event or programming offered (Davis et al., 2020). Snapchat can also provide fun and engaging ways like a game for outreach and engagement with Extension.

- **Instagram** is a social media platform created in 2010 that offers social networking and the ability to post videos and pictures (Carpenter et al., 2020). Users can send private messages and there is a twenty-four-hour story feature similar to Facebook. Instagram is reported to be used more than Facebook by teenagers (Anderson & Jiang, 2018) and is appealing to many for its focus on sharing visual content rather than only text. In one study of educators, Instagram was used with hashtags being reported as important ways to link content to others, to build community, increase professional knowledge, exchange emotional support, and increase their students' learning (Carpenter et al., 2020).

- **Facebook** is a social media platform that is attractive for its ability to offer closed groups and post short videos and pictures, update one's status, and tag friends. Typically, Facebook is viewed as creating a community with close connections (Laor, 2022). It can serve to provide both formal and informal learning in an ongoing way (Woodford et al., 2023) as well provide community support groups. In one study with college women, Facebook was used as a promising way to provide social support to increase physical activity (Rote et al., 2015).

- **YouTube** is a social media website that was acquired by Google in 2006 (Welbourne & Grant, 2016) and globally is the second most visited site (Arthurs et al., 2018), with 1.78 billion users being reported in 2020 (Statista, 2021). It has an age requirement to be thirteen years of age or older (Taylor & Cingel, 2023) and can be used to demonstrate and share information with clients and important stakeholders.

13.6   Social Media and Extension: A Reality in Today's World

With social media becoming almost a necessity in disseminating information, we have argued that its use in Extension is rapidly becoming the norm. We have noted several important considerations in its use, for instance, the context of the users and the characteristics of the cohort one is trying to reach. And just as Extension personnel have had to be mindful in messaging and dissemination, it is also critical to be intentional in the use of social media to maximize reach and effectiveness. In identifying the most useful and effective social media platform, it is important to first think of the outreach and engagement reasons as there are various ways that social media tools can be used within Extension. These are some aspects to consider (adapted from a survey in Wallace II, 2023):

- Conducting needs assessments
- Sharing information with clients
- Distributing announcements to clients about upcoming events and programs
- To have two-ways conversations with clients
- To request information and resources from clients
- Collect information from clients
- Attract potential users to Extension websites
- Market Extension programs
- Deliver Extension programs (e.g., YouTube or Facebook Live)
- Evaluate Extension programming and resources
- Communicate client success stories
- Enhance collaboration between specialists and clients
- Recruit volunteers
- Share different files such as photos and videos with clients
- Communicate with Extension advisory groups

13.7   Implications, Remaining Questions, and Looking Ahead

Extension's charge has long been to extend research, information, and innovative strategies and programs from land-grant university and research centers. Understanding how to utilize the various platforms and ever-changing technology will be critical in Extension's continued relevance and utility in carrying out its land-grant mission. Extension needs to ask itself several questions in the current era of information access and social media:

First, what is Extension's role in an era wherein information is now easily accessible? Whereas early Extension agents were critical in disseminating information from the land-grant universities and agricultural experiment stations to the community, people in the community today can easily go online to search for answers or check in on social media to find out what peers or influencers are saying about a topic. As we discussed in this chapter, along with information availability is misinformation availability. Media literacy and resources to delineate good sources from bad are needed today more than ever (e.g., De Paor & Heravi, 2020). We argue that Extension's charge to disseminate sound, trustworthy information, and that translates technical language for the lay audience remains critical. In addition to Extension's role in disseminating information, the need to curate information and educate the public on literacy regarding various topics will likely be even more necessary in the years to come.

Second, does engaging in social media entail a whole new set of skills and responsibilities that may introduce new challenges? Extension faculty and staff are generally hired based on a specific expertise (e.g., see Donaldson, this volume) and it is not typically the expectation that Extension Specialists and educators are social media experts. In a recent descriptive survey of Agricultural Extension Agents in North Carolina, results suggested that the majority (approximately 77 percent) of these agents agreed that social media made it easier to distribute information to their clients (Wallace, 2023). Results also suggested that training and support were needed to more effectively use social media in their work and that having a social media expert to consult with and assist with creating content, such as a social media specialist would be helpful. The reality is that engaging via digital and social media is a skill that is necessary in Extension and personnel will need support, training, and resources to do this effectively. We provided an example of engaging experts and their students to cocreate solutions and yield mutual gains (e.g., students gaining experience in handling a real campaign). Such partnerships may help navigate a potentially additional challenge of having media expertise in delivering Extension programming.

Third, what does engagement look like in today's information landscape? In many ways, we are in an era of reimagining engagement. Now more than ever, especially after the COVID-19 pandemic, there is an opportunity for Extension to use social media in a way that cocreates knowledge with community partners, clients, and stakeholders. Considering the historical shifts in media that we outlined earlier, those working in Extension who want to use social media need to think of ways to interact, cocreate, and personalize social media content so that social media outreach and engagement are successful. In keeping up with the shifts in social media to obtain and interact with information, Extension may benefit from collaborating with those who have social media expertise, as was done in the case study with the Jacht agency; as well as to continue highlighting Extension's relevance in the social media landscape.

Finally, just as Extension has in its first 100 years of existence, we need to ask the same questions in engaging audiences. How can we meet audiences where they are at? How can we build trust? How can we foster authentic engagement to support our clients' well-being? With the acceleration in how social media is communicating information, Extension can serve a critical role in supporting efforts to ensure that information is accurate and credible. Social media also offers Extension various ways to engage in the rapidly changing technological landscape with many avenues for research, programming, and disseminating information to support children, youth, families, and communities worldwide. With social media and technological advances, Extension can continue their reach but do so in innovative, impactful, and new ways.

References

Anderson, M., & Jiang, J. (2018, May). *Teens, social media & technology*. Pew Research Center. Retrieved from www.pewinternet.org/2018/05/31/teens-social-media-technology-2018/

Archrival: A Youth Culture Agency. (2023). *Algo Life*. https://archrival.com/insights/trends/algo-life

Arthurs, J., Drakopoulou, S., & Gandini, A. (2018). Researching YouTube. *Convergence*, 24(1), 3–15. https://doi.org/10.1177/1354856517737222

Auxier, B., & Anderson, M. (2021). *Social media use in 2021*. Pew Research Center. Retrieved from www.pewresearch.org/internet/2021/04/07/social-media-use-in-2021/

Baxter, G., & Dianne, T. (2023). "Parents don't need to come to school to be engaged": Teachers' use of social media for family engagement. *Educational Action Research*, 31(2), 306–328. https://doi.org/10.1080/09650792.2021.1930087

Brinkman, P., Kinsey, J., & Henneman, A. (2017). Increasing the capacity of social media to extend your outreach. *The Journal of Extension*, 55(1), 6.

Carpenter, J. P., Morrison, S. A., Craft, M., & Lee, M. (2020). How and why are educators using Instagram. *Teaching and Teacher Education*, 96, 103149. https://doi.org/10.1016/j.tate.2020.103149

Chau, M. M., Burgermaster, M., & Mamykina, L. (2018). The use of social media in nutrition interventions for adolescents and young adults: A systematic review. *International Journal of Medical Informatics*, 120, 77–91. https://doi.org/10.1016/j.ijmedinf.2018.10.001

Christensen, A., Hill, P., & Horrocks, S. (2015). The social media marketing map (Part 1): A tool to empower the digital leaders of extension. *Journal of Extension*, 53(4). https://tigerprints.clemson.edu/joe/vol53/iss4/29/

Chugh, R., & Ruhi, U. (2019). Social media for tertiary education. In A. Tatnall (Ed.), *Encyclopedia of education and information technologies*. Springer. https://doi.org/10.1007/978-3-319-60013-0_202-1

Davis, J., Rufener, S., Dennis, A., & Murphy, A. M. (2020, February). Marketing for next gen extension clientele through the use of geofilters abstract. *Journal of Extension*, 58(1).

De Paor, S., & Heravi, B. (2020). Information literacy and fake news: How the field of librarianship can help combat the epidemic of fake news. *Journal of Academic Librarianship*, 46(5), 102218. https://doi.org/10.1016/j.acalib.2020.102218

Dimock, M. (2019). *Defining generations: Where Millennials and Generation Z begins*. Pew Research Center. Retrieved from https://pewresearch.org/short-reads/2019/01/17/where-millennials-end-and-generation-z-begins/

Dimock, M. (2023). *5 things to keep in mind when you hear about Gen Z, Millennials, Boomers and other generations*. Pew Research Center. Retrieved from www.pewresearch.org/short-reads/2023/05/22/5-things-to-keep-in-mind-when-you-hear-about-gen-z-millennials-boomers-and-other-generations/

Doty, J. L., & Dworkin, J. (2014). Online social support for parents: A critical review. *Marriage & Family Review*, 50(2), 174–198. https://doi.org/10.1080/01494929.2013.834027

Fry, R., & Parker, K. (2018). *Early benchmarks show "post-millennials" on track to be most diverse, best-educated generation yet*. Retrieved from www.pewresearch.org/social-trends/2018/11/15/early-benchmarks-show-post-millennials-on-track-to-be-most-diverse-best-educated-generation-yet/#fn-25490-5

Garcia, A., Dev, D. A., McGinnis, C., Thomas, T., & The Learning Child Team. (2018). Impact of social media best practices toolkit: Effect on impressions and engagement of content for Extension professionals. *Journal of Extension*, 56(2). www.joe.org/joe/2018april/rb1.php

Gewirtz, D. (2018). *Technology that changed us: The 1990s, from WorldWideWeb to Google*. Retrieved from www.zdnet.com/article/technology-that-changed-us-the-1990s/

Gewirtz, D. (2019). *Technology that changed us: The 1970s, from Pong to Apollo*. Retrieved from www.zdnet.com/article/technology-that-changed-us-the-1970s/

Gottfried, J., & Shearer, E. (2016, May). *News use across social media platforms 2016*. Pew Research Center. Retrieved from www.journalism.org/2016/05/26/news-use-across-social-media-platforms-2016/

Hughes, J. (2020). *How to build a trustworthy social media reputation*. Retrieved from https://revive.social/social-media-reputation/

Institute for Public Relations. (2022). *Third annual disinformation in society report*. Accessed on November 28, 2024 from https://instituteforpr.org/wp-content/uploads/Disinformation-Study-MARCH-2022-FINAL.pdf

Joris, G., De Grove, F., Van Damme, K., & De Marez, L. (2021). Appreciating news algorithms: Examining audiences' perceptions to different news selection mechanisms. *Digital Journalism*, 9(5), 589–618. https://doi.org/10.1080/2167081 1.2021.1912626

Katz, E. (1957). The Two-Step Flow of Communication: An Up-To-Date Report on an Hypothesis. *Political Opinion Quarterly*, 21(1), 61–78. https://doi.org/10.1086/266687

Laor, T. (2022). My social network: Group differences in frequency of use, active use, and interactive use on Facebook, Instagram and Twitter. *Technology in Society*, 68, 101922.

Lau, A., & Kennedy, C. (2022). *Assessing the effects of generation using age-period-cohort analysis*. Pew Research Center. Retrieved from www.pewresearch.org/decoded/2023/05/22/assessing-the-effects-of-generation-using-age-period-cohort-analysis/

Liu, H., Liu, W., Yoganathan, V., & Osburg, V-S. (2021). Covid-19 information overload and generation Z's social media discontinuance intention during the pandemic lockdown. *Technological Forecasting and Social Change*, 166, 120600. https://doi.org/10.1016/j.techfore.2021.120600

Lou, C., & Yuan, S. (2019). Influencer marketing: How message value and credibility affect consumer trust of branded content on social media. *Journal of Interactive Advertising*, 19(1), 58–73. https://doi.org/10.1080/15252019.2018.1533501

Marciano, L., Ostroumova, M., Schulz, P. J., & Camerini, A.-L. (2022). Digital media use and adolescents' mental health during the Covid-19 pandemic: A systematic review and meta-analysis. *Frontiers in Public Health*, 9, 793868. https://doi.org/10.3389/fpubh.2021.793868

McCorkindale, T., & Henry, A. (n.d.). (rep.). *How Americans perceive intentionally misleading news or information* (3rd ed.). Third Annual Disinformation in Society Report.

Mohr, K. A. J., & Mohr, E. S. (2017). Understanding Generation Z students to promote a contemporary learning Environment. *Journal on Empowering Teaching Excellence*, 1(1), 9.https://doi.org/10.15142/T3M05T

Read, A., & Wert, K. (2022). *Broadband access still a challenge in rural affordable housing*. Pew Charitable Trust. Retrieved from www.pewtrusts.org/en/research-and-analysis/articles/2022/12/08/broadband-access-still-a-challenge-in-rural-affordable-housing

Roberts, J. (2023, January 27). *Where does Gen Z spend the majority of their time online?* Retrieved from https://later.com/blog/gen-z-social-media-usage/

Rote, A., Klos, L., Brondino, M., Harley, A., & Swartz, A. (2015). The efficacy of a walking intervention using social media to increase physical activity: A randomized trial. *Journal of Physical Activity & Health*, 12(1), 18–25. https://doi .org/10.1123/jpah.2014-0279

Rovira, C., Codina, L., & Lopezosa, C. (2021). Language bias in the Google Scholar Ranking algorithm. *Future Internet*, 13, 31. https://doi.org/10.3390/ fi13020031

Seemiller, C., & Grace, M. (2016). *Generation Z goes to college.* Wiley.

Simpson, C. K., & Donaldson, J. L. (2022). TikTok, tomatoes, and teenagers: Using new social media apps to connect extension education with younger audiences. *The Journal of Extension*, 60(3), 9.

Statista. (2021). *Number of YouTube users worldwide from 2016 to 2021.* Retrieved from Statista.com: www.statista.com/statistics/805656/number-youtube-viewers-worldwide/

Swinton, J. J. (2020). Extension needs outreach innovation free from the harms of social media. *Journal of Extension*, 58(2), 1.

Taylor, L. B., & Cingel, D. P. (2023). Predicting the use of YouTube and content exposure among 10–12-year-old children: Dispositional, developmental, and social factors. *Psychology of Popular Media*, 12(1), 20–29. https://doi .org/10.1037/ppm0000368

Thompson, L. J. (2018). Using short, silent "data story" videos to engage contemporary Extension audiences. *Journal of Extension*, 56(3).

Vogels, E. A. (2021). *Some digital divides persist between rural, urban, and suburban America.* Pew Research Center. Retrieved from www.pewresearch.org/ short-reads/2021/08/19/some-digital-divides-persist-between-rural-urban-and-suburban-america/

Vogels, E. A., Gelles-Watnick, R., & Massarat, N. (2022). *Teens, social media and technology.* Pew Research Center. Retrieved from www.pewresearch.org/ internet/2022/08/10/teens-social-media-and-technology-2022/

Wallace II, H. W. (2023). *Perceptions of North Carolina agricultural extension agents with regards to social media use in Extension.* [Doctoral dissertation]. North Carolina State University.

Welbourne, D. J., & Grant, W. J. (2016). Science communication on YouTube: Factors that affect channel and video popularity. *Public Understanding of Science*, 25(6), 706–718. https://doi.org/10.1177/0963662515572068

Woodford, H., Southcott, J., & Gindidis, M. (2023). Lurking with intent: Teacher purposeful learning using Facebook. *Teaching and Teacher Education*, 121, 103913. https://doi.org/10.1016/j.tate.2022.103913

Yao, Q., Li, R. Y. M., & Song, L. (2022). Construction safety knowledge sharing on YouTube from 2007 to 2021: Two-step flow theory and semantic analysis. *Safety Science*, 153, 105796. https://doi.org/10.1016/j.ssci.2022.105796

Zarnowiecki, D., Mauch, C. E., Middleton, G., et al. (2020). A systematic evaluation of digital nutrition promotion websites and apps for supporting parents to influence children's nutrition. *International Journal of Behavioral Nutrition and Physical Activity*, 17, 1–19. https://doi.org/10.1186/s12966-020-0915-1

Index

Printed in the USA
CPSIA information can be obtained
at www.ICGtesting.com
CBHW072013190924
14610CB00022B/359